The Mauritian Paradox
Fifty years of Development, Diversity and Democracy

EDITED BY

RAMOLA RAMTOHUL AND THOMAS HYLLAND ERIKSEN

University of Mauritius Press
Réduit, Mauritius

First published in 2018 by
University of Mauritius Press
Réduit, 80837
Mauritius
uompress@uom.ac.mu

Disclaimer: *The views and positions expressed in the chapters of this book are those of the individual authors/contributors and do not reflect or represent that of any organisation, institution, or agency or of the editors or publisher.*

Copyediting and proofreading by Dr Sachita Samboo.

Layout and Cover design: Doorga Ujodha

Typesetting: Madvee Armoogum-Sundhoo

Cover Photograph: Mr Avish Jungalee

ISBN 978–99903-73-48-6

TABLE OF CONTENTS

List of Tables

List of Figures

List of Abbreviations

ACHPR	African Commission on Human and Peoples' Rights
ACP	African, Caribbean and Pacific Group of States
AFM	Association des Femmes Mauriciennes
AJM	Association des Journalistes Mauriciens
APRM	African Peer Review Mechanism
ATI	Access To Information
BIOT	British Indian Ocean Territory
BLS	Best Loser System
BPO	Business Process Outsourcing
BV	Block Vote
CAM	Comité Action Musulman
CIIM	Common Ingroup Identity Model
COMESA	Common Market for Eastern and Southern Africa
CRG	Chagos Refugees Group
CSC	Chagossian Social Committee
DBM	Development Bank of Mauritius
ERCP	Economic Restructuring and Competitiveness Program
EPZ	Export Processing Zone
EU	European Union
FCOF	Front Commun Organisations Femmes
FDI	Foreign Direct Investment
FOI	Freedom of Information
FOIA	Freedom of Information Act
FPTP	First Past The Post
GATT	General Agreement on Tariffs and Trade
GDP	Gross Domestic Product
GIS	Geographic Information System
HDI	Human Development Index
IBA	Independent Broadcasting Authority
ICJ	International Court of Justice
ICT	Information and Communication Technology

ICTA	Information and Communication Technologies Authority
IFB	Independent Forward Bloc
IOC	Indian Ocean Commission
IIAG	Mo Ibrahim Index of African Governance
IMF	International Monetary Fund
IRS	Integrated Resort Scheme
LP	Labour Party
MAB	Mauritius Agricultural Bank
MAW	Mauritius Alliance of Women
MBC	Mauritius Broadcasting Corporation
MBS	Mauritius Broadcasting Service
MCB	Mauritius Commercial Bank
MCML	Multi-Carrier Mauritius Ltd
MEPZ	Mauritius Export Processing Zone
MFA	Multi Fibre Arrangement
MFP	Multi Factor Productivity
MHC	Mauritius Housing Corporation
ML	Mouvement Liberater
MLF	Muvman Liberasyon Fam
MLP	Mauritius Labour Party
MMM	Mouvement Militant Mauricien
MMSM	Mouvement Militant Socialiste Mauricien
MP	Member of Parliament
MPA	Marine Protected Area
MR	Mouvement Républicain
MSM	Mouvement Socialiste Militant
MWRCDFW	Ministry of Women's Rights, Child Development and Family Welfare
NEPA	Newspapers Editors and Publishers Association
NHS	National Health Service
NWC	National Women's Council
OAU	Organisation of African Unity
PMSD	Parti Mauricien Social Démocrate
PMXD	Parti Mauricien Xavier Duval

PR	Proportional Representation
RES	Real Estate Scheme
RM	Ralliement Mauricien
RPL	Relative Poverty Line
SADC	Southern African Development Community
SIT	Social Identity Theory
SAP	Structural Adjustment Program
SME	Small and Medium Enterprise
STV	Single Transferable Vote
TEST	Textile Emergency Support Team
TJC	Truth and Justice Commission
UNCLOS	United Nations Convention on the Law of the Sea
UNECA	United Nations Economic Commission for Africa
UNIDO	United Nations Industrial Development Organisation
USEP	Union Syndicale des Employés de Presse
WB	World Bank
WIN	Women in Networking
WIP	Women in Politics
WSHA	Women's Self-Help Association
WTO	World Trade Organisation

Notes on contributors

Thomas Hylland Eriksen is a Professor of Social Anthropology at the University of Oslo. He has done research on Mauritius since the 1980s, and has published books and articles about ethnic relations, national identity and cultural dynamics in Mauritius. Eriksen has also published in a number of other fields, and is a well-known anthropologist.

Ramola Ramtohul is a Senior Lecturer in Sociology and Gender Studies at the University of Mauritius. She has published on gender and politics, citizenship, higher education and elite migration in Mauritius. Ramtohul has received research awards from the University of Cape Town, American Association of University Women, University of Cambridge and University of Pretoria and is currently co-editor of *Journal of Contemporary African Studies*.

Milan J.N Meetarbhan is a Barrister who was previously Associate Professor of Law at the University of Mauritius, Senior Adviser to the Government of Mauritius, Chief Executive of the Financial Services Commission and Ambassador of Mauritius to the United Nations. His book, "Constitutional Law of Mauritius" was released in August 2017.

Tania Diolle is currently involved in active politics in Mauritius as a member of the *Mouvement Patriotique* political party. Until September 2017, she was Lecturer in Political Science at the University of Mauritius. She has carried out research on the electoral system and politics in Mauritius.

Roukaya Kasenally is a democracy scholar, CEO of the African Media Initiative (AMI) and Senior Lecturer in Media and Political Systems at the University of Mauritius. Since July 2015, she is a board director for the Electoral Institute for Sustainable Democracy in Africa (EISA). She has been a Reagan Fascell Democracy Fellow at the National Endowment for Democracy (Washington DC) (2011–2012) and a Draper Hills Democracy Fellow at Stanford University (2015). Kasenally has published widely on media and democratic systems.

Christina Chan-Meetoo is a Senior Lecturer in Media and Communication and Head of the Mediacom Studio which she has set up under the aegis of the UNESCO agency IPDC at the University of Mauritius. She has published on press freedom and media regulation, new media and gender-sensitive reporting. She is the editor of two books and was nominated to the International Visitors Leadership Program (IVLP) by the US Embassy of Mauritius in 2011. She blogs at www.christinameetoo.com.

Verena Tandrayen-Ragoobur is an Associate Professor in Economics at the University of Mauritius. Her research areas are international trade, labour markets, gender and development. She has published in the *Review of Development Economics*, *Journal of African Business*, *Journal of Chinese Economic and Foreign Trade Issues,* amongst others. She has been involved in various research consultancies funded by international and regional institutions including the International Labour Office, UNCTAD, World Bank and African Economic Research Consortium.

Harshana Kasseeah is a Senior Lecturer in the Department of Economics and Statistics at the University of Mauritius. She holds a PhD in Economics from the University of Nottingham. Her research areas include finance, growth and development, entrepreneurship, internationalisation of firms and firm exporting behavior with particular focus on micro, small and medium-sized enterprises. She has published a number of book chapters and articles in several international journals.

Patrick Neveling is a Senior Research Fellow at the Department of Anthropology, University of Bergen and researches capitalism from historical, anthropological and critical political economy perspectives. His PhD thesis on Mauritius is entitled *Manifestations of Globalisation - Capital, State, and Labour in Mauritius, 1825-2005*. He has published widely on the historical political economy of capitalism and is currently finishing a book on *Relocating Capitalism: Export Processing Zones and Special Economic Zones since 1947.*

Krish Seetah is an Assistant Professor of Anthropology at Stanford University and Director of the Mauritian Archaeology and Cultural Heritage (MACH) Project. He is a zooarchaeologist, whose focus is primarily on colonisation and colonialism. His research explores questions of technology, trade, and socio-economic attitudes in colonial contexts. He has worked in a wide variety of colonial contexts, including the North Crusades in the Baltic, Venetian Republican Expansion along the Adriatic, and European expansion in the Atlantic and Indian Ocean. His work in Mauritius aims to shed light, through the lens of archaeology, on the transition from slavery to indentured labour following abolition, the extent and diversity of trade in the region, and the environmental consequences of intensive monocrop agriculture.

Diego Calaon is a post-classical archaeologist. He is the site director of archaeological project in Torcello (Venice, Ca' Foscari University). Calaon has been Marie Skłodwska-Curie Fellows (REA-EU) to pursue his research in the anthro-ecological reappraisal of the Origin of Venice. For this investigation, he has been hosted by the Stanford University. He is an associated researcher on the "Mauritian Archaeological and Cultural

Heritage project" (MACH). Methodologically, his research focuses primarily on landscape transformations, working on the impacts of both short and long term migrations and ecological changes.

Saša Čaval is a Lecturer at the Department of Anthropology and Stanford Archaeology Center at Stanford University, USA, and a Visiting Researcher at the Scientific Research Center of the Slovenian Academy of Sciences and Arts, Ljubljana, Slovenia. Her research focuses on the archaeology of religion in historical societies. She has been studying the complexities of Mauritius since 2009, and is one of the founding members of MACH – Mauritian Archaeology and Cultural Heritage project.

Alessandra Cianciosi is a Postdoctoral Research Fellow at University Ca' Foscari of Venice (Italy). Her research area focuses on landscape archaeology and the development of settlements. She participated to archaeological projects, especially in Italy, managing different steps of research, from fieldwork to the design of museum exhibitions and workshops. Since 2012 she has been involved as field archaeologist in the Mauritian Archaeology and Cultural Heritage project (MACH) of Stanford University.

Aleksander Pluskowski is an Associate Professor at the Department of Archaeology in the University of Reading. His primary field is the integrated environmental archaeology of medieval Europe, but he has also worked on related questions of colonisation and ecological transformation in Mauritius as part of the MACH project since 2010.

Caroline Ng Tseung-Wong, PhD, is a Senior Lecturer in Psychology in the Department of Social Studies at the University of Mauritius. She obtained her PhD from Utrecht University, and her research interests and publications are on interethnic relations, multiculturalism, and cultural identities.

Patrick Eisenlohr is a Professor of Anthropology, Chair of Society and Culture in Modern India at the University of Göttingen. He has conducted research on Mauritius since the late 1990s where his main interests are language and social differentiation, nation-building and diasporization, as well as religion and media. He has published on transnational Hindu and Muslim networks in the Indian Ocean region, particularly between Mauritius and India, the relationships between religion, language and media, the sonic dimensions of religion, and the links between media practices and citizenship.

Gitanjali Pyndiah is a London based Mauritian writer and PhD researcher at Goldsmiths. She also teaches Media and Cultural Studies at Middlesex University London. Her research looks at decolonial historiographies in Mauritius and creative practices such as art, poetry and music. She has written on contemporary art, on roots reggae and the late seggae artist Kaya. Her latest creative piece Mother wounds, under the pen name Gitan Djeli, will be published in an Anthology on Indian Indenture by The Commonwealth Writers.

Julie Peghini is a Senior Lecturer at the University of Paris 8 (Vincennes-Saint-Denis, France) and a researcher at the CEMTI (Centre for Media, Technologies and Internationalisation Studies). She recently published a book about the island of Mauritius, "Île rêvée, île réelle. Le multiculturalisme à l'île Maurice" (PUV, 2016).

Laura Jeffery is a Senior Lecturer in Social Anthropology at the University of Edinburgh. She has worked with the Chagossian community (in Mauritius, Seychelles, and the UK) since 2002, publishing on topics including forced displacement and onward migration, the politics of victimhood, reformulations of home and the homeland, and human–environment relations.

Seán Carey studied sociology and social anthropology at Newcastle University. He has held a variety of academic positions and is currently honorary senior research fellow in the School of Social Sciences, University of Manchester and a fellow of the Young Foundation. He has written numerous articles on Mauritius for a number of publications, including The Guardian, The Independent, The Irish Examiner, Mauritius Times, African Arguments, African Business, Africa Investor and New African.

Introduction

Thomas Hylland Eriksen and Ramola Ramtohul

After 50 years of independence, proclaimed on the 12th of March 1968, peacefully, but under a shadow of uncertainty, the small and remote island of Mauritius soon turned into a beacon and miracle, to some a puzzle and paradox, for the developing world. The island's skilful management of diversity, political stability, sustained democracy and economic success earned it the labels of 'Mauritius Miracle' as well as 'African success story' (Bräutigam, 1999; Frankel, 2010). Mauritius has been described as an island nation that 'stands out in Africa for its lively civic culture, relative social harmony, equity and impressive economic growth' (Bräutigam, 1999: 137).

Yet, one must be forgiven for pointing out that in terms of history, economy, politics and social organisation, Mauritius cannot be considered a Sub-Saharan African society. It is neither founded in subsistence agriculture nor organised on the basis of kin groups. Mauritius has been a modern society for a very long time, dominated by a monetary economy and wagework, widespread literacy and reliance on modern institutions from the post office to the hospital. In this, Mauritius has far more in common with Caribbean island-states, which share a comparable history, than with continental Africa. In comparison with other island societies with a similar ethnic composition, Mauritius has nevertheless been described as 'all the more exceptional' since other previously colonised island nations such as Trinidad, Fiji and Sri Lanka experienced coups, a breakdown of democracy and ethnic conflict (Miles, 1999: 93).

By 1996, Mauritius had moved into the 'high human development' category of the UNDP's Human Development Index (HDI), a category generally monopolised by developed countries. Nobel Prize winning economists had contrasting visions of the future of the island where, on the one hand, the economist James Meade predicted doom and gloom in 1961. Fifty years later, another Nobel laureate, Joseph Stiglitz, praised the 'Mauritian miracle', which he described as a model for the USA and other countries to emulate. Mauritius was also described by *The Economist* (2008) as 'an isolated island [that] continues to reinvent itself and confound the sceptics'. In several key areas, from democratic practices and the freedom of expression to economic growth and peaceful ethnic diversity, Mauritius has continued to defy its early critics coining it the label 'Mauritius enigma' (Miles, 1999).

1

The most fundamental question we raise in this book is, simply, what next? Taking stock of the first fifty years, its successes and ongoing challenges, we ask what we have learnt and how contemporary history can help us predict or give advice as to possible or desirable developments over the next half century. This is a tall order, and predictions are naturally uncertain and risky. At the same time, the 50th anniversary represents a poignant moment in Mauritian history, a moment of reflection, retrospection and anticipation for things to come. How will Mauritius deal with climate change in the next decades? Will gender relations become more equal? Is more intermarriage likely, or will the ethnic community-based way of life continue to predominate? Will the economy shift towards more sustainable practices, and if so, how? These are some of the questions our contributors raise in the course of this book, and which are worth considering, even if no conclusive answer is available.

The first fifty years

Unlike most former colonies, independence, in the case of Mauritius, was not the result of a national liberation struggle, but was rather an internally contested matter. All of 44 per cent of the population opposed independence, and it was even argued that it was Britain that decolonised Mauritius (Houbert, 1981: 104). At the time of independence Mauritius was a classic case of dependency as an isolated, poor and economically dependent country that faced a number of major problems. These included the threat of ethnic conflict, economic stagnation, rapid population growth and high unemployment, all of which threatened its future as an independent nation, hence Meade's (1961) gloomy evaluation in his report to the government of Mauritius. These fears were also echoed in the novelist V.S. Naipaul's feature article in the Sunday Times Magazine of July 1972, where he described Mauritius as an 'overcrowded barracoon' that was 'incapable of cultural and economic autonomy' (1972: 4). Although independence entailed a transfer of political power, there was no visible transfer of wealth from the economic elites towards the deprived since wealth was not controlled by foreigners as was the case in other British colonies. Mauritian post-independence development rested on the same foundation that existed under colonial rule (MRC, 1999: 201).

Competition and conflict among the different communities created significant tension and hostility from the mid-1950s, which lasted until well after independence (Carroll and Carroll, 1999: 183). National identity was weak, and most Mauritians primarily identified with their ethnic and religious community. Divisions in the population and fear of Hindu hegemony in an independent Mauritius led to discord and the rejection of independence in some sections of the population, especially the so-called General Population (Catholics). For the Hindus, independence meant a final reversal of their former subordinated role under the Franco-Mauritian oligarchy and stronger control of the economy. However, for some of the other groups, it seemed to imply Hindu domination, few job opportunities for the in-group and no influence in government policy (Kaplan, 1967: 28). Seeing no future for themselves in Mauritius, many resourceful Catholics, both Franco-Mauritians and Creoles, emigrated, primarily to Australia, South Africa, Canada and Europe in the years following independence. Those who chose to stay traded off their past domination of political power for guarantees under the new system in an independent Mauritius. The Franco-Mauritians remained the land-owning elite, although they had to surrender political power.

In the wake of independence, with the help of the British, Mauritius had a specifically crafted electoral system to enable the management of diversity and ensure adequate representation of the different groups in parliament. How to reconcile majority rule with minority rights was actually a critical issue during negotiations leading to independence. Apart from multiple-member constituencies that were designed to ensure a balanced representation, the unique Best Loser System was also set up. This system allows for up to eight additional members of parliament from minority communities from candidates belonging to these groups who had narrowly lost in the election. The Best Loser System has however been critiqued for promoting and institutionalising communalism as well as legitimising the use of communal labels to predict the behaviour of individuals, thereby propagating stereotypes and being detrimental to nation building. (Mathur, 1991; Nave, 1998). Since independence, political parties have ensured membership and representation of the different communities, and have openly declared their support for the ideology of 'unity in diversity' (Hills, 2002: 289). These factors allowed for compromise and accommodation of ethnic diversity at the level of political structures in the country, which ultimately led to political stability. Regular democratic elections have been held since independence. Moreover, government investment in a comprehensive welfare system that provides free health and education as well as a wide range of social security benefits, played a major role in attenuating feelings of discontent among the lower income groups and in promoting an ethos on equal opportunity and meritocracy.

Despite the odds, Mauritius has been able to successfully accommodate the ethnic diversity of its population through different mechanisms, including institutional provisions, political conventions, as well as real and symbolic gestures that contributed to building a sense of belonging among the different groups. Successive government administrations have continued to fund cultural centres for each of the main ethnic groups in Mauritius as a gesture of public recognition and valuation of the contribution of each ethnic group to the country, although these cultural centres are also believed to play a more divisive role than anything else (Hills, 2002: 291). The policy of equal accommodation of all religions adopted by the state has nonetheless contributed towards fostering religious tolerance in the country. Since 1968, a formal accord was reached to keep communal conflict out of the political sphere, and it has by and large been driven underground and into small-scale rivalries of day-to-day life (Bates, 2000: 8), although it must be added that communalism occasionally raises its head in public, and that the lack of overt conflict does not mean that there is interethnic justice.

The success of Mauritius has been attributed to good luck, a favourable colonial inheritance and, good leadership that led to the development of a competent and representative state bureaucracy, restraint of population growth, economic diversification, the integration of minority communities into the policy process and the accommodation of diverse ethnic communities (Carroll and Carroll, 1999: 179). This led to the setting up of reliable institutions that protected property rights and ensured the rule of law, thereby favouring economic development. Political stability was also a key factor that was conducive towards progress in the country. The sharing of political power and the development of a vigorous opposition and media helped to ensure that no single elite or ethnic group was in a position to dominate (Svirydzenka and Petri, 2014: 7).

Sandbrook (2005: 561) describes the achievements of Mauritius as indicators of a successful and effective developmental state. These include economic diversification in response to changing global market conditions, broad based prosperity although not always inclusive, comprehensive free public services and benefits including safety nets for vulnerable groups, the rule of law and a vibrant democracy. The post-independence governments made a conscious effort to maintain a socially inclusive approach to development, while trying to avoid exacerbating the social exclusion of ethnic and economically disadvantaged groups. However, as the sociologists Carroll and Carroll observe, while the Mauritian democracy is a 'consolidated' one, it is indeed by no means perfect (1999: 179). Although the Mauritian success story has been praised, the island nonetheless faces a number of challenges that call for careful management of diversity as well as economic and environmental resources.

Economic transformation

The Mauritian economy has undergone major structural adjustments over the past 50 years, moving from a monocrop sugar economy at the time of independence to a more diversified base of economic activities and sources of revenue which included manufacturing, tourism and, more recently, information technology and offshore financial services. Visionary political and economic leadership together with the support of a national bourgeoisie are believed to have led to the successful transformation of the economy (Bunwaree, 2014: 579). Successive post-independence governments implemented economic policies leading to industrialisation and economic diversification, especially with export-oriented industrialisation and the setting up of the Mauritius Export Processing Zone (MEPZ) in the 1970s, which created employment on a large scale especially for women.

The development of the textile industry within the MEPZ helped Mauritius evolve from a low-income, heavily agricultural economy with mass unemployment and a per capita income of about $700 in 1970 to a middle-income economy with a per capita income of $12,715 in 2005 and a 'medium' human development index for 2007/2008 of 65 (Kothari and Wilkinson, 2013: 96). Due to its colonial linkages, Mauritius benefitted from preferential trade agreements from the European Union for its sugar and textile exports. Local capital from the sugar industry was transferred into the clothing and tourism sectors, thereby reducing the country's reliance on foreign capital. There were significant joint ventures between Asian and Franco-Mauritian investors (Bräutigam, 2008). These efforts to initiate structural change successfully led to significant growth levels, coining the term 'Mauritian miracle' (Stiglitz, 2011).

The phasing out of preferential agreements under the new regulations of the World Trade Organisation (WTO), which replaced Lomé 1 and 2, led to pressure on the sugar and textile industries to increase efficiency and restructuring of the economy. The Multi-Fibre Agreement for textiles expired in 2004 and the EU Sugar Protocol ended in 2009, whereas the price of sugar fell by 36 per cent between 2006 and 2010 (Svirydzenka and Petri, 2014: 1). The tourism sector was given a boost, to become a key sector of economic activity in the country. The signing of the Double Taxation Avoidance Treaty with India in 1983 which exempted Mauritian firms from Indian capital gains tax, catalysed the development of the offshore financial sector, and was instrumental in making Mauritius the largest source of Foreign Direct Investment inflows into India (Svirydzenka and Petri, 2014: 6). This treaty was however amended in May 2016 following pressure from Indian authorities, leading to significant concern in the Mauritian business sector. The amendments will affect investments as from 1st

April 2019 when capital gains will be taxed at the full Indian domestic rates of 15 per cent and 40 per cent[i].

In the 1990s, the offshore sector and a new knowledge-intensive 'cyber city' were established and more recently, the focus has been on the real estate sector as a significant source of Foreign Direct Investment. In an initiative to attract Foreign Direct Investment, the opening up of the real estate sector to high net worth foreign investors through the sale of luxury villas which grants permanent residence to foreign buyers has caused growing discontent among the local population, especially because of the belief that these schemes have pushed up the prices of property, thereby making it increasingly difficult for locals to become home owners (Ramtohul, 2016). This strategy is also believed to create little employment with minimal impact on the problem of high unemployment following the restructuring and consolidation of the sugar industry (Kothari and Wilkinson, 2013). The ocean economy, with its vast marine resources, is now being given increased focus as a new source of economic activity and revenue. Furthermore, government has approved the setting up of smart cities and technology parks in an initiative geared towards turning Mauritius into a smart island. There is also a policy effort initiated to turn Port Louis into a major seaport with increased sea connectivity.

The healthy performance of the Mauritian economy can be, to some extent, attributed to the mix of policies that the government and private sector pursued in order to cope with external challenges and demands of the global economy. These include tax reform, the review of legislation regulating business start-ups, and the further opening of the economy, which contributed to strengthening the competitiveness of the country on the global scene (NESC, 2010). However, the Mauritian economy and society face new challenges in the current global age. The vulnerability of the island to global economic and financial downturns, together with climate change and environmental problems, constitute major threats. Small scale is a major problem in a globally competitive economy and Mauritius struggles to cope with the limitations of size and scarcity of resources. Frankel (2010: 12) noted that Mauritius is more disadvantaged than Madagascar, along with eleven South Pacific countries, as the most remote in the world.

While the economy continued to grow, unemployment, poverty and inequalities have been rising, despite efforts made by government towards poverty alleviation. Here, Bunwaree (2014: 581) highlights the threat to governance posed by growing unemployment among women and the youth in the midst of rising inequality and the increasing number of foreign workers in the country. Furthermore, from the spectre of a Malthusian nightmare at the time of independence, total fertility rate is currently below the replacement rate, which is a growing concern for the country as the population ages. In 2015, the total fertility rate was 1.34 whereas the replacement rate is 2.1.[ii] The island currently faces a number of challenges to its sustained economic growth including: an ageing population, sustaining the welfare state, growing youth unemployment, rising labour costs, environmental degradation as well as ensuring sustainable economic growth and Foreign Direct Investment (FDI).

The fragility of the social fabric

The social fabric of a nation involves a complex set of interrelationships between its people and social institutions and it forms the basis for economic and social development in the country (MRC, 1999: 1). Despite daily interaction, ethnic groups in Mauritius tend to maintain distinct boundaries through dress, religious beliefs and traditions as well as through predominant endogamy within their ethnic communities (Hempel, 2009: 465). Moreover, the findings of a study of interethnic marriages in the island revealed that the rate of marriages across ethnic groups constituted less than 10 per cent of all marriages in Mauritius and even among those marriages occurring across ethnic groups, ethnic group boundaries were often later reproduced (Nave, 2000).

At the level of Mauritian society, although the country has not experienced long-standing or devastating ethnic conflict and violence, the often-praised 'unity in diversity' remains fragile and divisions persist in the country at all levels. Mauritius experienced ethnic riots before independence in 1964 and 1968, and after independence in February 1999. The 1999 riots, which left three people dead and 100 injured, began as a protest against state authority following the death of the Creole singer and icon Kaya in police custody. For many, Kaya's death symbolised the continued discrimination the Creole community faced (Eriksen, 2004). In fact, despite the rise in living standards in the country, poverty and social exclusion are a Mauritian reality, which is more pronounced among the Creole community. Back in 1993, the Creole priest Roger Cerveaux coined the term 'malaise créole', to describe the appalling conditions in which working class Creoles lived. There is also a widespread perception, documented time and time again in research, that the *ti-Creole* or working class Creoles are excluded from influential roles in the policy process and from government jobs. The riots had an adverse impact on the reputation of Mauritius as a paradise island as well as on its status as an ideal location for business, investment and tourism (Madhoo and Nath, 2013: 36).

1999 witnessed further smaller scale communal tensions in the country. In May 1999, Muslim football fans rioted after their team Scouts Club was defeated by the

Creole team Fire Brigade with a score of 1-0 following a disputed penalty. Following this communal sport-related violence, football was stopped for about eight months and government banned all teams that had traditionally represented the different ethnic groups in Mauritius (e.g. Cadets Club represented Hindus, Scouts Club - Muslims and Fire Brigade - Creoles). This measure led to a drop in public interest in domestic football in favour of European soccer, especially the English Premier League. Observers highlight that domestic soccer has been in decline ever since the teams based on ethnicity and religion were banned following rioting between rival fans[iii]. Muslim youth also burned down a Sino-Mauritian owned gambling club in Port Louis in which seven people died. Such violent communal outbursts are relatively uncommon occurrences, yet they nonetheless highlight the persistence of communal divisions in Mauritian society. In November 2017 for instance, one of the vice prime ministers had to resign because of derogatory and discriminatory communal references made towards the Creole community during a meeting held at the Ministry of Housing. Cardinal Piat, head of the Catholic Church, and Archbishop Ian Ernest, head of the Anglican Church, spoke out on this matter and met the Prime Minister, in view of avoiding a recurrence of the 1999 riots[iv]. This, according to Chan Low, helped to appease brewing tensions in the country[v].

Moreover, diversity in Mauritius also implies that the linguistic composition of Mauritius exacerbates the complexity of communal relations in the country. The 1983 census claimed that Mauritians spoke 22 languages, and 33 languages were identified as the mother tongues of ancestors of the population (Carroll and Carroll, 1999: 183-4). Multilingualism in the country actually reflects the historical and pluralistic profile of Mauritian society. Ethnic groups in Mauritius tend to maintain separate and distinct cultures, religions and ways of life and have different ancestral languages, in spite of the fact that they speak the common language *Kreol*. However, *Kreol* has traditionally been considered as a second-rated language in the country, including by Creoles and non-Creoles consider the official recognition of *Kreol* as a measure that would advantage the Creole community at their expense (Carroll and Carroll, 2000: 28). Language issues arise repeatedly in Mauritian politics and tend to amplify inter-communal tensions. Eisenlohr (2004: 60) examined the ethnicization of language in Mauritius, namely how language became attached to ethnic values and a means of ethno-national mobilisation. The 1995 crisis over the inclusion of ancestral languages in the ranking students for the Certificate of Primary Education examinations pitted group identity against scholastic imperatives. However, this conflict revealed that the primary concern of parents lay with the educational and employment prospects of their children, and not with the standing of their ancestral tongue or community and, also that politicians cannot automatically rely on ethnic languages to mobilise local political support (Miles, 2000). The successful management of the complex 'balance of languages' in Mauritius has thus been heralded as a 'hallmark of compromise, negotiation and proceduralism' (Miles, 1999: 97). Although power is wielded in different languages for different purposes, yet no single language can claim mastery or confer disproportionate power upon any particular community. English, which is the language closest to claiming official status, is not associated with any ethnic group, whereas French can be learned relatively easily by the native speaker of Kreol and it is the mastery of English and French that is correlated with access to education (Miles, 1999: 97).

These examples highlight the fact that the social fabric of Mauritian society remains fragile and that Mauritius is still an ethnically segmented society bound together within a state framework. Given that intermarriage between different communities is not encouraged albeit being more common at present, ethnic boundary maintenance and segregation are replicated from one generation to the next (MRC, 1998). Yet, at the same time, the Mauritian ethnic heterogeneity and experience incorporate inherent stabilising tendencies, especially the crucial role played by political, economic and social institutions towards promoting social cohesion and social capital in the country (Madhoo and Nath, 2013: 36). Ethnicity is also being gradually rivalled by other forces, processes, and institutions, most notably globalisation and its antecedents such as a consumerist culture, increased exposure to social and global media, migration and tourism, among others. The concluding observation of the Social Fabric Study Phase II (MRC, 1999: 212) that 'Mauritius has to deal with the problem of managing complexity at all times', therefore remains relevant in present day Mauritian society. Examining the issues and factors that on the one hand lead to contestation and on the other, prevent conflict, would enable a deeper understanding of managing diversity as well as how to foster a stronger sense of 'unity in diversity'.

Achievements and possible paths ahead

Given the circumstances of its publication, this book is largely a celebration of the first fifty years, though not an uncritical one. The chapter authors have different approaches and views, and at least one denies that it makes sense at all to talk of a 'Mauritian miracle'. Others take a critical view of the relatively marginal role of women in politics or the continued ethnic hierarchies that regulate much of both the economy and politics, while yet others raise critical questions as to the continued feasibility of the electoral system.

Currently, Mauritius has much to celebrate in terms of achievements. It has a free and vibrant printed press, the economy has continued to grow (though with uneven benefits for different parts of the population), and there is an international consensus about the stability of good governance in the country.

Not least, the development of politics of compromise at every scalar level, from the neighbourhood to the state, has prevented the country from erupting into serious ethnic conflict. Indeed, Mauritius is often invoked in academic debates about diversity and multiculturalism, offering models and practices which may be inspirational, thought-provoking and intellectually productive elsewhere. Indeed, in this and other areas, Mauritius may have a lesson to teach the world.

Yet at the same time, Mauritian multiculturalism remains paradoxical in at least three ways: (1) the encouragement of ancestral cultures renders it difficult for individuals to liberate themselves from cultural traditions, even if they should want to; (2) multiculturalism at the ideological and political level may conceal continued, or even increased, class inequalities at the social and economic level and; (3) the acceptance of multiculturalism can be a recipe for nepotism and corruption since it encourages kinship networks and ethnic obligations at the expense of more individualist and meritocratic practices. There is no simple solution to any of these problems, but they have to be dealt with, certainly if Mauritius is going to make the most of its human capital in the decades to come.

This book brings together many of the leading scholars of contemporary Mauritius, in an examination of the Mauritian transformations since 1968, analysing the 'model', the practices, and critically investigating its sustainability in the long run. In different ways, the chapters show how a combination of factors contributed to the present state of affairs, and what are the areas in which this small island nation did not succeed, examining the causes of failure in these instances. This volume takes stock of post-independence developments, offering a critical scrutiny of the present situation in 'miracle' multicultural island nation and will describe possible scenarios for the near future or, indeed, the next 50 years. This book also shows, hopefully, how the Mauritian case sheds new light on current and ongoing debates about diversity and multiculturalism, offering models and practices which may be inspirational, thought-provoking and intellectually productive elsewhere. Indeed, in this and other areas, Mauritius may have a lesson to teach the world.

References

Bates, C. (2000) *Communalism and Identity among South Asians in Diaspora*. Working Paper No. 2, September 2000. University of Heidelberg: Heidelberg Papers in South Asian and Comparative Politics.

BBC Sport (23.08.2006) *'Mauritian football seeks comeback'*. Available online at http://news.bbc.co.uk/sport2/hi/football/world_football/5278046.stm (accessed 30.12.17).

Bräutigam, D. (1997) 'Institutions, Economic Reform and Democratic Consolidation in Mauritius', *Comparative Politics* 30(1): 45-62.

Bräutigam, D. (1999) 'The "Mauritius Miracle": Democracy, Institutions and Economic Policy', in R. Joseph (ed) *State, Conflict and Democracy in Africa*. Boulder, London: Lynne Rienner.

Bunwaree, S. (2014) 'The Fading Developmental State: Growing Inequality in Mauritius', *Development* 57(3-4): 578-590.

Carroll, B.W. and Carroll, T. (1999) 'The Consolidation of Democracy in Mauritius', *Democratization* 6(1): 179-197.

Carroll, B.W. and Carroll, T. (2000) 'Trouble in Paradise: Ethnic Conflict in Mauritius', *Commonwealth & Comparative Politics* 38(2): 25-50.

Dedans, J.C. (2017) 'Chan Low: L'Église a su apaiser la fronde suscitée par l'affaire Soodhun', *Le Défimedia* 12 Nov 2017. Available online at http://defimedia.info/jocelyn-chan-low-leglise-su-apaiser-la-fronde-suscitee-par-laffaire-soodhun (accessed on 30.12.17).

Eisenlohr, P. (2004) 'Register Levels of Ethno-National Purity: The Ethnicization of Language and Community in Mauritius', *Language and Society* 33(1): 59-80.

Eriksen, T.H. (2004) 'Predicaments of Multiethnicity: Lessons from the Mauritian Riots of 1999' in S. May, T. Modood and J. Squires (eds) *Ethnicity, Nationalism and Minority Rights*. Cambridge: Cambridge University Press.

Frankel, J.A. (2010) *Mauritius: African Success Story*. HKS Faculty Research Working Paper Series RWP10-036. Harvard University: John F. Kennedy School of Government. Available online at http://web.hks.harvard.edu/publications /workingpapers/citation.aspx?PubId=7410 (accessed on 18.04.13).

Greig, A., Turner, M. and D'Arcy, P. (2011) 'The Fragility of Success: Repositioning Mauritian Development in the Twenty-First Century', *Island Studies Journal* 6(2): 157-178.

Hempel, L.M. (2009) 'Power, Wealth and Common Identity: Access to Resources and Ethnic Identification in a Plural Society', *Ethnic and Racial Studies* 32(3): 460-489.

Hills, M. (2002) 'The Formal and Informal Management of Diversity in the Republic of Mauritius', *Social Identities: Journal for the Study of Race, Nation and Culture* 8(2): 287-300.

Houbert, J. (1981) 'Mauritius: Independence and Dependence', *The Journal of Modern African Studies* 19(1): 75-105.

Kaplan, M. (1967) 'Mauritius: A place in the sun', *Transition* 28: 28-33.

Kothari, U. and Wilkinson, R. (2013) 'Global Change, Small Island State Response: Restructuring and Perpetuation of Uncertainty in Mauritius and Seychelles', *Journal of International Development* 25: 92-107.

Madhoo, Y.N. and Nath, S. (2013) *Ethnic Diversity, Development and Social Policy in Small States: The Case of Mauritius*. UNRISD Research Paper 2013-12. Geneva: UNRISD.

Mathur, H. (1991) *Parliament in Mauritius*. Stanley, Mauritius: Editions de l'Océan Indien.

Mauritius Research Council (1998) *Social Fabric Study Phase I*. Rose Hill, Mauritius: MRC.

Mauritius Research Council (1999) *Social Fabric Study Phase II*. Rose Hill, Mauritius: MRC.

Meade, J. (1961) *The Economic and Social Structure of Mauritius*. London: Methuen.

Miles, W.F.S. (1999) 'The Mauritius Enigma', *Journal of Democracy* 10(2): 91-104.

Miles, W.F.S. (2000) 'The Politics of Language Equilibrium in a Multilingual Society: Mauritius', *Comparative Politics* 32(2): 215-230.

Ministry of Foreign Affairs, Regional Integration and International Trade (2015) *Millennium Development Goals Report 2015*. Port Louis, Mauritius: MFARIIT.

Naipaul, V.S. (1972) 'Mauritius: The Overcrowded Barracoon', *Sunday Times Magazine* 16th July 1972, p. 4-16, 37-38.

National Economic and Social Council (2010) *Integration into the Global Economy: Socio-economic Challenges and Policy Implications for Mauritius*. NESC Report 14. Port Louis, Mauritius: NESC.

Nave, A. (1998) 'The Institutionalisation of Communalism: The Best Loser System in Mauritius', in M. Carter (ed) *Consolidating the Rainbow: Independent Mauritius, 1968-1998*. Port Louis, Mauritius: Centre for Research on Indian Ocean Societies.

Nave, A. (2000) 'Marriage and the Maintenance of Ethnic Group Boundaries: The case of Mauritius', *Ethnic and Racial Studies* 23(2): 329-352.

Permal, J.D. (2017) 'Démission de Soodhun: Mgr Ian Ernest se réjouit que sa rencontre avec le PM ait pu ramener la sérénité', *L'Express* 12 November 2017. Available online at https://www.lexpress.mu/article/320527/demission-soodhun-mgr-ian-ernest-rejouit-que-sa-rencontre-pm-ait-pu-ramener-serenite (accessed on 30.12.17).

Ramtohul, R. (2016) 'High Net Worth Migration in Mauritius: A Critical Analysis', *Migration Letters* 13(1): 17-33.

Sandbrook, R. (2005) 'Origins of the Democratic Developmental State: Interrogating Mauritius', *Canadian Journal of African Studies* 39(3): 549-581.

Singh (2015) 'What the changes in the tax treaty with Mauritius mean for India, investors', *The Indian Express* 12th May 2015. Available online at http://indianexpress.com/article/explained /what-the-changes-in-the-tax-treaty-with-mauritius-mean-for-india-investors-2795965/ (Accessed on 02.01.17).

Stiglitz, J. (2011) *The Mauritius Miracle*. Project Syndicate. Available online at http://www.project-syndicate.org/commentary/the-mauritius-miracle (accessed on 15.10.15)

Svirydzenka, K. and Petri, M. (2014) *Mauritius: The Drivers of Growth—Can the Past be Extended?* IMF Working Paper 14/134.

The Economist (16.10.2008) *Mauritius: Beyond Beaches and Palm Trees*. Available online at http://www.economist.com/node/12436181 (accessed on 16.10.15)

[i] Singh (2016) 'What the changes in the tax treaty with Mauritius mean for Indian investors', *The Indian Express* 12 May 2016.

[ii] Ministry of Foreign Affairs, Regional Integration and International Trade (MFARIIT, 2015).

[iii] BBC Sport (23.08.2006) 'Mauritian football seeks comeback'
http://news.bbc.co.uk/sport2/hi/football/world_football/5278046.stm

[iv] Permal (2017) 'Démission de Soodhun: Mgr Ian Ernest se réjouit que sa rencontre avec le PM ait pu ramener la sérénité', *L'Express* 12 Nov 2017.

[v] Dedans (2017) 'Chan Low: L'Église a su apaiser la fronde suscitée par l'affaire Soodhun', *Le Défimedia* 12 Nov 2017.

The Constitution at 50

MILAN J.N. MEETARBHAN

Introduction

The Constitution in force in Mauritius since March 12, 1968 was adopted by the United Kingdom Parliament.[i] Although the Constitution was largely based on the 'Whitehall model'[ii] used for adopting the Constitutions of a number of small island nations of the Commonwealth, it included several provisions that were unique to Mauritius. These provisions were often the result of the historical and demographic circumstances of the country. The constitutional status and the constitutional regime that came into force in 1968 should be considered in the light of the political struggles that started in the early part of the 20th century but more particularly of the preceding three decades.

Modern Mauritian constitutional history can be broadly divided into three periods of a decade each:

1. **1938-1948: The rise of Political and Trade Union movements**: notably the new Labour Ordinance of 1938 and new Constitution of 1948 enlarged suffrage with women being eligible to vote for the first time, although there were still property and literacy tests that had to be satisfied.

2. **1948-1958: The emergence of a new political class**: The 1948 election was a turning point in political emancipation but the results were frustrated by the appointment of nominees by the Governor to the Legislative Council. The 1956 Constitutional conference in London was followed by a new Constitution which granted universal suffrage in 1958.

3. **1958-1968: The Crucial Years, the Pre-Independence period:** Following the first election held under universal adult suffrage in 1958, the 1961 Constitutional Review, the 1964 Constitution, the 1965 Constitutional talks and the wide-ranging debates on the electoral system, the appointment of the Constitutional Commissioner and the decisive elections of 7 August 1967 led to the country's Independence in 1968.

Throughout these three decades, public debate on constitutional emancipation was marked by ethnic considerations. There was strong opposition to democracy, responsible government and majority rule with demands for separate electoral registers for each community, proportional representation on communal grounds and other quotas. During the constitutional talks leading up to Independence, the debate focused on the electoral system with competing views on safeguarding ethnic representation on one hand and on preventing perpetuation of divisions that could hinder nation-building on the other. The safeguards eventually provided in the Constitution went beyond the electoral system and also applied to various appointments and to independence of our institutions resulting namely in singular powers being conferred on the Governor-General.

Following the talks held at Lancaster House from 7 to 24 September 1965, 'between the advocates of independence and of continuing association with Britain on the ultimate status of Mauritius'[iii], the Secretary of State for the Colonies, announced that 'it was right that Mauritius should be independent and take her place among the sovereign nations of the world.'[iv] The UK Government decided that the future constitutional status of the country would not be decided by way of a referendum (which was demanded by some political parties but opposed by others who apprehended ethnic polarisation) but that a general election would be held following which the country would move towards Independence if a resolution asking for this was passed by a simple majority of the new Assembly.[v] At the election held on 7 August 1967, the Independence Party led by Sir Seewoosagur Ramgoolam won 39 seats with 54.13 per cent of the popular vote whilst the *Parti Mauricien Social Democrate*, led by Gaëtan Duval, which was opposed to independence and called for an "associate" status with the UK, won 23 seats with 43.99 per cent of the vote. At the first sitting of the newly elected Legislative Assembly on 22 August 1967, Sir Seewoosagur Ramgoolam's motion calling for Independence was adopted.[vi]

Mauritius became a sovereign State on 12 March 1968 with the last British colonial Governor, Sir John Shaw Rennie being appointed as Governor-General and Sir Seewoosagur Ramgoolam appointed as the country's first Prime Minister. The date of March 12 was chosen as a tribute to the struggle for Indian independence as the Salt March which is considered as a landmark in the freedom struggle started on this date in 1930. The Constitution provided for Her Majesty the Queen to remain as Head of State, represented in Mauritius by a Governor General and for a Legislative Assembly consisting of up to 70 members. The leader of the majority party in the Assembly would serve as Prime Minister and all Ministers in his Cabinet (except for the Attorney General) would be appointed from amongst members of the Assembly. The Privy Council which consists of members of the Judicial Committee of the House of Lords, the highest appellate court in the United Kingdom, would remain as the country's highest court.

1. 'Democratic State'

The Constitution of Mauritius is not programmatic or ideological to the extent that it does not provide for instance that the State shall be 'secular' or 'socialist', but the very first section of the Constitution does provide that Mauritius will be a 'democratic' State. Section 1 was given special status under the Constitution since it is one of the two provisions of the Constitution which can only be amended with the prior approval of the people in a referendum.[vii] The special procedure for amending section 1 thus elevates this section to one of the most fundamental provisions of the Constitution. The Privy Council has referred to this special status as 'an exceptional degree of entrenchment'.[viii]

The answer to the question of whether section 1 has any significant and judicially enforceable meaning has evolved over time. The initial thinking was that section 1 is merely in the nature of a Preamble, the contents of which are only defined by the other provisions of the Constitution. In other words, it is not a stand-alone provision but only proclaims the principle on which the remaining provisions of the Constitution are based. This has now given way to a different construction which in effect subjects interpretation of the rest of the Constitution to the requirements of section 1. The term 'democratic' would now be given real autonomous substantive meaning which makes it a justiciable provision of the Constitution.

In an early case[ix], the Supreme Court took the view that what section 1 proclaims in the abstract is 'concretised' by other provisions of the Constitution. 'Actually the idea of a democratic form of government which it proclaims in the abstract is concretised by those other provisions of the Constitution which create and regulate the essential components of a democracy. Such are those provisions which deal with fundamental rights and freedoms of the citizens, the composition, duties and functions of the executive, and of the Legislature, the election of members of the Legislative Assembly, the electoral system, the duration of the Assembly, an independent judiciary.'

In another case[x] a Judge said that, 'one must not go outside the Constitution to discover the form of democracy which obtains in Mauritius. The Constitution itself prescribes the form.' These pronouncements were mostly made in the first decade after Independence but later there was a judicial affirmation of the standing of section 1 as an operative provision of the Constitution. The Supreme Court and the Privy Council stated that this section was not just a mere Preamble, 'It is not simply a guide to interpretation. In this respect it is to be distinguished from many other constitutional provisions. It is of the first importance that the provision that Mauritius 'shall be ... a democratic State' is an operative and binding provision. Its very subject matter and place at the very beginning of the Constitution underlies its importance. And the Constitution provides that any law inconsistent with the Constitution is *pro tanto* void: section 2.'[xi]

It would be for the Courts to decide what is democratic and if anything done by the Legislative or Executive branches of Government are inconsistent with the constitutional provision that Mauritius is a democratic State. The Privy Council defined the three essential components of a democratic State as follows: 'The idea of a democracy involves a number of different concepts. The first is that the people must decide who should govern them. Secondly, there is the principle that fundamental rights should be protected by an impartial and independent judiciary. Thirdly, in order to achieve a reconciliation between the inevitable tensions between these ideas, a separation of powers between the legislature, the executive, and the judiciary is necessary.'[xii]

The Courts have declared attempts by the legislature to remove in certain cases the right of the judiciary to decide whether a person should be released on bail, as unconstitutional. The Supreme Court has stated that the Constitution clearly rests on two fundamental tenets, the rule of law and the juxtaposition (or separation as it is more often called) of powers and that it is not in accord with the letter or spirit of the Constitution to legislate so as to enable the Executive to overstep or bypass the Judiciary in its essential roles, namely those of affording to the citizen the protection of the law and, as guardian of the Constitution, to ensure that no person's human rights or fundamental freedoms are placed in jeopardy.[xiii] The Supreme Court made a vibrant defence of the doctrine of separation powers when it declared that an Act of Parliament which effectively overturned a decision of the Court[xiv] was in breach of the Constitution and null and void. The Court considered that the law enacted by Parliament was a frontal aggression on the highest Court in the land. 'Parliament did not merely usurp a purely judicial function in order to determine a private dispute between two parties. It set itself up as a Court of Appeal in order to reverse a judgment of the Supreme Court, and it did so long after the delays for an appeal were gone and the judgment had become final.'

In addition to setting out objectives, a Constitution may also specifically provide for Basic Features or Directive Principles.[xv] Although the Mauritian Constitution does not provide for Basic Features or Directive Principles which if breached would be inconsistent with the concept of a democratic State, it could be argued that some of the Basic Features or Directive Principles found in other Constitutions are enshrined in the concept of a democratic State.

The Courts may also be called upon to decide whether an amendment to the Constitution may itself be unconstitutional. Judges initially took the view that the test for validity of a constitutional amendment was only procedural. If the amendment had been adopted by the majority of members of the National Assembly as prescribed by the Constitution, the amendment would be valid. However, in 2003[xvi], the Supreme Court and the Privy Council were prepared to consider that even an amendment to the Constitution could not stand if it was inconsistent with the principle of a democratic State as set out in section 1 of the Constitution. This was a radical departure from earlier cases where the Supreme Court had taken the view that once a constitutional amendment had obtained the prescribed majority in Parliament, the judiciary would not question the validity of the amendment. There has been some debate amongst academics on circumstances in which judges may be called upon to decide whether a constitutional amendment may be unconstitutional.[xvii]

2. Protection of fundamental rights

Chapter 2 of the Mauritian Constitution protects the fundamental rights of the individual. It is significant that in spite of the debates preceding independence and pressure for special rights for specific groups, the Mauritian Bill of Rights provides for individual and not group rights (except for section 14 which guarantees the rights of a religious or cultural association to set up a school). It may be argued that even where there is a need to safeguard the rights of particular groups in a society, the protection of individual rights ultimately ensures that the rights of the members of these groups will be protected. These rights are justiciable rights and a judicial remedy may be available against any breach of these rights. Section 17 of the Constitution provides that where a person alleges that any of the provisions of Chapter 2 has been, is being or is likely to be contravened in relation to him, then, without prejudice to any other action with respect to the same matter that is lawfully available, that person may apply to the Supreme Court for redress.

The Bill of Rights is based essentially on the European Convention of Human Rights which was adopted in 1950.[xviii] Mauritian Courts have often been referred to judgments of the European Court on Human Rights and have been guided by the interpretation given by the European Court to various provisions of the Convention. The philosophy underlying the provisions of the Constitution relating to fundamental rights is clearly enunciated in the opening section of Chapter 2. The rights and freedoms guaranteed are subject to (1) the rights and freedoms of others and (2) the public interest. The general construct of the Bill of Rights is as follows:

a. the right or freedom is set out as the general rule;
b. there may be exceptions to the rule in specified circumstances or for specified purposes;
c. these exceptions are set out in the Constitution or they must be provided under a law and the law must be reasonably justifiable in a democratic society.

How will the Courts decide what is reasonably justifiable in a democratic society? The Supreme Court has followed the test laid down by the European Court of Human Rights in the case of *S and Marper v the United Kingdom*: 'An interference will be considered "necessary in a democratic society" for a legitimate aim if it answers a "pressing social need" and, in particular, if it is proportionate to the legitimate aim pursued and if the reason adduced by the national authorities to justify it are "relevant and sufficient"'[xix]. The Supreme Court has also referred to another ECHR decision, *Sahin v Turkey* in order to assess the 'necessity' for interference, 'the Court's task is confined to determining whether the reasons given for the interference were relevant and sufficient and the measures taken at the national level proportionate to the aims pursued'[xx].

The Supreme Court has stressed the need for limitations to fundamental rights not to be narrowly construed. Referring to the protection of the freedom of expression, the Court has pointed out that the provision setting out that protection is subject to the limitations contained in that provision, being limitations designed to ensure that the enjoyment of this right by any individual does not prejudice the rights and freedoms of others or the public interest. 'The necessity of any constitutionally permissible limitations must, like all derogations, be narrowly construed and must respond to what has generally been understood to be a "pressing social need". Thus, the application in practice of limitations which are permissible in principle must be closely monitored so as to ensure that they stay, in any particular case, within the limits proportionate to the legitimate aim pursued.'[xxi]

The test laid down in the Constitution for the validity of exceptions to the entrenched fundamental rights is whether the exception is reasonably justifiable in a democratic society. Section 3 lays down the principle that rights protected by the Constitution are subject to limitations designed to ensure that the enjoyment of these rights 'does not prejudice the rights and freedoms of others.' Thus, the Court has held that whilst freedom to practise one's religion is protected by the Constitution this is subject to the rights and freedoms of other people in the neighbourhood[xxii].

3. The electoral system

Mauritius has a unicameral legislature known as the National Assembly. It consists of 62 elected members (60 from 20 three-member constituencies and two from a two-member constituency) and of up to eight Best Losers. The electoral system was one of the most controversial issues during the constitutional debates in the 1960's, apart from the issue of independence or association with the UK. The debate over the electoral system was essentially driven by ethnic considerations and the need to ensure adequate representation of 'minority groups'. Various proposals were made regarding quotas, discrete electoral rolls, reserved seats and proportional representation.

In addition to the discussions that took place at the Constitutional conferences in London, (i) the issue was also canvassed during the visit of the Constitutional Commissioner Prof de Smith in 1964, (ii) representations were made to the Banwell Commission (the recommendations of the Commission were later vigorously opposed by the Mauritius Labour Party) and (iii) finally decided by the Secretary of State for the Colonies, Anthony Greenwood following the visit to Mauritius of his ministerial colleague, John Stonehouse. To allay the concerns about adequate representation of all sections of the population, two measures were envisaged:

- It was proposed to draw constituency boundaries in such a way as to ensure that certain 'minority groups' would still have an opportunity to elect members who might not otherwise get elected;
- The Best Loser system would ensure that additional Members would be appointed from amongst unreturned candidates belonging to under-represented communities in the Assembly following a general election.

The delimitation of constituency boundaries to meet the above objective resulted in wide disparities between the number of voters in different constituencies. Though all constituencies in mainland Mauritius are entitled to three Members of Parliament, some constituencies have almost three times as many voters as others.

For the purposes of determining which communities are under-represented among elected members and for appointing Best Losers, candidates at elections are required to state which of the four communities specified in the Constitution[xxiii] they belong to. The Electoral Supervisory Commission may then nominate from amongst unreturned candidates of the community it has deemed to be under-represented, the candidate with the highest percentage of votes as a Best Loser MP to ensure adequate representation of that community. In order to enable the Electoral Supervisory

Commission to allocate the additional seats, each candidate standing for election must, at the time of filing his nomination papers, state the community to which he belongs.

In 2007, members of a political party whose nomination papers for standing as candidates at a general election were turned down as they had not disclosed the community to which they belonged (deemed to be a mandatory requirement) complained to the UN Human Rights Committee that their rights under Articles 18, 25 and 26 of the International Covenant on Civil and Political Rights had been violated.[xxiv] Since the purpose of the declaration was to enable the Electoral Supervisory Commission to determine the adequate representation of each of the four communities and hence to nominate Best Losers, the Committee noted that community affiliation has not been the subject of a census since 1972. The Committee therefore found, 'that the continued maintenance of the requirement of mandatory classification of a candidate for general elections without the corresponding updated figures of the community affiliation of the population in general would appear to be arbitrary and therefore violates article 25 (b) of the Covenant.' In a case before the Privy Council it had been argued that allocation of seats to ensure adequate representation of communities 'based on figures now nearly forty years old makes no sense.'[xxv]

The allocation of seats to Best Losers has been one of the main issues discussed in wide ranging debates on electoral reform over many years. A Consultation Paper, 'Renewing Democracy, Electoral Reform - Modernising the Electoral System' published by the Government of Mauritius in March 2014, reviewed proposals on electoral system made (a) at the London Conference of 1956 and the resulting London Agreement of March 1957 and recommendations of the Trustram Eve Commission in the same year; (b) the Constitutional Review Conference of 1961 followed by the Constitutional Order 1964; (c) by the Constitutional Commissioner Prof SA de Smith in his 1965 Report; (d) the Banwell Commission report in 1966; (e) the recommendations of the Rt Hon John Stonehouse in 1966; (f) the Commission on Constitutional and Electoral Reform (the Sachs Commission) 2001/02; (g) the Parliamentary Select Committee Report 2002; and (h) the Carcassonne Report 2013. The Consultation Paper also set out the Government's own proposals for reform.[xxvi]

4. Parliamentary supremacy or constitutional supremacy

Section 2 of the Constitution provides that the Constitution is the supreme law of the land and any law inconsistent with the Constitution would be invalid. Thus, the Mauritian constitutional regime would be considered as one based on constitutional supremacy. However, in practice, Parliament may often have the last word.

Provisions of legislation voted by the Mauritian Parliament have been struck down as being inconsistent with the Constitution. As early as 1973 when the Constitution had been in force for only five years, the Supreme Court stated that, 'Of recent years more than a few cases have come to this Court in which the validity of enactments has been challenged on the ground of inconsistency with the Constitution and in which this Court has had the opportunity to observe and rule that the sovereignty of our Parliament was subject to the limitations placed on its Legislative freedom by the Constitution'.[xxvii] However, in the event that any law is found to be inconsistent with the Constitution, Parliament may alter the infringed constitutional provision to ensure that the impugned law stands valid. In addition, Parliament may where it proposes to adopt legislation that could fail the test of constitutionality, preemptively amend the relevant constitutional provision so that the law would be consistent with the Constitution.

Given that Mauritius has a parliamentary system where the Executive has an inherent majority, the Executive can, where a law or a section of the law has been struck down by the courts as being unconstitutional, obtain the support of the qualified majority prescribed under the Constitution to alter the supreme law itself to ensure consistency with the impugned law. On the other hand, when the Government introduces a Bill which it considers to be in breach of the Constitution or which could be challenged before the Supreme Court on grounds of inconsistency with the Constitution, it may seek to pre-empt such challenge by amending the Constitution upfront to remove or alter the relevant provision or add a new provision which specifically allows for the proposed bill to withstand any challenge. This is what the Government did in December 2015 when in view of doubts about whether the proposed Good Governance and Integrity Reporting Bill would stand the test of constitutionality, Government simultaneously introduced a Constitutional Amendment Bill which would specifically allow for confiscation of assets as proposed by the Good Governance and Integrity Reporting Bill.[xxviii]

In December 2016, when the Government was proposing to introduce legislation establishing a Prosecution Commission which would be empowered to review and overrule a decision of the Director of Public Prosecutions, the Government simultaneously introduced a Constitutional Amendment Bill that would ensure that the new legislation would not be declared unconstitutional.[xxix] In such circumstances, the constitutional amendments would effectively ensure that the Constitution would be made consistent with the proposed legislation instead of the legislation being consistent with the Constitution.[xxx]

A Constitution is often described as the supreme law that imposes limits on the powers of the three organs of government. It thus acts as a bulwark against the excesses of government. In Mauritius, the executive arm of government is part of the legislative arm and when it commands the required parliamentary majority it may amend the Constitution at any time. Thus, the supreme law which is meant to limit the powers of government and act as a bulwark against abuse by the government can at any time be amended by the Executive, acting solely through its parliamentary majority. In the same vein, it can further be argued that the Mauritian Constitution does not impose limits on the powers of the legislature as the National Assembly on its own and often acting through the majority party alone, may decide at any time to remove or extend the limits on its powers.

Judicial Review of Constitutionality

In exercising their powers of constitutional review, the Privy Council and the Supreme Court have consistently made two points:

(i) that a Constitution must be given a generous and purposive interpretation; and
(ii) the constitutionality of a parliamentary enactment is presumed unless it is shown to be unconstitutional.

The Privy Council[xxxi] has stressed that constitutions are not to be construed like commercial documents. 'The background of a constitution is an attempt, at a particular moment in history, to lay down an enduring scheme of government in accordance with certain moral and political values. Interpretation must take these purposes into account. Furthermore, the concepts used in a constitution ... may expressly state moral and political principles to which the judges are required to give effect in accordance with their own conscientiously held views of what such principles entail.'[xxxii]

Presumption of Constitutionality

With respect to whether legislation adopted by Parliament is consistent with the Constitution, the Mauritian Supreme Court has applied the principle of the presumption of constitutionality. The Supreme Court has generally followed the principle laid down by the Privy Council that the constitutionality of a parliamentary enactment is presumed unless it is shown to be unconstitutional, and the burden on a party seeking to prove invalidity is a heavy one[xxxiii]. The Supreme Court has also adopted a liberal approach to matters of form in its enforcement of constitutional rights so that procedural defects do not prevent Judges from protecting fundamental rights.

5. Perfecting the constitutional regime

The nation now has the benefit of almost half a century of constitutional practice and case law. We may therefore take a dispassionate view of how the Constitution has served us well or not well enough or simply needs to be updated to reflect modern trends, especially in the area of protection of fundamental rights.

Our Judges have since the early post-independence years built a solid body of constitutional case law asserting the doctrine of separation of powers, protection of fundamental rights and an increasingly wider scope of the notion of a democratic State.

Our Judges have consistently stood up for separation of powers, an essential pillar of a democratic State and have declared laws seeking to remove the power to grant bail from the judiciary, as inconsistent with the Constitution.

Our Judges have repeatedly stated that a Constitution must be given a generous and purposive interpretation and they have stressed the need for some flexibility on matters of form in constitutional cases.

The constitutional regime has overall, provided relative stability and promoted effective governance. However, there are major areas where the empirical evidence of the last 50 years suggests that serious consideration must be given to perfecting our democracy.

It has on some occasions been far too easy for ruling parties or alliances on their own to amend the Constitution as they please, often at very short notice and with little or no consultations.

It has even been possible for Governments having a majority in the legislature to remove constitutional obstacles to get through their legislative agenda or adopt constitutional amendment with retrospective effect validating all elections that have taken place since 25 years, so as prevent ant judicial challenge to the results of one previous election.

At times instead of enacting legislation which is consistent with the Constitution, the Executive has rushed in constitutional amendments to ensure that the Constitution is consistent with the proposed legislation.

The electoral system provided in the Constitution was the result of compromise between opposing views at a given point in our history. We need to revisit our electoral system to ensure greater equity and diversity. We also need to consider in this context, whether instead of increasing the number of MP's in the National

Assembly, we should have an upper house or a Council of State which can make a positive and meaningful contribution to the legislative process, especially in relation to constitutional amendments adopted by the legislature.

One major area of reform that should be considered is the mode of election of the President. After Independence, the Governor General was given some wide powers so as to give assurances to various sections of the nation that some functions will not be outside the realm of the political executive. When the country became a republic in 1992, these powers and others were given to the President. Whilst it may be in the interests of a democratic society that there is a proper allocation of power, yet when a Prime Minister has a mandate from the people and a President does not, the legitimacy of the exercise of certain powers by the President may be questioned. The President is for all intents and purposes a nominee of the Prime Minister and the mode of election of the President must be reviewed if an allocation of power leading to a healthier democracy is to be sustained.

Our Courts have generally provided constitutional redress to aggrieved citizens. However, we need to consider whether a specialised Constitutional Bench should be established and whether the rules on *locus standi* need to be re-examined so that citizens can seek constitutional redress in a wider range of cases than the present relatively restrictive rules would allow them to do.

Chapter 2 of our Constitution which is our Bill of Rights is based essentially on the European Convention of Human Rights which dates from 1950. There has been considerable global progress since then on the nature and scope of rights, not only political and civil rights but also economic and social rights. We need to reconsider our fundamental rights framework to expand the constitutional protection of individual rights in our country and to move from negative rights to more positive rights that include social and economic rights.

A review of the Constitution may also consider the following:

1. Whether the Right to life should be more than 'just animal existence', as some scholars and judges have put it. In one case, the Indian Supreme said that the right to life would include 'the right to food, clothing, decent environment and reasonable accommodation to live in. The difference between the need of an animal and a human being for shelter has to be kept in view. For the animal it is the bare protection of the body, for a human being, it has to be suitable accommodation which allows him to grow in all aspects- physical, mental and intellectual.'

2. Whether the constitutional protection of the freedom of expression is sufficient to include freedom of the press or whether we need a specific provision relating to freedom of the press.

3. Whether we need a specific protection of the right to privacy. Our Constitution protects the privacy of home and property but there is no constitutional protection of the right to privacy as such.

4. Whether the right to liberty should be only about physical liberty or be given a wider scope.

5. Whether the powers of the Electoral Supervisory Commission over the conduct of elections are sufficient or whether they should be enlarged so that the ESC has a greater say in the conduct of electoral campaigns.

These are by no means exhaustive but only set out some of the possible and desirable areas of reform.

Whilst we study the Constitution and how it has been applied and enforced we have to remind ourselves that over and above the text of the Constitution we must also apply the values of constitutionalism. Constitutionalism goes beyond a mere textual approach and includes values, norms and conventions. It is not just the letter of the Constitution that matters. A democratic State is not only one which complies with the strict requirements of its Constitution but also one which will at all times act in accordance with the core values of democracy and good governance.

The question that we can ask ourselves is whether courts can still promote these values and the spirit of the Bill of Rights even in the absence of any specific constitutional provision enjoining them to do so.

A revised Constitution will also have to address another lacuna in the present one: the absence of any reference to international law. Unlike many other Constitutions, ours does not state what is the relation between international and domestic law.

In the absence of any constitutional provision, our judges have had to determine the extent to which in applying the 'law' domestic courts will take into consideration or enforce norms of international law or treaty obligations depending on whether the treaty has been ratified by Parliament or arise only from an executive act. A modern Constitution for Mauritius should address the issue.

The fiftieth anniversary of Independence and of the Constitution would be an opportunity to start a review exercise to assess the merits of the existing constitutional regime and what additional measures are required to perfect and modernise the Constitution. Whilst the 1968 Constitution was not adopted by a Mauritian Constituent Assembly or by the people of Mauritius it is important that any review exercise should be carried by an independent body out in consultation with all Mauritians.

A revised Constitution would then have to be adopted by the people of Mauritius.

References

Dale, W. (1993) 'The Making And Remaking Of Commonwealth Constitutions', *International and Comparative Law Quarterly* 42(1): 67-83.

Landau, D. (2013) 'Abusive Constitutionalism', *University of California Davis Law Review* 47: 189-260.

L'Express (06.12.16) *'Milan Meetarbhan: "La Banalisation des Modifications Constitutionnelles"'*.

Meetarbhan, M.JN. (2017) *Constitutional Law of Mauritius: Constitution of Mauritius with Commentaries*. Mauritius: M.JN. Meetarbhan.

Po, J.Y. (2015) 'The conundrum of unconstitutional constitutional amendments', *Global Constitutionalism* 4(1): 114–136.

Report of the Mauritius Constitutional Conference September (1965), Sessional Paper No. 6 of 1965. Port Louis: J.E. Félix, Govt. Printer.

---

[i] The Parliament of the United Kingdom adopted the Mauritius Independence Act on 29 February 1968. An Order in Council, the Mauritius Independence Order was made on 4 March 1968, with the Constitution of Mauritius as an Annex. Prior to Independence, the colonial Government had granted Constitutions to Mauritius in 1825 (fifteen years after the start of British rule in 1810), a revised one in 1832 which remained in force until 1885 when a new Constitution providing for the first time for the election of some members of the Legislative Council was adopted. In February 1945, the Governor Sir Mackenzie-Kennedy appointed a Constitution Consultative Committee to discuss constitutional reforms and a new Constitution was granted in 1947. The first Constitution providing for universal suffrage came into force in 1958. In Mauritius, the Constitution was published as the Mauritius Independence Order 1968.

[ii] See William Dale: The Making And Remaking Of Commonwealth Constitutions, 42 Int'l & Comp. L.Q. 67 1993. The author cites Sir Kenneth Roberts-Wray who was Legal Adviser at the Commonwealth Office from 1945 to 1960.

[iii] 'Report of the Mauritius Constitutional Conference September 1965', Sessional Paper No.6 of 1965, at para.6.

[iv] Anthony Greenwood, Secretary of State for the Colonies, had emphasised at the opening of the Conference that he would not 'prejudge in any way the outcome of the present conference. No solutions have been ruled out in advance.' In their opening remarks, Sir Seewoosagur Ramgoolam stated that 'the Mauritius Labour Party wants the independence of Mauritius within the Commonwealth' whereas Jules Koenig Q.C stated on behalf of the Parti Mauricien that 'if we contend that decolonisation there must be, we discard independence as being fatal to the prosperity and the peaceful and harmonious development of Mauritius as part of the free world. We claim that it is the general wish of the people of Mauritius that as substitute for independence, close constitutional associations with Great Britain should be maintained within the framework of a new pattern.'

[v] Ibid.

vi The Salt March was called by Mahatma Gandhi to protest against the imposition of a salt tax by the British colonial government.

vii The special status was introduced in the Constitution by an amendment made in 1982.

viii *State v Khoyratty Abdool Rachid* [2004] PRV 59; [2006] MR 210.

ix Vallet v Ramgoolam [1973] MR 29.

x Lincoln & Ors v. Governor-General & Ors [1974] MR 112.

xi *The State v Khoyratty* [2006] UKPC 13.

xii Ibid.

xiii Noordally v Attorney-General [1986] MR 204.

xiv Mahboob v Government of Mauritius [1982] MR 135.

xv See for instance Part IV of the Indian Constitution and Article 45 of the Constitution of Ireland.

xvi *Police v Khoyratty*, Supreme Court [2004 MR 137]; *The State v Khoyratty*, Privy Council [2006 MR 210], [2004 PRV 59].

xvii For a comprehensive review of the arguments made in relation to what the 'conundrum of unconstitutional constitutional amendments', see Po Jen Yap: The conundrum of unconstitutional constitutional amendments *Global Constitutionalism (2015), 4:1, 114–136, Cambridge University Press, 2015*; D. Landau: Abusive Constitutionalism, *University of California, Davis Law Review* [Vol. 47:189].

xviii The United Kingdom ratified the Convention in 1951 and in 1953 extended the application of the Convention to a number of its colonies, including Mauritius.

xix [2008] ECHR 1581 (Applications Nos. 30562/04 and 30566/04 – 4 December 2008).

xx [2005] 41 E.H.R.R.8.

xxi Director of Public Prosecutions v Boodhoo[1992] MR 284.

xxii *Aumeer v Assemblée de Dieu [1988] MR 229.* In another case the Court held that, 'the right to property or the use thereof is not absolute but is subject to the limitations expressly and limitatively provided in section 3 of the Constitution, that is to say, limitations which draw their justification from the need to respect and protect the rights and freedoms of others and the public interest. Stone crushing plants inevitably generate stone dust and noise among other serious inconveniences, particularly in a residential and commercial area.' *(Ramdhony v Municipal Council of Vacoas Phoenix [1995] MR 103.*

xxiii The four communities specified in Section 3 of the First Schedule to the Constitution are: Hindu (2) Muslim (3) Sino-Mauritian (4) 'every person who does not appear from his way of life to belong to one or other of those 3 communities shall be regarded as belonging to the General Population'. In *The Electoral Supervisory Commission v The Honourable The Attorney-General* (2005 SCJ 252, 2005 MR 42), the Supreme Court declared that 'prospective candidates at a general election are under a legal obligation to declare on their nomination papers the communities to which they belong, failing which, their nomination papers will be held invalid by their respective Returning Officers.'

xxiv Communication No. 1744/2007

xxv Dany Sylvie Marie & Dhojaven Vencadsamy & ors v Electoral Commissioner & ors [2010] PRV 70; [2011] UKPC 45.

xxvi The Government's proposals were based essentially on recommendations made by Dr Rama Sithanen, a former Minister of Finance in a paper entitled 'Roadmap for a better balance between stability and fairness in the voting formula.'

xxvii Vallet v Ramgoolam [1973] MR 29.

xxviii The Bill provided for the confiscation of assets in cases of unexplained wealth through actions in rem which would consequently exclude constitutional safeguards available in criminal proceedings. Both the Constitutional amendment introducing the new Section 8(4)(aa) and the Good Governance and Integrity Bill were voted by the National Assembly on December 2 and 3, 2015. Introducing the Constitutional Amendment Bill to the National Assembly, the Prime Minister said, '... Government is mindful and respectful of the provisions of sections 1 and 2 of the Constitution and is aware that the Supreme Court, acting within its constitutional powers and functions, is empowered to strike down any law which breaches the Constitution. Government fully endorses that right and is committed to ensuring that any proposed legislation passes the test of constitutionality. We are also aware that Constitutions, insofar as rights are concerned, have to be interpreted generously. [..] It is with this perspective in mind that Government decided to come up with an amendment to section 8 of the Constitution in order to ensure that assets which are confiscated pursuant to the proposed Good Governance and Integrity Reporting Bill, when enacted, are confiscated pursuant to a law which meets the test of constitutionality.'

xxix The two Bills were subsequently withdrawn.

xxx See Milan Meetarbhan: 'La Banalisation des Modifications Constitutionnelles', *L'Express*, 6 December 2016.

xxxi [1998] UKPC 9; [1999] 1 AC 98.

xxxii *Matadeen v Pointu[1998] MR 172.* The Supreme Court had earlier held that, 'a Constitution, more particularly that part of it which embodies fundamental rights, should be interpreted in the light of its history, its sources and, wherever applicable, pronouncements on provisions similar to ours either by national courts or by international institutions. [..] These rights are not confined to any particular

xxxiii *Mootoo v Attorney-General of Trinidad and Tobago [1979] 1 WLR 1334] . Gooranah R. v The State [1968] MR 122; Philibert v. The State [2007] SCJ 274 ; Director of Public Prosecutions v Masson [1972 MR 204]).*

Stability and Dilemmas
The Mauritian Electoral System

TANIA DIOLLE

Introduction

Mauritius is often cited as a model of democracy and good governance in the African region. Indeed, factually, as given by The Economist Intelligence Unit's Democracy Index, whose indexes are built on five categories, namely, electoral process and pluralism, civil liberties, the functioning of government, political participation and political culture, Mauritius was ranked 18th out of 167 countries in 2015 and hereafter, the only African country to be recognised a full-democracy (Mathews, 2017). In relative terms, 'Mauritius has been and remains the top-ranking country in overall governance in Africa for the tenth consecutive year,' according to the Mo Ibrahim Index of African Governance (IIAG) 2016. Except for a brief suspension of elections in 1972, which took place in a context of civil unrest and following a state of emergency, it can be said that Mauritius has had regular elections and has been able to live up to its rankings and international reputation. The relatively most stable element of the Mauritian Democracy is an enduring electoral system, whose outcome is widely accepted among the different components of the Mauritian society.

The choice of an electoral system for any country is not a simple one and could be seen by many as a mechanism which simply translates votes cast by citizens into seats in the legislature at the national or subnational levels (Kunicoca and Ackerman, 2005). However, the literature on the subject has evolved since Duverger and more recent scholars such as Gallagher and Mitchell conceptualised electoral systems as a 'crucial link in the chain connecting the preferences of citizens to the policy choices made by government' (Gallagher and Mitchell, 2008: 4). An electoral system has to be seen as operating within a broader national governance framework and, as such, as influencing key governance dimensions and political dynamics (Duverger, 1952; Lijphart, 1994; Cox, 1997; Reynold, 2005).

In practice, electoral systems have implications on several aspects of political governance simply because of the political dynamics that they generate which actually affect not only governance but also accountability of policy makers of any given country. The electoral package that political actors have to adopt determines their incentives structure, thus affecting their behaviours when they are both in and outside the government. For example, the electoral system has considerable effects on the fragmentation of the party system, which in turn affects government effectiveness once the party gets into power (Menocal, 2011). The electoral system also has the power to ease or exacerbate conflicts between political contestants or the political constituencies (Menocal, 2011). Finally, the electoral system determines to whom the political contestant feels accountable to and therefore how and to whom the public resources will be allocated (Menocal, 2011). The key to understanding the linkages between the electoral system and governance lies in unravelling the channel within political context behind which a politician or a political party gets into power.

The assumption of this chapter is that the Mauritian electoral system was designed as part of an overall governance structure which aimed at promoting political stability and democracy in a context of high ethnicization of politics. The Mauritian electoral system has not been studied from an electoral engineering perspective. Past studies on the subject look at the system from a purely mechanical perspective, thus ignoring its role in the fragile governance structure put in place in Mauritius to channel ethno-religious interests. This chapter proposes to look at the Mauritian electoral system using *centripetalism* as the overall framework of analysis. This is a concept from political theory, often contrasted with consocialism (Lijphart, 1975) and communalism. Unlike the decentralised power-sharing of consocialism, or the entrenched competition of communalism, centripetalism strives to create stability and a shared political sphere at the centre (Reilly, 2006).

Centripetalism is about integrative power sharing and contends that political elites should be given incentives to appeal outside their ethnic constituencies, which is narrowly defined. The integrative power sharing mechanisms create the dynamics which will put the moderate multi-ethnic politician at an advantage when competing for political office, thereby giving incentives to politicians to be moderate. The Mauritian electoral system was one of the mechanisms introduced in Mauritius by the British to favour moderate politics at a time when they were anxious of the ethnicization of politics in Mauritius. The chapter will highlight the role of the Mauritian electoral system, its strengths and weaknesses. The aim is to bring new light on how the Mauritian electoral system can be reformed to address the features which, with the hindsight of 50 years, can be considered weaknesses of the Mauritian democratic model.

First Past The Post or Block Vote System

The literature on electoral systems converges towards three broad categories of systems which differ in their application depending on the socio-political context present at the time of their design or inception. As it stands the broad categories are: (1) the Plurality-Majority system, (2) the Proportional Representation system and, (3) the Semi-Proportional system (Norris, 1997; Gallagher and Mitchell, 2008; Menocal, 2011; Reilly and Norris, 1999).

The Mauritian electoral system has been classified by some as belonging to the First Past The Post (FPTP) category (Sithanen, 2012; Darga, 2004; Bunwaree, 2005; 2002) and categorized as Block Vote system by Reynolds (Reynolds et al., 2005: 44). While both systems have different district magnitudes, they broadly belong to the plurality-family of electoral systems. As specified above, the difference between the Block Vote (BV) system and the FPTP lies in the district magnitude; otherwise they are similar in their application and apply the same underlying principle. Under the FPTP system, the candidate who secures an absolute majority of votes is the winner, whereas under the BV system, there is more than one winner and the winners are those who secured the highest number of votes.

In the Republic of Mauritius, the district magnitude is of three representatives for 20 constituencies and of two for one constituency (Rodrigues). This means that the three or two candidates, depending on the constituency, securing the highest number of votes are declared the winners. For the purpose of this chapter the Mauritian electoral system will be referred to as the Block Vote System, which is conceptually closer to the mechanical application of the Mauritian electoral system.

Context leading to the establishment of the Mauritian electoral system

Mauritius adapted the Westminster model of government to its ethnically diverse population. This system was adapted to channel the expression of the societal divisions, which was the reflection of the social order under British colonial rule, and was determined by the peopling of Mauritius, itself largely driven by the needs of the sugar economy. Scholars such as Houbert described the pyramidal societal cleavages at the arrival of the indentured labourers as 'a small number of whites of French origin at the top, large numbers of black slaves at the bottom, and an intermediate group - in size as well as colour - in the middle' (Houbert, 1981: 78). The British were the apex which strengthened this pyramid. The abolition of slavery saw the replacement of the black slaves at the bottom of this pyramid by the indentured labourers. This pyramidal structure implied that there was little assimilation among the populations, who were of different ancestral origins, living in Mauritius.

Therefore, at the dawn of independence existing societal cleavages were further strengthened by the politics driving the movements for and against independence. At the time of the constitutional talks towards independence, there were concerns from both the British administration on the island and local politicians about the highly ethnicised twist that Mauritian politics took. As testimony, in one of his letters to the Governor General (1956), the President of the Labour Party expressed concerns on the adoption of Proportional Representation (PR) system of elections in Mauritius. He feared that implementing a STV (Single Transferable Vote) or a PR system *'would aggravate and perpetuate divisions among Mauritians on racial and religious lines'* (Forget, 1956) [i].

Today the Mauritian Constitution recognises four main ethno-religious groups, namely the Hindus, Muslims, Sino-Mauritians and the General Population, which is a category comprising of those who do 'not appear, from his way of life, to belong to one other of those 3 communities' (First Schedule, section 3(1)). The latest census to numerically list these four communities' dates back to 1972. This means that as at 1972 the Mauritian population comprised of 52 per cent Hindus, 17 per cent Muslims, 3 per cent Sino-Mauritian and 28 per cent General Population.

Main features of the Mauritian Electoral System

The talks and negotiations for the drafting of the Mauritian constitution and electoral system to move towards independence were initiated in 1956. The main milestones in the constitutional development of the Mauritian Political system are:

1. The 1957 London Agreement;
2. The setting-up of the Trustram Eve Electoral Boundary Commission in 1958;
3. The implementation of the Trustam Eve's recommendations in 1959;
4. The 1961 the Constitutional Review Conference with the appointment of Professor Smith as constitutional commissioner;
5. The 1965 holding of the decisive and crucial constitutional conference appointing the Banwell commission and;
6. The submission of the Banwell report in 1966

(Mathur, 1991; White paper, 2014).

However, the documents from the London Constitutional Talks seem to indicate that the main concern of the British administration and of some of the prominent local political figures at the time of the Constitutional Talks was to ensure that ethno-religious divisions did not prevent the implementation of liberal principles in Mauritian politics. For instance, the White Paper for an electoral reform of 2014 refers to the London agreement of 1957, where the main local political actors were represented, where it is quoted that:

*Whatever system of voting was introduced should be on the basis of **universal adult suffrage**, and should provide an adequate opportunity for all the **main sections of opinion** in Mauritius to elect their **representatives** to the Legislative Council in **numbers broadly corresponding to their own weight in the community**. It was also common ground that the system of voting should be such as to facilitate the development **of voting on grounds of political principle and party rather than on race or religion**[ii] (White Paper, 2014: 11)*

Therefore, the Mauritian electoral system was designed in a way so as to allow for the fair representation of the different ethnicities on the island but at the same time without rigidly institutionalising ethnic representation like it would in a Consociationalism system of governance as developed by the political theorist Arend Lijphart with Belgium as a test case (1969, 1975).

Universal Adult Suffrage was introduced in Mauritius in 1959 and the Mauritian electoral system, which is the Block Vote System, is an adaptation of the British Plurality/Majority First Past the Post electoral system inherited from the colonial administration. Since its inception in 1885, the Electoral System was changed four times (Sithanen, 2012) to respond to the changes in the Mauritian social structures. The present Mauritian electoral system dates back to 1967, where a 70-member legislative assembly was established with 62 Members of Parliament (MPs) directly elected and up to 8 nominated best losers. Depending on the constituency, voters express their preferences for three or two individual candidates from a list comprising of members of political parties and independent candidates. The three candidates winning the most votes are elected even if they did not obtain an absolute majority. Currently Mauritius is the only African country which has adopted the Block Vote system. This system actually counters the side effects of what Donald Horowitz (2003) refers to as 'ascriptive majority rule' which tend to be promoted under consociationalism.

The intention at the time of the elaboration of the Mauritian Electoral System was that one of its core elements should be to provide an adequate opportunity for the main 'sections' of the population to elect their representatives in numbers broadly corresponding to their own weight in the country. A mitigating component was to be introduced by facilitating the development of '*voting on grounds of political principle and party rather than on race or religion[iii]*', but at the same time ensuring that the main sections of the population felt included through representation. This principle being the introduction of multi-member constituencies, which had the effect of favouring a system which would mitigate existing ethno-religious divisions.

Delimitation of constituencies for the promotion of moderate politics

According to Raj Mathur, at the time of the London Talks, the constituencies were demarcated in a way to ensure adequate representation of the two numerically most important ethno-religious groups — the Hindus and the General Population (Mathur, 1997). He estimated that these two ethno-religious groups were divided into mainly rural and urban areas. To ensure the representation of the two other ethno-religious groups 'the national parties normally field a Muslim candidate in each of the constituencies in which that community constitutes a sizable section of the population and field one or two Chinese candidates in a Port Louis constituency, the only constituency in which the Chinese community represents an important ethnic group.' (Mathur, 1997: 62).

Broad-based necessity of the Mauritian electoral system

The electoral boundaries were designed in such a way as to ensure that political parties or alliances aiming to get into power have to engage in vote pooling. That is, they can't fish in only one group of constituents be it along ethno-religious or ideological lines if they aim to win power out of the electoral contest. Instead, they have to seek broad-based support for their programmes. These boundaries were designed to ensure fair representation of the main ethno-religious groups as defined in the Constitution of Mauritius by promoting geographic concentration of some ethno-religious groups in some constituencies, for instance in No. 2 - Port Louis South and Port Louis Central (Sithanen, 2012; Bunwaree, 2005).

The literature on the plurality systems in multi-ethnic societies highlights the contribution of its mechanisms in encouraging political parties to be 'broad churches' and engage in vote pooling so as to attract as many segments of society as possible. The Block Vote mechanism along with the delimitation of constituencies have indeed favoured the formation of alliances in Mauritius since independence. Parties aiming to be in the winning team to go for the 'winning formula', which inevitably means appealing to a broad range of voters by engaging in multi-ethnic alliances.

Mitigation of ethno-religious politics

Several other constituencies were designed in such a way that voters actually have to vote for candidates outside of their ethno-religious group to support a particular political party or alliances to get into power. Examples of such constituencies are No. 18 (Belle Rose/Quatre Bornes), No. 19 (Rose Hill) and No. 14 (Savanne/Black River) among others, where one ethno-religious group does not numerically dominate the constituency. Therefore, political parties or alliances have to make broad-based appeal to electors and propose candidates from two or three ethno-religious groups. Electors have to vote for a candidate outside his/her own ethno-religious group to enable a party to get into power. This feature is accentuated by the Block Voting system where a voter has to plebiscite his/her party by voting in block for the three candidates proposed by the party irrespective of the ethno-religious group to which it belongs. Therefore, in such constituencies appealing to only one ethno-religious group would actually be detrimental to the political party, alliance or even candidate.

The Best Loser System

The Mauritian Best Loser System (BLS) was introduced to ensure that in case the outcome of the Block Vote system leads to the underrepresentation of some ethno-religious groups, there will be a mechanism to redress the situation without altering the results of the election. The BLS mechanism consists basically of the allocation of 8 additional parliamentary seats to the best losers. The first four seats are allocated purely based on the ethno-religious belonging of the candidate and the last four seats are allocated based on the ethno-religious belonging of the best loser and his party affiliation. This has reassured the different components of the Mauritian society that they would be adequately represented along ethno-religious lines and has been attributed by members of Parliament such as Alan Ganoo (Hansard, 11 July 2014) as a lever of political and social stability in Mauritius. While also vehemently criticised by members of civil society and some members of Parliament, the BLS has been amended only twice since its inception. It has always been the subject of heated debate but no governments actually dared to fundamentally alter the system and take responsibility for its removal from the Mauritian electoral system. It was amended twice, in 1991 when the provisions regarding the seat allocation were changed and, in July 2014 following the United Nations Human Rights Commission's ruling in connection with the party *Rezistans ek Alternativ*'s ('Resistance and Alternative') complaint that their rights as a non-ethnic party were being violated by this provision.

As Sachs explains in his report on constitutional and electoral reform, the BLS is discussed with *'considerable emotion'* and is the subject of *'intense comments'* (Sachs, 2001: 30) by local politicians and members of civil society. The BLS has greatly contributed to appeasing social tensions and mitigating fears of under representation by some ethno-religious groups and therefore it has in many ways moderated fundamentalism tendencies by allowing for a democratic channel for the demand of ethno-religious representation.

Disproportionalities created by the Mauritian electoral system

While the Mauritian electoral system has accommodated the strong demand of ethno-religious religious at the time of independence, to be channelled democratically without the rigid institutionalisation of this demand, it has also been responsible for the failure of fair representation of women and of the opposition in Parliament.

Table 1: The most notable disproportionate elections results in comparison to the number of seats secured by the main opposition alliance since 1982

Year	Percentage of national votes	Number of Seats under the FPTP	Number of Seats under the BLS	Percentage of seats
1982	25.78	0	2	2.86
1995	19.7	0	0	0
2000	36.7	6	2	11.42
2010	42.9	17	2	27.14

Source: Electoral Commission Statistics (2015)

Table 1 shows that in 1982, the losing alliance did not win any seat in parliament despite having secured 25.78 per cent of the national votes. The BLS mechanism allowed for the representation of two members of the opposition in Parliament, which resulted in the opposition alliance holding 2.86 per cent of the parliamentary seats with 25.78 per cent of the national votes. The same exercise can be done for the 2010 elections where the opposition alliance secured 27.4 per cent of the parliamentary seats with 42.9 per cent of the national votes.

The underrepresentation of women has been a major cause of policy concern in Mauritius. Table 2 shows the percentage of seats secured by women in parliament, while they make up approximately 52 per cent of the voters in Mauritius.

The main reason behind the underrepresentation of women in parliament is the making of broad base and multi-ethnic alliances which tend to favour the most senior cadres of political parties. These most senior cadres of political parties tend to be males and faced to a shortage of tickets they are favoured in times of alliances.

Table 2: Women's Representation in Parliament from 1976 to 2015

Year	Total Seats	Women's Seats	Percentage women
1976	70	3	4.28
1982	66	3	4.55
1983	70	4	5.71
1987	70	5	7.14
1991	66	2	3.03
1995	66	5	7.58
2000	70	4	5.71
2005	70	12	17.14
2010	69	13	18.84
2014	69	8	11.59

Source: Gender links (2015)

Conclusion

The Mauritian electoral system was designed to promote liberal democratic ideals along party lines, while channelling the strong demand for ethno-religious representations at the time of independence. It has been praised by many for driving the enduring political stability that Mauritius has known for decades and which has actually helped the country make huge leaps forward. While the system promotes practices, which could be perceived as being close to power sharing principles, the fact remains that it favours instead integrative power sharing through its mechanisms, which promote the practice of moderate politics rather than the institutionalisation of ethnic representation. This was consciously designed in the system so as to give incentives to political actors to engage in vote pooling and for voters to vote in Block for the party or alliance which they support to get into government.

The main features of the Mauritian electoral system which mitigate ethno-religious politics in Mauritius have been identified as follows:

1. *The delimitation of constituencies*

Constituencies were designed in a deliberate effort to ensure the 'fair' representation of the main ethno-religious groups as defined by the Constitution of Mauritius.

Therefore, some constituencies are characterised by the concentration of one ethno-religious group while others are characterised by a plurality of ethno-religious groups. This force political parties to engage in vote pooling by forming alliances or by presenting a diverse list of candidates if they want to get into power.

2. *The Block Vote mechanism and the multi-member constituencies*

Some constituencies were designed in such a way that political parties/alliances have to align candidates from different ethno-religious groups to maximise support from the voters. Whether candidates, parties or alliances, they all have to engage in moderate politics to attract votes from different ethno-religious belonging. An ethnic-driven strategy does not usually work in such constituencies.

3. *The Best Loser System*

The Best Loser System has been instrumental in giving psychological comfort to the different ethno-religious groups mitigating any fear that their ethno-religious interests might not be represented in parliament. This in itself has had a huge contribution to the moderate nature of Mauritian politics compared to other ethnically diverse societies in the African region. The BLS has had such a strong psychological effect on the different ethno-religious groups in Mauritius that the Sachs Commission explicitly noted the emotional way in which and the intensity with which the removal of the BLS from the Mauritian electoral system has been discussed in the country (Sachs, 2001).

The use of integrative power sharing mechanisms that are inbuilt in the mechanism rather than institutionalised through laws, has worked well given the track record of Mauritius on democracy indexes. However, these provisions do not come without a price. The Block Vote System for example has had the effect of accentuating the disproportional low representation of the opposition parties and women in parliament.

After 50 years of independence, there is no doubt that Mauritius owes a lot of its stability to the Mauritian electoral system. However, many of these mechanisms were not formally institutionalised and instead democratic liberal principles were to prevail over ethno-religious politics. Considering the little amendments that were actually brought to an imperfect system and the hesitation with which elected officials embark on reforms, this leads us to the question of how much progress Mauritius made in breaking away from its deep societal divide which created the demand for mechanisms such as the Best Loser System.

References

Bunwaree, S. (2002) 'Economics, Conflicts and Interculturality in a Small Island State: The Case of Mauritius', *Polis/RCPS/CPSR* 9: 1-19.

Bunwaree, S. (2007) 'Electoral Reforms: For a More Gender Equitable Mauritius', *Journal of Mauritian Studies* 4(1): 50-64.

Bunwaree, S. (2010) *Governance, Gender and Politics in Mauritius.* Vacoas, Mauritius: Editions Le Printemps.

Central Statistical Office (2012) *Household Budget Survey 2012.* Port Louis, Mauritius: CSO.

Cox, G. (1997) *Making Votes Count.* Cambridge: Cambridge University Press.

Cuttaree, J. (2011) *Behind the Purple Curtain: A Political Autobiography.* Mauritius: Editions Le Printemps.

Darga, A. (2004) *Mauritius Electoral Reform Process.* EISA Occasional Paper 24.

Dinan, M., Nababsing, V. and Mathur, H. (1999) 'Mauritius: Cultural Accommodation in a Diverse Island Polity' in C. Young (ed) *The Accommodation of Cultural Diversity.* London: Macmillan.

Duverger, M. (1952) 'Les Partis Politiques', *The American Political Science Review* 46(2): 563-564.

Gallagher, M. and Mitchell, P. (2008) *The Politics of Electoral Systems.* Oxford: Oxford University Press.

Government of Mauritius (2014) *White Paper on an Electoral Reform: Modernising the Electoral System.* Port-Louis: Government of Mauritius.

Horowitz, D.L. (2003) 'Electoral Systems: A Premier for Decision Makers', *Journal of Democracy* 14: 115–27.

Houbert, J. (1981) 'Mauritius: Independence and Dependence', *Journal of Modern African Studies* 19(1): 75-105.

House of Commons Debates. Vol 566. Col 115w (8 March 1957); Mr Lennox Boyd.

Lijphart, A. (1969) 'Consociational Democracy', *World Politics* 29(2): 207-225.

Lijphart, A. (1977) *Democracy in Plural Societies: A Comparative Exploration.* New Haven: Yale University Press.

Lijphart, A. (1994) *Electoral Systems and Party Systems: A Study of Twenty-Seven Democracies, 1945–1990.* Oxford: Oxford University Press.

Mathur, H. (1991) *Parliament in Mauritius.* Rose Hill, Mauritius: Éditions de l'Océan Indien,

Mathur, H. (1997) 'Parliamentary Representation of Minority Communities: The Mauritian Experience', *Africa Today* 44(1): 61-83.

Menocal, A. (2011) *Why electoral systems matter: An analysis of their incentives and effects on key areas of governance.* Overseas Development Institute. Available online at https://www.odi.org/sites/odi.org.uk/files/odi-assets/publications-opinion-files/7367.pdf (accessed 28.11.17).

Mozaffar, S., Scarritt, J.R. and Galaich, G. (2003) 'Electoral institutions, ethno political cleavages and party systems in Africa's emerging democracies', *American Political Science Review* 97(3): 379-390.

Mozaffar, S. and Scarritt, J.R. (2005) 'The Puzzle of African Party Systems', *Party Politics* 11(4): 399-421.

Norris, P. (1997) 'Choosing Electoral Systems: Proportional, majoritarian and mixed systems', *International Political Science Review* 18: 297-312.

Reilly, B. (2006) *Democracy and Diversity: Political Engineering in the Asia-Pacific.* Oxford: Oxford Scholarship Online.

Reilly, B. and Reynolds, A. (1999) *'Electoral Systems and Conflict in Divided Societies'*, Papers on International Conflict Resolution No. 2. Washington, DC: National Academy Press.

Report of the Constitutional Commissioner, November 1964, Sessional Paper No. 2 of 1965 of the Mauritius Legislative Assembly.

Reynolds, A., Reilly, A. and Ellis, A. (2005) *Electoral System Design: The New International IDEA Handbook*. Stockholm: International IDEA.

Sachs Commission. (2001) *Report of the Commission on Constitutional and Electoral Reform 2001/02. Port-Louis: Government of Mauritius.*

Sithanen, R. (2012) *Initiative citoyenne pour une réforme réalisable à Maurice.* Quatre Bornes, Mauritius.

Smith, S. (1968) 'Mauritius: Constitutionalism in a Plural Society', *The Modern Law Review* 31(6): 601-622.

The Electoral Knowledge Network. http://aceproject.org/main/english/es/esd01.htm (accessed 15 June 2015).

---

[i] Cited in the White paper for an electoral reform, 2014, pp 11. Guy Forget was the President of the Mauritius Labour Party in 1956.

[ii] HC Deb Vol 566 Col 115w (8 March 1957); Mr Lennox Boyd cited in the White Paper for electoral reform, July 2014, pp 11.

[iii] HC Deb Vol 566 Col 115w (8 March 1957); Mr Lennox Boyd cited in the White Paper for electoral reform, July 2014, pp 11.

Political Leadership in Mauritius
The Trappings of the Poster Child Syndrome

Introduction

A number of qualifiers have been used to explain the Mauritian case: enigma (Miles, 1999), exceptionalism (Bräutigam and Diolle, 2009), fragility of success (Greig *et al.*, 2011). Others have celebrated the Mauritian democratic model, its cultural melting pot and its status as an economic miracle (Subramanian, 2001; Stiglitz, 2011). By all means, Mauritius, a small island famous for the dodo and its strategic position in the middle of the Indian Ocean, has been able, for a fair bit of its existence, 'to punch above its weight' and this, despite having no natural resources.

One feature that has been suggested to explain why Mauritius succeeded where other African countries failed - is its political leadership. Indeed leadership is key to steering a country onto a course of success, especially during moments of national importance such as independence, referendums or national tragedies. Speaking about the case of Mauritius, Bräutigam and Diolle (2009: 6) mention that 'today Mauritians looking back believe that they were blessed with good leaders as they started down the path toward prosperity'. This is further substantiated by the writings of Rotberg (2003: 30) who pinpoints the first Prime Minister's leadership capacity in steering Mauritius 'from a potentially explosive racial hothouse into a bustling, prosperous, politically hectic sustainable democracy'.

No doubt the Mauritian political leadership exhibited by the first Prime Minister - Sir Seewoosagur Ramgoolam was key in bringing on board a highly divided nation at independence and being the main architect of a government of national unity that came to life in December 1969. However, it would be rather short sighted to suggest that leadership operates in a vacuum and that it essentially centres around the specific personality of a given person. In fact, we are here reminded of Barack Obama's inaugural visit to Africa where he mentioned that 'Africa needs strong institutions, not strong men'. In the case of Mauritius, political leadership during the early post-independence years was strengthened by the investment in a series of key institutions: a strong bureaucracy, an independent judiciary, a partnership with the private sector and a number of important social engineering measures to ensure health, education and pension services for the majority of citizens.

The purpose of this chapter is to help shed light on the trajectory of political leadership as the island celebrates its 50 years of independence. The early political leaders of pre-independence Mauritius, motivated by the drive for liberation from an oppressive plantocracy society, had a unique capacity to come and work together for a common goal and what is interesting is that they transcended race, ethnicity and religion. Can this be said of modern Mauritian political leadership? How should we interpret the fact that in 50 years of independence, Mauritius has seen only two families 'rule' - Ramgoolam and Jugnauth?[i] That every single Prime Minister since independence has hailed from the Hindu community and more specifically from a particular caste? What should we make of the fact that in a country which by its Constitution is defined as secular but in its practice everything has a religious bordering on ethnic connotation? These are some of the questions that this chapter will attempt to answer.

Developing a leadership framework

One question that is often posed about Mauritius is how best to define it. An island state? A country of different peopling with no indigenous population that makes it unique but also at the same time complex. Is it African or not? Is it Indian? Historically, Mauritius bears a number of similarities to Caribbean island states such as Trinidad & Tobago and Guyana. The sequential presence of colonial powers, the double legacy of slavery and indentured labourers and the establishment of a sugar cane economy bring them even closer. Miles (1999: 93) is quite adamant in his assessment about Mauritius:

> *Although Mauritius is generally grouped within the African region, many observers reject its comparability with African societies on account of its island status and the immigrant origin of its peoples. Political success in Mauritius, goes the argument, has little to do with its Africanness. Rather, it is contended, small island nations have inherent advantages with respect to both ethnic tolerance and economic performance.*

The author believes that the African connection, especially when it comes to democratic and economic credentials, is conveniently used by Mauritius to demonstrate that it systematically tops the league board and this is evidenced in the work of Weltz (2013: 165):

Those who are in power, they feel of course closer to India because of origins. And for them Africa is just Africa. But Africa will be used when it suits the purpose.

Having said that, Sir Seewoosagur Ramgoolam was believed to have been a true Pan-Africanist and his support for the Organisation of African Unity (OAU) of which he was elected the Chairperson in 1976 was testimony of wanting Mauritius to be part of the African continent (Reddi, 2016). In more recent times, the African connection has been further strengthened with the Mauritius Africa Strategy[ii] which essentially acts as a conduit for business and investment facility. Therefore, by all accounts Mauritius is increasingly seeing itself through the prism of Africa.

Africa and Mauritius: The political leadership connection

Political leadership in Africa has known a number of lows and highs and has closely followed the different liberation and democratisation phases. The 1950s/60s saw the advent of liberation heroes who to a certain extent unshackled their people from the oppression of colonialism. Unfortunately, the excellent head start soon gave in to corrupt, war mongering and greedy leaders and this is eloquently captured by Adamoleku (1998: 95):

While the nationalist struggle phase witnessed the emergence of some first-rate political leaders, the nation-building phase has not only failed to produce leaders of comparable stature, but has also witnessed a decline in the achievements of those who, having won their laurels as great leaders during the earlier phase, retained the leadership mantle under the phase.

The advent of the third wave of democratisation in the 1990s saw a slow but steady change to the African political ecosystem - the presence of multipartyism, the holding of regular elections, investment in independent institutions, the introduction of term limits among other things. In fact, these democratic gains saw the coming of age of a new breed of leaders. Unfortunately, these gains are being reversed in a number of African countries (Gyimah-Boadi, 2015) and what is even more troubling is that it is happening in countries like South Africa, often invoked by other African countries as a model to emulate. Another worrisome trend is what Diamond, Plattner and Walker (2016) refer to as the return of authoritarianism in the world.

The literature on political leadership over the years has been significant but the difficulty lies in the fact that it is quite impossible to have a universally accepted definition or a well-developed theory of political leadership (Van Vyk, 2007). The understanding of political leadership becomes more focused when it is taken to mean 'the role of politicians in giving vision and strategies and creating a conducive environment for implementation of formulated policies' (Ngowi, 2009). This notion has a direct association with the principles and quality of governance.

Atomised or contextualised leadership

Over the years, certain political leaders have remained fondly as part of the collective memory of their respective citizens. To date we will remember the likes of Nyerere, Nkrumah, Kenyatta and Senghor. In the Mauritian memory bank, Sir Seewoosagur Ramgoolam is fondly remembered as the 'father of the nation', Sir Gaëtan Duval as the 'King Creole' and Sir Anerood Jugnauth as the 'father of the Mauritian economic miracle'. In certain cases there has been a tendency to focus on individual personalities, personal rule or biographical accounts of leaders. This has a predisposition to generate an often 'atomised' understanding of leadership (Tettey, 2012). Offering a critique to this, Morrell and Hartley (2006: 483) argue that:

> As well as potentially oversimplifying associated phenomena, such as charisma or effectiveness, the traditional psychological view privileges research from nomothetic paradigms, at the expense of interpretivist perspectives such as ethnography and social constructionism.

Grint (2000) provides a useful framework to further evaluate the manner in which leadership operationalizes itself, four theories of leadership - trait approaches, contingency approaches, situational approaches and constitutive approaches. He categorises these according to whether they emphasise the individual or the context as essential. Trait approaches emphasise certain characteristics that facilitate good leadership and assumes that leaders will exhibit a certain consistency in the use of their traits. Contingency approaches unlike trait approaches combine both individual character and context. They focus on how particular types of leaders are suitable for particular situations. As for situational approaches they champion the fact that leaders can rise and adapt to suit particular situations. Last but not least, in constitutive approaches both context and leader are contested, 'leadership must still be perceived as 'appropriate'', but what that means is an interpretive issue' (Grint, 2000: 3).

Transactional versus transformational leadership

The work of Burns (1978) was the first to reflect on these types of leadership which essentially are behaviourist by nature. Speaking about transactional leadership, Tettey (2012: 25) says that it is characterised 'by followers who give support to the leaders, by way of performance and other means, in return for rewards'. Here leaders lay a lot of emphasis on populist post-election perks such as maintaining subsidies, projects and jobs that go to their supporters. In fact, Schumpeter's work on leadership democracy indicates that 'democracy is only about the competition of leaders for votes' (cited in Mackie, 2009). The last 15 years have been marked by an accelerated presence of neoliberal market ideologies where leaders have been more concerned by form as opposed to content. Termed as the packaging of politics (McNair, 1995) where political spin, soundbites and rhetoric filled the political discourse.

As for transformational leadership, it is the 'capacity to mobilise followers on the basis of shared core values and principles, as well as the ability to cultivate future leadership and are not content with perpetuating a non-progressive culture of followership' (Tetty, 2012: 30). No doubt the current crisis in leadership experienced across the world within mainstream political parties is quite telling. Citizens are demanding a new way of doing politics and a clear rupture from the business as usual approach.

A quick cursory view of the predominant leadership traits in Africa points to the fact that they are mostly transactional leaders and Mauritius is no exception to this. However, one should be careful in not laying all the blame at the feet of political leaders as the advent of a critical and mobilised citizenry is equally important in ensuring the quality of leadership.

Leadership and Governance

Leadership is critical to governance. During the last decade or so a variety of indices/instruments have made their way within the African political and economic landscape - the African Peer Review Mechanism (APRM), the Mo Ibrahim Index of African Governance, the Afrobarometer Surveys and the UNECA African Governance Report.

In the case of the APRM established in 2003 by the African Union, its prime motivation is to have African leaders evaluate their peers. Nearly, 15 years down the line, the impact of the APRM remains mixed. To date, 35 countries have voluntarily acceded to the APRM, 17 of which have undergone their self-assessment process and are implementing their National Programme of Action. Critics have remained rather sceptical in terms of the quality of commitment to the process, at times merely being used as a means to receive a clean bill vis-à-vis the community of investors and donors. Others have deplored the state centric approach to the process (Jordan, 2006; Gruzd, 2007) or the absence of civil society's participation in the process (Rakner and Wang, 2007, Bunwaree, 2007).

Mukamunana and Kuye (2005: 596) sum up the mood of some of the African leaders when they mention that:

> For many African leaders, the idea of external evaluators coming to analyse and criticise the way a country manages its affairs is absurd. This is illustrated by these comments of President Wade [of Senegal]: 'it is unrealistic,' Wade said, 'How do you think I can tell a president in a country that his election or his treatment of the press was not regular?'

Championed as a continent grown and driven initiative, the Mo Ibrahim Index for African Governance has generated some interesting insights into the political, economic and social governance of African countries. Criticised by certain for its highly quantified assessment of an essentially supply side form of governance, the indices have in more recent times been supplemented by a more qualitative assessment of the state of governance. In addition to the Mo Ibrahim Index, there is also the Ibrahim Prize that celebrates excellence in African leadership. It was set up in 2006 with the aim of changing perceptions concerning African leadership and showcasing exceptional role models from the continent. Since its inception only four African leaders have been awarded the prize – Mandela and Chissano (2007), Mogae (2008), Pires (2011) and Pohamba (2014). In 2009, 2010, 2012, 2013, 2015 and 2016 no prize was awarded. One of the main criticisms that has been levied against the leadership prize is its monetary dimension. Recipients are awarded USD 5 million over ten years and subsequently USD 200,000 per year for life. The other criticism concerns the inability of the prize committee to give away the prize during six of the 10 years that prize has existed. Speaking to this, Mo Ibrahim the founder of the prize had this to say:

> From the very beginning, the bar set for the Prize has been extremely high. It recognises not good leaders—of which Africa has many—but truly exceptional figures which, by their nature, are rare ... So it is not surprising that there have been years when the Prize is not awarded (Quartz Africa, 2016).

The Forging of a Mauritian Nationhood: The Pre-Independence Decades

Mauritian heritage is constituted by its unique sequential colonial past. Frankel (2010) refers it as globalisation 'at its worst' – the Dutch (stripping the island of its ebony trees and killing the dodo) and the French (use of slaves to produce a plantocracy society) - and globalisation 'at its best' (importation of indentured labourers and expansion of the elite class). Three Constitutions have marked the painful struggle towards political emancipation and recognition, in 1831, 1885 and 1945. The Constitution of 1885 was supposed to be an improvement but, in reality, it remained restrictive in spirit and action. Out of a population of 360,000 only 4059 were registered as voters. The franchise was based on educational qualifications, ownership of immovable property of certain value, salary of at least Rs 50 monthly, and prescribed licence fees for trade activities among other things. Only males aged 21 and above with the ability to read and/or write were allowed to vote. These requirements resulted in only 1.5 per cent of the population entitled to vote.

The Rise of New Parties and Leaders - Anti Oligarchy

Politics in the first decade of the 1900s was essentially dominated by the Franco-Mauritians and a group of educated coloureds. In 1907, the first political party was created - 'Action Libérale' by Eugène Laurent with the aim of challenging the oligarchic establishment. Action Libérale attempted to cut across the racial and communal divide of the country but soon lost its ability to federate due to the rise of conservative forces within the party and growing demands for retrocession.

Laurent's 'Action Libérale' coincided with what can be called the political awakening of the Indo-Mauritians on the island. Their numerical presence was undeniable; by 1870 they represented some 216,000 out of a population of 316,000 (Varma, 2008). The visit of Gandhi in 1901 followed by Manilal Doctor, who stayed on the island between 1907 and 1910, was instrumental. Not only did Manilal Doctor educate the Indo-Mauritians on their rights but was also at the centre of the creation of the 'Hindustani', a newspaper that expressed the concerns of the Indo-Mauritian community. Here one must emphasise that the presence of newspapers in Mauritius is one of the longest tradition in the Southern hemisphere dating back more than 250 years. Newly created political parties, pro-independence groups as well as anti-independence all made use of this important tool to amplify and disseminate their messages. The presence and involvement of both Laurent and Manilal Doctor were viewed as a direct threat to the Colonial government and the oligarchs (Selvon, 2017).

The following three decades fomented by social agitations and labour unrest in a restrictive political system were fertile ground for the emergence of a structured political party. Dr Maurice Curé who had been militating for improved working and living conditions of labourers in sugar estates and advocating trade union legislation participated actively in politics since his return to the country at the end of the First World War. His socialist policies incurred the wrath of the plantocracy and local British administrators. In February 1936 he launched the Labour Party (LP) together with Pandit Sahadeo, Emmanuel Anquetil and others. Curé and his party members were positioning themselves as the new Mauritian intelligentsia concerned about unshackling the workers by appealing to them to be organised and structured. The LP also started to mobilise opinions around the urgency to push for independence and autonomy from the then British colony that was Mauritius.

One of the key earlier functions of the LP was to advocate for a new Constitution which became a reality in 1948. At the heart of this new Constitution was a widened franchise, a legislature with a higher elective element and an executive body having members appointed from the elected and nominated members of the Legislative Council. The right to vote was granted to any resident aged 21 or above who 'can speak and can read and write simple sentences in, and can sign his name in, any of the languages'. Two general elections (1948, 1953) were held under that constitution. Participation in the democratic processes could only result in legitimate demand for wider involvement in the governance of the country. Constitutional development in the other colonies of the Empire heightened the demand of the liberal/progressive politicians of the country. The major programme of the Labour Party for the 1953 General Elections centred on responsible Government and universal adult suffrage.

The period from 1900 to 1950 was important in a number of ways, creating an anti-establishment feeling that became vocal, changes albeit minimal ones in a new Constitution, the political awareness and participation of the Indo-Mauritians both an as an electorate and candidates within the Mauritian political landscape. However, what may be deemed as crucial was the coming together for a common cause which saw political leaders such as Laurent and Curé create parties that cut across the religious, ethnic and class divide. The next two decades would considerably put tension on this ability to rally.

Push and Pull between Consensual and Ethnic Politics

The late 1950s and 60s were eventful on a number of scores. As the country moved towards more vocal demands for independence, the creation of new parties populated the political landscape namely the Railliement Mauricien (RM) (1952), the Comité Action Musulman (CAM) (1957) and the Independent Forward Bloc (IFB) (1958).

Ramgoolam also assumed leadership of the LP in 1959 following that of Curé, Anquetil and Rozemont. These were decisive years as they witnessed a new Constitution in 1958 that finally delivered the universal suffrage, the participation of the political actors in the constitutional conferences in London and the proposal of an electoral model inclusive of a corrective variable – the Best Loser System (BLS) to ensure minority representation.

Reflecting on these years, a number of authors have provided varying interpretations - Bowman (1991) talks about consensual politics, Dubey (1997), Carroll and Carroll (2000) and Boudet (2003) refer to consociational democracy. No doubt all this was quite evident in the different negotiations as there was the need to accommodate all political actors and their concerns on board. However, at the same time what can be termed as the realities of Mauritian ethnopolitics (which would accentuate in the mid-1990s) was shaping the political landscape. In fact, the growing fear of the 'hinduization' of the LP under Ramgoolam's leadership earlier echoed in the very words of its founder, Maurice Curé – 'into a party for Indians rather than a party for labourers' (Curé cited in Simmons 1982: 77) was gaining ground. In fact, one cannot remain insensitive as to the creation of community-based parties such as CAM and the RM. Last but not least the disintegration of the term 'Indo-Mauritians' that had as backdrop ethno-religious and language demands for recognition caused a profound split in a population who had crossed the waters in search of a better life. This schism is eloquently described by Eisenlohr (2002: 109):

> To sum up, the disintegration of the 'Indian' or 'Indo-Mauritian' community in Mauritius has proceeded in two major shifts. First, due to religious nationalism and the intense interaction with religious nationalist organisations and missionaries from the subcontinent, the split between Hindus and Muslims became so profound that 'Indo-Mauritians' became either 'Hindu' or 'Muslim' by the 1940s. In everyday discourse the label 'Indian' (endien in Creole) has become a synonym for Hindus, but is never applied to Muslims despite their Indian background. In a second step, in the course of the 1950s and 1960s, the 'Hindu' community became further subdivided into 'Hindus' as such, meaning Hindus of North Indian, mainly Bihari background, who are the great majority among 'Hindus' in a wider sense and who are considered to be 'Hindi-speaking,' and the much smaller Tamil, Telugu and Marathi groups.

The Balancing Act - Politics of Accommodation and Consensus Building

We all know of the difficult moments that the island went through as it became independent - riots during the 1967 elections, a deeply divided nation with 44 per cent of the population voting against independence, the fear of the 'Hindu hegemony' materialising itself and the exodus of an important segment of the Mauritian elite. This was the powder keg that Rotberg (2003) was referring to and what Brautigam and Diolle (2009) termed as 'the crisis of confidence at independence'. However, this highly volatile situation was managed and negotiated under the leadership of Ramgoolam who allowed the island to build its reputation on a 'ballot not a bullet culture' (Bunwaree and Kasenally, 2005).

The Construction of a Development State

The main question that needed to be answered as the island became independent - was how to ensure unity, harmony and growth. In fact, political leadership in Mauritius had to contend with two rather bleak analysis as to the future of the island - 'poor development prospects' (Meade, 1961) and an 'overcrowded barracoon with little escape routes' (Naipaul, 1972). Ramgoolam realised that the only means to reverse the bad blood caused by a divisive independence was to push for a government of national unity by extending an olive leaf to the Parti Mauricien Social Démocrate (PMSD) to be part of the executive. Intense negotiations ensued backed by 'external brokers' (Bräutigam and Diolle, 2009) and the latter finally became a reality on 2nd December 1969. The aim was to forge ahead and ensure that all the imagination, creativity, talents and networks of those involved would be used for the betterment of the country. In fact, an important balance was maintained that between the political (Hindu) and economic (Franco-Mauritian) elite (Bunwaree, 2005).

A number of features have been cited as the reason behind the Mauritian success story: a participating private sector, an able and competent bureaucracy, the management of ethnic diversity, institutional development and the ability to ensure social dialogue (Carroll and Carroll, 1999; Bunwaree, 2005). From the onset there was an understanding that there was an urgent need to move away from economic monoculturalism. The setting up of the Economic Processing Zone (EPZ) and the development of tourism as a high-end destination were set in motion (Subramanian and Roy, 2001; Aumeerally, 2005; Bräutigam, 2008). The Mauritian state took the lead in promoting these new pillars of development with the support of the Mauritian private sector and foreign investors. This outward looking approach by deploying its 'peripherality to its advantage' (Aumeerally, 2005) was coupled with the strong

Fabianism that shaped Ramgoolam who put in place a fully-fledged and comprehensive welfare system and instituted a culture of government subsidy.

The first post-independence decade was a mixed picture: the postponement of the first post independent election (due in 1972), the promulgation of the Public Order Act in 1971, an economy highly fragilized by external shocks, the devaluation of the Mauritian rupee (1979), political repression and a growing intolerance vis-à-vis the media. This state of affairs was fertile ground for the advent of the Mouvement Militant Mauricien (MMM) into a full-blown political party.

The Coming of MMM - New Blood/New Ideas

The birth of the MMM took place just after the independence and to a great extent was influenced by the May 1968 protest march of students in Europe. According to its members, the MMM emerged as an alternative force to meet the aspirations of the youth of a newly independent country disappointed by old parties who were finding it difficult to deliver on the promises of independence. Just like the LP, the MMM appealed to the workers of the nation to support and rally behind them. In fact, the core group of the MMM supporters came from the trade unions whose workers were facing difficult working conditions. Indeed, the first formative years of the MMM would essentially be concerned with fighting for the rights and causes of certain categories of workers such as the port/harbour, transport and sugar workers. The emblematic leader of the MMM - Paul Bérenger, now in his 70s, was jailed together with some of his companions and it is believed that the year spent in jail help build his character. Bérenger's ethnic community, Franco-Mauritian, although not seen as an impediment at that time, would subsequently be the source of extremely communalist discourses especially during the two years (2003-2005) that he shared the Prime Minister position with Anerood Jugnauth following a pre-electoral deal on power sharing.

Despite being novice to the political game, the MMM contested its first by-election in 1971 and won against the ruling party. This early victory would set the scene to a much larger one - that of the first post-independence general election held in 1976, where the MMM scooped 38.65 per cent of the votes, won 34 out of the 70 seats in the Assembly thus making it the party with the highest percentage of votes ahead of the LP and a distant PMSD. Many political observers believe that these were among the best years of the MMM brilliantly performing the job of parliamentary watchdog. The hitherto staid tone of parliamentary debate was replaced by the vigour of combative sparing of the new MMM opposition; the latter used every parliamentary practice and procedure to hold the new government to account (Kasenally, 2017). The 1976 – 1981 period would in fact be MMM's springboard to its fabulous but short-lived victory when it won all the seats in the 1982 general elections.

The Search for Tigerhood: Boom Years of the 1990s

Political party splits have been a regular feature of the Mauritian political landscape. All the mainstream parties have undergone some split of some sort during the post-independence period. The MMM split in three occasions - 1973, 1983 and 1991; whilst the LP twice, which saw the advent of small parties; as for the PMSD it split once (Bunwaree and Kasenally, 2005). What effect have these splits had? As expected, they have weakened the party but at the same time they have caused what can be termed as a more autocratic form of leadership within the party. This will be further discussed in a later section.

Well what can be called as the boom years in Mauritius has often been associated with the leadership of Sir Anerood Jugnauth. Jugnauth was part of the pre-independence discussions and elected under the banner of the IFB. He joined the MMM in 1971 and took its leadership in 1976. After the 1983 split of the MMM, Jugnauth created the Mouvement Socialiste Mauricien (MSM) and remained its leader until 2003 when he assumed the post of President of Mauritius. As mentioned earlier, Jugnauth is often referred to as the 'father of the economic miracle'. Two important pillars of development were promoted under his leadership - the offshore sector and ICT. Unemployment dropped drastically from 20 per cent in 1983 to 3 per cent in the early 1990s. Jugnauth remained Prime Minister for an uninterrupted 12 years - 1983 to 1995 which then saw him defeated by the son of Sir Seewoosagur Ramgoolam, Navin Ramgoolam who took the leadership of the LP (rebranded New Labour Party) in 1990.

The trappings of success: Romanticising the past

Writings on Mauritius have been highly celebratory of its post-independence trajectory. As highlighted in the previous sections, Mauritius should be lauded for beating grim projections and for resisting some of the more damaging reform packages such as the Structural Adjustment Programmes (SAPs) imposed in the early 80s by international aid agencies (Bunwaree, 2004). A number of what can be termed as worrisome deficits have been recorded in such dynastic and authoritarian leadership; state capture, raw and undisguised ethnopolitics, absence of progressive reform among other things (Mistry, 1999; Kasenally, 2011; Bunwaree, 2015). The question that perhaps that one should ask is whether these are reversible trends and to what extent political leadership has been responsible for this state of affairs.

Coalitions and Alliances - The Certainty of Winning

Nine of the ten post-independence general elections involved pre-electoral coalitions. Often justified for national interest or in order to rally all communities, the intentions behind brokering a pre-electoral coalition have in fact been motivated by the need to stay in power or get into power. Kadima and Kasenally (2006: 74) discuss in detail the different approaches and idiosyncrasies that political leaders use to maintain the discussions and retain the upper hand during the negotiations:

> In any coalition a great deal depends on the breadth and depth of discussion and leverage of each party leader, which often defines the amount of bargaining capital to which he is entitled. It is not unusual to hear reports that a political party that has practically agreed on an alliance with another party is being 'courted' by or is 'courting' a third party.

What is interesting to note in the dynamics of pre-electoral coalitions and alliances is what can be called the senior and junior partners. As from the mid-80s, two leaders have 'monopolised' the political space - Anerood Jugnauth and Navin Ramgoolam - both leaders of a political party that has as its core voting base - the Hindus. In fact, both leaders brokered a number of pre-electoral coalitions/alliances where they retained the prize trophy - that of being the Prime Minister. Table 3 provides a breakdown as per the different general elections.

The above is indicative of the fact that all the mainstream political parties have entered in a pre-electoral alliance (and more than once) with each other. Does this point to the politics of accommodation or that of convenience? Another important element to bear in mind is that all pre-electoral alliances (except that of 2000) disintegrated sometime after forming government. Is it the dominant character of the leader of the stronger (numerically) party that pushes the other partner out of the alliance? Is it that the discourse of rallying parties in the name of national unity and stability is no more relevant once in power? Is it the clash of leaders? Is it due to the fact that other parties outside the alliance are being courted? It seems to be a combination of all these factors that makes alliances fragile once they have won an election.

The Leader is Supreme

Collegiality is often touted as one of the key features that a leader should possess. Reflecting on the evolution of political leadership in the last 50 years or so, it seems to be the case that decisions are now taken in a unilateral manner - the notion of the leader as supreme has made its way. This is evidenced by the fact, that it is the leader who decides when and which party to contract a pre-electoral alliance, who nominates candidates for an election and it is again the leader who controls the party purse (Bunwaree and Kasenally, 2005; Kadima and Kasenally, 2006). None of the mainstream political parties have a process for electing their leaders nor do they have any form of succession planning put in place. Paul Bérenger remains the historical leader of the MMM since its creation, Navin Ramgoolam 'inherited' the leadership of the LP from his father and this happened in the case of Xavier-Luc Duval (son of Gaetan Duval, PMSD) and Pravind Jugnauth. Such automatic leadership has over the last 15 years given rise to dynastic politics where not only leadership is 'restricted' or 'reserved' but also other positions are allocated to offsprings of past political cadres. This sheds light on what can be viewed as a closed and restrictive system of party political membership often accessible to those with political lineage as well as those who can 'buy' their way into politics.

Table 3: Prime Minister under different pre-electoral coalitions

Year	Coalition / Alliance	Prime Minister
1983	• MSM - LP - PMSD • MMM	Anerood Jugnauth
1987	• MSM - LP - PMSD • MMM + others	Anerood Jugnauth
1991	• MSM - MMM • LP - PMSD	Anerood Jugnauth
1995	• LP - MMM • MSM - RMM	Navin Ramgoolam
2000	• MSM - MMM • LP - PMSD	Anerood Jugnauth (3 years) Paul Bérenger (2 years)
2005	• LP - PMSD • MSM - MMM	Navin Ramgoolam
2010	• LP - MSM - PMSD • MMM	Navin Ramgoolam
2014	• MSM - PMSD + others • LP - MMM	Anerood Jugnauth (2 years) Pravind Jugnauth (January 2016 - ongoing)

Source: Electoral Commission Office, Mauritius

In fact the advent of big money in politics has had devastating impact on the manner in which politics is understood and practised. The relational power between politicians and voters has been significantly altered due to big money, which to a large extent is premised on a clientelist approach and this has essentially accentuated during the early 1990s.

The Ethnicized Leader

A number of authors have commended Mauritius for its capacity to manage the island's unique ethnic diversity. Terms such 'rainbow nation', 'unity in diversity', 'convivial and cosmopolitan', 'melting pot' have peppered the collective memory of locals and foreigners. We saw in earlier sections that the transition from pre- to post-independence was managed by the political leadership with the intention to accommodate and include everyone (especially the minorities) on board. In their official discourses, political leaders have been sure to cast the net wide enough to demonstrate that their parties are representative and inclusive by fielding candidates across the different ethnic groups. However, a more introspective view validates the point made by Miles (1999: 93):

> *Political parties in Mauritius have tended to reflect the country's ethnic divisions. Only the Mauritian Militant Movement (MMM) under the leadership of Franco-Mauritian Paul Bérenger has consistently espoused a class-based, transethnic platform with any degree of persuasiveness, and even it has been beset by ethnic factionalization and calculation. The Mauritian Social Democratic Party (MSDP) is a thinly veiled Creole movement that initially opposed British withdrawal from the island, fearing independence under a Hindu majority. The Labour Party, despite its origins as an ethnically open syndicate has become transformed into the favored party of an identifiably Hindu electorate. Even the ironically named Mauritian Socialist Movement (MSM), which held power under Sir Aneroood Jugnauth from 1983 until 1995 and advocated a distinctive free-market pathway, was seen as the party of the Hindu bourgeoisie.*

Another relevant point worth highlighting is the smouldering fear of a 'Hindu hegemony' that has translated itself into a reality where 'all three prime ministers have hailed from the same caste' (Miles, 1999) and 'where one may go so far as to say, tentatively, that the Indian electorate will never accept a prime minister other than an Indian' (Bucktowar, 1979). In fact, Bérenger faced the full wrath of a section of the Hindu community when he became Prime Minister in 2003. The latter was the target of the most vitriolic and communalist attack.

Last but not least, one has witnessed the growing influence of socio-cultural groups on political leaders. These socio-cultural groups are in fact powerful religious lobby groups who claim to influence and represent specific ethnic segments of the Mauritian society. Certain of the leaders of these groups say that they have the authority to influence how certain ethnic communities vote. Over the years, political leaders, especially when they are in power, have cosied up to them and have given them a certain legitimacy. Despite the country's secular status, these groups receive important subsidies from the state.

Maintaining the Status Quo: Transactional Leadership

There is no doubt that the tiny island under successive governments has known considerable progress bringing it to its current status of a middle-income country with clear ambitions of moving towards a high-income status. Bunwaree (2014) speaks of the fading Mauritian developmental state and the growing inequalities and asymmetries within the Mauritian society. A clear sign of the quality of political leadership is its ability to question the status quo and to promote a progressive agenda based on programmatic as opposed to merely clientelistic or populist ideas. As Flinders (2016) aptly says 'politics is complex but populism is simple'. In the last two decades, a number of key issues have been put in abeyance by successive governments namely that of electoral reform, a targeted welfare state and the introduction of a Freedom of Information Act (FOIA).

It is more than 15 years, since the retired Judge, Albie Sachs was called upon to set up a commission to make recommendations on electoral and constitutional reform for Mauritius. Although the remit of the Sachs Commission was quite broad and included that of political party funding and strengthening the role of the Electoral Commission and Electoral Supervisory Commission amongst others, the discussion was mostly focused on the 'proposals regarding representation in Parliament on a proportional basis within the existing electoral system' (Sachs, 2002). What ensued were two Parliamentary Select Committees set up to study the recommendations on 'Electoral and Constitutional Reforms' and another on 'Public Funding of Political Parties'. Unfortunately, nothing changed as political consensus did not materialise. Nearly 10 years after Sachs, in 2011, the then Prime Minister (Navin Ramgoolam) commissioned Professor Carcassonne to make recommendations on electoral reform which was followed by an extensive report by Rama Sithanen, an electoral systems expert and once an active politician. The coming into power of the current ruling coalition at the end of 2014, saw the setting-up of a Ministerial Committee to make recommendations on electoral reform and more precisely 'the introduction of a dose of proportional representation in the National Assembly, and guarantee better women representation; the mandatory declaration of community; anti-defection measures; the widening of the powers of the Electoral Supervisory Commission and the Financing of Political Parties Bill'. Till date the process remains stalled.

Mauritius is one of the very few countries in the world that offers such a comprehensive welfare system - universal old pension, free health, free education, subsidies on flour and rice and free transport for the elderly and students. This is a considerable burden on the state coffers especially given that the island is facing the crisis of an ageing population. Governments in power have been very hesitant to deal with this issue as they believe any targeting or alteration of the current welfare state which over the years has been consolidated, would result in political suicide. However, there is a need for a dispassionate discussion but no political leader wants to be remembered as the one responsible for demise of the welfare state in its current form.

Another case in point is the introduction of a Freedom of Information Act (FOIA). The promise of the enactment of such a piece of legislation has been long in the waiting. The latter has appeared in the electoral manifesto of all the mainstream political parties but has never been enacted. It seems that there is a draft law that has been prepared by the current ruling alliance but the main bone of contention is that if ever an FOIA will be in enacted it will be done with no public consultation - a matter of deep concern to a number of observers who see it as a mere piece of window dressing!

Corruption and State Capture

The advent of an impersonal state is fundamental to a fair and merit based democratic society. Political leadership often seizes state resources to its advantage and over time this has been visible in varying ways in Mauritius. Fukayama (2015: 13) aptly captures this when he refers to the fact that 'neopatrimonialism can co-exist with democracy, producing widespread patronage and clientelism in which politicians share state resources with networks of political supporters'. In fact, this brings us back to initial argument about what type of democracy prevails and its ability to speak truth to power.

In the case of Mauritius, political patronage and clientelism have become a big issue which seems to have permeated many segments of the Mauritian society. Indices pertaining to level of corruption, point to the fact that Mauritius is among (together with Botswana, Cap Verde and Seychelles) the least corrupt countries in Africa. The CPI 2015 (Transparency Index) ranked Mauritius 45th out of 168 countries and gave it a score of 53 on 100 (0 being most corrupt and 100 least corrupt). But once again, indices offering the numerical scoring do not tell the whole picture.

Perhaps the most tangible example of the citizen's reactionary approach to corruption within the political class was the results of the 2014 general elections. To a number of observers the previous regime headed by Navin Ramgoolam of the MLP lost the elections due to a combination of incumbency fatigue, political patronage and impunity. The current ruling party rode to victory on an electoral promise 'of clean and corrupt free government' and at mid-mandate is facing their own fair share of corruption related scandals. It therefore seems that high-end corruption is endemic within the Mauritian political class and that the small island has not escaped from the infamous 'politics of the belly' syndrome (Bayart, 1993).

What Now?

Mauritius has 'suffered' at the hands of a highly romanticised version of democracy. This has unfortunately made democracy a rather uncontested, linear, placid and taken for granted principle. This state of affairs has in turn played to the advantage of the dominant/mainstream parties, especially allowing for at times unbridled and uncontested leadership to settle in. The current leadership is ailing (Bérenger and Ramgoolam are in their 70s), dynastic (Xavier Duval and Pravind Jugnauth) and increasingly shaped by big money. The latest 'handing over' of Prime Ministership between father (Aneerood Jugnauth) and son (Pravind Jugnauth) was widely criticised for lacking the legitimacy of the popular mandate and this does not augur well for meritocracy and fair competition.

The demand for political change and renewal is becoming increasingly audible and this is more visible on the social media platforms. A number of these initiatives have used the presence of social media, notably Facebook, to generate a community of followers. The most visible ones are as follows: *Nou Republik* (Our Republic), *Ennsellepep* (One Nation), Mauritius Society Renewal and Young Thinkers Mauritius. Even certain of the mainstream parties are trying to reinvent themselves by opening up to new blood and ideas. However, this is being done without really addressing the very core of the issue: fair, open and merit based access to the position of leader. As Mauritius turns 50, let us hope that the quality of political leadership will be addressed in a serious manner.

References

Aumeerally, N.L. (2005) '"Tiger in Paradise": Reading Global Mauritius in Shifting Time and Space', *Journal of African Cultural Studies* 17(2): 161-180.

Bayart, J.L. (1993) *The State in Africa: The Politics of the Belly*, 2nd Edition. USA: Wiley.

Bowman, L.W. (1991) *Mauritius: Democracy and Development in the Indian Ocean*. Boulder: Westview Press.

Boudet, C. (2003) 'L'émergence de la Démocratie Consociative à Maurice, (1948-1968)', *Annuaire des Pays de L'Océan Indien* XVII: 325-336.

Bräutigam, D. with Diolle, T. (2009) '*Coalitions, Capitalists and Credibility: Overcoming the crisis of confidence at independence in Mauritius*', Research Paper 4, Development Leadership Programme.

Bucktowar, L. (1979) *Democratic Government in Mauritius*. Mauritius: Rainbow Print.

Bunwaree, S. (2004) 'Export oriented employment and social policy in Mauritius', in S. Razavi, R. Pearson, R and C. Danloy (eds) *Globalization, Export-Oriented Employment and Social Policy: Gendered Connections*. New York: Palgrave Macmillan.

Bunwaree, S. (2005), '*State-Society Relations: Re-engineering the Mauritian Social Contract*', Paper presented at the 11th CODESRIA General Assembly, 6-10 December 2005, Maputo.

Bunwaree, S. and Kasenally, R. (2005) *Political Parties in Mauritius*. Johannesburg: EISA Publications.

Bunwaree, S. (2007) *The African Peer Review in Mauritius: Lessons from Phase 1*. AfriMAP, OSISA.

Bunwaree, S. (2014) 'The Fading Development State: Growing Inequality in Mauritius', *Development* 57(3-4): 578-590.

Bunwaree S. (2015) 'The Democratic Deficits of Mauritius: Development and Justice Threatened', in S. Adejumobi (ed) *National Democratic Reforms in Africa*. New York: Palgrave Macmillan.

Burns, J.M. (1978) *Leadership*. New York: Harper and Row.

Carroll, B.W. and Carroll, T. (1999) 'The Consolidation of Democracy in Mauritius', *Democratization* 6(1): 179-197.

Carroll, B.W. and Carroll, T. (2000) 'Accommodating ethnic diversity in a modernizing democratic state: The Mauritian example', *Ethnic and Racial Studies* 23(1): 120-142.

Diamond, L., Plattner, M. F. and Walker, C. (2016) *Authoritarianism goes Global*. USA: John Hopkins University Press.

Dubey, A. (1997) *Government and Politics in Mauritius*. Delhi: Kalinga Publications.

Eisenlohr, P. (2002) 'Language Identity and in an Indian Diaspora: "Multiculturalism" and ethno-linguistic communities in Mauritius', *Internationales Asienforum* 33(1-2): 101-114.

Flinders, M. (2016) *The failure and farce of American Politics*. OUP Blog: Oxford University Press's Academic Insights for the Thinking World.

Frankel, J.A. (2010) '*Mauritius: African Success Story*', Paper presented at the NBER Conference on African Successes, Accra, Ghana, 18-20 July 2010.

Fukayama, F. (2015) 'Why is Democracy performing so badly?', *Journal of Democracy* 26(1): 11-20.

Gyimah-Boadi, E. (2015) 'Africa's Waning Democratic Commitment', *Journal of Democracy* 16(1): 101-113.

Greig, A., Turner, M. and D'Arcy, P. (2011) 'The Fragility of Success: Repositioning Mauritian Development in the Twenty-First Century', *Island Studies Journal* 6(2): 157-178.

Grint, K. (2000) *The Arts of Leadership.* Oxford: Oxford University Press

Gruzd, S. (2007) *The African Peer Review Mechanism: Assessing Origins, Institutional Relations and Achievements.* South Africa: SAIIA.

Jordan, E. (2006) 'Inadequately Self-Critical: Rwanda's Self-Assessment for the African Peer Review Mechanism', *African Affairs* 105(420): 333-351.

Kadima, D. and Kasenally, R. (2006) 'The Formation, Collapse and Revival of Political party Coalitions in Mauritius', in D. Kadima (ed) *The Politics of Party Coalitions in Africa.* South Africa: EISA & KAS Publication.

Kasenally, R. (2011) 'Mauritius: Paradise Reconsidered'. *Journal of Democracy* 22(2): 160-169.

Kasenally, S. (2017) 'The 1976 - 1981 Parliament: An Insider's View', *L'Express*, (https://www.lexpress.mu/idee/293856/1976-1981-parliament-insider-view)

Mackie, G. (2009) 'Schumpeter's Leadership Democracy', *Political Theory* 37(1): 128-153.

McNair, B. (1995) *An Introduction to Political Communication.* London and New York: Routledge.

Meade, J. (1961) *The Economics and Social Structure of Mauritius - Report to the Government of Mauritius.* London: Methuen.

Miles, W.F.S. (1999) 'The Mauritian Enigma', *Journal of Democracy*, 10(2): 91-104.

Mistry, P. (1999) 'Commentary: Mauritius- Quo Vadis?, *African Affairs* 98(393): 551-569.

Morrell, K. and Hartley, J. (2006) 'A model of political leadership', *Human Relations* 59(4): 483-504.

Mukamunana, R. and Kuye, J.O. (2005) 'Revisiting the African Peer Review Mechanism: The Case for Leadership and Good Governance in Africa', *Journal of Public Administration* 40(4.1): 590-604.

Naipaul, V.S. (1972) *The Overcrowded Barracoon.* London: Random House.

Ngowi, H.P. (2009) 'Economic Development and Change in Tanzania since Independence: The Political Leadership Factor', *African Journal of Political Science and International Relations* 3(4): 259–67.

Quartz Africa (2016) *"Why we haven't given Africa's most prestigious leadership award"* (https://qz.com/714618/why-we-havent-given-africas-most-prestigious-leadership-award-for-two-years/)

Rakner, L.R. and Wang, V. (2007) *'Governance Assessments and the Paris Declaration'.* A CMI Issues Paper Prepared for the UNDP Bergen Seminar September.

Reddi, S. (2016) *"SSR's Conception of Mauritius and its African Identity"*, Paper presented at the African Studies Seminar Series, University of Mauritius.

Rotberg, R. (2003). 'The Roots of African Leadership Deficit', *Compass: A Journal of Leadership* 1(1): 28-32.

Sachs, A. (2002) *Report of the Commission on Constitutional and Electoral Reform.* Mauritius: Government Printing.

Selvon, S. (2017) 'The true nature of the retrocession movement in Mauritius ...prior to the birth of the Mauritius Labour Party', *L'Express* (https://www.lexpress.mu/node/300754)

Simmons, A.S. (1982) *Modern Mauritius: The Politics of Decolonisation.* Bloomington: Indiana University Press.

Stiglitz, J.E. (2011) *The Mauritian Miracle.* [Prague]: Project Syndicate.

Subramanian, A. (2001) 'Mauritius: A Case Study', *Finance and Development* 38(4). Available online at http://www.imf.org/external/pubs/ft/fandd/2001/12/subraman.htm (accessed on 20.12.17).

Subramanian A. & Roy, D. (2001) *Who can explain the Mauritian Miracle: Meade, Romer, Sachs, or Rodrik.* Washington, D.C.: International Monetary Fund.

Tetty, W.J. (2012) 'African Leadership Deficit: Exploring Pathways to Good Governance and Transformative Politics', in K. Hanson, G. Kararach and T. Shaw (eds) *Rethinking Development Challenges for Public Policy.* London: Palgrave Macmillan.

Transparency International (2015) *Corruption Perception Index – 2015 - Mauritius.* Available online at https://www.transparencymauritius.org/corruption-perception-index/corruption-perception-index-2015/ (accessed on 20.12.17).

Van Wyk, J.A. (2007) '*Political Leaders in Africa: presidents, patrons or profiteers?*', African Centre for the Constructive Resolution of Disputes (ACCORD) Occasional Paper Series, vol 2, no. 1. Durban: ACCORD.

Varma, M.N. (2008) *The Making of Mauritius.* Mauritius: Editions Le Printemps.

Weltz, M. (2013) *Integrating Africa: Decolonization's Legacies, Sovereignty and the African Union.* London and New York: Routledge.

---

[i] There was a slight exception following a pre-electoral deal which saw Paul Bérenger, leader of the Mouvement Militant Mauricien (MMM) share the Prime Ministership with Anerood Jugnauth and became the Prime Minister from 2003 - 2005.

[ii] Part of the 2015-2019 Government Programme aimed at developing new economic measures to participate in Africa's growth.

The Media as Agents of Democracy in Mauritius
Issues and Challenges since Independence

CHRISTINA CHAN-MEETOO

Introduction

Journalism is deemed to play key roles in the functioning of all modern democracies. As part of the public sphere, the media purport to inform citizens about decisions that can affect their everyday life, to report and to act as watchdog on decision-makers, to denounce abuse and scandals, as well as to sensitise and educate the population about grand ideas and challenges. In practice however, such objectives are often not entirely fulfilled due to several obstacles and constraints, whether linked to the intrinsic setup of media houses which tend to be closely related to the wealthy because of their ownership structures and reliance on advertising revenues (Herman and Chomsky, 1988; Foley, 2000) or to external factors such as political interference, creation of pseudo-events by the marketing world (Boorstin, 1963), unwritten social and cultural guidelines (McQuail, 2000) inter alia. Further, the challenges faced by the journalistic profession in a changing technological world are constantly evolving and thus complicate matters (Wahl-Jorgensen, Williams, 2016), with increased fragmentation, polarisation and partisanship (Hollander, 2008; Leeper, 2014).

Mauritius is no exception. Yet, it is worth exploring the specificities of its mass media which operate in a particular context: that of a small island state in the Indian Ocean which has been colonised by the French and the British successively, which has inherited and cultivated multicultural and multilingual legacies and whose modern history has been marked both by somewhat peaceful economic development and subtle socio-ethnic undercurrents. Many scholars have written about the hybrid nature of Mauritian society (Boswell, 2005) and the dilemma of multiculturalism associated with its polyethnic makeup[i] (Eriksen, 1998). This living paradox is what defines the country and the local mass media are an inherent part of the mix with their own share of ambivalence whether in terms of their history, actors or choice of editorial line.

This chapter thus seeks to explore the key evolutions, issues and challenges that are specific to the Mauritian media. I first focus on the key periods preceding independence in order to examine the position of significant media actors within the colonial plantation economy, from the first free newspapers associated with the economically dominant Franco-Mauritian minority, to the introduction of titles associated with more diverse communities, and the growing popularity of pro-independence newspapers in the 1940-1960's period. I then examine the post-independence phase: the difficult periods for the written press which was subjected to heavy censorship in the early 1970's and governmental attempts at financial stifling in the 1980's, but also the more positive periods of diversification of politically engaged media titles and subsequent state support for the training of media workers, followed by the introduction of private radio stations in 2002 and live parliamentary coverage in 2017.

The chapter highlights the ambivalent linkages that the private media entertains with both the political and corporate actors of the country: for the first through patronage and advertising revenue, and for the second through the strong affinities and regular nominations of advisers from the ranks of media workers. The chapter shows that the legal and regulatory frameworks within which the media operate are themselves flawed. Despite electoral pledges from governing parties, legislation related to access to information is still missing. The media have no agreed upon code of ethics nor any self-regulatory system to take care of unethical and unprofessional reporting, despite various commissioned reports recommending industry-led regulation. Yet, overall, the Mauritian democracy enjoys a relatively positive global outlook with honourable performances in indices relating to press freedom and the opportunities heralded by broadened participation of citizens in the public sphere.

The early days of free press in the colony: Ethnic, economic and political linkages

The first newspaper published on the island of Mauritius (then known as *Isle de France*) also happens to be the pioneer paper in the Southern hemisphere and on the African Continent (Chan-Meetoo, 2011). *Affiches, Annonces et Avis Divers (des Isles de France et de Bourbon)[ii]* was launched in 1773 by the Frenchman Nicolas Lambert under the French colonial rule in association with the French business venture, the *Compagnie des Indes[iii]*. It was an official publication for both Isle de France and Bourbon (now known as Reunion Island, a neighbouring island which has remained a French overseas territory) and it contained primarily advertisements for freshly imported goods on sale including slaves as well as other official announcements by the colonial power and the *Compagnie des Indes*. The early media on the island thus targeted the economic and intellectual elites with commercial advertisements, later adding on literary and cultural pages.

British colonial rule which started in 1810 and lasted for 158 years, was marked by continuity in the public sphere for people of French origin for much of the time as the British preferred to keep the peace with the dominant sugar barons. In 1831, the lawyer Adrien d'Epinay was sent by his peers to London to negotiate financial compensation for the abolition of slavery for plantation owners. He also negotiated for the creation of a Colonial Assembly to include Mauritian representatives (that is the descendants of the French colonisers[iv]), obtained authorisation for the latter to work in the public administration and also freedom of the press, which was until then censored by the British administration. Upon his return to the island, d'Epinay launched the daily newspaper *Le Cernéen* and also created the first private Bank of Mauritius which was subsequently replaced by the Mauritius Commercial Bank (Piat, 2002).[v]

The history of the introduction of a free Mauritian press is marked by a strong linkage with sugar plantation owners and associated private banking, thus carrying a significant class and ethnic bias within the context of a colonial capitalist system. Political participation and press freedom became more open thanks to (but also initially limited to) the White opinion leaders of French origin. A coloured man named Berquin, belonging to the community known as the 'gens de couleur' as per Allen's terminology (1999: 82), established a newspaper called *La Balance* in 1832 in association with the secretaries of the Procureur and Advocate General John Jeremie, who had been entrusted with the task of the abolition of slavery in the colony. The paper however disappeared in 1835. Meanwhile, in 1833, *Le Mauricien* was founded by Jules Eugène Leclezio, another representative of the White community and director of the Mauritius Commercial Bank[vi] (Toussaint, 1943). In 1843, Rémy Ollier, a *métis*[vii] (half-caste of mixed blood, son of a French captain and a former slave), founded his own paper when the prevailing papers associated with the White oligarchy, *Le Cernéen* and *Le Mauricien,* refused to publish his response to a critical review of a theatre play which had been printed in these anti-abolitionist papers. The initial review expressed indignation about the fact that authorisation had been given to stage *Antony,* a play by Alexandre Dumas, the famous mixed French writer with 'negro' blood in his veins, just like Ollier. The latter's pamphlet, *La Sentinelle,* a scathing denunciation of racism, became a regular publication championing the cause of the *gens de couleur* and claiming seats for them in the Assembly.[viii]

Newspapers associated with the other ethnic groups include *The Hindustani* launched in 1909 by Manilal Doctor to defend the cause of Indian migrants who were being ill-treated on sugar plantations as attested by the report submitted by Frere and Williamson in 1875[ix] . The first papers in Mandarin for the Chinese migrants also appeared around 1920. As noted by Idelson (2007), as from the 1930s, newspapers became increasingly imbricated in the ethno-political discourse of the public sphere as represented by the four groups identified in the Constitution of Mauritius: Hindus, Muslims, Sino-Mauritians and General Population. By the middle of the 19th century, it had become apparent that the demographic setup of the country had drastically changed with the numerical domination of people of Indian origin followed by those of African roots as evidenced by official censuses carried out in the period (see table 4). The proportion of Indo-Mauritians first exceeded the 50 per cent mark between 1851 and 1861. According to the International Organisation for Migration 2013 Migration in Mauritius report (p. 31):

> When the British conquered Mauritius in 1810, the population was almost 100,000; however, more than 80 per cent were slaves. The abolition of slavery a quarter of a century later – in 1830 – reduced the size of the population, probably because most slaves returned to Madagascar or the African continent. More than 100,000 Indians were recruited to replace the slaves, which is the main reason why Mauritians of Indian origin still make up the largest segment of the population today.

Table 4: Census figures between 1846 and 1952

Census Year	General population	Indo-Mauritian population	Chinese population	Total	Indo-Mauritian as % of population
1846	102,217	56,245	-	158,462	35
1851	102,827	77,996	-	180,823	43
1861	115,864	192,634	1,552	310,050	62
1871	97,497	216,258	2,287	316,042	68
1881	107,323	248,993	3,558	359,874	69
1891	111,517	255,920	3,151	370,588	69
1901	108,422	259,086	3,515	371,023	70
1911	107,432	257,697	3,662	368,791	70
1921	104,216	265,524	6,745	376,485	71
1931	115,666	268,649	8,923	393,238	68
1944	143,056	265,247	10,882	419,185	63
1952	148,238	335,327	17,850	501,415	67

Source: Central Statistics Office

It became inevitable for the British Colonial Office that it had to reform the mode of suffrage, which it did only almost a century later by introducing voting rights for any citizen who could sign his/her name in 1947. This was the conclusion of a long series of evolutions involving a growing consciousness of the working class as an exploited group and marking the start of the process of decolonisation. Significant events during the period include the 1871 protests by Indian indentured labourers, the ability to purchase small plots of land due to the declining interest of the Franco-Mauritians in the sugar industry, the awakening of a Hindu conscience with the celebrations marking the arrival of the first coolies in 1935, the creation of the Labour Party by Dr Maurice Curé associated with massive strikes organised with Emmanuel Anquetil and Pandit Sahadeo in 1936. The suffrage reform radically changed the face of Mauritian politics with the entrance of the first Hindu representative, Dr Seewoosagur Ramgoolam, who took over the Labour Party and led the negotiations for the conditions associated with the granting of independence to the island[x] (Piat, 2002).

It is in this context that the newspaper *Advance* was created in 1940 by the Labour Party, and it quickly became an outlet for the growing demands of the Hindu community and a strong advocate of independence. Some of its illustrious protagonists such as the poet and novelist Marcel Cabon (Editor-in-Chief of *Advance* between 1958 and 1970) and the poet and artist Malcolm de Chazal were regarded as traitors to the Creole Community, which was, at that time, largely opposed to the idea of independence due to the fear of the 'péril hindou' or 'Hindu menace' (Callikhan-Proag, 1996; Boudet, 2007: 2012). According to Boudet (2007), the leitmotiv of the Hindu menace was initiated between 1953 and 1955 by Noël Marrier d'Unienville, Editor-in-Chief of *Le Cernéen*. On 4th June 1953, the latter wrote the following in an editorial:

> *Le suffrage universel ici veut dire, personne n'en doute, le suffrage hindou. Le suffrage hindou veut dire l'hégémonie hindoue. L'hégémonie hindoue signifie fatalement... l'annexion, dans un temps plus ou moins long, de l'île Maurice à l'Inde.*

> [*Nobody can deny that universal suffrage here means Hindu suffrage. Hindu suffrage means Hindu hegemony. Hindu hegemony inevitably means... annexation of Mauritius to India in the longer term.*][xi]

The modern-day paper *Le Mauricien*, then headed by famous writer and politician Raoul Rivet positioned itself against independence together with *Le Cernéen*, although it later rallied the cause. As for the paper *L'Express,* it was created in 1963 by Sir Guy Forget, member of the Labour Party, although it was touted as a distinct media house with a professional product which would demarcate itself from the more politically-oriented *Advance*. Forget subsequently distanced himself from the Labour Party after 1968 when the party agreed to form a coalition with the *Parti Mauricien Social Démocrate* (PMSD) which had initially campaigned against independence. The linkage of the publication with the political sphere still remained though. Several members of *Mouvement Militant Mauricien* (MMM) who became members of parliament (MPs) and ministers were at some point editors at *L'Express*.

Post-independence period: Tense relations between the press and the State

After having obtained independence from British rule, Mauritius went through very difficult economic and political periods which negatively impacted on press freedom. On the economic front, the country had been experiencing declining real per capita income, high population growth and high unemployment since the 1950's (Yeung Lam Ko, 1998). Yeung Lam Ko (1998: 8) notes that the government's diversification strategy failed due to 'lack of capital, shortage of skilled workers and lack of enterprise and risk taking regarding new industrial activities (most probably due to the deeply ingrained sugar mentality in the country)'.

On the political front, following the by-elections of 1970 which boosted the opposing MMM, government instituted a state of emergency and a moratorium on elections and arrested the leaders of the MMM. Public gatherings were forbidden through a Public Order Act, MMM presses were confiscated while the whole written press was heavily censored in 1971 (Bräutigam, 1997). Journalists needed to bring their texts to the Line Barracks (police headquarters) for vetting by the Police Commissioner and his team. *L'Express* decided to publish blank spaces to show to the readers that texts had been censored. The state of emergency was subsequently lifted in 1972. The rest of the 1970s and the 1980s saw the golden age of political media with a flurry of titles associated with particular parties such as *Le Populaire* for the PMSD, *The Sun* for the MSM, *Le Militant* for the MMM as well as the existing *Advance* of the Labour Party. In 1984, however, government proposed the introduction of a Newspaper and Periodicals (Amendment) Bill which would require large cash deposits of Rs 500,000 for newspapers to be allowed to operate. This was opposed by journalists through a sit-in protest in front of Parliament. 44 journalists were arrested and detained for four hours. The Bill was subsequently repealed in 1985 (Selvon, 2012).

A decade later, as if to atone for the harm done to the profession, the government introduced the Media Trust Act which provided for the institution of the Media Trust, whose main objective is to organise seminars, conferences, workshops and training courses for media professionals using primarily government funding. Its board mainly consists of elected representatives of the press although the chairperson is designated by government[xii]. The organisation was however paralysed for more than ten years between 2004 and 2015 as no chairperson had been appointed by government despite the holding of elections by the press corps to designate other board members. It was revived in 2015 with the change of government and it has since then launched several training courses for working journalists. The latest controversy pertains to the nomination of a chairperson who has never been in the private media and has instead been director of the Government Information Service. This is perceived as a move to punish the private media which have been overtly critical of the current government. Government's response has been that the law stipulates that the chairperson is appointed by the Minister and that no mention is made of a particular profile.

21st century developments

The beginning of the 21st century was marked by a new era in the media landscape with the liberalisation of the airwaves although this event intervened at a very late stage in the history of a country which purports to be a democracy when compared with the history of other democracies. Indeed, until 2002, broadcast media was monopolised by the State through the Mauritius Broadcasting Corporation (MBC). Radio had initially been started as a private venture by the Mauritian citizen Charles Jolivet under the latter part of the British colonial rule (broadcasts were primarily in French despite being under the British rule). The venture was absorbed in the State company, the Mauritius Broadcasting Service (MBS), which subsequently became the MBC which is still an important player, especially in television broadcasting.

With the adoption of the Independent Broadcasting Act in 2002, three private radio stations, namely Radio One, Radio Plus and Top FM emerged. All are officially highly regulated (by the IBA, the ICTA and MCML[xiii]) but there is in practice a limited scope of intervention, except at critical periods such as election campaigning. There is still no private television operator although the IBA law technically provides for broadcasting licences for private television[xiv]. This is probably due to the high capital investment required to operate a television station and the restrictive cap of 20 per cent on foreign investment and shareholding. Interestingly, in the mainstream media and the public sphere, the prevailing perception is that the legislation does not provide for private television, thus fuelling the notion that the different governments have deliberately omitted the provision in order to oppose such a possibility. This is factually wrong. Part II of the IBA Act has clear provisions for the granting of private commercial television broadcasting licences. Section 22 of Part IV states that the duration of a licence would be for 5 years.

However, it is true to say that governing parties would prefer television to remain under State monopoly, especially after seeing the effects of private radio shows which have opened up their microphones to the public. When in power, all political leaders have systematically been critical of the radio stations and the private media in general for what they refer to as an abuse of airwaves, publication of false news, lack of fairness and impartiality, etc. Early in 2004, shortly after the liberalisation of airwaves,

71

the then Prime Minister Paul Bérenger expressed discontent about the alleged abuses by the private radio stations. He publicly announced the setting-up of a special committee to investigate radio content and the introduction of a Broadcast Delay Apparatus in all stations to prevent airing of unwarranted comments by audience members who participate in phone-in shows[xv].

On the positive side, it is worth noting that the government introduced Parliament TV in 2017, which is accessible both through a dedicated television channel and an online platform (https://parliamenttv.govmu.org/). This Parliament TV provides live coverage of National Assembly proceedings as well as access to archived coverage. This is actually a surprising move on the part of government given that there was no obligation to introduce Parliament TV as there was no such commitment in the winning coalition's electoral manifesto. Although there may be flaws with regard to the quality of the coverage (in particular the restrictive choice of camera angles and framing), this undoubtedly represents a major step towards access to information for all citizens.

Current state of the media: Incestuous links with the corporate and the political

Beyond their tense relationships with political power, there are various systemic issues which continue to be faced by the so-called Mauritian Fourth Estate. Not least of those being their inherent structures and operations. The mainstream media tend to entertain strong links and incestuous dependency on the corporate world, mostly itself a legacy of the sugar industry barons. *La Sentinelle* which is advertised as the premier media group of the country, is currently run by a former CEO of the biggest private bank, the Mauritius Commercial Bank (MCB), itself linked to the history of big sugar estates. As shown by Bagdikian (2004) on the international scene, the mainstream mass media tend to be characterised by economic concentration which includes both vertical and horizontal integration. The same patterns can be observed in Mauritius as the big media houses such as *La Sentinelle* and the *Défi Media Group* expand their activities and member companies to cover pre-press, printing, publication, distribution, events management, billboard advertising, etc. Buy overs and mergers are used to absorb competing publications and consolidate a hegemonic presence by exploiting new market niches with high commercial potential. The market is currently dominated by two big media conglomerates, *La Sentinelle Ltd* and *Le Défi Media Group*, and a smaller one, *Le Mauricien Ltd.*

As mainstream media strive to improve their levels of profitability, investment in quality journalism is weakened and easy to replicate simplistic reporting and entertainment media become the norm to woo increasingly fragmented audiences, leading to more 'He said, She said' reporting[xvi], sensationalist and magazine style content under the guise of infotainment and bordering on the voyeuristic style of reporting. The pursuit of likes and shares through social media and fad apps on technological platforms become an obsession and, instead of exploiting the possibilities of collective intelligence promised by the web 2.0, we are faced with a dumbing down on average with more clickbait journalism, native advertising, sponsored content, and a lack of in-depth investigation, let alone serious fact-checking.

This is complicated by a high turnover rate in the profession and also another type of incestuous relationship: that of the press with the political world. Indeed, the majority of political communication advisers of ministers and parastatal bodies are drawn from the news desks of private media and are nominated shortly following the proclamation of election results and appointment of ministers. This seems to suggest that these professional journalists turned advisers had significant affinities with the ministers in order to obtain their appointments and puts a question mark on their claims of neutrality when they were in their respective news desks during election campaigns. Similarly, one can wonder how objective their subsequent coverage of political news is when they return to their respective employments as journalists. It should be noted that none of the journalists make any statement about their appointment as political advisers to their audiences at any moment whatsoever.

Cynically, as highlighted in the country report in the *Report on the State of Right to Information in Africa 2017* (Chan-Meetoo, 2017: 164-173), one can say that within the ranks of journalists who have been political advisers, all mainstream political parties are represented, thus creating an artificial balance in coverage though arguably, the coverage of any particular regime tends to be more critical than positive given that those journalists who stay in the news desks are those who do not have the required level of affinity with the governing parties. Thus the critical role of oversight/reporting by the media is existent, albeit in an unorthodox manner.

As can be seen, ambiguity and ambivalence are present at all levels of the mainstream media. Media owners and managers essentially fray with the economic power whilst media workers do so with the political power.

Legal and regulatory constraints

One could also argue that the legal and regulatory frameworks within which the media operate are themselves flawed. Whereas an increasing number of countries, including on the African continent and in less democratic states, have introduced legislation related to Freedom of Information (FOI) or Access to Information (ATI), Mauritius is still a long way towards achieving the same. There is, as yet, no legislation pertaining to FOI/ATI in Mauritius. Section 12 of the Constitution[xvii] does specifically guarantee freedom of expression which it defines as the freedom to impart ideas and information but it does not go any further in defining this freedom and in fact, refers to a long list of constraints such as national security, public safety, morality and health as well as the protection of reputation, privacy, court proceedings, confidential information and regulation of public communication channels. It also clearly refers to imposition of restrictions on public officers.

Indeed, civil servants in Mauritius are governed by the Official Secrets Act[xviii] and the Human Resource Management manual[xix] (prepared by the Ministry of Civil Service and Administrative Reforms) which clearly prohibit the dissemination of information related to government matters without authorisation from supervisory levels. This creates a chilling effect on members of public administration who could act as potential whistle-blowers and conversely leads to an unhealthy reliance by the media on officious sources from inside who may be prone to hidden agendas and manipulative information leakages.

The ever-elusive Freedom of Information Act

All winning political parties and coalitions have regularly referred to freedom of information as a goal in their electoral manifestos prior to being elected. The earliest which can be documented is that of the 2005 *Alliance Sociale* comprising the Labour Party (*Parti Travailliste* – PTr), *the Parti Mauricien Xavier Duval* (PMXD), the Mouvement Républicain (MR), *Les Verts Fraternels* and the *Mouvement Militant Socialiste Mauricien* (MMSM). This winning coalition, with the Labour Party as the leading partner, specifically referred to freedom of information in its political manifesto[xx]. This was subsequently transcribed in the official government programme 2005-2010[xxi] which was read by the President of the Republic in Parliament:

> *'My Government will provide citizens with a right of access to personal information held by State agencies and to information relating to government business by enacting a Freedom of Information Act.'*

However, no legislation was introduced. In fact, new elections took place in 2010 and the winning coalition called *L'Alliance de l'Avenir* comprised of, again the Labour Party, with the PMXD restyled as *Parti Mauricien Social Démocrate* (PMSD) and a new partner, the *Mouvement Socialiste Militant* (MSM). The manifesto for this winning coalition did not refer at all to the previous pledge for freedom of information.[xxii]

This can be explained by the confrontational relations which prevailed during the 2005-2010 period between the political actors (ruling parties and opposition alike) and the press of the country. Confrontations have sometimes led to unpleasant attitudes and reactions on the part of the political actors such as intimidating interpellations by the police following broadcasting of news items related to the health of a Prime Minister in 2008, the symbolical burning of newspapers in 2009, the boycott of a group's papers at press conferences in 2010, and the temporary ban of one journalist to the National Assembly in 2016. On the other hand, the press often have recourse to their editorial content and even selective reporting and agenda setting tools to retaliate against specific political actors and parties depending upon their own prevailing interests, affinities or biases.

We have currently reached a stage where such confrontations have become part of the system and are even secretly enjoyed by the press (as these are conducive to sensationalist content and thus heighten their media's reach and sales) and this is undoubtedly unhealthy and constitutes an impediment to the realisation of a more mature democracy. Furthermore, political parties have become accustomed to having undisputed hierarchies within their own ranks (party leaders have never been replaced except by their own progeny despite claims of having democratic elections within the party structures). A Freedom of Information Act is thus a very difficult step for political parties to take as such legislation could result in constant scrutiny and questioning of decision-making at state level by the mass media and by ordinary citizens.

As the government of the day was very unhappy with the coverage it was being given by the privately owned media, Prof. Geoffrey Robertson, a high profile human rights barrister, academic, author and broadcaster, was specially appointed in 2013 as consultant to review the media sector and to consolidate all media laws and introduce regulation of the media through the institution of a Media Commission. However, the consultant went beyond the mandate and made three main recommendations in April 2013 in his preliminary report 'Media Law and Ethics in Mauritius'[xxiii], namely:

- The review of all laws related to the media (sedition, defamation, contempt of court, etc.);
- The introduction of a code of ethics for the media and a Media Commission to regulate the media;
- The introduction of Freedom of Information legislation.

At the last general elections organised at the end of 2014, the *Alliance Lepep* comprising the MSM as leading partner in coalition with the PMSD and a new party called *Mouvement Liberater* (ML) won. Surprisingly, the pledge for a Freedom of Information Act resurfaced in this coalition's manifesto[xxiv]:

> *Un 'Freedom of Information Act' sera introduit pour garantir la transparence et permettre la libre circulation des informations [A Freedom of Information Act will be introduced to guarantee transparency and allow the free circulation of information.][xxv]*

This was again transcribed in the official government programme 2015-2019 which was read by the President of the Republic in Parliament:

> *254. The Constitution of Mauritius guarantees fundamental rights and freedom of a citizen of the country, such as: freedom of expression and speech, political opinion, assembly and association. Government is determined to protect these rights and widen the contours of our democracy.* (Government Programme 2015-2019, p. 56).

And further:

> *258. A Freedom of Information Act will be brought forward to promote transparency and accountability in public administration and more particularly in contract allocations.* (p. 57).

All political coalitions that have been in power have pledged at some point in time to introduce such legislation under the appellation of Freedom of Information Act but none have made much visible significant progress. Under the present government, there has been a slight progress as the decision to introduce FOI was announced at the level of Cabinet as the very first item on 22 January 2016[xxvi]:

> *1. Cabinet has taken note that the Freedom of Information Bill, as announced in the Government Programme 2015-2019, is being prepared. The main objective of the Bill will be to promote transparency and accountability in public administration.'* (Cabinet Decisions, 22 January 2016, p. 1).

The commitment has been reiterated within the last African Commission on Human and Peoples' Rights (ACHPR) Mauritius country report for 2009-2015 submitted in March 2016. The section on implementation of recommendations from previous periodic reports comprises the following item:

20.0 To finalise the drafting of the Freedom of Information legislation and pass it into law. In the Government Programme 2015-2019, it is stated that a Freedom of Information Act will be enacted to promote transparency and accountability in public administration in contract allocations. Given that the nature and scope of such legislation is an evolving one, Government is presently doing the necessary groundwork for the preparation of a legislation which will adopt innovative processes to improve access to information. Once this initial process is completed drafting instructions will be given to the Attorney-General's Office to proceed with the preparation of the Bill.[xxvii] (p. 76)

It is thus possible that the groundwork for the law is indeed currently being done at the level of the State Law Office in order to propose a draft but there is no further information about the status of the work being done.

The last ACHPR country report also states that:

42.0 Section 12 of the Constitution provides for freedom of expression, that is freedom to hold opinions and to receive and impart ideas and information without interference, and freedom from interference with his correspondence. The local media enjoy a long tradition of freedom and pluralism with a number of dailies, weeklies, fortnightlies and monthlies whilst the audiovisual landscape consists of the national radio and television, the Mauritius Broadcasting Corporation and equally private radio stations. Freedom of the press is guaranteed and is an essential component of the right to freedom of expression provided for under section 12 of the Constitution. (p. 14)

All in all, it is true to say that there is relative diversity in the Mauritian media landscape if we consider that all factions are more or less represented (ethnic, economic, political, etc.) albeit in incomplete ways.

Lack of consensus on professional standards

One can however hardly rejoice about such a situation as all of those stakeholders (media, corporate actors and politicians alike) derive some kind of benefit but at the expense of democracy and the general public. It is the latter which suffers the most from the incestuous relationships between the press and economic and political powers, which are aggravated by the obvious lack of professional standards. The absence of a unified ethical framework for the journalistic profession has been highlighted by many observers and official reports have been commissioned to address the issue, one by Kenneth Morgan, former director of the former British Press Complaints Commission, and the other by Prof. Geoffrey Robertson.

Morgan was entrusted by the Media Trust (then under the direction of the editor-in-chief of *L'Express*) in 1998 to formulate proposals for the local media. He strongly recommended the setting-up of a self-regulatory system by media houses who would be represented on a board instituted under a revised version of the Media Trust Act. But, the recommendations were never adopted as the rival editor-in-chief of *Le Mauricien* and other media houses opposed the idea on the basis that self-regulation was supposed to be already in place within individual media houses and that there was no need for a common self-regulation system. Competing egos thus stood in the way of a proposed attempt at rationalised industry-led regulation (Chan-Meetoo, 2013: 17). Similarly, ego wars have impeded the sustainability of associations and unions of media workers. Some of them (AJM, NEPA, USEP[xxviii]) have been launched with much hope and hype, especially in times of harsh criticism against the media industry but none have survived the lack of solidarity on core issues for media workers and puerile turf wars.

Fifteen years after the Morgan report, the idea of a regulatory system was further developed by Robertson who had been employed as consultant by the government. In his preliminary report, he proposed a broad spectrum of measures to sanitise but also consolidate the professional practice of journalism. These included the review of all laws affecting the media (such as on defamation, sedition, publication of false news, inter alia), the appointment of an independent Ombudsperson and a Media Commission under a consolidated Media Trust that would be co-financed by the State and the industry for a regulatory system involving participation of civil society, as well as the introduction of Freedom of Information Act. To date, the final report has not been published and it is not known whether it has been effectively submitted or just cast aside by government.

The paradox of a globally positive outlook

Overall, despite the absence of FOI in Mauritius, the country fares well in terms of governance trends with commendable performance in freedoms for political rights and civil liberties, average performance for press freedom and transparency. It has been categorised as generally free by Freedom House. The latest Freedom House 2017 survey classified Mauritius as a "free" country with a score of 89 per cent placing it within the top 50 countries of the world. Mauritius has also performed honourably in the Reporters Without Borders Press Freedom index despite a decline in absolute scores. For Reporters Without Borders, the country is ranked 56th, thus gaining 5 places since 2016 but there has been loss in its score due to a decline in respect for freedom of information following some threats from governing parties, a jail sentence against a print media editor-in-chief and warnings to state media journalists who expressed their opinion about their media house during public debates.

Under the different political regimes over the past two decades, the private media have been regularly criticised and sometimes verbally threatened by governing coalitions but there have never been direct repression, arrests or outrageous abuses against the local media. In spite of the absence of FOI/ATI laws, the State does release a wealth of data, albeit not always complete, user-friendly or well organised. The State does provide extensive information on its official portal at http://govmu.org/ whereby all ministries, departments, parastatal and other government bodies are present and produce a website as part of the domain. There is no outright censorship (except for an unfortunate day in 2007 when the Information and Communication Technology Authority blocked access to Facebook because of a fake profile of the then Prime Minister). The media landscape is also quite well developed in comparison with other island states, especially in the sector of print media which has been in existence since nearly 250 years and with a diversity of media titles over the years after independence. The official figures from Statistics Mauritius count an average of 40 publications every year, a surprising figure for a small country with a population of around 1.3 million inhabitants.

Finally, opportunities and new trends, in particular related to new entrants, new digital tools and new journalistic practices do exist. Online platforms have recently allowed for a flurry of new entrants, bloggers, citizen journalists and tiny media companies, some serious, others less so. The upcoming configuration heralds what could be termed in French a *'joyeux désordre'* [joyful disorder], further spiced up by the possibilities offered by the participation of 'The People Formerly Known as the Audience' as famously coined by Prof. Jay Rosen from NYU. The 'Paul Lismore' phenomenon, a mysterious and anonymous whistleblower and commentator, is but one of its manifestations. Mainstream papers and politicians alike have obsessed over his/her identity in vain and seem fearful of the impact of such lone runners who are able to command the attention of the many. Such thorns in the side may perhaps incite media actors and decision-makers alike to try and get their acts right.

References

5-Plus Dimanche (2004) *'Bérenger cible les radios privées'.* Available online at
http://www.5plus.mu/node/19323 [accessed 1 October 2017].
Allen, R. (1999) *Slaves, Freedmen and Indentured Laborers in Colonial Mauritius.* UK: Cambridge
University Press.

Alliance de l'Avenir (2010) *Programme gouvernemental de l'Alliance de l'Avenir*. Available online at:
https://web.archive.org/web/20100601212558/http://www.bleublancrouge.mu/files/Programme.pdf [accessed 1 October 2017].

Bagdikian, B. (2004) *The New Media Monopoly*. Boston: Beacon Press.

Barbeau, V. (2002) 'Presse écrite et télévision à Maurice: Espace de débats ou enjeu communautaire?' in J. Simonin (ed) *Communautés périphériques et espaces publics émergents. Les médias dans les îles de l'Océan Indien*. Paris: L'Harmattan.

Boswell, R. (2006) 'Unraveling Le Malaise Créole: Hybridity and Marginalisation in Mauritius', *Identities: Global Studies in Culture and Power* 12(2): 195-221.

Boudet, C. (2007) 'Les Franco-Mauriciens: Une diaspora pollinisée', *Migrations internationales et vulnérabilités* 23(3): 109-132.

Boudet, C. (2012) 'Le rôle du "péril hindou" dans la mise en place de la démocratie consociative à l'île Maurice (1947–73)', *Canadian Journal of African Studies* 46(2): 177-193.

Bräutigam, D. (1997) 'Institutions, Economic Reform, and Democratic Consolidation in Mauritius', *Comparative Politics* 30(1): 45–62.

Cabinet Decisions, 22 January 2016. Available online at:
http://pmo.govmu.org/English/News/Pages/Cabinet-Decisions---22-January-2016.aspx [Accessed 5 September 2017].

Callikhan-Proag, A. (1996) 'De Marcel Cabon à Malcolm de Chazal. Deux perdi bande', *Sur Malcolm*. Vizavi/Ether Vague, Maurice/Toulouse: 31-54.

Chan-Meetoo, C. (2017) 'Mauritius country report', in Africa Freedom of Information Centre (AFIC) (ed) *Report on the State of Right to Information in Africa 2017*.

Chan-Meetoo, C. and Kasenally, R. (2011) *Enhancing Democratic Systems: The Media in Mauritius. A Dialogue Session*. Cameroon: Langaa RPCIG.

Chan-Meetoo, C. (2013) *Media Ethics and Regulation: Insights from Africa*. Cameroon: Langaa RPCIG.

Chan-Meetoo, C. (2013) 'Improving Democracy in Mauritius. The need to remove information boundaries and enhance the media', *OSSREA Journal of Social Policies and Development OSSREA Mauritius Chapter Special Issue: 21-27*

Eriksen. T.H. (1998) *Common Denominators: Ethnicity, Nation-Building and Compromise in Mauritius*. Oxford: Berg Publishers.

Foley, M. (2000) 'Press regulation', *Administration* 48(1): 40-51.

Government Programme 2005-2010. *Address by the President of the Republic* (2005). http://mauritiusassembly.govmu.org/English/Pages/Address%20by%20the%20President/Government-Programme-2005.aspx [accessed 5 September 2017].

Government Programme 2015-2019. *Achieving Meaningful Change. Address by the President of the Republic of Mauritius* (2015). Available online at:
http://mauritiusassembly.govmu.org/English/Documents/Add%20president/govprog2015.pdf [accessed 5 September 2017].

Herman, E.S. and Chomsky, N. (1988) *Manufacturing Consent*. New York: Pantheon Books.

Histoires Mauriciennes (2015) [Website]. *Remy Ollier, le métis flamboyant*. Available online at: http://histoiresmauriciennes.com/remy-ollier/ [Accessed 5 October 2017].

Hollander, B.A. (2008) 'Tuning out or tuning elsewhere? Partisanship, polarization, and media migration from 1998 to 2006', *Journalism & Mass Communication Quarterly* 85(1): 23-40.

International Organisation for Migration (2013) *Migration in Mauritius: A Country Profile.*

Idelson, B. (2007) 'La presse réunionnaise et mauricienne au moment des décolonisations', *La Réunion dans l'océan Indien. De la décolonisation au XXIᵉ siècle, Revue Historique de l'Océan Indien* AHIOI 3: 131-143.

L'Alliance Lepep (2014) *Manifeste Electoral.* Available online at: http://pages.intnet.mu/meetoo/elections2014/programmes/programme-16.pdf [Accessed 5 October 2017].

Leeper, T. (2014) 'The Informational Basis for Mass Polarization', *Public Opinion Quarterly* 78(1): 27-46.

L'Express (2007) *'L'alliance sociale à la croisée des chemins'.* Available online at: https://www.lexpress.mu/article/lalliance-sociale-%C3%A0-la-crois%C3%A9e-des-chemins [Accessed 5 October 2017].

Mauritius: 6th to 8th Combined Periodic Report, 2009-2015, submitted: 5 May 2016 at 59th Ordinary Session of the African Commission on Human and Peoples' Rights, 21 October - 4 November 2016.

Mauritius National Assembly. (March 2016) *The Constitution of the Republic of Mauritius.* Available online at: http://mauritiusassembly.govmu.org/English/constitution/Pages/constitution2016.pdf [Accessed 1 October 2017]

Media Trust Act. Available online at: http://attorneygeneral.govmu.org/English/Documents/A-Z%20Acts/M/Page%207/MEDIATRUST1.pdf [accessed 25 September 2017].

Ministry of Civil Service and Administrative Reforms (2011) *Human Resource Management Manual.* Available online at: http://civilservice.govmu.org/English/Documents/HRM%20Drectory/HRMM_08042011.pdf [accessed 5 October 2017].

Official Secrets Act. Available online at: http://attorneygeneral.govmu.org/English/Documents/A-Z%20Acts/O/OFFICIAL%20SECRETS%20ACT.pdf [Accessed 20 October 2017].

Piat, D. (2002) Association France Maurice [Website].*'Résumé de l'histoire de l'île Maurice'.* Available online at: http://www.association-france-maurice.net/spip.php?article8 [accessed 5 October 2017].

Report of the Royal Commissioners appointed to enquire into the treatment of immigrants in Mauritius - Presented to both Houses of Parliament by command of Her Majesty, 6th February, 1875. London: William Clowes and Sons.

Robertson, G. (2013) *Media Law and Ethics in Mauritius. Preliminary Report.* Available online at: http://gis.govmu.org/English/Documents/Media%20Law%20-%20Preliminary%20Report.pdf [Accessed 1 October 2017].

Rosen, J. (2009) PressThink [Blog]. *'He Said, She Said Journalism: Lame Formula in the Land of the Active User'*. Available online at:

http://archive.pressthink.org/2009/04/12/hesaid_shesaid.html [accessed 30 October 2017].

Selvon, S. (2012) *A New Comprehensive History of Mauritius Vol 1.* Mauritius: MD Selvon.

Toussaint, A. (1943) *Dictionnaire de biographie mauricienne – Dictionary of Mauritian Biography*, no. 8, March 1943: 250-251.

The Independent Broadcasting Authority Act 2000. Available online at:

http://www.iba.mu/documents/IBA%20Act_2016.pdf [accessed 10 October 2017].

Wahl-Jorgensen, K., Williams, A. *et al.* (2016) 'The Future of Journalism. Risks, threats and opportunities', *Digital Journalism* 4(7): 809-815.

Yeung Kam Lo, L. (1998) *'The Economic Development of Mauritius Since Independence'*, Working Paper, School of Economics, University of New South Wales, Australia.

i The Constitution of Mauritius refers to four communities for representation in the National Assembly as follows: (i) the Hindu community which constitutes the majority of the population with 51.8 per cent, (ii) the Muslim community with 16.6 per cent, (iii) the Sino-Mauritian community with 2.9 per cent and (iv) the General Population, a residual category with 28.7 per cent. These figures are drawn from the 1972 census and are used to allocate best loser seats for general elections in order to guarantee representation of the four groups in the National Assembly.

ii [Posters, Advertisements and Other Announcements of the Isles of France and Bourbon] The translation is mine.

iii The island was a French colony for almost a century between 1715 and 1810. It became a British colony after the Battle of Grand Port in August 1810. Independence was granted in March 1968.

iv The descendants of the French colonisers seem to have retained the appellation *'colons'* [French word for 'colonisers'] in spite of the fact that the British were the new colonisers, aptly signalling the continuing domination of the community.

v http://www.association-france-maurice.net/spip.php?article8

vi Dictionnaire de biographie mauricienne – Dictionary of Mauritian Biography, no. 8, March 1943, p. 250-251.

vii The French term 'métis' is here retained to distinguish from the gens de couleur insofar as the person's father is a White man, carries the paternal patronym, and visible phenotype.

viii http://histoiresmauriciennes.com/remy-ollier/

ix Report of the Royal Commissioners appointed to enquire into the treatment of immigrants in Mauritius: presented to both Houses of Parliament by command of Her Majesty, 6th February, 1875., p. 420-463.

x http://www.association-france-maurice.net/spip.php?article8

xi The translation is mine.

xiihttp://attorneygeneral.govmu.org/English/Documents/A-Z%20Acts/M/Page%207/MEDIATRUST1.pdf

xiii The Independent Broadcasting Authority (IBA) was established in 2000 to regulate radio and television broadcasting. The Information and Communication Technologies Authority (ICTA) was created in 2001 to regulate the provision of telecommunications and ICT services. Multi-Carrier Mauritius Ltd (MCML) was set up in 2000 under the IBA Act as the sole Terrestrial Transmission Company in Mauritius which is responsible for the allocation of frequencies.

xiv See the IBA Act (available at: http://www.iba.mu/documents/IBA%20Act_2016.pdf).

xv See 'Bérenger cible les radios privées´ in 5-Plus Dimanche, http://www.5plus.mu/node/19323.

xvi According to New York University Professor Jay Rosen, this refers to reporting which merely seeks to exploit a public dispute, especially in cases of polarised extremes which are exposed symmetrically without fact-checking any of the claims despite the possibility of doing so. (*He Said, She Said Journalism: Lame Formula in the Land of the Active User*, PressThink, 2009).

[xvii] http://mauritiusassembly.govmu.org/English/constitution/Pages/constitution2016.pdf

[xviii] http://attorneygeneral.govmu.org/English/Documents/A-Z%20Acts/O/OFFICIAL%20SECRETS%20ACT.pdf

[xix] http://civilservice.govmu.org/English/Documents/HRM%20Directory/HRMM_08042011.pdf

[xx] https://www.lexpress.mu/article/lalliance-sociale-%C3%A0-la-crois%C3%A9e-des-chemins

[xxi] http://mauritiusassembly.govmu.org/English/Pages/Address%20by%20the%20President/Government-Programme-2005.aspx

[xxii] https://web.archive.org/web/20100601212558/http://www.bleublancrouge.mu/files/Programme.pdf

[xxiii] http://gis.govmu.org/English/Documents/Media%20Law%20-%20Preliminary%20Report.pdf

[xxiv] http://pages.intnet.mu/meetoo/elections2014/programmes/programme-16.pdf

[xxv] The translation is mine.

[xxvi] http://mauritiusassembly.govmu.org/English/Documents/Add%20president/govprog2015.pdf

[xxvii] Mauritius: 6th to 8th Combined Periodic Report, 2009-2015

[xxviii] The Association des Journalistes Mauriciens (AJM), an association for Mauritian journalists, was created in 2006. The Newspapers Editors and Publishers Association (NEPA) was set up by editors-in-chief and newspaper publishers in 2007. The Union Syndicale des Employés de Presse (USEP), a trade union for media workers, was created in 2012.

Mauritius' Economic Success Uncovered

VERENA TANDRAYEN-RAGOOBUR AND HARSHANA KASSEEAH

Introduction

Mauritius has achieved remarkable economic growth since independence, effectively transitioning from an agriculture-based economy to a middle-income country. Over the 50 years since independence, the Government adopted a gradual outward-looking, export oriented strategy leading to the diversification of the economy carving out niches in the textile industry, tourism sector and developing a vibrant financial services sector. Emerging sectors such as Information and Communication Technology, seafood and real estate have also contributed to sustaining economic growth. Alongside the diversification strategy, aggressive policy reforms in the past decade have been instrumental in building resilience against external economic shocks namely the dismantling of the Multi-Fibre Agreement, the EU sugar reforms and the 2008 financial crisis.

The country has consistently maintained its position as a top performer in several global indices such as the Mo Ibrahim Index of African Governance where Mauritius remains the top ranking country in overall governance in Africa for the tenth consecutive year (with a score of 79.9 in 2016) (Mo Ibrahim Foundation, 2016). From the Africa Human Development Report (2015), Mauritius with a Human Development Index (HDI) of 0.77 has already achieved the high medium development status and performs well above the African average value of 0.52 and the Southern Africa sub-region average HDI value of 0.57 (UNDP, 2016). However, being a small island economy, Mauritius is still highly vulnerable to external shocks such as changes in climatic conditions, recent financial crisis, rising food and oil prices, among many others.

Although Mauritius has achieved outstanding economic performance over the 50 years since independence, the country is presently stagnating in a middle-income trap. After 20 years of remarkable performance, the economy has fallen off a high growth plateau of about 6 per cent towards the 2-3 percent range. Unemployment, income inequality and poverty have been on the rise in the past years. The headcount poverty level was 6.9 per cent in 2012 while the Gini coefficient, a measure of inequality, has increased from 0.388 to 0.414. In addition, the small island economy is plagued by an increasing trade deficit, low investment, declining savings, an ageing population, low fertility rate and high youth unemployment.

The objective of this chapter is to analyse the Mauritian pathway towards economic development and also identify the numerous challenges that confine the country to slow growth and into the middle-income trap. We first analyse the sources of growth of the economy since independence. Then the chapter attempts to explain the present socio-economic situation of the Mauritian economy using macroeconomic indicators. Lastly, policy options are discussed to face the challenges and the factors that can hinder/help the economy to move to its expected high-income category by 2030. Our methodology rests on the use of macro-economic data for Mauritius for the past five decades to analyse the socioeconomic situation of the country.

The chapter is structured as follows: The next section reviews the existing growth literature which has explained the economic miracle of Mauritius. We then move on to analysing the Mauritian development path via macroeconomic and social indicators, followed by a comparative analysis of Mauritius with other upper middle-income countries. Subsequently, we discuss challenges and policy options, before the brief conclusion.

Economic growth and development

The growth literature advances several factors explaining growth. The Harrod-Domar growth model proposes that accumulation of labour and capital is the single factor that promotes growth. The Solow (1956) growth model for instance advances that apart from accumulation of capital and labour, technology is also an important factor influencing growth. The endogenous Solow growth model proposes that technology, captured by total factor productivity matters the most for economic growth.

In trying to understand how economic development occurs and what strategies can be adopted to foster that process, Rostow (1959) suggested that countries can be placed in one of five stages in terms of their level of growth: (i) stage 1 is dominated by traditional societies, characterised by subsistence economy, with output not traded or even recorded, the existence of barter, high levels of agriculture, and labour-intensive agriculture; (ii) stage 2 comprises societies with preconditions to growth, where there is an increase in capital use in agriculture, the development of mining industries, and some growth in savings and investment; (iii) stage 3 englobes societies in take-off mode, with higher levels of investment and industrialisation, accumulation of savings, and a decline in the share of the agricultural labour force; (iv) stage 4 consists of societies that drive to maturity and where wealth generation enables further investment in value adding industry and development - growth becomes self-sustaining, industry is diversified, and more sophisticated technology is used; and (v) stage 5 is the mass-consumption societies that achieve high output levels and where the services industry dominates the economy. It has been pointed out in the literature that not all countries necessarily go through all these five stages. Some countries can also skip some stages (Lin, 2011). Furthermore, Rostow's evolutionist model has been criticised for not taking change and diversity into account.

Mauritius at the time of independence was a monocrop economy, prone to terms of trade shocks, witnessing rapid rise in population growth rate and susceptible to ethnic tensions (Subramanian and Roy, 2001; Zafar, 2011). The main ingredients in the Mauritian success story have been summarised by various researchers to comprise advantageous initial conditions, openness and institutions (Subramanian and Roy, 2003). The country's political and economic situation has been stable since its independence in 1968 and this has also been a major contributing factor to the Mauritian 'miracle'. The country has delivered high growth rates along with macroeconomic stability and low inflation environment. The country's economic transformation hence mirrors closely the different stages as proposed by Rostow (1959).

As proposed by Ramdoo (2014) 'economic' transformation of the Mauritian economy was conducted in such a manner that the economic landscape, society and institutions were modernised simultaneously, though at various speeds taking into consideration the political, human, institutional and economic realities and constraints of the time. Ramdoo (2014) advances that the Mauritian development model can be summarised by five distinct phases: 1970s where the economy was dominated by sugar cane and the consequent move to manufacturing; the 1980's dominated by the textile boom; the 1990's were led by tourism and financial services; the 2000s saw the advent of ICT/BPO-real estate and finally in the 2010's the emergence of the ocean economy and Africa strategy.

Being a small island economy, Mauritius has relied heavily on trade. While there is some debate as to how 'trade' actually contributed to growth, it is generally agreed that openness to exports (Rodrik, 1999), foreign direct investment (Romer, 1993) and trade policies (Sachs and Warner, 1997) have been at the heart of trade being a major contributor to growth. At the outset, the country tried to use an import-substitution strategy to curb imports. However, this strategy failed as the country was still a low-income economy and the market was limited. Policy makers recognised that export strategy would be better suited for the small economy. At the same time, the country was benefiting from trade policies such as the Lomé convention and the Multi-

Fibre Arrangement (MFA). These two trade policies helped the country develop its sugar sector further and consolidate its position as one of the leading exporters of textile and clothing into the EU region.

Rodrik (1997) and Subramanian (2009) find that a key ingredient of the Mauritian success story was the preferential market treatment of its exports in EU and the US markets. Rodrik (1997) qualified Mauritius as having a "heterodox opening", that is, the policy of encouraging exports through various incentives while maintaining high barriers to imports. A main component of this heterodox opening was the establishment of the Export Processing Zone (EPZ) in 1970. Firms operating with an EPZ certificate benefited from tax advantages, elimination of tariffs on imported inputs used by manufacturers, and laxer labour standards for EPZ workers and a lower minimum wage (Frankel, 2010).

The base of diversification of the Mauritian economy lies in the success the country had from exports of sugar that generated the wealth, which was then used by the private sector to diversify their activities into textile, tourism and financial services among others. However, on 30 September 2009, the Sugar Protocol of the Lomé Convention (which provided ACP countries with guaranteed access to the EU markets for fixed quantities and preferential prices) expired. The Mauritius sugar industry has not only reinvented itself with modern plants but has also witnessed industry consolidation over the last two decades, with about 20 small and medium groups having come together under four large banners – Omnicane, Terra, Medine and Alteo. Also, the industry has moved up the value chain, exporting refined sugar for higher revenues, instead of the raw sugar, which fetches lower returns (Financial Times, 2013).

With the coming of the World Trade Organisation (WTO) and the consequent erosion of trade preferences, and the phasing out of the MFA, EPZ firms in Mauritius have had to adjust to competing in a world market without any artificial support. The Multi-Fibre Agreement had previously limited China's exports of textile and clothing. As proposed by Ancharaz and Kasseeah (2014), in the run-up to 2005, Mauritius saw a large number of closures in its textile and clothing sector, with a sharp increase in unemployment, especially among women. This prompted the Government to put forth a package of measures aimed at restructuring the economy and helping the ailing clothing sector, which many have qualified as a "sunset industry" (Loong-Yu, 2005).

Acemoglu et al. (2001) and Subramanian et al. (2004), propose the idea that 'institutions' are a key determinant of development. Indeed apart from geography and trade, it has been shown in the literature that properly working institutions are a major factor contributing to growth. North (1991) defines institutions as humanly devised constraints that structure human interaction. They are made up of formal constraints comprising explicit rules such as constitutions, laws and property rights; and informal constraints comprising social norms and conventions.

Mauritius owes it success to properly working institutions that have supported the growing sectors of the economy (Subramanian and Roy, 2003). Rodrik *et al.* (2004) estimate the contributions of institutions, geography and trade in determining income levels around the world, using recently developed instruments for institutions and trade. The results obtained indicate that institutions 'trump' everything else. Hence, once institutions are accounted for, measures of geography will have at best weak effects on incomes, although they have strong indirect effects by influencing the quality of institutions. In the same vein, Subramanian and Roy (2003) examine different explanations for the Mauritian growth experience since the mid-1970's and find that institutions are the single most important explanation for the economic success story, particularly the presence of 'robust' institutions.

Further explanations proposed for the success of the economy include the presence of efficient administration, political stability, favourable regulatory environment and a well-developed financial system (Frankel, 2010). The favourable environment led to the emergence of a number of sectors including sugar, tourism, manufacturing (particularly textile and clothing) and financial services. Recently, Svirydzenka and Petri (2014) use a growth accounting framework to analyse the sources of past growth and project potential ranges of growth through 2033. The authors find that growth has average 4.5 per cent over the past 20 years and their baseline projections suggest that future growth rates would be around 3.25 per cent, which could be increased using proactive policies.

Mauritius has been quite resilient to economic shocks. This is often attributed to the highly diversified economy and appropriate fiscal and monetary policies adopted at the right time. However, most studies tend to gloss over the role of agency or 'debrouillardise' that is the resourcefulness of the Mauritian population. In the last decade, emphasis has been placed on the promotion of a business culture in Mauritius (Kasseeah and Tandrayen-Ragoobur, 2017). To further attract investment in the country, particularly foreign direct investment, a number of reforms have been undertaken to make it easier to do business in Mauritius.

Other explanations have also been put forward to explain the economic success of Mauritius. As proposed by Subramanian and Roy (2001), cross-country growth regressions cannot capture country-specific idiosyncratic effects. For instance,

Mauritius has certain peculiarities that somehow made the country what it is today. Among these idiosyncrasies, the diversity of the population turned out to be a blessing for the country as it was able to make excellent use of the diasporas to further its economic agenda. In addition, the sugar sector, termed the 'cash cow' was protected since the beginning while in other African countries the sector was stifled with high tax burdens. The generous welfare system helped to provide effective social protection. Furthermore, the maintenance of stability, law and order and rule of law and mediation of conflict also contributed to the economic success.

The Mauritian development path - An analysis

The economic success of Mauritius has been explained by multiple factors and there are often nuances and controversies on the real factors that underpin this success (Romer, 1992; Sachs and Warner, 1995, 1997; Subramanian, 2001, 2009; Subramanian and Roy, 2007; Frankel, 2010; Stiglitz, 2011; Zafar, 2011; Svirydzenka and Petri, 2014). In fact, Mauritius went through five phases of development (Makoond, 2011). In the early 1970s, Mauritius was mainly a monocrop economy with sugar and basic manufacturing but in the 1980s, Mauritius diversified to other sectors namely textile and tourism along with local manufacturing. Then, the 1990s saw greater diversification via the services sector with the financial services and the freeport. The fourth stage of development is based on the small island economy being perceived as a business platform for Information and Communication Technology (ICT)/Business Process Outsourcing (BPO), real estate, seafood, alongside the existing sectors namely sugar, textile and tourism. The fifth phase saw further diversification, with Mauritius being an integrated business platform for financial services, ICT/BPO, real estate, medical services, knowledge industry, seafood hub, hospitality, cane industry, renewable energy, as well as textile and fashion (Makoond, 2011).

One major lesson from Mauritius for other countries is the country's ability to identify the major turning points of the various stages of structural transformation: agriculture to manufacturing and to services. The discussion in this chapter is mainly concerned with the 'second' phase of industrialisation onwards, hence looking at the period starting early 1980s. This industrialisation process has been intensively discussed since the early 1990s, for instance Romer (1992); Sachs and Warner (1995 and 1997); Subramanian and Roy (2007); Frankel, (2010); Zafar (2011); Svirydzenka and Petri (2014) and all have postulated various factors or combination of factors that have contributed to the economic success of Mauritius. However, the small island economy is currently facing a number of challenges and there is a need to address the important long-standing economic weaknesses in the medium term in order to progress towards becoming a high-income economy within the next decade.

The Structural Economic Transformation of Mauritius

The different stages of development can be shown in Figure 1 below through the structural economic transformation of the small economy. Over the years, the share of the primary sector to GDP has declined substantially, while the share of the services sector has followed an upward trend.

Figure 1: Structural Economic Transformation, 1976-2015

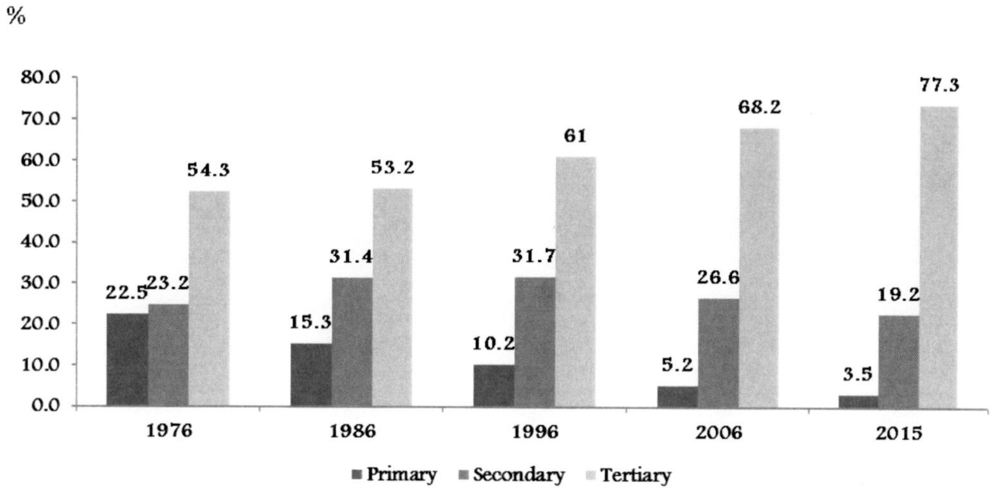

%

Source: Authors' Computation - Statistics Mauritius, National Accounts - Various Issues

Mauritius has undergone a structural change over time, reflecting a successful economic diversification strategy. The primary sector has been on decline since independence. Its contribution to GDP has fallen from 22.5 per cent in 1976 to 3.5 per cent in 2015 (see table 5). This is mainly explained by the contraction of the sugar industry which has faced difficult challenges with the end of the EU Sugar Protocol. To ensure its survival, there have been important reforms under the Multi Annual Adaptation Strategy to reduce costs, enhance competitiveness and diversify into high value added activities such as the production of special sugars, electricity generation from bagasse and production of ethanol and spirits. The share of secondary sector output rose from 24.8 per cent in 1976 to 31.4 per cent in 1986 but it has since fallen back to around 19.2 per cent in 2015. The performance of the secondary sector is closely linked to the performance of the EPZ sector whose growth averaged 17.5 per cent annually between 1977 and 1986 and down to 6 per cent in 2011 and 0.2 per cent in 2015. The downfall is attributed mainly to the end of the Multi-Fibre Agreement with the closures of factories, increased labour costs and rising competitive pressures from other countries.

Table 5: Main Sectors, 1976 - 2016 (Percentage Distribution of Gross Value Added by industry group at current basic prices)

Sector of economic activity	1976	1980	1985	1990	1995	2000	2005	2010	2015	2016
Agriculture, forestry and fishing	22.5	12.4	15.3	12.9	10.4	6.5	5.7	3.7	3.5	3.6
of which sugar cane	17.8	8.1	11.1	8.0	5.7	3.3	3.0	1.2	0.9	0.8
Manufacturing	15.2	15.2	20.6	24.4	23.0	22.5	19.2	18.0	14.7	13.9
Sugar	5.5	2.4	3.2	3.4	1.6	0.8	0.8	0.3	0.2	0.2
Food	-	-	-	-	-	3.9	4.9	6.3	5.1	4.9
Textiles and clothing	2.6	4.3	9.5	12.0	11.5	11.5	6.8	5.1	4.6	4.1
Construction	8.0	7.6	5.6	6.7	6.4	5.3	5.4	6.9	4.4	4.2
Wholesale and retail	11.3	14.2	13.2	13.0	12.8	11.5	11.9	11.8	12.0	11.9
Hotels and restaurants	1.8	2.3	2.4	3.9	5.1	6.0	7.1	7.0	7.4	7.8
Transport, Storage and Communications	8.5	11.3	10.9	10.4	11.4	12.7	11.9	9.5	6.2	6.3
Financial intermediation	5.7	5.0	4.7	4.9	6.5	8.8	9.2	10.0	12.0	12.1
Real estate, renting and business activities	10.2	12.7	11.1	8.9	8.5	8.4	9.8	8.4	5.0	4.8

Source: Author's Computation – Statistics Mauritius (2016)

The share of the tertiary sector in Gross Domestic Product (GDP) has in turn increased from 52.3 per cent in 1976 to around 77 per cent in 2015. The rise is linked to the expansion of sectors like Tourism, Financial and Business Services and Information and Communication Technologies (ICT). Tourism represented 7.8 per cent of GDP in 2016 compared to a mere 1.8 per cent in 1976. The share of Financial and Insurance Activities in GDP has increased to 12.1 per cent in 2016. In essence, the top pillars of the Mauritian economy over the last five years are Manufacturing, Financial and Insurance activities, Wholesale and Retail Trade, Tourism and Accommodation and Food Services activities.

The Growth Performance

The immediate years following independence was a period of low economic growth averaging an annual growth rate of 1.8 per cent. The sugar boom coupled with the promotion of the EPZ sector led to a spell of very high growth in the mid-1970s. With a 23 per cent decline in sugar prices in 1976 and the oil crisis in 1979, Mauritius experienced a major economic downfall by the end of the 1970s. The economic growth contracted by 10.1 per cent in 1980 (see Figure 2). Substantive reforms were undertaken between 1980 and 1986 under the Stabilisation and Structural Adjustment Programme. Mauritius benefitted from a period of high growth rate in the mid-1980s, reaching 9.7 per cent in 1986. From the late 1980s to the mid-1990s, the economy underwent further diversification and the development of the Services sector was earmarked as an avenue for higher growth. In 1990, GDP growth stood at 7.2 per cent. The three major sectors of the economy namely, Sugar, EPZ and Tourism as well as the new growth areas in Financial and Business Services provided the main engines for a robust growth performance during the 1990s.

Figure 2: Economic Growth (GDP Growth Rate), 1976-2016

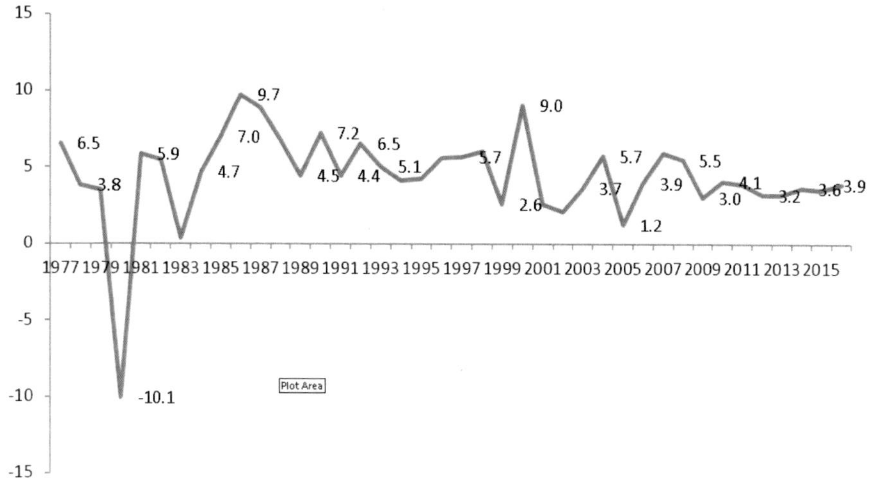

Source: Statistics Mauritius, 2016

However, by the turn of the century, Mauritius was faced with eroding trade preferences, increased global competition and a less favourable international economy compounded by rising oil prices. As a result, the growth rate slowed considerably. In 2005, GDP growth rate was 5.7 per cent. The policy response came in the form of broad-based economic reforms to enhance global competitiveness and increase growth. The growth performance effectively improved between 2006 and 2008, reaching 5.9 per cent in 2007. In the aftermath of the global financial and economic crisis and the Euro zone sovereign debt crisis, the growth rate has averaged around 3 per cent from 2009 to 2015. The challenge to the Mauritian economy remains to increase its GDP growth rate which turned around 3.9 per cent by the end of 2016. Growth has been undermined by uncertain economic environment and low domestic investment, high unemployment rate and low productivity.

Productivity and Labour Market Situation

With regard to labour productivity, the growth rate has been low over the years, with an average rate of 4 per cent per annum since the 1980s. In 2016, global labour productivity stood at 2.6 per cent (UNECA, 2017) but still, compared to Mauritius some African countries registered productivity growth between 4 and 4.7 per cent in 2016, namely Côte d'Ivoire, Democratic Republic of Congo (DRC), Ethiopia, Ghana, Nigeria, Rwanda, Liberia, Sierra Leone and Zambia. In turn China's figure stood at 6.6 per cent while India had a 4.7 per cent growth in labour productivity. Overall, the gains in labour productivity have not been sufficient to offset the growth in average compensation of employees. Similarly, capital productivity has been declining whilst the Multi Factor Productivity (MFP)[i] index has been rising over the years. In addition to labour and capital inputs, it takes into account qualitative factors such as better management and improved quality of inputs through training and technology. A growth of 0.7 per cent has been observed in MFP from 2003 to 2013, indicating very low growth in MFP and thereby depicting limited availability of new knowledge or less effort to take advantage of existing knowledge. MFP growth is central to sustained growth of labour productivity and is a central focus in supply-side policies.

Figure 3: Productivity Indices, 1982-2015 (base year 2007: index = 100)

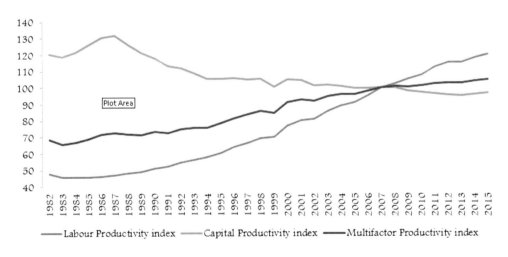

Source: Statistics Mauritius, 2016

On the employment side, unemployment rose rapidly towards the end of the 1960s and the early 1970s from 7,472 in 1968 to 34,408 in 1972[ii]. However, the subsequent economic boom led to the number of registered unemployed being halved by the late 1970s. In the early 1980s unemployment rose again, reaching a peak of more than 79,000 individuals registered as unemployed. From Figure 4, the unemployment rate was estimated at nearly 20 per cent in 1983. Thereafter, followed a remarkable progress towards full employment, which was duly achieved by the start of the 1990s. Unemployment rate averaged 3.5 per cent yearly during 1989 and 1994. The past two decades, though, have seen the return of the problem of unemployment. The unemployment rate stood at 9.6 per cent in 2005 and has increased at a rate between 7 and 8 per cent annually from 2006 to 2016.

Figure 4: Female and male unemployment from 1983 to 2016

Number of Unemployed

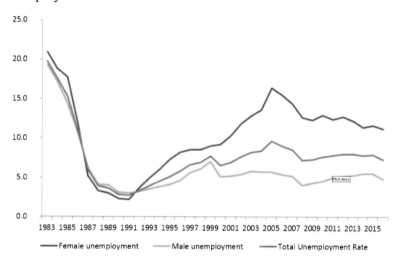

Source: Data Computed from Statistics Mauritius (2016)

Much of the rise in unemployment can be traced back to the sizeable increase in the number of women out of work. In effect, the labour market situation as at date is characterised by an overall unemployment rate of 7.3 per cent (4.8 per cent for male and 11.2 per cent for female). The age composition of the unemployed has also changed over time. In particular, youth unemployment is a major concern in Mauritius (Tandrayen-Ragoobur and Kasseeah, 2015), being around 19.3 per cent in 2008, it has reached 23.9 per cent in 2016. Youth unemployment rate for women has been consistently higher than that of men. During the period 2006 to 2009, the gap between male and female youth unemployment rate decreased as a result of a sharper decline in female unemployment rate. The gap then widened due to a higher increase in female unemployment rate. The young unemployed in 2016 numbered 18,900 of whom 8,200 were men and 10,700 women.

Domestic and Foreign Investment

The trend in domestic and foreign investment is closely linked to local and external economic conditions. During the period 1970 to 1976, the investment rate (that is the ratio of Gross Fixed Capital Formation to GDP) more than doubled, from 12.2 per cent in 1970 to 27.4 per cent in 1976. Resources from the sugar boom served to finance the development of the EPZ and Tourism sectors. However, a downtrend in investment followed thereafter. On the back of the economic crisis of the late 1970s and beginning of the 1980s, the investment rate reached 17.9 per cent in 1982. Investment picked up after the adoption of the Stabilisation and Structural Adjustment Programme and maintained a robust growth between 1983 and 1990 when it peaked at 30.6 per cent. The investment rate remained quite high during the 1990s averaging almost 27 per cent. It has since then considerably declined, reflecting a worsening of economic conditions caused by the end of trade preferences, lasting economic uncertainty and slowdown in the aftermath of the 2009 global crisis. It has averaged 22.5 per cent over the period 2000-2015 and has fallen to 17.3 per cent in 2016. Further, the private sector has always accounted for the bulk of investment in Mauritius. Private investment represented 72.7 per cent of overall investment in 2015 (see Figure 5).

Figure 5: Private and public investment rate of the Mauritian Economy, 1976-2016

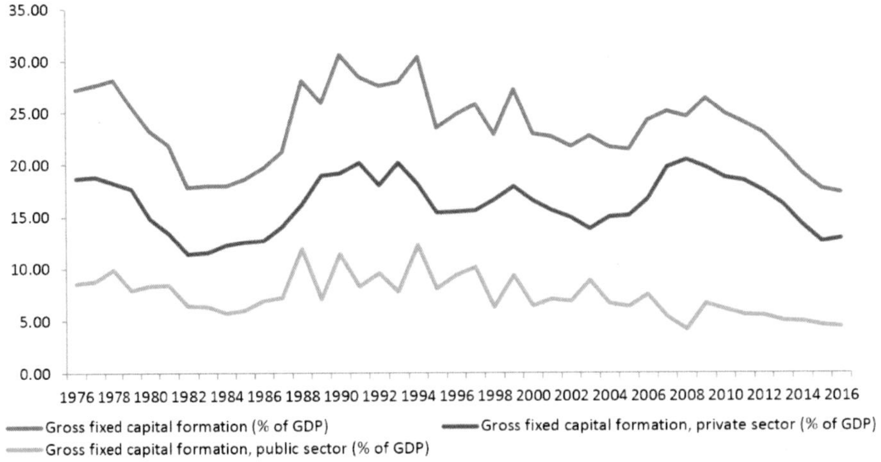

Source: Statistics Mauritius, 2016

96

With respect to Foreign Direct Investment (FDI), it is only from the mid-1980s that FDI started entering Mauritius mostly in the EPZ and Tourism sectors. The latest FDI figures show that inflows into Mauritius recorded for 2015 were to the tune of Rs 9.627 billion.[iii] On a fiscal year basis, FDI inflows have been estimated at Rs 15,413 million during 2016/17, higher than the Rs 12,878 million recorded during 2015/16. More than two-third of the inflows were directed to the 'Real estate activities' sector. The 'Financial and insurance activities' and 'Construction' sectors received Rs 3,255 million and Rs 931 million, respectively, during the same period. Nearly 30 per cent of the direct investment inflows originated from France, while those from South Africa and China amounted to Rs 2,044 million and Rs 1,118 million, respectively. FDI inflows from 2006 to 2015 are shown in Figure 6.

Figure 6: Foreign Direct Investment in Mauritius by sector, 2006-2015

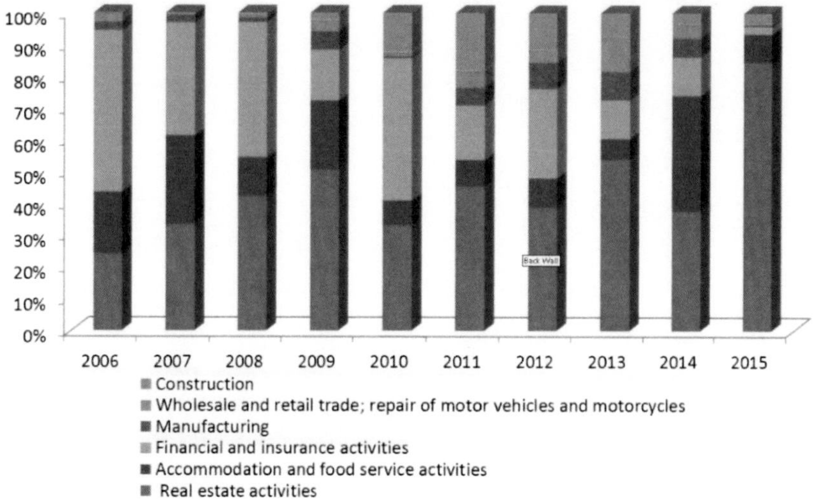

Source: Board of Investment and Bank of Mauritius, 2016

Different policies have been implemented in these sectors to attract FDI. In particular, FDI has surged in real estates under the Integrated Resort Scheme (IRS) and Real Estate Scheme (RES) projects. The IRS plan was developed in 2002 to allow foreigners to buy property in Mauritius. It targets the high end of the international property market whereby the recipient automatically receives a residence permit. In 2008, the government introduced the RES plan, which is a mini-version of the IRS. Non-citizens can also invest in a list of qualifying business activities namely construction, fishing and marine resources, infrastructure, marina development, power industry, leisure, tourism and warehousing, among many others. However, the different resort schemes have brought only one off investment in the country. Although the schemes are often portrayed as crucial for poverty alleviation and making a contribution to the local community development via the creation of jobs and opportunities for small local businesses, the IRS scheme is, however, not always a blessing (Bundhoo, 2013).

From the grassroots standpoint the scheme, instead of alleviating poverty, appears to be deepening the unequal distribution of resources. The schemes are neither creating jobs for the locals nor encouraging small local businesses and even if jobs are created, they are of poor quality and essentially unskilled jobs such as waiters, housemaids, cooks, all of which are paid very low wages. Fishermen on the coastal regions have also reported losing their catch, local inhabitants being deprived of access to the beach, growing price of land in the locality and environmental degradation are the gloomy sides of the coin as the number of IRS multiplies taking over the most attractive view of the island (Bundhoo, 2013). It is also argued that the concept of the IRS is enlarging the gap between the rich and poor. The development process thus resembles more of a rapidly growing 'inequalisation' process rather than reducing poverty and the rising threat that increasing plots of land are being sold to foreigners (Bundhoo, 2013).

Trade: Composition and Direction

With the exception of 1974 and 1986, the Mauritian trade balance has always shown a deficit since independence. After a brief improvement between 1982 and 1986, the balance of trade deficit has continually worsened over time. In fact, exports have declined over the past 15 years mainly because of large negative terms of trade shocks, the phasing out of the Multi-Fibre Agreement in 2004/2005; reductions in sugar price guaranteed from the European Union starting in 2006; high world commodity prices, especially for food and oil products; the financial crisis 2007-2008 and increase competitiveness from emerging countries. The negative trade balance from 1976 to 2016 is shown in Figure 7.

The composition of domestic exports is today more diversified where the heavy reliance on sugar (93 per cent of total domestic exports) has decreased considerably. The proportion of sugar exports represented 13 per cent of domestic exports in 2015. Articles of apparel and clothing accessories have emerged as the country's most important export, representing more than 42 per cent of total domestic exports. The destination of domestic exports is also more diversified. Europe (in particular UK and France) represents the largest export market with 42 per cent of total domestic exports. Food, beverages and mineral fuels make up the bulk of the country's imports. In 2015, they represented around 34 per cent of total imports. The main sources of imports (accounting for around 36 per cent of total imports in 2015) are China and India.

Figure 7: Exports, Imports and Trade Balance, 1976-2016

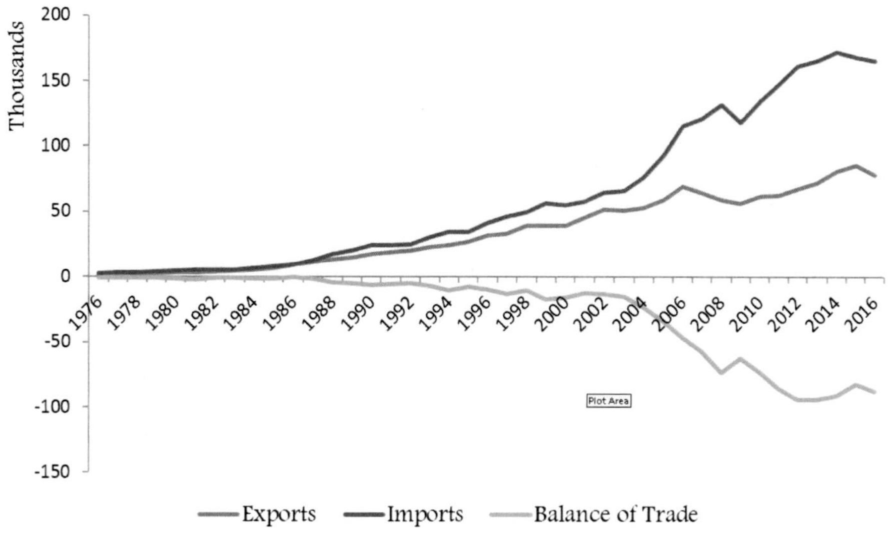

Source: Statistics Mauritius, 2016

Social Indicators: Income Inequality and Poverty

From the social indicators, it is observed that income inequality has increased between 2006/07 and 2012. The Gini coefficient has risen from 0.388 to 0.414 in 2012 (see Table 6). The share of total income going to the 20 per cent of households at the lower end of the income range decreased from 6.1 per cent in 2006/07 to 5.4 per cent in 2012. On the other hand, the share of the upper 20 per cent of households increased from 45.6 per cent to 47.4 per cent (Statistics Mauritius, 2012).

Table 6: Income inequality and median income from 2001 to 2012

	2001/02	2006/07	2012
Median monthly income (Rs)	11150	14640	21790
% of households earning less than 50% of ½ median monthly income	13.1	14.3	17.1
Gini Coefficient	0.371	0.388	0.413

Sources: Statistics Mauritius, Household Budget Surveys 2001/02, 2006/07, 2012

Likewise, relative poverty as measured by the 'proportion of households below the half median monthly household income per adult equivalent' increased from 7.7 per cent in 2001/02 to 7.9 per cent in 2006/07 and 9.4 per cent in 2012. Similarly, the proportion of poor persons in relative poverty increased from 7.8 percent to 8.5 per cent and 9.8

per cent during the same period (Statistics Mauritius, 2015). Hence, around 122,700 people live on less than Rs 5,652 per month (the relative poverty line) in 2012 (see Table 7). In terms of relative poverty, a Relative Poverty Line (RPL) is set at half of the median monthly household income per adult equivalent.

Further, the average income of households in relative poverty was Rs 9,800 per month, ten times less than that of the richest 10 per cent of households (Rs 97,400). The average monthly consumption expenditure of households in relative poverty was Rs 8,300, seven times less than that of the richest 10 per cent of households (Rs 53,600). Further, one out of every five households (20 per cent) in relative poverty was in debt. Among indebted households, poor ones disbursed around one-third of their income (Rs 3,200) on debt repayment per month. In 2012, children were more prone to poverty than older people. There was an estimated 42,100 children in relative poverty out of a total of 285,900 children. Households with 3 or more children, households headed by divorced/separated persons or female headed households as well as households headed by persons with low educational attainments were more likely to be in relative poverty. More specifically, poverty is higher amongst women and in households headed by females and by those with education below the secondary level.

Table 7: Indicators of relative poverty, 1996/97- 2012

	1996/97	2001/02	2006/07	2012
Relative poverty line (Rs) per adult equivalent per month	**2,004**	**2,804**	**3,821**	**5,652**
Estimated number of households in relative poverty	23,800	23,700	26,100	33,600
Proportion of households in relative poverty (%)	8.7	7.7	7.9	9.4
Estimated number of persons in relative poverty	92,700	93,800	105,200	122,700
Proportion of persons in relative poverty (%)	8.2	7.8	8.5	9.8
Income gap ratio (%)	21.0	22.6	21.9	24.0
Poverty gap ratio (%)	1.7	1.8	1.9	2.3
Annual amount required to move people out of relative poverty (Rs Mn)	300	450	700	1,300

Source: Statistics Mauritius, Poverty Analysis (2015)

Comparative Analysis with other Upper Middle-Income Countries

It is of utmost importance to compare Mauritius with other upper middle-income countries in terms of socio-economic indicators. The selected nations are South Africa, Gabon, Botswana, China, Malaysia and Thailand. From Table 8, it can be observed that

Mauritius does well in terms of exports as a share of GDP as compared to South Africa, Gabon and Botswana but lags behind South-East Asian economies such as Malaysia and Thailand. In terms of FDI as a share of GDP, Mauritius lags behind all the selected countries except South Africa. In fact, over the years the share of FDI has been declining and the country has registered only investment targeted to real estates which neither creates jobs nor transfers knowledge and innovations nor creates backward and forward linkages in the domestic economy. The other indicator is GDP growth where Mauritius fares better than South Africa, Botswana and Thailand but still lingers behind Malaysia, Gabon and China. Similarly in terms of income inequality, it is observed that the small island economy compares favourably to most countries in the sample. For the poverty headcount ratio, Malaysia and Thailand have a lower index relative to Mauritius but the later still does better that the rest of the other countries. However, as discussed above, youth unemployment remains a major concern and when compared to other upper-middle income economies, Mauritius faces high female and male youth unemployment rates compared to the East Asian nations but is still better relative to the African nations. Youth unemployment remains a major problem for the African continent.

Gauging the Challenges and Policy Focus

Understanding how countries go through their socio-economic development sequence is a continuous quest for policy makers. Most often, the sequence is from low-income to middle-income and, ideally, to high-income. In some cases, however, countries get stuck in the low- or middle-income group for a long time period and cannot move up. The transition of an economy from middle-income status to the high-income status is a major leap, and the necessary conditions and policies must prevail to push this evolution. Mauritius is presently trying to cross the middle-income bar and is finding it difficult to make it into the high-income group. Subsequently, the country finds itself in a 'middle-income trap'. Different reasons as shown by the above macroeconomic indicators in terms of low investment, low productivity growth, stagnating GDP growth rate, high trade deficit, high youth unemployment rate, lack of innovations and research and development, increased income inequality and poverty may explain the present situation. Hence, the reasons that prevent this jump are numerous and interconnected.

Firstly, being a small island economy, vulnerable to external economic situations, Mauritius has attempted to build its resilience via a number of policies. Different reform packages were implemented since 2010 aimed at stimulating the economy. The continuing slow growth in the EU propelled the Government to set stimulus packages which were to enhance competitiveness via diversification towards new sectors and markets; promoting efficiency and productivity gains at the firm level; reducing leverage by most firms; developing the capital market and financial instruments; encouraging long-term corporate planning; improving the diversity of skills in line with the vision of knowledge-based economy; and speeding up the implementation of infrastructure projects. Further, the creation of a new Economic Restructuring and Competitiveness Program (ERCP) comprising of 100 policy measures aimed at shifting export growth to new markets, restructuring and deleveraging enterprises, retraining retrenched workers, upgrading public infrastructure and improving the regulatory environment for competitiveness.

Table 8: A snapshot of main indicators across similar upper middle income economies in 2016

	Exports % of GDP	FDI % of GDP	GDP Growth (%)	Real GDP per capita (US$)	Gini Index (2010)	FYUR	MYUR	TYUR	Poverty gap at $3.10 a day (%)	Poverty headcount ratio at $3.10 a day (% of population)
Botswana	49.7	2.7	-0.3	7,080.1	60.5	39.7	28.5	33.9	13.96***	35.7
China	22.4	2.3	6.9	6,416.2	42.1	8.5	12.1	10.5	9.05**	27.2
Gabon	45.9	4.4	3.9	10,735.8	42.0	40.8	30.9	35.5	7.23*	24.4
Malaysia	71.0	3.7	5.0	10,876.7	46.3	7.5	6.1	6.7	0.49***	2.7
Mauritius	49.8	1.8	3.5	9,134.8	35.7	27.9	16.0	21.2	0.65#	2.96
S. Africa	30.9	0.5	1.3	7,575.2	63.4	57.1	48.8	52.6	13.09|	34.7
Thailand	69.3	2.0	2.8	5,774.7	39.3	4.7	3.3	3.9	0.19#	1.2

Note: (1) * 2005 Figures;** 2010 Figures; *** 2009 Figures; # 2012 Figures; | 2011 Figures
(2) FYUR- Female Youth Unemployment Rate; MYUR- Male Youth Unemployment Rate; TYUR - Total Youth Unemployment Rate
Source: World Bank Development Indicators (2016)

In recent years, the economic strategy has focused on the objective of turning Mauritius into a high-income country. A new vision namely Vision 2030 was devised to bring a second economic miracle and achieve the high-income status. The main objectives were to address unemployment; alleviate if not eradicate poverty; open up the country and new air access policies; and promote sustainable development and innovation. Core areas on which the development of Mauritius are centered are a revamped and dynamic manufacturing base, the development of the Ocean industry, revisit the services sector and position Mauritius as the regional platform for trade and investment in Africa. Economic transformation to an inclusive high-income economy may not happen as proposed by the government in its national plan. There are many grey areas that would not allow easily the economy to take off as rapidly as proposed in the Vision 2030.

The question of when Mauritius will be able to join high income country status will depend on its ability to improve the skill set of its labour force, the quality of infrastructure, and the speed of technology adoption (Svirydzenka and Petri, 2014). First, Mauritius will need to address some important long-standing economic weaknesses in the medium term namely skill shortages and mismatches, high youth unemployment and the low participation of women in the workforce. The island suffers from a shortage of skilled workers, weak productivity growth stemming from a lack of creativity and innovation in the workforce, and an over-reliance on unskilled and low-wage migrant workers. Likewise, reforms for pensions, public enterprises, social benefits, and the tax system are needed to make the public sector more efficient, while macro policies to increase public and private savings can create the room for further productive investments (Svirydzenka and Petri, 2014). The public finances may require more discipline. The plan to invest massively in the different sectors of the economy may exacerbate pressure on tax payers, government debt and borrowings.

In addition, improvements in business environment are essential for foreign and domestic investment and improve Mauritius' image as an open, stable, and well-functioning place to do business (Svirydzenka and Petri, 2014). Measures to improve small and medium enterprise (SME) productivity are needed. Another key area that constitutes an important challenge is the ease of doing business which has been deteriorating over the recent past. While the competitive ranking of Mauritius has improved significantly and is now ranked 45th out of 138 countries compared to 57th in 2008/9 out of 134, its labour market efficiency has remained the same (4.4) while financial market development (5 in 2008/9 v/s. 4.3 in 2016/17) and institutions (4.7 in 2008/9 v/s 4.5 in 2016/17) have deteriorated. The main areas of concern that have a significant bearing on productivity and hence competitiveness are government bureaucracy, lack of innovation, corruption, inadequate infrastructure and access to finance. These factors have a clear bearing on the ease of doing business, enhanced productivity and competitiveness.

Further, with respect to the huge trade deficit over the years, Mauritius has to look for niche markets for its textile products. Innovative skills and the production of market high value commodities in line with international standards will help in boosting competitiveness and exports. Mauritius must take advantage of the several trade agreements with the SADC, COMESA and IOC and reduce dependence on traditional European markets. Relocation of local-based resources such as investments, labour and expertise on the African continent, may provide broader business avenues and employment opportunities in the region.

Conclusion

On the eve of independence, Mauritius was a sugar dependent economy, with high unemployment. Over the years following independence, Mauritius tried to address its problems by setting up import substitution industries to address the concerns of the economy. This policy was unsuccessful. Following this, the country successfully implemented export-oriented strategies. The country was able to transform its economy, within a very short period of time, from a low-income economy to an upper middle-income economy with relatively high HDI, macroeconomic stability and proper institutions. Mauritius is among the top performers in Africa today and this has been termed by several researchers as the 'Mauritian miracle.'

Over the past 50 years, the country and its people have shown their resilience. First, this resilience was shown when the country showed its capacity to ride out the ending of the Sugar protocol. Second, the country dealt with the effects of the termination of the MFA wherein it lost its competitive edge in its exports to the EU and relevant markets. Third, Mauritius adapted to the financial and euro crises, which severely affected export markets including tourism. The Mauritian economy has evolved to constantly adapt to changing international conditions, with new sectors emerging and existing sectors transforming themselves in their quest for survival.

After almost years of outstanding economic performance, the Mauritian economy has fallen off a high growth plateau of about 6 per cent towards the 2 to 3 percent range. It is now facing emerging challenges such as youth unemployment, income inequality, poverty, an ageing population, a huge trade deficit and unsustainable public debts. In view of its objective to move to a high-income status, there is a pressing need for the island economy to apply medium term and long term measures like the ones presented above and strategies to move the country to this higher development track.

References

Ancharaz, V.D. and Kasseeah, H. (2016) 'Surviving Chinese Competition in a Post-Multi-Fibre Arrangement World: Experience of Clothing Exporters from Mauritius', *Global Journal of Emerging Market Economies* 8(1): 35-59.

African Development Bank (2015) *'Empowering African Women: An Agenda for Action'- Africa Gender Equality Index 2015.* Abidjan, Côte d'Ivoire: African Development Bank Group.

Bundhoo, S. (2013) 'Disability, Poverty and Sexual Violence', *Le Mauricien* 18.10.13. Available online at http://www.lemauricien.com/article/disability-poverty-and-sexual-violence (accessed on 26th October 2017).

Frankel, J.A. (2010) *'Mauritius: African Success Story'*, NBER Working Papers 16569, National Bureau of Economic Research, Inc.

Hamuth, S. (2016) 'Economic Evolution since Independence', *Le Defi Media Group.* Available online at http://defimedia.info/economic-evolution-independence (accessed on 3rd September 2017).

Lin, J.Y. (2011) 'New Structural Economics: A Framework for Rethinking Development', *The World Bank Research Observer* 26(2): 193-221.

Loong-Yu, A. (2005) *'The Post MFA era and the rise of China'*, Global Monitor. Available online at https://www.asienhaus.de/public/archiv/post-mfa-era-china.pdf (accessed on 1st December 2017).

Makoond, R. (2011) *Mauritius Economic Trajectory.* Port Louis, Mauritius: Joint Economic Council.

Meade, J.E. (1961) *The Economic and Social Structure of Mauritius - Report to the Government of Mauritius.* London: Methuen.

Mo Ibrahim Foundation (2016) *Ibrahim Index of African Governance - A Decade of African Governance 2006-2015.* Mo Ibrahim Foundation.

Naipaul, V.S. (1972) *The Overcrowded Barracoon.* New York: Random House Inc.

Ramdoo, I. (2014) 'Economic Transformation in Mauritius', *GREAT Insights*, Volume 3, Issue 5. Available online at http://ecdpm.org/great-insights/value-chains-industrialisation/economic-transformation-mauritius-heterodox-journey/ (accessed on 1st December 2017).

Rodrik, D. (1997) *'Trade Policy and Economic Performance in Sub-Saharan Africa'.* Paper prepared for the Swedish Ministry for Foreign Affairs, November.

Rodrik, D., Subramanian, A. and Trebbi, F. (2004) 'Institutions Rule: The Primacy of Institutions over Geography and Integration in Economic Development', *Journal of Economic Growth* 9(2): 131-65.

Romer, P.M. (1992) 'Two Strategies for Economic Development: Using Ideas and Producing Ideas', *The World Bank Economic Review* 6(1): 63-91.

Rostow, W.W., (1959) 'The Stages of Economic Growth', *The Economic History Review* 12(1): 1-16.

Sachs, J., and Warner, A. (1995) *'Economic Convergence and Economic Policies'*, (No. w5039) National Bureau of Economic Research.

Sachs, J., and Warner, A. (1997) 'Sources of Slow Growth in African Economies', *Journal of African Economies* 6(3): 335-76.

Solow, R.M. (1956) 'A Contribution to the Theory of Economic Growth', *The Quarterly Journal of Economics* 70(1): 65-94.

Statistics Mauritius (2015) *Poverty Analysis 2012*. Port Louis, Mauritius: Ministry of Finance and Economic Development.

Statistics Mauritius (2016) *Digest of Labour Statistics 2015*. Port Louis, Mauritius: Ministry of Finance and Economic Development.

Statistics Mauritius (2016) *Household Budget Survey 2012 - Poverty Analysis*. Port Louis, Mauritius: Ministry of Finance and Economic Development.

Statistics Mauritius (2016) *National Income Accounts September 2016*. Port Louis, Mauritius: Ministry of Finance and Economic Development.

Statistics Mauritius (2016) *National Income Accounts, Historical Series 1976 - 1993*. Port Louis, Mauritius: Ministry of Finance and Economic Development.

Stiglitz, J.E. (2011) 'Rethinking Development Economics', *The World Bank Research Observer* 26(2): 230-236.

Subramanian, A. (2009) *'The Mauritian Success Story and its Lessons'*, Working Papers UNU-WIDER Research Paper, World Institute for Development Economic Research (UNU-WIDER).

Subramanian, A. and Roy, D. (2003) 'Who Can Explain the Mauritian Miracle: Meade, Romer, Sachs, or Rodrik?' in D. Rodrik (ed) *In Search of Prosperity: Analytic Narratives on Economic Growth*. Princeton, NJ: Princeton University Press.

Svirydzenka, K. and Petri, M. (2014) *'Mauritius: The Drivers of Growth - Can the Past be Extended?'* IMF Working Paper No. 14/134. Washington D.C.: International Monetary Fund.

Tandrayen-Ragoobur V. and Kasseeah H. (2015) 'Youth Unemployment in Mauritius: Tile Ticking Bomb', in P.B. Mihyo and T.E. Mukuna (eds) *Urban Youth Unemployment in Eastern and Southern Africa: Features, Challenges, Consequences and Cutback Strategies*. Addis Ababa, Ethiopia: OSSREA.

Tandrayen-Ragoobur, V., and Kasseeah, H. (2017) 'Is Gender an Impediment to Firm Performance? Evidence from Small Firms in Mauritius', *International Journal of Entrepreneurial Behavior & Research* 23(6): 952-976.

UNECA (2017) *Urbanization and Industrialization for Africa's Transformation*. Economic Report on Africa. Addis Ababa, Ethiopia: United Nations.

Zafar, A. (2011) 'Mauritius: An Economic Success Story,' in P. Chuhan-Pole and M. Angwafo (eds) *Yes Africa Can: Success Stories from a Dynamic Continent*. Washington D.C.: The World Bank.

---

[i] Multifactor productivity (MFP) measures the changes in output per unit of combined inputs. It shows the rate of change in 'productive efficiency'.

[ii] The data is not available by gender.

[iii] The current exchange rate is 1 EURO= Rs 40.20.

Genealogies of a Miracle
A Historical Anthropology of the
Mauritian Export Processing Zone

PATRICK NEVELING

Introduction

History, society, economy, and politics in independent Mauritius are inextricably linked with the macroeconomic success of the nation's Export Processing Zone (EPZ) in the 1980s. Likewise, this EPZ success profoundly altered and continues to shape the international image of Mauritius as it earned the island status recognitions as 'first African tiger' (Morna, 1991) and 'economic miracle' (Alladin, 1993). Since then, the trajectory of independent Mauritius has become enshrined in the iconography of theories, policies, and best-practice recommendations for postcolonial development. This chapter reconstructs the Mauritian EPZ story, not only with a view to its international reception but also with an emphasis on the *longue durée* of the many variables that enabled such success. The new, critical light shed on the enshrinement of Mauritian development as a miracle brings to the fore those histories that have been out of focus in previous appraisals.

In order to advance this analysis, it is first and foremost important to identify those who fabricated the shrine for the Mauritian miracle. At the turn of the 1990s, two high-profile World Bank publications set the tone for a series of leading economists, development studies scholars, and political scientists descending on Mauritius to analyse the rapid growth rates in EPZ manufacturing since the mid-1980s (Subramanian and Roy, 2001; Alladin, 1993; World Bank, 1990 [1989], 1992). Yet, most publications were the result of short-term visits with datasets limited to what the Mauritian Central Statistical Office and the many World Bank (WB) and International Monetary Fund (IMF) surveys had produced on the heels of the supposedly successful, and thus rather unique structural adjustment programs of the early 1980s.

Those reports and publications came at the peak of the now worn-out and largely discredited neoliberal policies that brought the world the many national and regional financial crises continuing since 2008 and, what may be even worse than those crises, a ramping up of inequality across all tiers of national economies (Piketty,

107

2014). Not surprisingly, given that the WB and the IMF were hotspots of neoliberal policy implementation across the globe, those reports on Mauritius very much reflected the neoliberal agenda and set out to whitewash histories of economic development in Mauritius by establishing a simplistic juxtaposition that does justice neither to the Mauritians whose daily labour shaped the growth rates that made for the 'miracle' nor to the debates and struggles that paved the way for the economic policies required for capitalist world-market manufacturing to thrive in the Mauritian EPZ.[i]

What is more, a Mauritian success story has been nurtured since the early 1990s that ascribes clear-cut and largely mistaken roles of good guys and bad guys. IMF staffers Arvind Subramanian and Devish Roy were among the first to front a narrative that juxtaposed the rapid growth rates of the 1980s and 1990s with the analysis of a British colonial survey mission of the years 1959 and 1960 under the leadership of the renowned Keynesian later Nobel-laureate James Edward Meade. Simply put, and Subramanian and Roy put it very simple indeed, Meade was said to have predicted an inevitably bleak future for Mauritius, because limited access to external markets and a monocrop sugar economy at peak capacity meant that rapid population growth would result in ever-increasing unemployment and shrinking per capita income and this would ultimately stipple any prospect for peaceful coexistence of a multi-ethnic population already ripe with internal political conflicts. Yet, "history, or rather Mauritius, proved the Nobel Prize winner, James Meade's, dire prognostication (...) famously wrong" (Subramanian and Roy, 2001: 4).

This narrative, juxtaposing the mistaken Keynesian development economist commissioned by the late colonial state with the postcolonial nation's miraculous EPZ program, has been repeated time and again. Supatchai Panitchpakdi, then Director-General of the World Trade Organisation (WTO), offered Mauritian politicians and the nation's wider public a slightly reworded version of that neoliberal success story when he spoke as honorary guest at the national independence celebrations of 2004. With a simple equation, he sought to soothe the pain that preferential export quota cessation in the wake of the 2005 changes to the WTO regime had caused for the island and its quota-dependent EPZ and sugar sector; never mind dozens of factory closures, tens of thousands of newly unemployed or further crisis scenarios, if world-leading economists such as Meade had been wrong in 1960, why should their dire predictions be right in the 2000s (Neveling, 2016).

As the Mauritian nation celebrates its fiftieth independence anniversary, this chapter seeks to set the record straight and proposes a genealogy of the Mauritian miracle that abandons schematic and mistaken neoliberal equations and instead highlights the achievements of all Mauritians and those who have helped the nation grow and prosper over the past decades.

The argument develops as follows. First, I introduce a genealogy for the Mauritian EPZ program that stretches back to the Meade mission and, further, to the colonial sugar sector and to the rising Mauritian labour movement, whose struggles forced the introduction of a pioneering labour law in the British Empire after the so-called Uba-riots of 1937. Second, I provide an overview of the research approach of the Meade mission and outline how policies and institutions implemented on Meade's recommendation radically changed the political economy of Mauritius. Third, I show how the Mauritian EPZ Act of 1970 emerged from national and international efforts alike and, not least, how this benefitted from the rise of a new agency in the UN system, the United Nations Industrial Development Organisation, which gave important backing to the Mauritian government and private sector's push for international funding for an EPZ. Fourth, this chapter contends that Mauritian workers and their families, first and foremost, kept the EPZ going, as they not only provided the labour for the assembly lines, but also remained vigilant and resistant against escalating exploitation in the hundreds, if not thousands, of factories that have opened and closed shop in Mauritius in the decades since 1970. I conclude, that there was no Mauritian miracle and that we should instead dismantle the shrine that enforces those disembodied histories of Mauritian development detailed above. Instead, conclusive and future-oriented lessons to draw from the Mauritian developmental success emerge from viewing the 1980s peak period of EPZ growth as a convergence of favourable international and national conditions at the time coupled with the island's readiness for world-market production, which was owed to historical and contemporary struggles against escalating exploitation in Mauritius.

Setting the stage for change

Few would disagree that Mauritius was in a fairly dire and desperate situation at the turn to the 1960s. Sir Hilary Blood, Governor and Commander-in-Chief of Mauritius from 1949 to 1954, published a full-page stocktaking of the island's socio-economic condition and predicament in the London Times' British Colonies Review section in early July 1959, calling for a 'New Deal for Mauritius' (Blood, 04/07/1959). His elaborations illustrate well Britain's late imperial policies of the time, which focused not on maintaining imperial rule, but on creating conditions for colonies such as Mauritius to become independent and at the same time remain part of the capitalist arena of production and trade despite an increasingly tri-polar differentiation of the world into alliances between capitalist, socialist and non-aligned nations. In line with the neo-Malthusian approach of the 1950s, Blood identified rapid population growth as a problem across British colonies, especially so in small island colonies with limited capacities for economic expansion. Mauritius was a paradigmatic case to him. The contemporary output of 500,000 to 600,000 metric tons of sugar was the industry's limit both in terms of production and international marketing capacities. Yet, one ton of sugar provided the revenue to fund the basic social services for one inhabitant and with the island's population increasing from 500,000 in 1952 to 600,000 in 1958, the third-fastest growth rate worldwide, Mauritius was on the brink of collapse. The situation was aggravated by the threat of ethnic cleavages, a diagnosis Blood put forward by stating that Mauritians were 'politically minded' and that the socio-political setting of Mauritius shaped by 'differences in race, colour, economic conditions and religion'.

Nevertheless, the problems that Blood identified for Mauritius in 1959 were the effect of nearly 150 years of British colonial rule, and not of an inherent tendency of humans to identify in terms of ethnicity alone and then go to war with each other over some imagined essential differences (this is a historical perspective on the common denominators approach to Mauritian ethnicity, see Eriksen, 1998).

After invading against limited French resistance in 1810 and once Napoleon had been defeated in 1815, the British rulers altered the island's economic trajectory profoundly. In contradistinction, they left the internal social and political stratification largely intact. Mauritius' thriving privateering economy of the eighteenth century and the Port Louis free port were shut down and the island turned into a plantation-only economy focusing increasingly on sugar cane as the single export crop. In the process, mainly French but also other European colonisers morphed into a self-declared 'native' population and their leaders' position became structurally similar to that of other subjects under the British imperial system of indirect rule. As owners of plantations and mills, the island's resident capitalist class of foremost French origin entered into joint ventures with British businesses in shipping and trade. Those new Euro-Mauritian alliances reaped good profits from sugar, especially so after 1825, when Mauritian produce was awarded the preferential customs rates for sales to the British market that had previously been reserved for the Caribbean colonies. Yet, a conflict of interest remained and profitable business ventures seemed to matter little to the plantation owners' irrational, violent, armed uprising against the abolition of slavery, even though the latter earned them compensations of around two million Pound Sterling (Neveling, 2013; North-Coombes, 2000).

The supply of dependent, exploitable labourers was secured via the mostly seamless transition to the new regime of indentured labour from South Asia and

Eastern Africa. Compensation fees furthered the globalisation of the Mauritian sugar sector as larger estates introduced the new global standard of vacuum pan extraction in the 1840s and mills centralised at ever-increasing capacity and yield from a 1863 peak of 303, processing an average of 450 metric tons of sugar, to 38 in 1937, processing an average of 8210 metric tons of sugar (combined data from Teelock, 1998: 96; North-Coombes, 2000: 141). In the process of nineteenth century globalisation, numerous smaller Euro-Mauritian establishments went bankrupt or were swallowed up by larger players during the fiscal crisis of the 1840s and during the El Nino waves of the 1870s. Whereas those bankrupt businesses released staff for higher management positions in the larger estates and mills, small and medium scale cane cultivation was increasingly outsourced to former indentured labourers, whose households bore the risks of bad crops from soil erosion and potential destruction of all yields during the annual cyclone season.

As owners of the majority of mills, the Euro-Mauritian bourgeoisie retained control of an important bottleneck in the sugar commodity chain; the processing that turned canes into commodities for export. The real estate market for smallholder plots boomed because rights to residence for indentured labourers after the ends of contracts were favourably tied to property ownership. With those wishing to stay in Mauritius somewhat pushed into compulsory land purchases, the *petite* and *grande morcellements* of the 1840s and 1870s were forerunners to the short-lived and tragic boom of Mauritian smallholders in the years before the end of indenture in 1923. The percentage of total acreage under cane held by smallholders rose from 26.61 in 1914 to 41.09 in 1922, only to decline rapidly to 30.83 per cent in 1930. The rapid decline of sugar prices on the world markets after 1923 pushed many new businesses went into receivership and of the 14,495 small and medium cane plantations operational in 1930, most were highly indebted and would suffer more with the continuing decline of global sugar prices during the 1930s (Neveling, 2013, North-Coombes, 2000).

Other authors have already hinted at the long historical roots of the Mauritian EPZ success story. Yet, the focus of Deborah Bräutigam, Ryan Saylor, and Tania Diolle, and to some extent also of my own work, has been on the role of institutions and transcolonial and transnational networking of the Mauritian bourgeoisie (Saylor, 2012; Bräutigam, 2005; Bräutigam with Diolle, 2009). While the emphasis on quota politics for sugar and their extension to EPZ manufacture exports under the multi-fibre arrangement of 1974 is crucial, as evidenced also in the introductory references of the speech by the WTO Director-General in 2004, the question of how the spoils from such preferable quota are divided and how this translates into the social fabric of colonial and postcolonial Mauritius is as important.

The 1930s crisis and the plight of tens of thousands of smallholder households are focal points to answer that question and to better understand the success of the Mauritian EPZ. Historical research highlights the importance of the 1937 so-called Uba riots, an island-wide uprising that began in the Lallmatie region and took its name from a so-called small-planters cane. Until this day, historical research clads the riots in utilitarian terms. On one side are the small planters, who did not benefit in the same way as larger estates from the scientific crossing of cane varieties in the Royal Botanical Gardens of Pamplemousses and therefore engaged in their own clandestine cane breeding practices with the Uba cane emerging as a high net-weight and robust cane that guaranteed optimum revenues. On the other side are the millers, especially the Indian family owning the mill in the Lallmatie region, which for some time purchased the Uba canes at the same price as other canes despite their lower sucrose content. This caused them a loss, supposedly, which is why the further decline in sugar prices after 1935 forced them to lower the purchasing price for Uba canes (Storey, 1997).

Yet, the story told so far is incomplete and completing it is crucial for our understanding of the development policies of the late colonial and the early postcolonial Mauritian state. A focus solely on scientific breeding techniques that yielded higher sucrose content and from which the small planters were excluded casts the miller's price reductions in a rational and also somewhat benevolent light – they shouldered a loss as long as they could, whereas the small planters in somewhat clandestine ways had focused their efforts to better their situation on the breeding techniques alone and were thus likewise somewhat techno-centric utilitarians. Instead, millers and small planters alike were aware that the constant improvement of crushing and refining machines also improved sucrose extraction ratios across all cane varieties.

More importantly, while the crises of the 1920s and 1930s affected all actors in the Mauritian sugar sector, the colonial state's support initiatives catered first and foremost for the larger estates and millers. A conference on the future of the sugar sector pushed for tax rebates for larger estates, which were granted in 1927. When the 1930s crisis nullified the positive impact of these subsidies, the British finally set up the Mauritius Agricultural Bank (MAB) in 1937, which bailed out many estates held under receivership by offering new credit lines at much lower interest rates and the transfer of current loans from commercial banks to the MAB. Adding to this, the ratification of the International Sugar Agreement of 1937 by the leading European colonial powers of the time offered security for Mauritian preferential quota in a time of uncertainty. The 1938 report of the Hooper Commission, which had been appointed by the British colonial state for an enquiry into the Uba riots and their spread from

Lallmatie across the island and into other sectors, was very explicit about the fact that nothing had been done for smaller and medium sized cane plantations (Hooper, 1938; for a detailed analysis see Neveling, 2012).

Perhaps the most important outcome of the Uba riots and the recommendations of the Hooper Commission was that the colonial administration for the first time in Mauritian history took the concerns of small business owners and workers seriously and thus shifted from facilitator of preferential market access for the sugar plantocracy and its umbrella organisation, the 1921-founded Mauritius Sugar Syndicate, to a however reluctant arbitrator for social justice and a however limited redistribution of wealth. Even though it excluded cane workers and many other professions, the Mauritian Trade Union Ordinance of 1938 allowed dockworkers and craftspeople to unionise and would become a blueprint for improved labour rights legislation across the British Empire. In other words, more than three decades before the beginning of the Mauritian EPZ-miracle, the struggles of Mauritian workers created what has rightly been identified as a "milestone in colonial trade union legislation" (Croucher and McIlroy, 2013). Turning to the Meade Commission of 1959/60 in the following section reveals how the events of 1937 and after ushered in further pioneering changes that made the Mauritian EPZ boom possible.

Implementing change

The Second World War affected Mauritius in considerable ways. A German blockade and the bundling of the Empire's resources to support the war efforts in Europe and Asia radically changed the island's economy. Several estates freed considerable land for producing everyday foodstuffs and, as elsewhere across Sub-Saharan Africa, new industries emerged to substitute imports that were no longer available. While many of the latter vanished soon after 1945, some factories remained in operation into the 1970s. Yet, by the end of the 1950s it was already evident that none of these industries were viable alternatives that could generate significant revenues and employment alongside the sugar sector. The Quatre Bornes based government processing plant for aloe fibres, for example, continued to produce the hemp bags for packaging Mauritian sugar with significant government subsidies. Its closure in the early 1970s was the first major industrial dispute led by the rapidly expanding *Mouvement Militant Mauricien* (MMM), the then socialist party that would seek to put an end to Mauritian communalism in the 1970s and, for a short time in 1982/83 oversee the democratisation of national budget negotiations despite the increasing pressure from the Structural Adjustment Program (SAP) that the World Bank and the International Monetary Fund imposed on Mauritius in exchange for keeping the cash-strapped nation afloat and secure imports of basic commodities.

Yet, in between these two major external interventions in the Mauritian political economy came a series of small and medium-scale interventions in which Mauritians had a much more significant say than they had had during the war and the SAP. Most of these interventions had to do with the successive implementation of the Meade mission's recommendations during the 1960s and the establishment of the EPZ in 1970.

Several scholars have written about the rather informal beginnings of the EPZ in 1965, when the Mauritian entrepreneur Jose Poncini opened Micro Jewels and established an early export-oriented enterprise processing parts for Swiss watches in Mauritius, an undertaking for which he received crucial backing from Meade with obtaining permits from the London Colonial Office (Burn, 1996; Dommen and Dommen, 1999; Neveling, 2014; Hein, 1989; Yin *et al.*, 1992). The same authors have also emphasised the pioneering efforts of Mauritian economist Edouard Lim Fat, who brought home recommendations for opening an EPZ from survey missions to rapidly industrialising territories of the time, such as Hong Kong, Puerto Rico and Taiwan, which he published prominently in the *Revue Agricole* and the sugar industry's *PROsi-Magazine* in an effort to convince Mauritian sugar magnates and politicians to pave the way for industrial expansion via state-backed diversification (for a detailed analysis Neveling, 2017; original publications are Lim Fat, 1969; Lim Fat - November, 1969).

Yet, so far only Bridget and Edward Dommen, Meade's daughter and son in law respectively, and Yeung Lam Ko (Yeung Lam Ko, 1998) have given more detailed consideration to the relevance of the commission's recommendations for what would later be known as the Mauritian miracle. In fact, Yeung Lam Ko goes as far as suggesting that Mauritius' independence day on March 12, 1968, may have been chosen to mark the day of the arrival of the members of the Meade commission in Mauritius (Yeung Lam Ko, 1998: 1). While we cannot be certain whether he used this as a rhetorical figure or whether that date in any way motivated the decisions in 1968, there is a lot to be gained from a closer examination of the commission's preparation for and their actual research in Mauritius.

A visit to the archives of the London School of Economics, where the Meade collection of personal papers and notes is held alongside the collections of many other famous economists, will bring to light for the interested researcher a total of twelve well-stocked boxes on Mauritius with notes, correspondences, research papers and drafts informing the 1961 published Meade report. These include, for example, around 40 letters and statements received by Meade and his five collaborators in response to advertisements they had placed in Mauritian newspapers in 1959. Those advertisements invited all Mauritians to share their views on the major blockages to economic prosperity and to suggest measures for improving the situation. The answers received are witness to a people with diverse, engaged, and highly developed views on the island's economy and its problematic embedding in the global system. One company suggested to resolve transport problem by importing used Goggomobiles, microcars produced by a German manufacturer in Bavaria from 1955 to 1969, to Mauritius and they argued that this would also create good business for garages and other car repair and service outlets. Another company, Happy World Foods, alerted Meade to the fact that Mauritius was lacking cold storage facilities and suggested the subsidised import of freezers to broaden the scope of foodstuffs on offer. Coincidentally, Happy World Foods is now the Altima Group and the largest food and grocery wholesale distributor in Mauritius.[ii]

The correspondences with Meade's employer, the London Colonial Office, seem much less innovative in comparison to these letters. The commission's tasks are detailed in a letter dated July 13, 1959, and largely mirror what Blood had said in his London Times op-ed. In fact, the Colonial Administration had been aware of the Mauritian crisis for quite some time and a five-year plan to stimulate economic development and diversification had been implemented in 1957 already. Yet, despite such awareness, the Meade commission's report might have had the same limited impact as many other similar endeavours of the European late colonial powers and the wider project of industry-driven development during the Cold War decades.

The situation and setting changed radically, however, when two deadly and devastating cyclones, Carol and Alix, struck Mauritius in early 1960, only weeks before Meade and his team arrived. Around 40 per cent of all dwellings were destroyed, many lost their lives and vital supplies could only be secured following a major relief effort by the British Air Force and a wave of donations and support letters coming from the UK mainland (Times; 03/03/1960). Significant funding was released for reconstruction and the coverage in the London Times and other leading UK newspapers shows that Mauritius became a paradigmatic case; the Empire wanted to show that although it was crumbling and ridden with conflict, a colony in dire need could nevertheless be salvaged. Meade and his team were thus at the heart of a disaster relief effort and became involved in a major rebuilding project. This ranged from plans for the Victoria power station, funded by the first ever World Bank credit line to Mauritius, secured by the UK government and underwritten on the London markets in 1963, to the establishment of the Mauritius Housing Corporation (MHC) in 1960, which would build the many cités across the island that were to finally give a home to the many landless families that had settled on the outskirts of the cities in the aftermath of the 1920s and 1930s crises in the sugar sector (for the story of such a cité and the conditions of living, see Delforge, 1971).

Yet, it would still be a long way to move from rebuilding the island to setting up an EPZ. Planning for economic diversification so that Mauritius would have a second pillar for export commodities and employment beyond sugar would prove an arduous task as this required an institutional layout, selecting the right measures from a number of policies available, and convincing both the Colonial Office and the Mauritian bourgeoisie to lend their support. The flurry of policies and debates circulating at the time is evidenced, for example, in the letters that Meade exchanged with the nascent development agencies of other British colonies. A first indication towards the plans for an EPZ comes to light in the Jamaican development corporation's very positive response to Meade's query about the success of their tax rebates and other subsidies for new industries. The Jamaican programme of 10-year tax and customs holidays and state-funded building of industrial estates may have well served as the template for the pioneering industries programme that the Colonial Office implemented on Meade's recommendation. These measures, plus Meade's recommendations to fuse the MAB and the MHC in the 1964 founded Development Bank of Mauritius (DBM) so that Mauritius would have an industrial development bank, paved the way for the Mauritian parliament's EPZ-Act in 1970.

Yet, the Jamaican policies were the brainchild of a US-marketing corporation, Arthur D. Little Inc., who had been the driving force behind the opening of the world's first EPZ in Puerto Rico in 1947 and carried Puerto Rican policies forward to Jamaica upon a contract with the local government in 1957 (Neveling, 2015). This means that when Mauritian economist Edouard Lim Fat went to survey the Puerto Rican economic success story of the time in the mid-1960s, he was not looking at something radically different from Meade's pioneering industries policies, as the World Bank narrative outlined in my introduction would have it, but instead Lim Fat returned to the roots of the same export-oriented industrialisation policies that Meade had encountered in his exchange of letters with the Jamaican authorities. In fact, the export-oriented development policies in the EPZs of Taiwan, Singapore and Hong Kong that Lim Fat also surveyed likewise originated in the Puerto Rican programme of 1947.

The Mauritian shift from the Pioneering Industries Act of the early 1960s to the EPZ-Act of 1970 was therefore a gradual one. Rather than initiating a radical reversal, the paramount achievement of Lim Fat and others working towards the zone policies was to commit the leading figures in the sugar sector and in the early postcolonial administrations to carry forward in more explicit ways what Meade had begun in 1960. Beyond that, the uphill path towards creating a viable EPZ in Mauritius had to do with convincing international development organisations to commit credit lines and technical assistance to the EPZ. As Deborah Bräutigam with Tania Diolle have pointed out, a World Bank technical assistance mission had voiced concerns about the feasibility of an EPZ in Mauritius (Bräutigam with Diolle, 2009).

When another mission, this time funded by the newly founded United Nations Industrial Development Organisation (UNIDO), recommended an EPZ the World Bank made a U-turn and opened credit lines for completing work on the industrial zone in Plaine Lauzun and for developing the estate in Coromandel. While the DBM that Meade had recommended became the main liaison for handling World Bank money on the Mauritian side, the location for the Coromandel zone was chosen with explicit reference to the *cités* nearby, whose inhabitants would make for the workforce and have a short walk to and from home. On an international level, technical assistance to the Mauritian EPZ would serve UNIDO to showcase their consultancy work and, hence, Mauritius again became somewhat of a blueprint for a trend across the Third World (Neveling, 2015; 2017).

Maintaining change

During the 1990s, Mauritian scholars distinguished four phases of EPZ development. Take-off years during the 1970s, crisis years from the late 1970s to around 1982, boom years from 1983, and efforts at consolidating the high growth rates in the EPZ during the 1990s (Yin *et al.*, 1992; Hein, 1996). From the vantage point of 2018, 50 years after Mauritian independence, two further phases can be identified. The decline of EPZ employment from around 1999 to 2005, and the recent revival of EPZ-like operations, now in close collaboration with the People's Republic of China.

A closer look at these phases brings to light the interlinked development of postcolonial Mauritius and its EPZ. The zone was always a particular one in global comparison as from the early stages onward it was never a clearly demarcated zone, confined to a given number of fenced off industrial estates. Instead, the legal provision that an EPZ enterprise could be registered anywhere on the island meant that the zone businesses could not but embed themselves into the everyday life on the island. During the take-off phase in the 1970s, the number of EPZ workers grew rapidly to around 20,000. Zone workers soon engaged in the struggles for a better life led by the MMM and became known as Amazons when they confronted riot police with great bravery during the strike waves of the 1970s. Major points of contention were very bad working conditions and the lack of social security provisions that Mauritians had won successively since the struggles of the late 1930s. Also in those years, Mauritian sugar businesses, flush with cash due to the high sugar prices from the 1973 world food crisis, entered EPZ operations with numerous joint ventures, commonly with European and Hong Kong based textile and garment corporations. Workers would soon be sought after and factories offered prize draws for applicants.

Fortunes seemed to change for good with the second oil crisis of 1978 and 1979 and the rapid decline of sugar prices after 1975. The first and second Ramgoolam administrations spent heavily on social housing in an effort to appease the growing discontent among a population that was longing for betterment of their lives in the postcolonial state. Yet, the 130,000 jobs promised at the beginning of the 1970s had not materialised in 1980 and instead, the island was facing debt default and struggling to import basic commodities. When the 1982 landslide victory gave the MMM all openly elected seats in parliament, Mauritius was already under control of the World Bank and the IMF. While structural adjustment forced EPZs onto the governments of many other African and Latin American countries during the 1980s and 1990s, it may have been a blessing that Mauritius already had set up such a zone on rather independent terms and during a period when workers were fairly strong and able to limit the worst excesses in labour rights violations that have made EPZs ill-famous worldwide as sweatshops where the life of a worker or a trade unionist counts for little.

Along with the economies in the US and the UK picking up steam from 1983 onward, the Mauritian zone entered the very boom phase that earned it the label 'miracle'. The relocation of businesses from Hong Kong to Mauritius in the early wake of the 1998 handover to the People's Republic of China has often been listed as another important factors for the boom (Meisenhelder, 1997). While this certainly has merit, it is important to again reference a global system of quota allocation that played into the cards of Mauritius. With the multi-fibre arrangement of 1974, Western countries had introduced import quota for textiles and garments in order to protect their own industries and to reward firm alliances of Third World nations with the capitalist bloc during the Cold War heydays. As a close ally, Mauritius had received a beneficial quota and with the EPZ-nations/regions Hong Kong, Singapore and Sri Lanka reaching quota limits (and plunging into civil war in the latter case), Mauritius became a highly attractive destination. The boom also meant that workers' wages rose considerably and the Mauritian government (on recommendation of the World Bank) waved minimum wage differentials between the zone and the "normal" national economy, which facilitated the larger scale entry of male workers. Another significant development of those years was the opening of numerous factories in rural regions, again an effect of companies struggling to find workers (Neveling, 2012).

Consolidation from around 1990 onward was facilitated when the Mauritian government opened the EPZ to contract workers from South Asia and later also People's Republic of China and Eastern Africa. These workers were often employed under harshest conditions, which drew comparison with the situation of indentured workers in Mauritius during the nineteenth century. Yet, their low wages and hard labour kept the zone competitive in an international setting that saw the entry of an increasing number of postcolonial nations. In this period, many male workers left the zone for the construction sector and the bustling tourism sector offered more attractive employment to young Mauritians with higher education.

Yet, higher education had often been funded by the wages that mothers had earned in the EPZ and when the zone went into crisis as the WTO regimes introduced the phasing out of preferential quota from 1997 onward, two entire generations of workers still employed in the EPZ faced a bleak future. The government responded in the 2000s with a *Textile Emergency Support Team* (TEST) and offered vocational training and microcredit schemes. Many of the women workers I spoke to during my year of ethnographic research from 2003 to 2004 emphasised, however, that at 40 years of age and beyond, they could neither see any realistic chances for a second career in tourism nor as independent shop owners (on this period see Ramtohul, 2008). Thus, as Mauritius turned 40 in 2008, the nation looked back on recent years also as a period when every closure of a larger EPZ factory, not least those of Mauritian flagship companies such as Floreal Knitwear, had sent shockwaves across the island. Other than during the wildcat strikes of the 1970s, however, it did not seem feasible to imagine a future for the Mauritian EPZ and this, in my view, gave the protests against the closures during the mid-2000s an atmosphere of a nation saying farewell to the development policy scheme that had helped it out of the dependency on sugar and doing so at the same time as the sugar industry itself was also facing closures of mills and estates due to the quota ending in that sector, too.

A window into the future

Tourism, the Ebène cyber-city, and the tax haven status acquired in the early 1990s have certainly added many pillars to the Mauritian economy. It is nowadays virtually impossible to imagine the island could ever again enter into a crisis scenario similar to those of the turn to the 1960s or of the early 1980s. Still, as more new sectors may become established on the island, it is important to remember that the Mauritian EPZ never generated a 'miracle' in the strict sense of the term. Instead, what I hoped to show with the above was that the 1980s boom years have genealogies that stretch back to the early 1800s as regards the links of Mauritius with beneficial quota systems for export commodities. Another strand of that genealogy goes back to the 1930s when

119

Mauritians, only recently freed of the chains of indenture, became very explicit about their discontent with the immediate suffering they were experiencing during the global crisis of the time and due to the lack of attention that the colonial administration paid to their plight. In a sense, the wildcat strikes in the EPZ and the wider national uprising of the 1970s could be regarded as structurally similar, for, again, Mauritians had won a great new sense of liberty with independence and yet there was a global economic crisis and a government and a private sector that were both too busy with themselves to show sufficient care for their plight. In both periods of struggle in the face of global crises, then, Mauritians not only won rights that made their own lives better, but they won rights that helped the island move forward and made it the template for changes across the global south.

Referencing the EPZ success story merely as a 'miracle' does little justice to those struggles and their lasting impact. Likewise, it is important to remember that there are many good explanations for the 1980s boom-years. In fact, in percentage figures, the growth rates in the EPZ during the 1970s were probably higher than those of the 1980s. What is more, the neoliberal narrative emerging in the 1990s that has the economists err and Mauritians prevail may be true only in the sense that Mauritians, and others, not least the members of the Meade commission, took the time to carefully analyse the past, present and future prospects of their island's economy and thus prevailed over the supposedly invisible hands of global markets. I would hope these endeavours might continue as Mauritius moves towards the centenary of its independence in 2068.

References

Alladin, Ibrahim. (1993) *Economic miracle in the Indian Ocean: Can Mauritius show the way?* Stanley, Mauritius: Editions de l'Océan Indien.

Blood, Hillary. 04/07/1959. "*New Deal for Mauritius.*" The Times.

Bräutigam, Deborah. (2005) 'Strategic Engagement: Markets, Transnational Networks, and Globalization in Mauritius', *Yale Journal of International Affairs*: 63-77.

Bräutigam, Deborah with Tania Diolle. (2009) *Coalitions, Capitalists and Credibility: Overcoming the Crisis of Confidence at Independence in Mauritius.* Development Leadership Programme Research Paper 4.

Burn, Nalini. (1996) 'Mauritius', in Uma Kothari and Vidula Nababsing (eds) *Gender & Industrialisation: Mauritius, Bangladesh, Sri Lanka.* Stanley, Mauritius: Editions de l'Océan Indien.

Croucher, Richard, and John McIlroy. (2013) 'Mauritius 1938: the origins of a milestone in colonial trade union legislation', *Labor History* 54(3): 223-239.

Delforge, Guy. (1971) *Enquête sociale: la vie sociale dans les cités C.H.A. et E.D.C. des Plaines Wilhems.* Port Louis: Institut pour le Développement et le Progrès.

Dommen, Bridget and Edward Dommen. (1999) *Mauritius: An Island of Success. A Retrospective Study 1960-1993*. Oxford: James Currey.

Eriksen, Thomas Hylland. (1998) *Common Denominators: Ethnicity, Nation-building and Compromise in Mauritius*. Oxford: Berg.

Hein, Philippe. (1989) 'Structural Transformation in an Island Country: The Mauritius Export Processing Zone', *UNCTAD Review* 1: 41-57.

Hein, Philippe. (1996) *L'économie de l'île Maurice*. Paris: L'Harmattan.

Hooper, C.A. (1938) *Report of the Commission of Enquiry into Unrest on Sugar Estates in Mauritius, 1937*. Port Louis, Mauritius: Government Printer.

Lim Fat, Edouard. (1969) 'Free Industrial Zones in Taiwan and Puerto Rico', *Revue Agricole et Sucrière de l'île Maurice* XLVIII: 337-348.

Lim Fat, Edouard. (1969) 'Commentary', in *PROsi* 3-5. Port Louis, Mauritius: The Public Relations Office of the Sugar Industry.

Meisenhelder, Thomas. (1997) 'The Developmental State in Mauritius', *The Journal of Modern African Studies* 35(2): 279-297.

Morna, C. (1991) 'Africa´s First Tiger', *Africa Report* 36: 42-44.

Neveling, Patrick. (2012) *Manifestationen der Globalisierung. Kapital, Staat und Arbeit in Mauritius, 1825-2005* (DPhil Thesis, engl.: Manifestations of globalisation. Capital, state, and labour in Mauritius, 1825-2005). Halle/Saale: Martin-Luther-University Library.

Neveling, Patrick. (2013) 'A Periodisation of Globalisation according to the Mauritian Integration into the International Sugar Commodity Chain (1825-2005)', in Jonathan Curry-Machado (ed) *Beneath and Beyond the Commodities of Empire*. Basingstoke (UK), New York: Palgrave Macmillan.

Neveling, Patrick. (2014) 'Three shades of embeddedness, state capitalism as the informal economy, emic notions of the anti-market, and counterfeit garments in the Mauritian Export Processing Zone', *Research in Economic Anthropology* 34: 65-94.

Neveling, Patrick. (2015) "Export processing zones, special economic zones and the long march of capitalist development policies during the Cold War." In Leslie James and Elisabeth Leake (eds) *Negotiating Independence: New Directions in the Histories of the Cold War & Decolonisation*. London: Bloomsbury.

Neveling, Patrick. (2016) 'Beyond Sites and Methods: The Field, History, Global Capitalism', in Simon Coleman, Susan Hyatt and Ann Kingsolver (eds) *Routledge Companion to Contemporary Anthropology*. London: Routledge.

Neveling, Patrick. (2017) 'The political economy machinery: toward a critical anthropology of development as a contested capitalist practice', *Dialectical Anthropology*: 163-183.

North-Coombes, M. D. (2000) *Studies in the Political Economy of Mauritius*. Moka, Mauritius: Mahatma Gandhi Institute.

Piketty, Thomas. (2014) *Capital in the Twenty-First Century*. Cambridge: Harvard University Press/Belknapp.

Ramtohul, Ramola. (2008) 'Trade Liberalisation and the Feminisation of Poverty: The Mauritian Scenario', *Agenda* 22(78): 55-67.

Saylor, Ryan. (2012) 'Probing the Historical Sources of the Mauritian miracle: Sugar Exporters and State Building in Colonial Mauritius', *Review of African Political Economy* 39(133): 465-478.

Storey, William Kelleher. (1997) *Science and Power in Colonial Mauritius*. Rochester: University of Rochester Press.

Subramanian, Arvind, and Devesh Roy. (2001) '*Who can explain the Mauritian miracle: Meade, Romer, Sachs or Rodrik?*' IMF Working Paper 01/116.

Teelock, Vijaya. (1998) *Bitter Sugar: Sugar and Slavery in 19th Century Mauritius*. Moka, Mauritius: Mahatma Ghandi Institute.

The London Times. 03/03/1960. '*Aid for Mauritius, Cyclone relief fund opened*'. The Times.

World Bank. (1990) [1989]. *Mauritius: Managing Success*. Washington D.C.: The International Bank for Reconstruction and Development/The World Bank.

World Bank. (1992) *Mauritius: Expanding Horizons*. Washington D.C.: The International Bank for Reconstruction and Development/The World Bank.

Yeung Lam Ko, Louis. (1998) '*The Economic Development of Mauritius since Independence*', UNSW School of Economics, Working Paper Series 1998(6).

Yin, Pierre, Donald Ha Yeung, Deshmuk Kowlessur and Mirella Chung. (1992) *L'île Maurice et sa Zone Franche: la deuxième phase de développement*. Stanley, Mauritius: Editions de l'Océan Indien Ltée.

---

[i] With this in mind, I want to recommend the World Bank open-access repository of published and declassified reports to interested readers, nevertheless. Despite their often academic jargon and policy-driven assessments, Bank reports are mostly very readable historical sources on the Mauritian economy and give a good sense of the motivations for policies at a given time (for an introduction see Neveling, 2017).

[ii] All letters referenced can be found at: London School of Economics Archives, Meade Collection, Box 5/9.

Small is beautiful, but is it viable?
Scale and Mauritian options for the next 50 years

THOMAS HYLLAND ERIKSEN

Introduction

It is often said, and it is difficult not to agree, that Mauritius is a small country in the global context. In terms of area, it ranks 179th of 196; in terms of population it is 156th. QED.

OK, so it's small. But just how small? This is a less straightforward question than one might assume. And, to follow up: when do size and scale matter – and when are they irrelevant? These are the two questions I'd like to reflect upon on this occasion, where we have the chance to lift our gaze from the everyday and think along longer lines and loftier visions; past, present and future. My contention will be that small scale sometimes matters and sometimes doesn't, and when it does, it can be both an advantage and a handicap.

In an article published in 1966, with the rather cumbersome title 'Sociological characteristics of small territories and their implications for economic development', the anthropologist Burton Benedict refers to Mauritius on several occasions. After all, he cut his teeth as a fieldworker in the cane fields of Mauritius, studying small-scale economics among rural Indo-Mauritians. Benedict makes a number of shrewd observations about scale and size in his article. For example, he points out that whereas a strike at a factory in England would have no noticeable effect on the wider society, a similarly-sized strike at a Mauritian sugar mill would send ripples throughout Mauritian society. So, modest scale does create a certain vulnerability. Only so many persons and institutions are available to carry out particular tasks, and when someone disappears, finding a replacement can be hard.

Benedict also makes a related point about internal differentiation – that is, how many forms of specialisation can be maintained in a small society as opposed to a large one. He also claims that a society like Luxembourg, although it had just half the population of Mauritius, was of larger scale owing to its tight integration into the European Economic Community, now the European Union. I will eventually return to these arguments and see to what extent they can help in making sense of

123

contemporary Mauritius, but allow me first of all to make a couple of final initial points about scale, namely that it is relative, and it can refer to different kinds of phenomena. So you can have a place which is small scale in some respects, but not in others.

And scale has a relative, or rather relational aspect (see Anderson, 1998). Whether you come across as David or Goliath depends on who you are comparing yourself to. In my native Norway, if we feel the need to be a big country, we just look to Iceland rather than to Sweden or Germany. Indeed, it may be claimed that Mauritius has its own colonial problem in Rodrigues, and when I started to work here more than thirty years ago, people were always quick to distinguish between *ilois* from Chagos and *iliens* from Mauritius. In Trinidad, which has about the same population as Mauritius, people may tell jokes about small-islanders from Tobago or St Vincent which are quite similar to jokes told here about people from Rodrigues. Mauritius is much smaller than Madagascar, but a lot bigger than Seychelles. Indeed it is a major player among the island-states and territories of the Western Indian Ocean. Besides, it is not smaller-scale than Madagascar in every respect. Owing to its higher level of economic and institutional development, Mauritius can offer a wider range of occupational and career opportunities to its 1.2 million citizens that Madagascar, with a population of 25 million, cannot. So let us keep this in mind; scale is not just about size, it is also about complexity and connectivity (cf. Eriksen, 2016).

I will now take a closer look at different facets of scale and their implications for individuals, society and the economy of Mauritius.

The individual

Let me start at the level of the individual. How does small scale affect your opportunities in life? To many, scale is rarely relevant in everyday life; Mauritius is small, but it isn't tiny. Most people, no matter where they live, spend most of their time in small-scale settings anyway. For example, people generally get married within an hour's travel from where they live, whether that place is Mauritius or India.

Yet scale is not entirely irrelevant. In larger countries, you may be advised to take your driver's license in a small town with just one roundabout and two traffic lights. All other things being equal, complexity is less in a smaller than in a larger place. At a more general level, it needs mentioning that a classic problem confronting ambitious people in small places is the big fish/small fish dilemma: Are you happy being a big fish in a small pond, or would you rather try your luck as a small fish in a big lake? Yes, you can go abroad if you feel suffocated by the smallness of this place; but you can also contribute to your own society in a multitude of ways. Given the small size of the population, it is necessary for many to wear several hats, as when – for example – the Prime Minister is also in charge of two or three further portfolios. A third option in today's digital world with its possibilities for instantaneous, global communication, is to go transnational, staying at home but you can wear several hats; you can go transnational, staying at home but actively cultivating relations to the outside world. A country like Mauritius, small but not tiny (see Gingrich and Hannerz, 2017 for a discussion of the difference), produces flexible and versatile individuals ready to take on new tasks. Whereas big countries produce specialists, small countries produce generalists. In Mauritius, unlike in the US, you cannot make a living as an expert on Turkish foreign policy, but you can be someone who knows a bit about the foreign policy of many countries.

A different aspect of smallness concerns anonymity, which is notoriously difficult in a small place. Can you, for example, rob a bank and get away? In the case of Mauritius, the answer is probably no, since the cashier knows your mother and will tell you to go home and behave yourself, or else she'll report you to the police. Besides, even if you were for some miraculous reason able to get away with a few million rupees in cash, how would you spend it? Surely, if you – as a youngish man with little documented income – walked into Leal & Co's showroom with a suitcase full of banknotes, demanding the newest BMW, that would raise a few eyebrows.

A more general point about anonymity and scale is the fact that you run into the same people all your life, and the extent of networks is limited. If you fall out with them, they can still be hard to avoid, and there are few, if any, others to associate with. In larger countries, there would be many alternatives. Say you work at a university and have a strained relationship with your dean; in a larger country, you could move to another university, while in Mauritius this may not be possible. So if your career plans are halted by a personal conflict or similar, you cannot necessarily just find other associates to work with. And you cannot escape your reputation unless you leave the country.

Yet, Mauritius is just big enough for some degree of anonymity to be possible. Consider, by way of comparison, the Faroe Islands, a North Atlantic dependency of Denmark with a population of less than 50,000. Yet the Faroese have their own language and a few local mass media. Be this as it may: Some Faroese may proudly declare that they have no gays, prostitutes or drug addicts. The answer is simple; it is because they are all in Denmark, mainly Copenhagen which is big enough for anonymity to be possible. You can't be a burglar in the Faroes, since everybody knows who you are. And not least, they know your mother, so by becoming a deviant from the norm, you bring shame not only over yourself, but also over your family. It is also a fact that if you are Faroese and suffer from a chronic disease, you have to move to Denmark. Here, the critical threshold has been surpassed in this respect. Seychelles sends patients to Mauritius for treatment which requires specialist interventions. Again, we see that Mauritius is small, but not tiny.

To sum up the argument so far, the range of options for an individual living in a small society is narrower in some respects, but in other respects it may indeed be wider. A Norwegian friend of mine, a fellow academic who works in the USA, fears that he would become lazy were he to return to provincial, small Norway. This view is a version of Karl Marx' concept of rural idiocy: By living in a small, rural place, Marx argued, you acquire a limited horizon and a narrow range of experience. This view may have been true when it was first formulated, but modern education, media and cyberspace change everything. Moreover, people who live in big countries can be shockingly ignorant of the world outside, and those who live in small countries are often extremely interested in the outside world, sometimes to the point of obsession. For example, you may find that many Mauritians know more about Emmanuel Macron's politics than many Frenchmen, or more about English football than many Englishmen.

Politics and society

Smallness encourages people to discover that they are multitalented. Perhaps exaggerating slightly, Marcelle Lagesse wrote that 'L'île Maurice compte 1 million d'habitants et autant d'écrivains' (quoted in Peghini, 2016: 251), signalling that you need to make a special effort to keep cultural life fully assorted and vibrant in a small country. It nevertheless remains a fact that the number of people involved in politics, music, the arts and civil society organisations is limited here. The dependence on individuals creates vulnerability: when someone disappears, it can send ripples throughout the sector (similarly to the strike alluded to by Benedict). Given their small scale and the dominance of often tiny political and intellectual elites, small islands are especially prone to social epidemics, i.e. processes of change that are both fast and highly consequential (Gladwell, 2000). Just think about the violent riots which erupted in Mauritius in 1999, following the controversial death of Kaya, which brought the entire country to the brink of chaos, only to die down within a few days. This sobering experience shows how a relatively minor event taking place in a small island-state can have serious repercussions throughout society, because of its modest scale.

The closely knit networks resulting from small scale do not only create vulnerability, however, but also strong relations of trust and mutual obligation, ensuring that things get done. Trust nevertheless has two faces; it can be constraining as well as enabling. It places obligations on you as well as giving you opportunities for social mobility. As observed by Benedict, shopkeepers and small businessmen often have a different ethnic or religious identity from the majority, not so closely connected through kinship and friendship, so they can more easily collect debt than others. Trust also creates role dilemmas in politics and public life in general, leading to accusations of nepotism and corruption. In fact, a major challenge for Mauritius in the future consists in overcoming the limitations imposed on politics and social life through network structure. Social distances are short, 'everybody knows each other', and there are not a great number of alternatives.

V.S. Naipaul, known in Mauritius mainly for his dismissive analysis in *The Overcrowded Barracoon* (to which I shall soon return), was also markedly unenthusiastic about his own country, and had the following to say about it: 'Superficially, because of the multitude of races, Trinidad may seem complex, but to anyone who knows it, it is a simple colonial philistine society' (Naipaul, 1973b). By this, he means that social life, culture and politics are conformist, regulated by common norms inherited from colonialism. While it may be easy to argue against this simplistic view of culture and diversity, whether it concerns Trinidad or Mauritius, Naipaul neglects the significance of race and ethnicity. The closed circles of the small country are often ethnic, precluding the full participation of people with the wrong ethnic identity (see Boswell, 2006 on *le malaise créole*). People with talents, but without the right networks, may easily be excluded from the possibility of social mobility in this kind of society. This is a problem not least in small countries which are also ethnically diverse.

However, on the positive side, we should keep in mind that small places often punch above their weight. Think of Iceland. The population is just over a quarter of that of Mauritius – about 350,000 – and yet, like Mauritius, they have produced a Nobel laureate in literature, several internationally famous popular musicians, dancers and designers, and a national football team which is almost inexplicably good by European standards.

Also, Mauritius boasts a larger scale, if we define it as complexity, than many larger societies. The media pluralism is considerable for such a small population, notably with respect to the print media. On the whole, the press is critical and independent, and both dailies and weeklies encourage debate by printing op-ed articles and letters contributed by readers. This cannot be taken for granted: The city of Perth in Western Australia has about the same population size as Mauritius, but just one daily newspaper, the *West Australian*.

But of course, in other ways, small scale does create vulnerability; it cannot be conjured away. Mauritius relies crucially on its connectedness to world markets. It has no military force, and is thus incapable of protecting its vast oceanic territory in a situation of crisis. Yet Mauritius is more self-sufficient than many other island societies. It is small, but not super small, and it is diverse not just in terms of demography, but also economically. To this I now turn briefly.

Economy

Small islands are always expensive places to visit, whether they are in the Caribbean, the Pacific or the Indian Ocean. The reason is simple; nearly all consumer goods have to be imported. But by this token, Mauritius is not a small island. During colonialism, the domestic market was judged large enough to justify import substitution, and a range of light industries aimed for the local market were established. Biscuits and soap, therefore, do not have to be imported, nor do mangoes or beer. This marks a contrast to much smaller Seychelles, which cannot compete in a deregulated global market in these contexts. Although small-scale agriculture is perfectly feasible in the Seychelles even if the country is hilly and soils relatively poor, getting your mangoes from India is cheaper than growing them yourself.

Yet scale will be a challenge for Mauritius too in the years to come. One reason is the slow but sure disappearance of protective measures, quotas and special arrangements that we witnessed worldwide in the 1990s, when the free-trade ideology of the World Trade Organisation (WTO) took over from the General Agreement on Tariffs and Trade (GATT) and Lomé agreements. When everybody has to compete on the same, level field, the larger players tend to win owing to the economy of scale; the more units you produce, the lower the cost of the last unit produced, distributed or consumed. But we cannot blame it all on global neoliberalism; we should also look at the incredible reduction in transportation costs since the 1970s. Here in Mauritius, many remember how the building of the 'vrac' terminal – the introduction of automated, machine-based loading of sugar and the unloading of wheat and other imports – led to massive unemployment and social unrest in the Port-Louis docks. Around the same time, the container ship became the standard mode of transport of goods around the world, throwing hundreds of thousands of stevedores worldwide into unemployment and reducing transport cost by more than ninety per cent. This development is good news for huge economies like China, but problematic for small economies.

We should also keep in mind that although Mauritius has diversified its economy in admirable ways since the 1970s, it relies crucially on imports. Anything from cotton and linen to machine parts and – in some cases – specialised knowledge, has to be imported. Likewise, self-sufficiency with respect to food and energy is utopian and unlikely. These factors, like the military weakness and the relative lack of specialisation, are a strong reminder of the necessity to maintain strong ties to other countries – unlike larger countries which might chug on even if they become fairly isolated, like South Africa did in the final stages of apartheid.

Communication and cognitive scale

In some respects, Mauritius is far more deeply integrated in larger networks than many Mauritians are aware of. I grant you that Kreol is a small language (but again, it isn't tiny!), but English and French are emphatically not. In some ways, one could argue that many European peoples are more isolated since their command of foreign languages is more limited. In Norway, the vast majority of Facebook users communicate only in Norwegian; in the Czech Republic, the majority of citizens can only communicate comfortably in Czech. As a general rule, we may posit that the larger the language you speak, the less likely is it that you will acquire fluency in another language. So, as I have pointed out already, Marx' concept of rural idiocy, or any permutation thereof, does not work in a context like this one. On the contrary, in terms of communication, Mauritius is less isolated, less parochial than many larger, more centrally located places. It is permeated by a world-awareness that comes from being on the outskirts of a global system. If you live in a small country, chances are that you will be more interested in the outside world than had you lived in a larger country. Briefly, then, in terms of communication, Mauritius is not a small-scale place.

The non-scalable

Scale does not always matter. Many large countries are far more isolated than a small island-state like Mauritius. For one thing, the ocean has been a highway of connectedness since time immemorial. Oceans connect; mountains divide. For another, Mauritius has been an integral part of global systems since the first attempt at colonisation. Even the failed colonisations presupposed global connections. Thirdly, and no less importantly, Mauritius is firmly connected to the world through its migration history. Mauritians have ancestors from Guangzhou, Patna, Madagascar and Bretagne, and these thin webs of significance and attachment matter not only to the persons in question, but ideally to the Mauritian people. Finally, Mauritius is connected to the world through language. Although 'le mythe de quinze langues pour une population d'un million' was debunked by Père Henri Souchon more than thirty years ago, it is a pretty polyglot place, with the international languages of English and French foregrounded, but more than a smattering of major Asian languages as well.

Tourism is not scalable. A good waiter, a lovely beach and so on is just as good here as in Thailand or Mexico. Unlike sugar, beaches are not scalable. With sugar, it doesn't matter to the consumer if his kilogramme of sugar has been produced on a large plantation or a small farm; it can be scaled up indefinitely, with a declining price and increased competitiveness as a result. This does not work with services. Anything with a local flavour, anything handmade or unique, cannot be scaled up without losing its specificity. So David can often beat Goliath; in art and handicrafts, in quality of life, in other domains such as food.

The environment is also not scalable, simply because it is not man-made. The vastness and purity of the ocean, its biodiversity and uniqueness; the climate, the crops and plants that thrive in Mauritius itself are resources which are becoming globally precarious and rare; they cannot be transplanted to anywhere, and are unique.

So Mauritius is not just a small society. It is a fully paid-up member of large scale systems, it communicates easily and smoothly with much of the world through the global languages of English and French, and many Mauritians maintain strong ties to other parts of the world through origins and ancestry. Yet it is small scale in other ways, which creates its own kinds of vulnerability. And again, there are important domains where scale does not matter or where smallness can indeed be an asset, that is to say anything unique.

Conclusion

The 'spectre of comparisons' originally described by the nineteenth-century Filipino author and freedom fighter José Rizal (see Anderson, 2002) is nearly always a cause for concern, but especially in small countries which are : Whatever is beautiful or impressive at home is immediately dwarfed when it is compared to the achievements of larger, metropolitan countries. The challenges are thus threefold: Securing social cohesion and equality without obliterating cultural diversity – one could say promoting social equality without demanding cultural similarity; developing a pride in the local as something unique, not as an inferior copy of the metropolitan; and finally, developing a local politics which grows out of domestic concerns proper, not of political projects developed overseas.

The author of more than one book dismissing small island culture as derivative and inauthentic, V.S. Naipaul paid Mauritius a visit, leading to the locally infamous essay 'The Overcrowded Barracoon' (Naipaul, 1973). Written with characteristic cynicism, the essay depicts an island where virtually everybody wants to leave – it is too remote, too poor, too boring, and of particular interest to Naipaul, there is no future for ambitious people in this overpopulated, sugar-dependent place. Naipaul paints a picture where hordes of young Mauritians train as nurses, since it may give them a one-way ticket out.

Now, we all know that this was not the end of the story. Only fifteen years later, the situation had changed dramatically, following the establishment of the Export Processing Zone (EPZ), a slow but sure growth in tourism as air travel here became more reliable and affordable; and a few years later, Mauritius was connected to the world through internet and mobile telephony as well. By the early 1990s, many of the young Mauritians I met admitted that they wanted to leave, but only for the experience, or the education, and that they were certain to return. Only five years earlier, the picture was different and less upbeat with regards to Mauritius' future.

So we should be cautious about making predictions about the next fifty years – after all, if we look fifty years back, it is easy to see that recognised experts, like Meade, Titmuss and Benedict, were mainly wrong in their predictions. But I think we know two or three things about Mauritius, three hundred years after settlement and fifty years after independence, that might come in handy when reflecting on options and opportunities, and which have a bearing, however obliquely, on scale.

John Donne famously wrote that 'No man is an island, entire of itself' in 1624. A poem warning against Little Englanderism and isolationism, it could almost be seen as a poem against Brexit, four hundred years *avant la lettre*. In a very real sense, no island is an island either, if by island you mean a bounded, isolated entity (Eriksen, 1993). And this is where Benedict was wrong in his comparison between Mauritius and Luxembourg. Mauritius was part of a global network from day one – even the failed attempts at colonisation, by the Portuguese and the Dutch, relied on global connections. Seen by itself, it is small scale, but it is thoroughly woven into a much larger tapestry and has always been so. A mountain valley in the USA, say, would by most criteria be more small scale, less complex and more isolated, than Mauritius.

Regarding internal differentiation, it is true that many small-scale societies rely overwhelmingly on one product, or crop, rendering them exceptionally vulnerable to market fluctuations. As is well known, this is no longer the case in Mauritius, which has a far more diversified economy and educational system than it did a generation ago. Take the university. It was truly a small, even tiny institution when I first visited it in the 1980s; today, it is much larger with a far greater range of study programmes now and strong ambitions to make its mark internationally in a wide range of research areas.

So, to try to answer my own question: What are the options for the next fifty years? Well, Mauritius has no choice other than continuing to punch above its weight in different ways.

Should one remain content through being incorporated into global systems, like the little cog providing sugar for the French and later British empire – or are there other options? The answer is definitely yes. It is perfectly possible for a small country like Mauritius to define international agendas and to serve as a model for others. Notably, there is a rising demand globally for services, goods and places with a distinctive local feel, and let me add that this demand, importantly, is not just about selling stuff, but also about the quality of life locally. Some time ago, the American sociologist George Ritzer (2003) wrote a funny, and also insightful book called *The Globalization of Nothing*. He defines 'nothing' as anything – goods, services, people, places – which could have been anywhere in the world, where the personal touch and the local flavour have been washed away. He contrasts the *grobalisation of nothing* with the *glocalisation of something*: In touch with the outside world, but without losing oneself. Producing a good experience for tourists cannot be scaled up. At its worst, it becomes a kind of globalisation of nothing,

But this is not just about tourism, or development in a conventional sense. In this day and age, there are also many reasons to keep human development and ecological issues in mind. Back in 1986 when I first arrived in Mauritius, 'Green Island' was just a liquor brand; now, this lovely country could reinvent itself as a green lantern showing how a robust economy can be combined with a high quality of life for everyone – regardless of their ethnic identity or religion – and ecological sustainability. There is no reason at all why it shouldn't become a model for others to emulate along these lines. After all, Mauritius reinvented itself after independence. The historical compromise between Ramgoolam and Duval ensured communal peace, followed by the diversification of the economy and the growth of a vibrant, democratic public culture. It could well reinvent itself again. And there is no determinism involved; the future is what we make of it. In the case of Mauritius, isolation is not an option, as three hundred years of history have shown; and a pretty radical change of direction is possible, as fifty years of independence have demonstrated.

Finally, let me point out that there is an important aspect of small scale which I have not addressed directly until now, but which can prove to be a major asset for Mauritius in the coming years and decades: Smaller entities can change and adjust to new circumstances much faster than larger ones. If a large cargo ship is brought off course and is heading towards a reef, it may run aground even if the problem was discovered an hour earlier, while a smaller speedboat can change its course in a matter of seconds.

This logic applies to almost any kind of entity, including companies and not least countries. The Mauritian leadership decided to diversify the economy a generation ago, and did so, successfully, at breakneck speed; it will be possible to change course again. Larger and more sluggish countries lack this luxury. Being a small country, globally integrated and with a collective vision, can in this way be an enormous advantage.

Acknowledgements

This chapter is a revised version of the keynote lecture delivered at the conference 'Mauritius after 50 years of independence' in June 2017. My revisions are based on the stimulating presentations and discussions of the subsequent days. I would like to thank the organising and scientific committees of the conference for having made this important event possible, and in particular Roukaya Kasenally, Christina Chan-Meetoo and Ramola Ramtohul.

References

Anderson, Benedict. (1998) *The Spectre of Comparisons*. London: Verso.

Benedict, Burton. (1966) 'Sociological characteristics of small territories and their implications for economic development', in M. Banton (ed) *The Social Anthropology of Complex Societies*. London: Tavistock.

Boswell, Rosabelle. (2006) *Le Malaise Créole: Ethnic Identity in Mauritius*. Oxford: Berghahn.

Eriksen, Thomas Hylland. (1993) 'Do cultural islands exist?', *Social Anthropology* 2(1): 133-147.

— (2011) "A simple colonial philistine society': Cultural complexity and identity politics in small islands', in T. Curtis (ed) *Islands as Crossroads: Sustaining Cultural Diversity in Small Island Developing States*. Paris: UNESCO.

— (2016) *Overheating: An Anthropology of Accelerated Change*. London: Pluto.

Gingrich, Andre and Ulf Hannerz. (eds) (2017) *Small Countries: Structures and Sensibilities*. Philadelphia: University of Pennsylvania Press.

Gladwell, Malcolm. (2000) *The Tipping Point: How Little Things Can Make A Big Difference*. London: Abacus.

Naipaul, V.S. (1973a) 'The Overcrowded Barracoon', in *The Overcrowded Barracoon and Other Articles*. Harmondsworth: Penguin.

— (1973b) 'London', in *The Overcrowded Barracoon and Other Articles*, pp. 9–16. Harmondsworth: Penguin.

Peghini, Julie. (2016) *Île rêvée; île réelle: Le multiculturalisme à l'Île Maurice*. Paris: Presses Universitaires de Vincennes.

Ritzer, George. (2004) *The Globalization of Nothing*. London: Sage.

Transcending Intersectional Identities
The Women's Movement in Postcolonial Mauritius

RAMOLA RAMTOHUL

Introduction

This chapter focuses on the evolution and trajectory of the women's movement in postcolonial Mauritius. Mauritius has a plural society with its population presently composed of four ethnic groups and four major religious groups[i]. The Mauritian nation is often depicted as a rainbow nation, which is nonetheless fragile with a facade of unity in diversity. The Mauritian society can be described as a typical plural society which, following Fenton's definition (1999: 38) is not only composed of many cultures, but also lacks or has historically lacked any strong impulse towards social and cultural integration. In such societies, the removal of an external constraining force, especially colonial rule, leaves behind a society with no integrative mechanisms[ii]. Anticolonialism in Mauritius was not a clear-cut matter as was the case in most postcolonial nations. While the British represented political rule imposed from the colonial power, economic and cultural domination was imposed by Francophone Mauritians. British governance for the Hindus and Muslims represented a check on the Franco-Mauritian and upper-class Creole aristocracies. However, with the rise in the political prominence of the Hindus, the allegiance of the Franco-Mauritians and Creoles shifted towards the British colonial power.

The accession of Mauritius to independence in 1968 was the result of three decades of active political manoeuvring and negotiations rather than that of a national liberation struggle. It entailed a number of high-level political consultations and negotiations between the different parties representing the local interests of the different ethnic groups and the British colonial authorities. Political leaders and negotiators in these consultations were all men. Hence the role of women in the political debates and campaigns that preceded independence was not clear. Apart from the brief period of communal riots on the eve of independence proclamation, Mauritius became a sovereign state in a rather peaceful manner, in the absence of a national liberation struggle. The approach of independence did not lead to any form of political nor national unity and Mauritians were instead highly divided over the issue of independence, with 44 per cent of the population opposing independence. This opposition stemmed from minority ethnic groups who feared for their future in an independent Mauritius (Moutou, 2000). The forging of a spirit of nationalism and unity was consequently fractured, causing manifold effects on the social and political affairs of the newly independent Mauritius.

Intersectionality becomes a key concern for the women's movement in Mauritius as Mauritian women carry multiple and conflicting identities mainly based on class, religion, caste and ethnicity, all of which affect their involvement and action in women's organisations. This chapter analyses the conditions under which women in Mauritius decided to transcend intersectional identities and form feminist movements advocating women's rights, often going against cultural norms. Primary data for this research was sourced from oral history interviews with senior members of the main women's organisations in the country.

Intersectionality and women's movements

The theory of intersectionality and identity has shown that identities are complex, comprising multiple intersections of class, gender, race, nationality and sexuality, causing individuals to react differently at different times (Crenshaw, 1991; Hill Collins, 2000). Differences of education, job opportunities and cultural possibilities also get filtered through the lenses of class and ethnicity which structure the individual experiences of women (Spelman, 1988). In much of the postcolonial world, nationalist movements provided an impetus for women's mobilisation and activism. The development of a feminist consciousness is imperative for women's movements to be able to successfully transform social power relations (Lerner, 1993). In a plural society such as Mauritius, the forging of feminist consciousness would require women to transcend intersectional identities to achieve feminist demands. Here, the extent of unity and solidarity among different communities of women becomes a key factor that will determine the success of the actions of the women's movement, especially whether it will be able to present its demands clearly and forcefully.

Views on the impact of women's multiple identities on female solidarity diverge. Basu (1995: 3) on the one hand, posits that differences exert a strong influence on the nature of women's perceptions and types of mobilisation and have been divisive to women's movements within and across nations. The pervasiveness of wide divisions among women separates them into interest blocks and identity groups, making it difficult to mobilise women as a cohesive group. Basu (1995: 1) further notes that many middle-class women's movements failed to mobilise poor women because they assumed that class interests could be subordinated to gender interests. On the other hand, Mouffe (1992: 372), in a neo-Marxist analysis, talks of a 'multiplicity of relations of subordination', where a single individual can be a bearer of multiple social relations, which may be dominant in one relation and also subordinated in another. When constructed as relations of subordination, social relations can become the source of conflict and antagonism and eventually lead to political activism or a 'democratic revolution' (Laclau and Mouffe, 1985). Hence, despite women's multiple identities, they are often caught up in relations of subordination, which have the potential to challenge the status quo by crossing boundaries and forming feminist alliances.

It therefore becomes central to understand when and why different women's groups act in a coordinated way in a plural context. On this issue, Salo (1999: 124) introduces the notion of 'strategic alliances' which women form, despite their multiple identities and differences. Here, the focus is on the moment at which disparate groups within the movement coalesce in such a way that they operate as a movement that is distinct from other political forces. Mohanty (1991: 7) puts forward the notion of a 'common context of struggle' which brings together disparate women's groups to form an alliance. Moreover, Baldez (2002: 6) introduces the 'tipping' model to define the point at which diverse organisations converge to form a women's movement to challenge the status quo. National liberation struggles appear to have been the 'tip' that got women working together in the movement in much of the post-colonial world. Baldez (2002: 4) also argues that all women's movements share the decision to mobilise as women on the basis of widely held norms of female identity. These norms comprise a set of understandings that reflect women's widespread exclusion from political power. Issues such as reproductive rights, women's representation in politics, equal pay, childcare and domestic violence therefore have the force to unite women from different backgrounds and ideologies.

The status of women in Mauritius

Under 19th century Mauritian law, the state treated women as the inalienable property of their husbands, thereby restricting any attempt towards autonomy by women. The 'Code Napoleon[iii]' or 'Napoleon's Civil Code of 1804', adopted in 1808 in Mauritius, imposed the status of 'minor' on a married woman and was characterised by severe patriarchalism, restricting women to the private domestic sphere. Marriage was considered to be the definitive fate of girls and there was little concern for gender issues, except from the perspective of health, fertility and welfare (Gunganah *et al.*, 1997). Concern over poor health, high maternal mortality and overall welfare led to the creation of the social welfare department and the establishment of social welfare centres throughout the rural areas, which aimed at improving the living conditions of the rural population (Gunganah *et al.*, 1997).

The Mauritian state has been modelled on the British colonial model, which is characterised by male hegemony at all levels of its structures. At independence, Mauritius therefore inherited a structure whose ideology was designed to systematically promote male privilege and power while consolidating women's subordination. The gendered quality of the state becomes clearly visible in its institutions, such as cabinet, parliament, the judiciary and the police force which remain male dominated institutions. Moreover, gender-based subordination has been and is still deeply ingrained in the consciousness of men and women in Mauritian society, and tends to be viewed as a natural corollary of the biological differences between them. Gender-based subordination is reinforced through religious beliefs, cultural practices, and educational systems that assign to women lesser status and power. A sexual division of labour persists in the country, with domestic and reproductive work still considered to be 'women's work'.

The response of Mauritian postcolonial leadership to cumulative gender inequalities that were historically embedded in the stratified and pluralist society consisted primarily of a policy of breaking down formal barriers to women's access to legal, political, educational and economic institutions, assuming that this would bring about significant changes in women's participatory roles. Wide-ranging opportunities became available to women. These included improved access to health services and reproductive health facilities, state provision of free education at all levels, employment opportunities and legal amendments to eliminate sex discrimination. However, it was the setting up of the Export Processing Zone in the 1970s that created mass employment opportunities for women with low levels of education, and was the trigger to the economic empowerment and autonomy of Mauritian women from working class backgrounds.

The early women's organisations

Mauritian women have been engaged in civil society organisations since the early 18th century, when the country was under colonial rule. Most of the early civil society organisations were social, cultural and religious organisations that had branches and activities dedicated to women. The focus at that time was mainly on social, religious and cultural activities in specific communities where different communities worked with or supported specific organisations in most cases. The majority of the early women's organisations were either connected to socio-religious bodies that were headed by men or were class-based.

Muslim women were involved in women's associations such as the Mauritius Muslim Ladies Association, formed in 1940 and the Ahmadist Muslim Women's

Association, set up in 1951 (Emrith, 1994; Orian, 1980). These women's organisations worked towards the physical, mental and spiritual emancipation of Muslim women in the country and activities included religious education and charitable work. Hindu women were involved in the Arya Samaj[iv] movement since 1912 and in the Bissoondoyal 'Jan Andolan'[v] movement since 1942. Both movements promoted education for girls in their endeavour to preserve the Indian culture and languages in Mauritius. The Mauritius Arya Samaj movement launched a campaign against child marriage and denounced the dowry system. The education made available to Hindu girls at that time primarily focused on the inculcation of cultural and religious values. And yet, according to Rughoonundon (2000: 38), this was the only way to obtain the agreement of conservative families to send their daughters to school. Women from bourgeois Indo-Mauritian families in the movement often volunteered as educators and encouraged families to send their daughters to school, thereby breaking taboos which had so far excluded Indo-Mauritian girls from access to education.

The Catholic Church sponsored and supported the *Écoles Ménagères*, a women's organisation founded in 1956 by the social worker, France Boyer de la Giroday (Orian, 1980). The Écoles Ménagères was created to focus on respectable domesticity and it catered to the needs of young girls in terms of providing training in household management 'skills' to become good wives in accordance with Christian gendered ideology. Activities of the Écoles Ménagères gradually progressed beyond the domestic front, to include literacy classes, civic education including the history and culture of Mauritius, kitchen gardening and entrepreneurship[vi]. Women from bourgeois or high-income households volunteered as trainers at the Écoles Ménagères.

Apart from the religious-based women's groups, some of the early women's organisations had class dimension. There were numerous smaller women's associations in rural areas which had been operational since the late 1940s (Rughoonundon, 2000: 159). These small rural women's associations were dealing with social issues such as marriage, burial, betrothal amongst others. Membership of these associations mainly comprised women from low income groups with little or no literacy skills. The activities of these organisations nevertheless disclose attempts made by working class women to group together and exert some form of agency over issues governing their daily lives and thereby access different spaces outside the home. This can be qualified as an early form of conscious raising and feminist activism among the working class women.

Among the class-based women's organisations, there was the Women's Self-Help Association (WSHA), set up in 1968[vii] which had an upper-class membership. In the 1960s, the WSHA set out to promote textile handicraft production at home. It provided free training to women and girls in embroidery and basket making skills with the aim of enabling them to earn their living. This association had a significant impact since its training programmes reached hundreds of young girls in the villages, who would have otherwise had to live a life of economic dependence on their fathers and husbands. According to Dommen and Dommen (1999), efforts of the WSHA prepared women both in terms of skills and psychologically, to seize the new employment opportunities in the Export Processing Zone (EPZ) that emerged in the 1970s. However, the WSHA did not open up skills held by men to women nor did it challenge patriarchal authority. It sought to improve the lives of women and girls in the country by extending educational access to them. Working with women from disadvantaged and low-income backgrounds and from different communities nevertheless made the founders of WSHA more aware of the problems these women faced on a daily basis largely because of women's inferior legal status[viii]. The training and grouping together of women also created a forum where these women were able to have discussions about their rights and become conscious of the need to work together as women in order to press for legal changes (Dumont, 1976). This marked the start of the growth of a feminist consciousness among these women.

The social segregation of women along communal and class lines had slotted Mauritian women into interest block and identity groups, which was a major obstacle towards meeting the necessary conditions for the development of feminist consciousness. Furthermore, a common feature of the predominant religions in Mauritius - Hinduism, Islam and Christianity - is an ideology of male authority over women and the endorsement of women's role in the family as caregiver, wife and mother. As such, there was little space for women's organisations to challenge patriarchal authority, transcend intersectional identities and engage in feminist activism that extended beyond the inclusion of women into education and domestic skills training. Rather, there appeared to be an implicit 'patriarchal bargain' which guided the activities of these women's organisations to focus on practical gender needs such as nutrition, health, hygiene, basic literacy and child care. The socio-religious organisations were controlled backstage by men, whereas the WSHA had strong connections with government and did not challenge conservative notions of respectable femininity. Moreover, structural constraints such as gender differences in access to economic resources and until the establishment of the EPZ in the 1970s, limited employment opportunities for women with low levels of literacy, meant that very few women dared abandon the very institution that they might seek to critique, namely the family and community. The absence of a nationalist ideology and national unity in Mauritius was an additional disadvantage which, if present, had the potential to impel the different women's groups to work together and develop a strongly forged feminist and political consciousness.

The start of a feminist movement

The start of a core women's movement in Mauritius involving a feminist struggle geared towards the improvement of women's rights began after independence in the mid-1970s. This period witnessed a crisis of the state as government appeared to be corrupt and increasingly inept, poverty and unemployment were rampant, and the population frustrated. There was a rise in political consciousness in the country as leftist organisations such as the *Mouvement Militant Mauricien* (MMM) and trade unions became increasingly popular and powerful. This created the necessary political space for women's and gender issues to be brought up as the leftist organisations focussed on national unity and not on ethnic and religious issues and also made space for women. The government's decision to institute a state of emergency in 1971 and postpone elections in order to quell the trade union manifestations, the censorship of the press and the arrest of MMM leaders in 1972 caused further disarray. In 1975, the country also witnessed mass student revolt.

Anger at political elites and lack of confidence in state institutions led to a blossoming of movement politics during this period. The women's movement was part of this surge as the wider context of political unrest created the necessary space for women to challenge the status quo and imagine different realities. Movement politics therefore became an alternative to party politics in Mauritius and the growth in non-party organisations seeking rights and empowerment for the powerless developed from the belief that the state was no longer able to create meaningful economic development, power for the poor and those who, like women, exercised limited political influence than their numbers warranted. During that brief period of political repression, movements provided an avenue for political participation for women and a number of autonomous and non-ethnic/religious women's organisations emerged. These organisations inspired a gendered identification among women as opposed to the ethnic and religious as had been the case in the past.

One of the prominent women's groups was *La Ligue Féministe*, founded by Shirin Aumeeruddy-Cziffra in 1974[ix]. The principal aims included: achieving equality of the sexes in the laws, abolition of sex discrimination, equal chances for boys and girls to education and training, equal salary for work of equal value, respect for human beings, promotion of family planning, liberty of women over their bodies, freedom of action for the youth and fostering an active participation of women in the economic, social and political affairs of the country[x]. La Ligue Féministe held meetings all around the island, as explained by Shirin Aumeeruddy-Cziffra:

The idea was to work with the masses, try and engage in awareness programmes to get women to think about their own status, let them own this thing, and become you know, empowered.[xi]

Many of the members, including Shirin Aumeeruddy-Cziffra, had studied overseas and had been exposed to European socialist ideologies and feminism. Eriksen (1998: 117) however notes that the European-inspired feminism promoted by the Ligue Féministe, had little popular support because of hegemonic patriarchal values that disapproved of feminist ideologies and of women's involvement in formal politics. Despite being a feminist movement, La Ligue Féministe nonetheless had male members as the belief was that men could also be feminists and therefore support women's issues.

Another autonomous women's organisation was the *Association des Femmes Mauriciennes* (AFM), set up in early 1975 by a group of women from upper and middle class backgrounds[xii]. The latter were already engaged in social welfare activities, trade unions and women's associations. The aim of AFM was to promote women's welfare by making women conscious of their status and rights. The founder members realised that it was better to work together to foster common action than work in isolation. The association worked to educate women especially at grassroot level in rural areas so that the latter became conscious of their exploitation and took action to remedy any injustice. In an interview, the president of the organisation in 1980, Marie-Josée Baudot explained:

Women are very slow to make a move, to distance themselves from traditions which sometimes oppress them, from customs, and all these established issues that make up their reality. They are not sufficiently interested in events outside their daily life.[xiii]

Members sought the help of the small rural women's associations to reach out to women in rural areas where educational seminars for women were organised, informing women about their rights through debates, seminars and discussions with lawyers (Orian, 1980). They also encouraged women to forge solidarity between themselves and to take action on issues and conditions that oppressed them.

The *Muvman Liberasyon Fam* (MLF) was set up in 1976 after some of its founder members left the MMM and La Ligue Féministe. In similar vein, the MLF adopted a Marxist feminist ideology and worked more intensively with the working classes. Since its inception, the MLF was mainly involved in trade union activities, adult literacy courses for women, campaigns against laws that discriminate against women, campaigns for women to have a voice in the media and campaigns to gain reproductive rights. It has been engaged in a wide range of actions, some of which were somewhat radical, for example hunger strikes, women's rallies and sit-ins on public roads in the late 1970s and early 1980s.

The women's organisations set up soon after independence focused on the empowerment of women through employment creation and consciousness-raising on women's rights. During this period, Mauritius witnessed societal changes such as a decline in infant mortality, maternal death rates and in the number of births. There was also an increase in women's life span and access to education. According to Lerner (1993), such changes allow more women to live in economic independence and are crucial to the development of transformative feminist consciousness. Activities and demands of women's organisations in Mauritius became more militant and the women's movement grew in strength, unity and organisation. A greater sense of solidarity began to develop as women from different socio-economic and educational backgrounds, religious and ethnic groups began working together on a common platform, especially on issues pertaining to women's rights. Moreover, by this time, Mauritius had a generation of young women, especially among the upper classes, who had had access to quality education and thus had a different outlook of life.

The growth in feminist consciousness in the country was also enhanced by global attention on women's rights in the 1970s, especially with the proclamation of 1975 as International Women's Year and the decade 1975-1985 as the Decade for Women by the United Nations. The UN Declaration of 1975 as the Year of Women provided a much-needed boost to the activities of the various women's organisations in the country, as explained by Shirin Aumeeruddy-Cziffra:

> In 1975 the United Nations came out, all of a sudden declared the year of women and it was such a good opportunity for us … we used this year, UN year for women to have exhibitions, to tell people about women's rights and it became OK because UN is giving us a sort of, you know, backing indirectly because this is the Year of Women.[xiv]

The patronage of the UN facilitated the organisation of seminars and discussions on women's rights as it became more politically acceptable in the conservative and patriarchal Mauritian society and was associated with modernisation. The UN Decade for Women was also instrumental in making space for leaders of women's organisations in Mauritius to interact with women activists from different countries.

Women's collective action

The formation of strategic alliances among women's groups took place in 1978, which was a key historical moment in the country. It was shaped by structural events of the time, namely the rise in social movement (leftist politics and trade unions) activity and the growth of global feminism in the 1970s. This was when two powerful women's fronts and an alliance of women's organisations were formed: the Front Commun Organisations Femmes (FCOF), Solidarité Fam and the Mauritius Alliance of Women (MAW).

The *Front Commun Organisations Femmes* (FCOF), set up in 1977, was the first women's front in Mauritius[xv]. This women's front was set up with the exclusive aim of fighting against the amended Immigration and Deportation Act which was discriminatory towards women. In 1977, amendments to the Immigration and Deportation Act were made so that all foreign men married to Mauritian women lost their right of residence in Mauritius. This Act was discriminatory since it did not apply to foreign women married to Mauritian men. According to the MLF (1988), the aim of these amendments was to safeguard the economic interests of a class of Mauritian men who felt threatened by the highly qualified foreign husbands of Mauritian women. The discriminatory legislation was a significant threat towards women and family stability, causing indignation among women's organisations. This pushed them to converge onto a common platform and fight for women's rights as a stronger unified group. They organised their actions locally in the form of petitions and demonstrations in front of parliament, but they were not able to take their case to court in Mauritius because at that time, 'sex' was not included in the definition of non-discrimination in the Constitution[xvi]. The women's front then sought international action and took their case to the United Nations Human Rights Committee on Sexual Discrimination in May 1978[xvii]. This case set a precedent internationally as it was the first case on sexual discrimination that was put before the UN Human Rights Committee. The UN Human Rights Committee concluded that the new immigration law discriminated against women on grounds of sex and the Mauritian government was asked to amend the law.

The success of the lobby of the FCOF against the discriminatory government policy and legislation led to the formation of a wider platform called *Solidarité Fam*, which was also known as the 'Women's Liberation Movement'. The women's organisations that set up the FCOF were the core group that had founded Solidarité Fam in 1978 to celebrate International Women's Day. More women's organisations gradually joined in, namely Mauritius Alliance of Women, Association des Femmes Mauriciennes, SOS Femmes and Soroptimist. Women in trade unions and in small regional women's associations supported this platform. Solidarité Fam was a strong women's platform that worked towards changing the civil law - the Code Napoleon - on marital laws and to give women a legal status that was equal to men. It had members who were close to both the opposition MMM party (e.g. La Ligue Féministe) as well as members who were close to the governing Mauritius Labour Party (MLP) party (e.g. Mauritius Alliance of Women). Despite their links with different political groups and ideologies, these women lobbied together for a change in the status of women in Mauritius, demonstrating a growth in feminist consciousness as women pooled their efforts together to strengthen their actions. Public meetings were held in the Port Louis botanical gardens and women were encouraged to speak in public. Solidarité Fam was a popular and unmistakably feminist movement that appealed to women in all sections of Mauritian society as it gave them an opportunity to voice out their grievances, share common concerns and most of all, lobby for an improvement in the status and rights of women. Moreover, given its broad founder membership, it was a movement that the majority of Mauritian women could identify with and it was able to bring together women from different educational, class, religious and political backgrounds into the public arena to lobby for women's rights. Solidarité Fam was particularly active from 1978 to 1985.

The third alliance of women's groups is the Mauritius Alliance of Women. Its origins lay at the celebrations of International Women's Day in March 1978 when thirty-two women's organisations got together at Continental Hotel in Curepipe. Many of these women leaders had attended the 1975 International Women's Year Conference in Mexico City and three years later, were frustrated with the slow progress in regard to changes in the laws governing women's rights in marriage. The women leaders realised that although the objectives of the various women's associations were welfare oriented, there was considerable duplication of efforts and this lack of unity and fragmentation had weakened the women's movement. They agreed to come together under a federation which came to be known as the Mauritius Alliance of Women (MAW)[xviii]. The latter came into full existence as an umbrella organisation in 1978 with the primary aim of helping women obtain an equal place in society. One of the first tasks undertaken by the MAW was to rally women's support towards changing the legislation governing marriage, which was discriminatory towards women and treated married women as minors. The MAW worked together on this issue with left-oriented women's organisations, MLF and Solidarité Fam.

The women's platforms lobbied as a stronger group for the legalisation of religious marriages to protect women's rights. These areas of overt discrimination against Mauritian women prompted them to transcend intersectional identities, form strategic alliances and together fight for women's rights. The formation of these stronger

145

women's alliances and the seminal work done by them marked the forging of feminist consciousness in Mauritius during this period, as women got together, breaking down ethnic, religious, political and class boundaries, and fought together as women. The unifying factor here, or 'tip' according to Baldez's (2002) 'tipping model', was the struggle for women's rights and equality under the law and all women felt concerned by this issue. This common context of subordination got women to group together under a stronger unified body in a movement to challenge the status quo. Following the widespread protest action and petitions, the Mauritian government called in a French legal expert to advise on amending the Code Napoleon. The Code Napoleon with respect to marriage laws was eventually amended in 1980 and 1981 and the legal amendments gave religious marriages the same status as civil marriages. Married women were given equal rights with regard to conjugal and parental decisions and also professional and economic autonomy.

State feminism and diluted activism of women's groups

The early 1980s witnessed the formation of the Mauritian version of state feminism or the women's national machinery, namely the Ministry of Women's Rights, Child Development and Family Welfare (MWRCDFW)[xix]. The Ministry was given responsibility for legal issues and changes concerning women, children and the family as well as to initiate policy for the welfare of women and children. It also attempted to work together with women's organisations, by grouping them under a council, thereby taking over the role of the earlier women's fronts/alliances and weakening existing ones. One of the units of the Ministry, the National Women's Council (NWC), acts as coordinator and communicator between the state and women's associations. Women's associations that are registered with the NWC obtain a small grant and do their own fundraising[xx]. They are expected to work together and form a pressure group, advocate for women's issues and concerns and recommend actions that the Ministry can then take up at a higher level.

However, women's associations have not been assuming the role they were meant to, largely because of their ageing membership and the fact that most members are housewives[xxi]. These women are mainly under patriarchal control and have to adhere to conservative notions of respectable femininity. They therefore do not propose transformative ideas and plans for women. The lack of feminist orientation and activism on the part of these women's groups can also be explained by their lack of autonomy as many are linked to socio-religious organisations and are communal based, whereas others are linked to political parties (MLF, 1988). Each political party has its group of women political agents heading the small women's associations all over the island. Hence, the endeavour of the Ministry to group women's organisations together has not been able to build a strong and focused women's pressure group which would raise the critical feminist consciousness. Unfortunately, the resources and space created within the Ministry has been taken over by women political agents acting in the interest of men in political parties. This has alienated autonomous women's organisations and dampened women's critical voice. It has also weakened the existing women's fronts and alliances as the Ministry has taken over the role as the central institutional body representing women's rights and welfare in the country.

Despite the diluted activism of women's associations, serious and life threatening problems, namely domestic violence and backstreet abortion that affect women across class and community, led to the resurgence of feminist activism. Although the outreach was not as strong as in the 1970s as the Ministry eventually took control of the matter, these problems nonetheless brought women's groups together. Domestic violence has culminated in widely reported deaths in the country over the years. SOS Femmes played a primordial role in making this *private* issue a public and national concern[xxii]. Other women's organisations that supported this cause include Genderlinks and Women in Networking (WIN). Genderlinks raised awareness on this issue through the press and WIN did fundraising for SOS Femmes. Following the sustained pressure from the women's groups, the MWRCDFW took the matter to parliament and domestic violence became a criminal office with the enactment of the Protection from Domestic Violence Act in 1997. However, domestic violence remains a major social problem in Mauritius and so far actions have been taken on an adhoc basis and implementation of the law is not thorough.

Activism in favour of abortion has been more divisive among women's groups. Abortion has been illegal since colonial rule and successive governments have been reluctant to take up this matter in parliament because of strong resistance from the Catholic Church and Muslim religious groups. A few women's organisations have been lobbying for an amendment of the penal code which criminalised abortion. A Common Front on Abortion was set up in 2009 in order to demand immediate suspension of the existing law following the tragic death of photographic reporter, Marie-Noelle Derby. This women's front included MLF, Mauritius Family Planning Welfare Association and Women in Networking (WIN). SOS Femmes, Genderlinks as well as human rights, health and labour organisations supported this cause. A Bill proposing the legalisation of abortion under specific conditions was brought to the National Assembly in 2012[xxiii]. A common religious front led by the Catholic Church and supported by the Anglican Church and representatives from the Muslim and Buddhist communities opposed the bill. This front also included women representatives of these religious groups, highlighting identity divisions in women's voices. The law was finally passed with only

20 per cent of MPs voting against. This was a victory of the women's front, although the law does not fully legalize abortion and poor women are still vulnerable.

Mobilisation for women's political representation

The 21st century witnessed a shift in the energy and focus of women's organisations towards lobbying for feminist issues within the formal political sphere as they became more closely aligned with global women's movements. New feminist oriented women's organisations that lobbied for a greater presence of women in parliament were formed during this period. Their actions were very bold, transgressing dominant conservative cultural values and notions of respectable femininity.

FédèrAction, a women's platform set up in March 2005 by a group of women from an elite background (academics, barristers, consultants and journalists), lobbied for a more equitable society and a real democracy where the rights and dignity of women would be respected and upheld. FédèrAction organised a public protest walk on 28th March 2005 in Port Louis to lobby for the respect of women's rights and for all political parties to field one woman candidate in each constituency in the upcoming national election. The press reported that the protest march had about 150 participants to 200 participants[xxiv], mainly women. Although the march began as a neutral and non-political manifestation, it later took on a partisan stand with negative slogans directed the then Minister of Women's Rights, Arianne Navarre-Marie, asking her to "come out" of her office and join the march[xxv]. Women politicians from the governing parties were, on the one hand, alienated by the action and language of some members of FédèrAction, which they considered to be too radical. On the other hand, they may have been restricted by their political duties and party discipline. FédèrAction is no longer active mainly because of funding and time constraints, yet its initiative to raise awareness on the issue of women's marginal presence in parliament was an important component of the women's lobby for political space. However, the mass identification and participation of women from all sections of society was lacking. The small gathering of women at the march indicates that the bulk of the women population either did not identify with this movement and its cause or was unwilling or fearful to transgress conservative cultural norms of respectable femininity.

The 'Majority Party', set up by Paula Atchia in March 2005, was the first women's party of Mauritius[xxvi]. It aimed specifically at securing a critical mass of women in parliament in the 2005 general elections. The Majority Party functioned as an autonomous women's group and claimed to be feminist in inspiration since it recognised the unique political contribution women could make given their cognitive specificities[xxvii]. During its political campaign, the Majority Party carried out information and sensitisation campaigns to encourage women to register as voters and also to vote for women and made extensive use of email to reach out to people. Funding was a major problem and the party also experienced difficulties during its electoral campaign. The Majority Party had planned to present a maximum of 20 candidates, with one in each constituency[xxviii]. It had also opened its doors to women candidates from the other political parties, who had not been given a ticket but still wanted to stand for election[xxix]. However, the party finally presented only four candidates for the 2005 election. Apart from Paula Atchia, the other three candidates[xxx] of the Majority Party stood for election in the constituencies where they resided.

The very low candidature highlights the fact that the party experienced major difficulties in attracting a good number of potential candidates for the election. Patriarchal forces acting through threats of physical violence and alienation from the family proved to be major obstacles to most women who wished to join the Majority Party and stand for election. Moreover, since it was a feminist body, the party was also viewed with suspicion by men as well as by women. None of the candidates of the Majority Party was elected and the party received very little support from the women population it was working so hard to represent. Paula Atchia acknowledges that the main weakness of the party and its strategy was the failure to 'get all the women together'[xxxi]. The party thus appears to have operated in complete isolation. The experience of Paula Atchia and her party highlight the lack of female solidarity and shared political interests of women. The only accomplishment of the Majority Party was its contribution towards raising general awareness on the need for a greater number of women in parliament.

MediaWatch Organisation, formed in 2003 and later known as Genderlinks Mauritius, has also been actively lobbying for an increased presence of women in parliament. It has organised talks, seminars and published articles about women's marginal presence in parliament. It is a branch of Genderlinks Southern Africa, which is an African feminist network and has benefited from financial support, foreign expertise and training. It has been lobbying for the Mauritian Government to abide by its commitment to the 1997 Southern African Development Community (SADC) Gender Protocol which mandates a 30 per cent presence of women in parliament. On the eve of elections, it has organised workshops and seminars where political leaders were invited to present their parties' commitment towards gender equality. However, there was often considerable political bickering at the workshops with political leaders not attending[xxxii].

Another women's organisation - Women in Networking (WIN), set up in May 2006, has also been lobbying for an increased presence of women in the Mauritian parliament through its affiliated branch Women in Politics (WIP). The main goal is to empower women so that they were able to enjoy the rights and freedoms mentioned in article 1 of the Universal Declaration of Human Rights[xxxiii]. One of its aims is to develop 30 women leaders per annum who will be able to influence decision-making in all spheres, and lead to the transformation of politics in Mauritius with the doubling of the number of women in Parliament. WIP has been organising training courses for women, mentoring and training them to assume leadership positions and participate in active politics. Debates and seminars on the theme of 'women and politics' however do not draw large audiences, indicating that the majority of the women in the country are either not aware of the importance of having a gender balance in parliamentary representation, or they do not foresee the presence of more women in parliament as spearheading any meaningful change to their lives.

Women's parliamentary representation was 17.1 per cent with 12 women members of parliament (MPs) following the 2005 election. The figure rose to 18.8 per cent with 13 women MPs in 2010 whereas it dropped to 11.4 per cent with 8 women MPs following the 2014 election. These figures highlight the fact that the issue of parliamentary representation has proven to be highly divisive among the various women's organisations in the country due to competing political ideologies, women's multiple identities and conflicting demands on their loyalty. Intersectionality becomes a major obstacle to the endeavours of women's organisations seeking to enhance women's political space. Women are often sympathetic to the feminist demand for more women in parliament but are loyal to the political parties that their families support. Hence, on the issue of women's representation in parliament, there is a need for conscientisation to be done at all levels and greater collaboration among the different groups of women.

Conclusion

The experience of women's organisations and the women's movement in postcolonial Mauritius highlights the significance of autonomy for successful mobilisation and safeguarding of women's rights and entitlements, particularly in the context of the Mauritian plural society. Women's groups have historically been connected to patriarchal bodies, especially religious organisations and political parties, which have hindered the realisation of a critical feminist consciousness and the forging of a strong women's lobby necessary for change in regard to women's rights. The autonomous and semi-autonomous feminist-oriented women's organisations of the 1970s were able to forge strategic feminist alliances that successfully lobbied for women's rights. The trajectory and experience of the women's organisations also show that women's rights issues have the potential to unite women from different backgrounds and communities. 50 years after independence and for the future, a strong women's lobby that gives priority to women's gendered interests and rights remains crucial. Religion and politics have proved to be largely divisive in Mauritian society and women's rights and entitlements have often consequently been marginalised. This is pertinent when it comes to women's representation in parliament, women's sexual and reproductive rights and the longstanding problem of backstreet abortion in Mauritius. The experience of the more recently formed women's organisations to lobby for political space for women also highlights the need to reach out women across all levels of society as was done by the women's groups in the 1970s. Only then will the women's lobby be strong and representative of the women population of the country.

References

Baldez, L. (2002) *Why Women Protest: Women's Movements in Chile.* UK: Cambridge University Press.

Basu, A. (2005) *Women, Political Parties and Social Movements in South Asia.* Occasional Paper 5, Geneva: UNRISD.

Becker, H. (1995) *Namibian Women's Movement 1980 to 1992: From Anti-colonial Resistance to Reconstruction.* Frankfurt: Centre for Intercultural Communication.

Bissoondoyal, U. (1990) *Promises to Keep.* Mauritius: Editions de L'Ocean Indien; India: Wiley Eastern Ltd.

Collins, P.H. (2000) *Black Feminist Thought: Knowledge, Consciousness and the Politics of Empowerment.* 2nd Edition. New York: Routledge.

Crenshaw, K. (1991) 'Mapping the Margins: Intersectionality, Identity Politics and Violence against Women of Color', *Stanford Law Review* 43(6): 1241-1299.

Dommen, E. and Dommen, B. (1999) *Mauritius: An Island of Success – A Retrospective Study 1960–1993.* New Zealand: Pacific Press; Oxford: James Currey.

Dumont, C. (1976) 'Aujourd'hui! Avec la "Women Self-Help Association... Et la ligue féministe"' *Virginie – Le Magazine de la Mauricienne.* No.2, pp. 22 – 24.

Emrith, M. (1994) *History of the Muslims in Mauritius.* Mauritius: Editions Le Printemps.

Eriksen, T.H. (1998) *Common Denominators: Ethnicity, Nation-Building and Compromise in Mauritius.* Oxford, New York: Berg.

Fenton, S. (1999) *Ethnicity: Racism, Class and Culture.* UK: Macmillan.

Gunganah, B., Ragobur, S. And Varma, O.N. (1997) *Beyond Inequalities: Women in Mauritius.* Mauritius & Harare: MAW, SARDC.

Jayawardena, K. (1986) *Feminism and Nationalism in the Third World.* London & New Jersey: Zed Books.

Jeffery, P. (1998) 'Agency, Activism and Agendas' in P. Jeffery and A. Basu (eds) *Appropriating Gender: Women's Activism and Politicized Religion in South Asia.* London and New York: Routledge.

Laclau, E. and Mouffe, C. (1985) *Hegemony and Socialist Strategy.* UK: Verso.

Lerner, G. (1993) *The Creation of Feminist Consciousness: From the Middle Ages to Eighteen-seventy.* Oxford, New York: Oxford University Press.

L'Express (24.05.06) *'Mlle France de la Giroday évalue 25 ans des écoles ménagères'*.

Le Mauricien (16.03.05) *'Politique: Création d'un parti composé uniquement de femmes'*.

Le Mauricien (20.03.05) *'Parti de la majorité: Présentation officielle des candidates lundi'*.

Mauritius Research Council. (2003) *Study on the Evolution of Women and Gender Development over Three Generations in Mauritius*. Rose-Hill, Mauritius: MRC.

Mohanty, C.T. (1991) 'Catrographies of Struggle: Third World Women and the Politics of Feminism' in C.T. Mohanty, A. Russo and L. Torres (eds) *Third World Women and the Politics of Feminism*. Bloomington and Indianapolis: Indiana University Press.

Mouffe, C. (1992) 'Feminism, Citizenship and Radical Democratic Politics' in J. Butler and J.W. Scott (eds) *Feminists Theorize the Political*. London and New York: Routledge.

Moutou, B. (2000) *Ile Maurice: Récits de son Histoire Contemporaine*. Mauritius: B. Moutou.

Muvman Liberasyon Fam. (1983) 'The Need for an Independent Women's Movement in Mauritius.' in M. Davis (ed) *Third World – Second Sex*. London: Zed Books.

Muvman Liberasyon Fam. (1988) *The Women's Liberation Movement in Mauritius*. Mauritius: Ledikasyon pu Travayer.

Nursimloo, A. (1979) 'Le Silence des Femmes' *Virginie – Le Magazine de la Mauricienne*. No.16, pp. 44 – 54.

Oodiah, M. (1989) *MMM 1969 – 1989: 20 ans d'histoire*. Mauritius: M. Oodiah.

Orian, M. (1980) 'L'année 1979 au féminin: Réalisations, problèmes, difficultés, projets.' *Virginie – Le Magazine de la Mauricienne*. No.15, pp. 37 – 43.

Ramtohul, R. (2009) *'Women and Politics in a Plural Society: The Case of Mauritius'*, (PhD thesis) University of Cape Town, South Africa (unpublished).

Rughoonundon, S. (2000) *La Femme Indo-Mauricienne - Son Cheminement*. Mauritius: Editions Capucines.

Salo, E. (1999) 'From Woman to Women: Feminist Theory and the Diverse Identities of South African Feminists' in K.K. Prah (ed) *Knowledge in Black and White*. South Africa: Centre for Advanced Studies of African Society.

Simmons, A.S. (1982) *Modern Mauritius: The Politics of Decolonization*. Bloomington: Indiana University Press.

Spelman, E. (1988) *Inessential Woman: Problems of Exclusion in Feminist Thought*. Boston: Beacon Press.

---

[i] The Franco-Mauritians and the Creoles are Catholic, the Indian community - Muslim and Hindu, and the small Chinese community - Buddhist and/or Catholic. While the Franco-Mauritians, Hindus, Muslims and Chinese have retained cultural ties to their original homelands, the Creoles who are descendants from the slaves brought to Mauritius from East Africa have no such ties (Simmons, 1982).

[ii] Furnivall (1948), Smith (1965) – cited in Fenton (1999).

[iii] The Code Napoleon, backed by the Catholic Church and enacted in 1804, classified married women with children, the insane and criminals as politically incompetent. It restricted women's legal and civil rights, made married women economically and legally subject to their husbands and declared that they belonged to the family, not to public life. This legislation also forbade women to attend political meetings or to wear trousers (Lerner, 1993).

[iv] The Arya Samaj movement draws on the teachings of Maharishi Dayanand who emphasised equal rights in marriage for men and women (MRC, 2003). It launched its first women's association in Vacoas in 1912,

geared towards promoting education among women and a school for girls was opened in the village of Bon Accueil in 1922. In 1931, the group launched another women's association in Port Louis. It also held conferences for women in 1933, 1965 and 1970. When the Arya Samaj movement started, Hindu women suffered from low status, lack of access to education and discrimination. Indo-Mauritian girls were being married from ages 9 to 12 and boys from ages 14 to 18 (Rughoonundon, 2000). Child marriage was prevalent, thus causing many Hindu women to face early widowhood and poverty (MRC, 2003).

[v] The Jan Andolan movement was launched by the Bissoondoyal brothers - Basdeo and Sookdeo. The Jan Andolan movement aimed at defending the cause of people of Indian origin, the promotion of Indian culture and literacy among the Indians and the propagation of Indian languages. The movement was highly involved in the struggle for the rights of the Indian community in Mauritius and it encouraged Hindu women to participate as voters in the elections preceding independence.

[vi] L'Express (24.05.81) – reprinted in L'Express (24.05.06).

[vii] Interview with Sheela Baguant, founder member of Women's Self-Help Association – 25.01.07.

[viii] Dumont, C. (1976) 'Aujourd'hui! Avec la "Women Self-Help Association... Et la ligue féministe"' *Virginie – Le Magazine de la Mauricienne*. No.2, pp. 22 – 24.

[ix] It was previously known as La Ligue Féminine du MMM, which was the women's section of the *Mouvement Militant Mauricien* (MMM). After a few months, Shirin Aumeeruddy-Cziffra took the movement out of the MMM, to function autonomously as *La Ligue Féministe*. This strategy was adopted because as a women's section of the MMM, most of the women were assuming a secondary role to their male colleagues, thereby defeating the purpose of a feminist organisation (Interview with Shirin Aumeeruddy-Cziffra – 31.01.07). The Ligue Féministe nevertheless remained close to the MMM.

[x] Dumont (1976), Oodiah (1989).

[xi] Interview with Shirin Aumeeruddy-Cziffra – 31.01.07.

[xii] Founder members include Marie-Josée Baudot and Annie Cadinouche.

[xiii] Interview with Marie-Josée Baudot in Orian, M. (1980) 'L'année 1979 au féminin: Réalisations, problèmes, difficultés, projets.' *Virginie – Le Magazine de la Mauricienne*. No.15, p 42 (translated from the French text).

[xiv] Interview with Shirin Aumeeruddy-Cziffra – 31.01.07.

[xv] It was formed by four women's organisations: the MLF, the Ligue Féministe, the women's section of the MMMSP led by Loga Virahsawmy, and the women's section of the Christian Movement for Socialism led by Jocelyne Minerve.

[xvi] It was only in 1995 that the Constitution was amended to include sex in the definition of non-discrimination.

[xvii] The case is called Shirin Aumeeruddy-Cziffra and nineteen Mauritian women against the Government of Mauritius. Available online at http://www.bayefsky.com/pdf/100_mauritius35a.pdf (accessed on 5th October 2008). There were 20 Mauritian women involved in this case, three of whom were married to foreign husbands - Shirin Aumeeruddy-Cziffra, Patty Craig and Nalini Burn (Interview with Shirin Aumeeruddy-Cziffra – 31.01.07).

[xviii] The MAW had the collaboration of France Boyer de la Giroday, founder of Écoles Ménagères, from Association des Femmes Mauriciennes, as well as from the small rural women's associations. The leftist women's and political organisations, namely La Ligue Féministe and MLF, were not part of the MAW. This was the main difference between MAW and Solidarité Fam since the latter had the membership of both autonomous and political women's organisations.

[xix] The establishment of the MWRCDFW was catalysed by the adherence of the Mauritian state to the United Nations and also by the proceedings of the 1975 World Conference on Women. In 2010, the appellation of the Ministry of Women's Rights, Child Development and Family Welfare was changed to Ministry of Gender Equality, Child Development and Family Welfare.

[xx] Interview with Mohini Bali – Head of Women's Unit, MWRCDFW – 09.02.07.

[xxi] Interview with Mohini Bali – Head of Women's Unit, MWRCDFW – 09.02.07.

[xxii] SOS Femmes was set up in 1989 by the late Rada Gungaloo. It offered free legal advice to victims and also operated a shelter for women where battered women could seek refuge.

[xxiii] The bill, which was approved by the government's Council of Ministers on 4th May 2012, would legalize abortion in cases of danger to the woman's 'mental health,' a vague concept that can be used to justify virtually any abortion. It would also permit abortions in cases or rape, or statutory rape of a minor under the age of 16, as well as eugenic abortions in cases of fetal deformity. Source: https://www.lifesitenews.com/news/christians-muslims-buddhists-unite-to-fight-legalization-of-abortion-on-isl (accessed on 01.04.15).

[xxiv] L'Express (29.03.05).

[xxv] L'Express (29.03.05). "Marche pacifique: FédèrAction n'attire que 200 personnes".

[xxvi] Paula Atchia was also a founder member of FédèrAction and had participated in the protest march.

[xxvii] Manifesto of the Majority Party (2005: 1).

[xxviii] Le Mauricien (16.03.05) 'Politique: Création d'un parti composé uniquement de femmes.

[xxix] Le Mauricien (20.03.05) 'Parti de la majorité: Présentation officielle des candidates lundi'.

[xxx] Marina Mohun was teaching in a private primary school, while Valérie Vengrasamy was in charge of a pre-primary school. Rozy Kheddoo was at one time a political activist for the MMM, and was vice-president of the Sugar Industry Labour Welfare Fund.

[xxxi] Interview with Paula Atchia – 05.07.07.

[xxxii] Interview with Loga Virahsawmy - 10.01.07.

[xxxiii] Article 1 of the Universal Declaration of Human Rights states that 'All human beings are born free and equal in dignity and rights'.

The Materiality of Multiculturalism
An Archaeological Perspective

KRISH SEETAH, DIEGO CALAON, SAŠA ČAVAL,
ALESSANDRA CIANCIOSI AND ALEKSANDER PLUSKOWSKI

Introduction

The power of materials, of materiality, lies in the nuances and contours of how objects can be read, and interpreted. The trend in archaeology has seen an important transition from observing finds as static objects, to having their own biography (Appadurai, 1986), with a distinct capacity to connect people through time and across space (Joy, 2009). More than this, as we look more closely at what an object biography actually entails, it becomes clear that the ability to connect people, by design, creates a network (Meskell, 2013: 338) and that performance can be an integral part of the production, consumption and discard of 'things' (Shanks, 2004). This is the theoretical position from which the authors approach the study of artefacts as discussed in this chapter. When engaging with materials in this way, there is an obvious aim of providing a voice to the groups, the workforce, that made up the larger part of the diaspora to the island; specifically, a voice in addition to the historic narrative, be that complementary or contradictory. Ultimately, this view of materials places a particular emphasis on hybridity, the coming together of different ethnic groups, with disparate social and economic positions. The chapter will develop to discuss a range of more commonly considered artefact groups; however, rather than an object *per se* we start with a commodity, one that shaped the lives and landscape of Mauritius.

Sugar defined the colonial economies of the Atlantic and Indian Ocean from the period of European expansion, marking the transition of sugar from a luxury product limited to high-status consumers to a widely available commodity with a global market. This transformation of the commercial and social value of sugar, which took place over the course of the 16th century, also involved a dramatic shift in the infrastructure associated with its production; from small-scale Mediterranean installations to Atlantic plantations powered by large numbers of slaves. Sugar production, originating most probably in India, spread to the Middle East and following the Arab conquests, was introduced to North Africa and the Mediterranean islands (Galloway, 1989). Following the establishment of the crusader states in the Levant from the end of the 11th century, Europeans also adopted cane sugar production, provided a growing market for it and became heavily involved in its trade. The direct material traces of sugar production centres consist of assemblages of ceramic sugar mould vessels and molasses jars, as well as the remains of presses and mills. However, a crucial component was their supporting settlements which provided the labour, and which remain less well known (Burke, 2004). In the western Mediterranean, sugar production was adopted following the incremental Christian conquests of Iberia. The shift occurred when the Portuguese and Spanish established sugar plantations on the eastern Atlantic islands, particularly in the Canaries where the rapid expansion of the industry in the early 16th century reflected the exploitation of the enslaved indigenous population for labour and the clearance of native woodlands for fuel and fields. Sugar cane and its associated production culture were then transported to the Caribbean. Whilst sugar-processing technology changed in the 17th century, its reliance on slave labour also resulted in a new, integrated relationship between processing centres, settlements, communication networks and landscapes (Singleton, 2016). The sugar economy of Mauritius, which grew rapidly in the last decades of the 18th century and after a short hiatus again from 1815, must be situated in this broader context (Teelock, 2009: 88, 226). Growing, processing and exporting sugar cane defined the physical relationship between settlements, landscapes, and people in Mauritius. For example, the demand for labour following the growth of the industry and the abolition of slavery prompted plantation owners to contract indentured workers.

Objects of Memory

Having briefly set the stage for how objects and commodities have come to have meaning and formed a bridge between the wider global context and Mauritius, the following now looks at how materials can serve as a form of memory to help us better understand the nuances of colonialism, and the post-independence period. Moving from the level of landscape to specific personal objects, the next section traces the ways in which material studies can shed light on the modern island.

Landscape: materiality of settlement and the roots urbanisation

The Old Labourers' Quarters at Trianon were listed as National Heritage on the 22nd July 1974 (Peerthum, 2010). The monument is one of the few standing structures that witnesses the daily-life of the sugar plantation workers brought to the island during the period of indenture (Green, 1976; Teelock, 2001: 229-30). As such, Trianon barracks represent a significant heritage structure connected with the indenture experience (Andiapen and Nemchand, 2011; Nemchand, 2014). Archaeology has added to this idea, highlighting the complexity of the social relations that the monument incorporates (Calaon *et al.*, 2013). The barracks' materiality demarcates the shift from slavery to indenture. The monument reveals the multifaceted notion of 'house', and 'private or social space', during a period that was pivotal to the development of contemporary Mauritius. Archaeology undertaken on the topography surrounding the barracks evidences a transformation in the use of land and its relationship with the local workforce. The barracks' design depicts contested negotiations between different social agents: colonial elites, slaves, and indentured labourers. If we enlarge the picture, it is possible to use archaeological tools not only to describe Trianon sugar estate, but also to rethink the development of urbanism in contemporary Mauritius.

Trianon Barracks are rectangular stone accommodations with vaulted roofs arranged in terrace fashion. They present serial dwelling units, slightly elevated from the soil, with front and back doors, and a window on the façade (Calaon *et al.*, 2013: 123-4). The design is derived from the well-known military British colonial architecture (Home and King, 2016). Following an army cantonment model, the architecture follows a principle by which similar buildings are orthogonally organized around a courtyard, creating functional and organized spaces hierarchically positioned on the estate. The organisation of the cantonment model addresses key social issues in the colonial settlement, such as racial segregation and ethnic superiority (Mitter, 1986). The design also tackles public health concerns (Home, 2013: 122-5). The model fits with the need to house groups of people, probably divided by gender, who were supposed to spend only their nights and short spans of free time in the barracks. Kitchen, privies, and work-related spaces were meant to be collective and were placed in specific common areas.

This architectural arrangement provided good control over the workforce. Scholars related the military type of housing with the impacts of abolition: with the contraction in the number of workers, the planters were mandated to improve conditions for their workforce and, at the same time, control them in an effective manner (Nelson, 2016: 116). The historical documentation shows that the idea of a salubrious space in the masters' mind, collided with the sense of 'a good' place to live for the labourers; they abhorred the barrack-type building, essentially because they were not adequate for a family unit and they did not address health standards (RCIM, 1875: 2098-99). In other words, masters and landlords were providing dwellings to the new contract workforce using an old notion of housing, suited for the late slavery era, which diverged from the ethnic, social and religious requirements that the mainly north-Indian workers were looking for in a house.

Archaeological research has demonstrated that, when Trianon barracks were seeded to the indentured labourers, substantial improvements were made to house single-family units. For example, wooden divisions and a garret were set up to create interior rooms. A canopy was added to the back to be used as a kitchen area (Calaon *et al.*, 2013). Family type groups, also marked by a significant degree of religious and caste varieties, disliked living in such communal environments and they preferred single hut-type dwelling units, with straw roofs. The huts were less robust, but they provided much more flexibility in the internal division, and, being positioned in the landscape of the camp in a less structured and hierarchical way, they offered the possibility to have a private courtyard for cooking and social activities.

Were the stones barracks the standard slave dwelling type in late 18th and early 19th century Mauritius? At this stage of the research, we do not have an unequivocal answer, but historical, landscape, and archaeological surveys have pointed to similar structures, previously not identified. Examples from other estates have similar stone dwellings constructed during the early period of indenture, some of which have survived. Additional examples are documented in the historical sources (RCIM, 1875). It is unlikely that all were as monumental as those at Trianon, and probably many of the barracks were built with simple dry-stone walls. This seems to be the case, for example, on the Bras d'Eau sugar estate. Archaeological surveys point to two different areas of dwellings, with two different construction types. Barrack-terrace type units, with shared spaces, characterize one form. The second is clearly defined by the presence of several basements of single huts, with small family courtyards and private open-areas. Subsequent phases of archaeological excavations will prove if the chronological/typological data can be used to distinguish slave and indenture dwellings.

Undoubtedly less than 5 per cent of the indentured labourers in Trianon lived in the barracks; 95 per cent inhabited huts distributed around several camps (Calaon *et al.*, 2013; Seetah *et al.*, 2017 - see maps as part of Figure 11). The fact that the perishable construction materials of those camps did not last, and, on the contrary, the stone barracks are still standing today, provoked an overexposure of the barracks themselves. In the historical narrative, they became the prototype of habitation for the indentured experience. Archaeology is helping to provide a new narrative, re-contextualizing the setting of the estates, and focusing on the material and spatial evidence.

As seen in the Atlantic, where the archaeology of slavery has been able to describe the passage from barrack style co-residential dwellings to family-unit-type architectures (e.g. Chesepeake area in Virginia, with the representative case of Monticello; see also Singleton, 1985; Vlach, 1992; Morgan, 1998; Fesler 2004; Heath, 2010), material culture and Geographic Information System (GIS) analyses are helping to better explain the intricate spatial hierarchy that shaped the Mauritian sugar estate landscape, and the built environment. Taking a broader view, Trianon serves as a point of departure for assessing the development of urbanization on the island as a whole. The built area of the estate, constructed after abolition but obviously retaining colonial design cues, is structured around the master's house, detached by a garden from the other parts of the estate. We can define this model as the 'Big House and Slave quarters' pattern, well known from the Atlantic context. The monumental master's house sits as the top of a private territorial system, governing the workforce through a physical and material juxtaposition: hierarchy became a physically reinforced social distinctions, substantiated through design and materiality of the buildings (Anthony, 1976; Ellis & Ginsburg, 2010). Stables and service areas were located near the workforce, but not too far from the master. The plantation was understandably distant, but still within eyesight. The barracks were located between the house and plantation. The design mandate foresaw that at least a group of workers needed to reside in the vicinity, providing services, and serving as a liaison between the master's family and the sugar mill. We can imagine that this setting was almost the standard during the French period in Mauritius. The main shift in spatial organization during the period of indenture was the introduction of camps. These were located some distance from the master's house, connected to both the plantation fields and the chimneys, and were well defined and enclosed. New rural landscapes started to appear: groups of family houses, internally organized according to social/religious elements rather than hierarchy/working needs. Roads and paths were opened to connect the new settlements, proto-villages, to the core of the estate and to specific areas, i.e., the temple, the river, etc.

When considering the general urbanisation of the island through time, one can appreciate how critical the landscape/material perspective is. During the French period, the estates were hierarchically orientated around the master's house, with the slave quarters and the infrastructures centralised. During the British period, a dispersed settlement gradually started to emerge with camps/villages scattered around the property: a direct result of increasing numbers of indentured labourers. After the sugar crisis at the end of the 19th century, many workers purchased land to build their own homes (Allen, 1999: 115-30). The distribution of the recent, self-generated, rural villages replicates the design of the camp. In the absence of urban planning, the new villages were constructed along the main thoroughfares, and strongly connected to family ties, i.e., the next generation building adjacent or above the parent's property, much more than hierarchical social patterns.

In concluding this section, it is worth briefly applying the same principles developed from a GIS approach to other aspects of the island's built environment. French Port-Louis followed an ordered design, built along military cues. Government and martial zones dominated the space between the city and the harbour. Free people were settled in a European style planned city, with public spaces, churches, the theatre, squares, etc., and houses open to the street. Slave and other non-free individuals employed in the city had their quarters nearby (AGTF, 2014). This urban model did not fit with the new society created after the transition to indenture and the implications this had on settlement design. The communion between the master's house and the camp did not form the same bond as during the period of slavery. Since the beginning of the 20th century, Mauritius has abandoned the French Port-Louis city-like landscape, adopting a progressively dispersed settled pattern. Rural villages, production areas, and affluent, mainly coastal, residential areas now form distinct settlement types. This has created a unique landscape that typifies Mauritius, encompasses in its materiality tangible features of the negotiated social history of the island.

Religion: the intersection of tangible and intangible

While we readily observe the possibilities for using changes in landscape to understand urbanisation, for the Mauritian context specifically, the 'religious landscape' is also of particular relevance to any assessment of how the modern island developed. The Mauritian iteration captures Christianity, Islam, Hinduism, Buddhism, and *Longanis*, the local syncretic religious practice (Vaughan, 2005; Seetah, 2015a; 2015b; Allen, 2015; Teelock, 2009; Čaval, 2018). Since all identified religious structures (i.e., churches, temples, mosques, shrines) in present-day Mauritius are still in use, archaeological excavations of these locations are unnecessary. In the (temporary) paucity of religious material culture associated with the past and obtainable through archaeological excavation, landscape is a fundamental point of departure from which to undertake research into religious plurality.

The context of landscape occupancy plays a significant role in shaping the dynamics of diaspora. Economy, and particularly land use, guided the location of migrants' settlements and thus indirectly influenced the spread of religions around the island. In Mauritius, this is exemplified in settlement distribution following indenture. Facilitating an imagined sense of continuity with the past is an important function of religion during periods of diaspora. As part of the territorialisation of communities on the island, sacred structures were erected, initially corresponding to the religious denominations of workers on respective sugar estate. Eventually settlements were named according to meaningful places from, mainly but not exclusively, the workers' homeland. With the adoption of imported geographical terminology, the villages became markers of identity, and also served as waypoints for other communities and religions within the context of public space. The significant factors for the distribution of such names were the status of religion in society, social attitudes towards cultural pluralism, the numbers of 'co-ethnic' and 'co-religion' people settled in an area, and the size and presence of other religious and ethnic groups. Such was the practice not only by Hindus, who adopted geographical names (such as Benares, Gohkoola, Tranquebar, etc.) but also by Christians (e.g., Verdun, Britannia, Albion, Helvetia) and Muslims (e.g., Medine, Yemen) (Trouillet, 2012; McLaughlin, 2005).

Religion is a unique cultural resource that frequently marks ethnic identity much more distinctively than customs. Religious beliefs and practices have been essential to immigrants for adaptation and reorganising their domestic and public lives in a new environment. Having come to Mauritius, either as estate owners, merchants, and craftsmen, or as slaves and indentured labourers, settlers gradually transformed and reinvented their rituals, festivals, traditions, and ceremonies. People turned to religion, particularly when the new setting was unfavourable (Mol, 1979; McLaughlin, 2005; Fogelin, 2007).

During slavery, the prohibition of slave gatherings made it almost impossible for slaves to stay connected to their religious practices. In 1685, the French king, Louis XIV issued the Code Noir, regulating slaves' main (non)rights: the life, death, purchase, religion, and treatment of slaves in all French colonies. The significance of religion is exemplified by the fact that the first seven of 59 articles focused on the religion of slaves, providing an idealized picture of religious life for enslaved peoples. Subsequently other Code Noirs were designed to define the conditions of slavery for individual French colonies respectively. The Code Noir for the Mascarene Islands was issued in 1723. Article I. indicated that all slaves had to be baptized within the first week of arrival, but only as Catholics, and not Protestant. Compared to Madagascar and Mozambique, where slaves were baptised before embarkation, in Mauritius, the Order of St. Lazarus was given responsibility to baptize slaves within two years of arrival. This directive was only moderately observed, although the names of slaves were changed to traditional Christian ones. The fact that many slaves had not actually been baptized became evident after abolition, with the missionary work of Père Laval (Tamby, 2011; de Vaux, 1801; Nagapen, 1984; Boswell, 2006). Seeking to emphasize the differentiation toward slaves and their descendants, with whom they ultimately shared the same religion and denomination, French planters started to practice Roman Catholicism more traditionally, for example celebrating Mass in Latin or French (Boswell, 2006; Nagapen, 1984; Eriksen, 1998). However, it is noteworthy that during this time, *Longanis*, a religious practice unique to Mauritius, was formed. Slavery has been referred to as 'social death' for bonded people; however, elements of intangible heritage, alongside traditional knowledge and customs which slaves incorporated into local *Longanis*, helped them in dealing with hardship and adversity (Čaval, 2018).

In contrast, during the period of indenture, especially relevant in the Mauritian case as the administration implemented a distinctive system, labourers were permitted to retain links to their own religions (Younger, 2009; Benedict, 1980). During the early stages of the indentured system, from 1834, men heavily dominated the migrant population, which in turn facilitated the emergence of Hanuman worship in Mauritius. Hanuman was and still is venerated as a great village deity in north India; however, he became particularly important for Hindu immigrants in Mauritius. The god was known for its celibacy, was mainly venerated by men, and was seen as a deity who could provide strength to overcome daily struggles. These are plausible reasons for his popularity among early indentured labourers. Popularly known also as Mahabir Swami, his shrines are still found in almost every Hindu Mauritian home (Hazareesingh, 1966; Ramhota, 1998; Selvam, 2012).

Contrary to other destinations of indentured labourers, such as Trinidad, where Indian customs and religious practices on plantations were derided and even forbidden, the immigrants in Mauritius were free to perform their religious practices. Initially, indentured workers sharing the same or similar identity were distributed between sugar estates in small numbers. As the need for labour grew, more people from the same region were employed on a single estate. Workers became more confident in expressing their religious identity, initially through the construction of shrines, and subsequently in more substantial structures, such as temples, churches, and mosques. Yet, to maintain their religious identities in the long term, they had to temporarily relinquish certain segments of their religion/culture (McLaughlin, 2005). *Lesser* traditions (i.e. Marathi, Tamil, Telugu Hinduism) had to be sacrificed so that the central ones (i.e. Hinduism) could survive: in the first decades of the indentured system, all Hindus shared the same places of worship, which hosted pan-Hindu deities. Gradually the Hindu subgroups individualized, and as soon as they were granted some land, they began with the construction of their own shrines and temples (Knott, 1986: 13; Ramhota, 1998). Hindus started crafting small shrines around their homes and in sugar cane fields (Figure 8) so that they could perform their daily *pujas*.

Realistically, the smallest object of public worship, a shrine, requires a negligible, if any, financial contribution compared to the construction of a larger structure, yet it provides the devotees with considerable religious consolation (Čaval, 2018). Shrines are a vital and the most abundant part of the cultural/religious landscape of Mauritius (Colwell-Chanthaphonh & de Salle-Essoo, 2014), a proper and accurate exhibit of the all-encompassing plurality of Mauritius. Set up by a religiously entangled community, they clearly display everyday needs and pragmatism. Often two or even three different religious denominations share one shrine structure. When developed even further, we observe a shrine structure of an architectural form, standardized by one denomination and used by another, as is the case of the Vishnu shrine in the former sugar estate l'Espérance, which employs the Christian architectural form of 'grotto' for a Hindu monument (Figure 9).

Figure 8: Cherie - Central structure in a Hindu shrine/ temple in a sugar cane field	**Figure 9a: The Christian 'grotto' architectural form used as a Hindu sacred architecture**

Figure 9b: Christian shrine in Triolet

Figure 9c: Hindu shrine in a sugar cane field of the former L'Espérance estate

A number of written sources highlight the instrumental role that planters played in facilitating workers' access to and maintenance of their religious customs and identities. Sugar estate owners allowed shrines, temples, mosques and churches to be built for and by immigrants. Planters were aware of the workers' dedication to their religions and were motivated to offer assistance in the construction of temples on estates. They provided the land upon which to build the temples, the building materials, financial contributions, and skilled workers to help in the construction. However, these were not acts of generosity, but rather a conscious expediency to motivate the labourers to perform better. In 1872-73 the Royal Commissioners stated that:

> On Stanley Estate, we saw a Roman Catholic chapel built for and by the immigrants in their camps; but, on the other hand, on Stanley, as well as on several other estates, there are Hindu temples [...] Many of these temples are well and solidly built, and equal to the majority of those built in country villages in India." (Frere & Williamson, 1875: paragraph 2880).

The same patterns continued into the 20th century: for the construction of a Shivala in the 1950's, the land and building materials were donated by the "large Franco-Mauritian owned estate which [...] gives employment to many villagers," village residents, including some non-Hindus, covering other expenses (Couacaud, 2012; Trouillot, 2012; Ramhota, 1998). Ultimately, the particular development of religious identity in Mauritius reflects the array of influences that have come to characterise the religious landscape of the island, with now a rich mosaic of temples, mosques and churches.

Personal materiality

As this chapter has developed, certain themes should by now be implicit. One in particular, identity, whether informed from a tangible landscape view or intangible personal one, forms a critical topic of enquiry. Identities in Mauritius were and remain multiple and fluid. They are the result of movement of people under colonialism, whether through forced or voluntary migrations. Diaspora can be traced through material culture, as tangible remains of a process that 'is about creating and maintaining identity in communities dispersed amongst other peoples. It is about local and non-local and how through processes of hybridity and creolization some groups of people can be both at the same time' (Lilley, 2004: 287).

As described above, religion is one of the most important characterisations of identity and culture. In Mauritius we can see the complexity of religious practices, in particular when observed within the context of burial practice, the result of a dynamic interchange of cultures and at times can be interpreted as symbols of community power, and resistance. The best-known archaeological example of this particular phenomenon in Mauritius is the site of Le Morne, located in the extreme southwestern corner of the island. It was particularly important for maroons, because it offered an isolated place to settle for runaway enslaved people (Seetah, 2015a).

165

Between 2009-2013 a planned excavation was carried on the 'Old Cemetery' of Le Morne. The cemetery itself is located on a small sandy islet, which is regularly cut off from the mainland by tidal oscillations. The archaeological finds, alongside the fact that the region was a stronghold for marooned slaves from the latter part of the 18th century (Allen, 1999) and the cemetery's first appearance on regional maps in 1880 (Descubes, 1888), suggests that the cemetery dates to the mid 1830s, around the period of emancipation (Seetah, 2015a). An initial survey revealed 49 grave structures, of which 24 structures were excavated, resulting in the recovery of 26 skeletons. Basalt rocks delineated the graves. Well-constructed trapezoidal coffins made of wooden panels, held together with iron nails, were recovered with regularity. Few additional objects were found, but they are incredibly meaningful given what they represent: the very essence of personal materiality for a heavily marginalized and disenfranchised group. The recovered artefacts include a series of bone buttons, mother-of-pearl buttons, glass bottles, a small number of French coins dating from 1812 to 1828, clay tobacco pipes, accompanied by related flints, manufactured in Britain. Gold earrings and other metal dress elements were sporadically recovered.

Figure 10: Le Morne, Grave 42

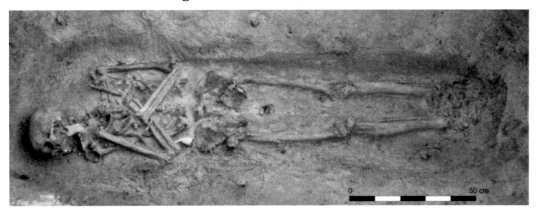

Even though the cemetery was marked with a cross on the map dated to 1880, the burial traditions do not reflect Christian practices. Furthermore, there is no evidence that the cemetery was consecrated. The orientation of the bodies to the west, the burial of neonatal and newborn individuals, and the inclusion of grave goods would suggest that African traditions were being followed (Seetah, 2015a). In particular, among the items recovered in the burials, we can distinguish objects connected with clothing (especially buttons) from objects placed deliberately inside the grave. The mother-of-pearl buttons suggest that they were dressed in relatively fine clothes; the tobacco pipes and occasional flints could be interpreted as 'slave material culture'. In fact they are often found in slave graves in the Atlantic region, but they are not documented in cemeteries associated with people of European descent (King, 2006: 310-311; Katz-Hyman and Rice, 2011). The burials themselves appear to reflect a population of some means, at least to the extent to which they could provision their deceased. The dead were buried in well-constructed coffins and they were placed in clearly delineated graves, which were maintained and cared for. This would seem to indicate that they were free people, but whether they had previously been enslaved remains unclear (Seetah, 2015a). We can tentatively conclude that the cemetery contains the remains of the first generation of freeborn Mauritians.

The material culture found in the graves concretely establishes that people buried in Le Morne 'Old Cemetery' participated in the British commercial economy. Most of the objects found, were clearly mass-produced outside Mauritius and widely marketed throughout the world. Pipes, buttons and glass bottles had similar wide networks of distribution during the early 18th century and at present there is no way to determine how these were obtained. The most significant point is that these objects were selected, and perhaps even purchased, by a group with some (likely small) means. Other objects may have been included, those that were perishable and which have not survived long enough for archaeological recovery. In particular, inside a burial equipped with many different objects (Figure 11), we found a glass bottle that was deliberately placed close to the head of the deceased, probably inside a pouch, close to a sequence of bone buttons. The particularity of this item is the shape of the bottle, typical of those used within a toiletry context. Indeed, the find was a cologne bottle, probably of French manufacture.

Glass bottles, along with pipes, ceramic sherds, and iron nails, were the most frequently recovered artefact types on colonial archaeological sites. The ubiquity of glass bottles in these contexts is the result of rapid technological innovation and commercialization in the glassmaking industry during the early colonial period (Hume, 1969: 60–71; Jones & Sullivan, 1989; Jones, 2011; Herremens *et al.*, 2014). Europeans not only consumed the alcohol contained in the glass bottles, but also traded it with slaves and labourers. Once this class of object entered into slaves' cultural practices, the bottles came to have particular significance as spiritual items, often appearing as grave goods (Rubertone, 2001) or as raw materials used to create tools (Porter, 2015).

Figure 11: Le Morne, Grave 23

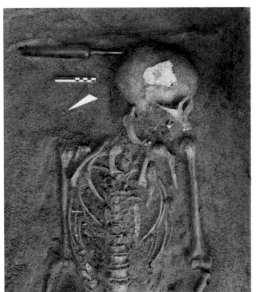

Figure 12: Detail of the glass bottle

Connections to a global context

The material culture of Mauritius expresses a high degree of connectivity with colonial and post-colonial trading networks. Whilst various products were imported to the island, the dominant export was sugar. This became the primary crop cultivated in Mauritius during the period of British rule, particularly after 1825 when colonial officials facilitated the export of Mauritian sugar to Britain's protected markets, which in turn prompted the rapid growth of sugar estates on the island. Production peaked in the mid-19th century and sugar remained the principal export through to the mid-20th century (Bräutigam, 2008: 139-140). As a result, sugar played a vital political role in state formation and Mauritius' transition from a colonial to independent state, but it also defined the cultural landscapes of the island, which today represent a palimpsest of slavery, indenture and the assertive break from the colonial past. Although sugar itself is largely invisible archaeologically, the material remnants of plantations whether as collections of buildings that now represent national monuments like Trianon, bounded spaces, fields and communication networks, represent one of the most striking material expressions that bridge the colonial and post-colonial past in Mauritius. Here, on estates such as Trianon, the daily lives of many Mauritians were organised and concentrated, and came to influence the island at large. This is well illustrated by the patchwork of religious structures that occupy virtually every type of settlement and habitat on the island, from the coast to the heart of plantation fields.

The mono-crop landscape of the sugarcane fields maintains the legacy of the colonial sugar estates, in which old Hindu shrines and temples still exist, and moreover, are still in use. Even though the former labourers' camps have been discarded, and the people have moved on, the old temples and shrines are regularly visited and provide spiritual comfort. Likewise, the religious structures in the urban locations have the advantage of never being out of sight; thus, their continuity is unquestioned. The 1968 Constitution's *'Freedom of creed and of religious belief'* gained another dimension with economic growth of the modern Mauritian population. New sacred structures, private and public, for all religions and beliefs, are being built consistently, continuing to connect people through time and across space via intangible heritage. As a complement, the material culture, some of which we observe in the most poignant of settings (the grave itself), was generated by these historic communities. Whether enslaved, indentured, free, part of the colonial administration, or the increasingly global mercantile world, it provides a tangible connection to the construction of the island's multi-ethnic and multi-social identities.

As archaeology becomes more systematic (Seetah, 2015b), and responds to a wider archaeological agenda, one that speaks to a slave and indentured past well beyond the boundaries of historic European monuments and estates – crucial elements, but unrepresentative of a common past – the subject has increasing relevance. New approaches are revealing the influence of disease and the relationship to climate (Seetah, 2018), and in the future will connect these ancient epidemics with the modern context. Archaeology is also playing an ever more important role in recognizing, promoting and valorising a broader range of heritage. A particularly noteworthy example is the Le Morne Old Cemetery, a site that is critical to our understanding of the slave past, but entirely detached from the 'estate' context. While the power of scientific, historical, and anthropological archaeologies are brought to bear under the umbrella of 'the archaeology of Mauritius', far more important than methods and theory is a movement, one that is gaining ground each year: a recognition of what archaeology means by the local population. All too often, archaeology has been seen as simply a complement to history or anthropology; it is not. When tens of thousands of visitors to the Aapravasi Ghat Interpretation Centre see the still-exposed excavations, painstakingly protected and integrated into the broader narrative in a tangible way, they observe direct evidence of the past: that is the true impact of archaeology. In this way, the subject becomes a vehicle for nationhood.

References

AGTF (2014) *A unique Place in Time and Space. A Pictorial Presentation of the Aapravasi Ghat World Heritage Site and the Indenture Experience in Mauritius (1834-2014)*. Port Louis: Aapravasi Ghat Trust Fund.

Allen, R.B. (1999) *Slaves, freedmen and indentured laborers in colonial Mauritius.* Cambridge: Cambridge University Press.

Allen, R.B. (2015) *European slave trading in the Indian Ocean, 1500–1850*. Ohio: Ohio University Press.

Andiapen, R. and Nemchand, A. (2011) 'The Conservation of Trianon Barracks', *Aapravasi Ghat Trust Fund Newsletter* 9: 23-24.

Anthony, C. (1976) 'The big house and the slave quarters, Part 1, Prelude to New World architecture', *Landscape,* 20(3): 8-19.

Appadurai, A. (ed) (1986) *The Social Life of Things*. Cambridge: Cambridge University Press.

Benedict, B. (1980) 'Slavery and indenture in Mauritius and Seychelles', in J.L Watson (ed) *Asian and African Systems of Slavery*. Oxford: Basil Blackwell.

Bossche, W.V.D., and Weegenaar, F. (2001) *Antique Glass Bottles: Their History and Evolution (1500-1850) Comprehensive, Illustrated Guide with a Worldwide Bibliography of Glass Bottles*. Antique Collector's Club.

Boswell, R. (2006) *Le Malaise Créole: Ethnic identity in Mauritius*. New York: Berghahn Books.

Bräutigam, D.A. (2008) 'Contingent capacity: export taxation and state-building in Mauritius', in O.H. Fjeldstad, D.A Bräutigam and M. Moore (eds) *Taxation and State-Building in Developing Countries: Capacity and Consent.* Cambridge: Cambridge University Press.

Burke, K.S. (2004) 'A Note on Archaeological Evidence for Sugar Production in the Middle Islamic Periods in Bilād al-Shām', *Mamlūk Studies Review* 8: 109-18.

Calaon, D. *et al.* (2013) 'Archaeological insights of the `indentured experience': The case of Trianon Barracks', in V. Teelock, A. Janoo, G. Summers, M.S. Rivière, & S. Nirsimloo-Gayan (eds) *Angajē: Explorations into the history, society and culture of indentured immigrants and their descendants in Mauritius*. Port Louis: Aapravasi Ghat Trust Fund.

Colwell-Chanthaphonh, C., & de Salle-Essoo, M. (2014) 'Saints and evil and the wayside shrines of Mauritius', *Journal of Material Culture* 19(3): 253-277.

Couacaud, L. (2012) 'Recognizing Mauritius's Unique Heritage: The Relevance of Estate Temples and Shrines', in V. Teelock, A. Janoo, G. Summers, M.S. Rivière, & S. Nirsimloo-Gayan (eds) *Angaje: Post-Indenture Mauritius*. Port Louis: Aapravasi Ghat Trust Fund.

Čaval, S. (2018) (in press). 'Archaeology and religious syncretism in Mauritius', in K. Seetah (ed) *Connecting Continents: Archaeology and History in the Indian Ocean*. Ohio: Ohio University Press.

Vaux, C.G. (1995) *The History of Mauritius, Or, The Isle of France and the Neighbouring Islands from Their First Discovery to the Present Time: Composed Principally from the Papers and Memoirs of Baron Grant*. Asian Educational Services. London: W. Bulmer and Company.

Descubes, A. (1880) *Map of the Island of Mauritius*. Mauritius: Dept. of Public Works.

Ellis, C. and Ginsburg, R. (2010) *Cabin, quarter, plantation: architecture and landscapes of North American slavery*. New Haven Conn.: Yale University Press.

Eriksen, T.H. (1998) *Common Denominators: Ethnicity, Nation-building and Compromise in Mauritius*. Oxford, New York: Berg Publishers.

Fesler, G.R. (2004) *From Houses to Homes: An Archaeological Case Study of Household Formation at the Utopia Slave Quarter, ca. 1675 to 1775*. Ph.D. Dissertation, Department of Anthropology, University of Virginia.

Fogelin, L. (2007) 'The Archaeology of Religious Ritual', *Annual Review of Anthropology* 36: 55-71.

Frere, W.E. & Williamson, V.A. (1875) *Report of the Royal Commissioners appointed to enquire into the treatment of immigrants in Mauritius: Presented to Both Houses of Parliament by Command of Her Majesty, 6th February, 1875*. London: William Clowes and Sons. Volume 1.

Galloway, J.H. (1989) *The Sugar Cane Industry: An historical geography from its origins to 1914* (Vol. 12). Cambridge: Cambridge University Press.

Green, W.A. (1976) *British slave emancipation: the sugar colonies and the great experiment 1830-1865*. Oxford: Clarendon Press.

Hazareesingh, K. (1966) 'The religion and culture of Indian immigrants in Mauritius and the effect of social change', *Comparative Studies in Society and History* 8(2): 241-257.

Heat, B. (2010) Space and place within plantation quarters in Virginia, 1700-1825, in E. Clifton and R. Ginsburg (eds), *Cabin, quarter, plantation: architecture and landscapes of North American slavery*. New Haven Conn.: Yale University Press.

Hellemans, K., Vincke, A., Cagno, S., Herremans, D., De Clercq, W., & Janssens, K. (2014) 'Composition and state of alteration of 18th-century glass finds found at the Cistercian nunnery of Clairefontaine, Belgium', *Journal of Archaeological Science* 47: 121-133.

Home, R. and King, A.D. (2016) 'Urbanism and Master Planning: Configuring the Colonial City', in G.A. Bremnre (ed), *Architecture and Urbanism in the British Empire*. Oxford; New York: Oxford University Press.

Home, R.K. (2013) *Of Planting and Planning: The Making of British Colonial Cities*. New York: Routledge.

Jones, O., Sullivan, C., & Miller, G.L. (1985) *The Parks Canada Glass Glossary for the description of containers, tableware, flat glass, and closures*. National Historical Parks and Sites Branch. Parks Canada. Environment Canada; Canadian Government Publishing Centre.

Joy, J. (2009) 'Reinvigorating object biographies: Reproducing the drama of object lives', *World Archaeology* 41(4): 540–556.

Rice, K.S., & Katz-Hyman, M.B. (eds) (2010) *World of a Slave: Encyclopedia of the Material Life of Slaves in the United States* [2 volumes]: Encyclopedia of the Material Life of Slaves in the United States. ABC-CLIO.

King, J.A. (2006) 'Household archaeology, identities and biographies', in D. Hicks, & M. C. Beaudry (eds), *The Cambridge Companion to Historical Archaeology.* Cambridge : Cambridge University Press.

Knott, K. (1986) Religion and Identity, and the study of ethnic minority religions in Britain. Australia: Australian Association for the Study of Religions.

Lilley, I. (2004) 'Diaspora and identity in archaeology: moving beyond the Black Atlantic', in L. Meskell and R. Preucel (eds), *A Companion to Social Archaeology*. Oxford: Blackwell.

McLoughlin, S. (2005) Migration, Diaspora and Transnationalism: Transformations of Religion and Culture in a Globalising Age', in J.R. Hinnells (ed) *The Routledge companion to the Study of Religion*. New York: Routledge.

Meskell, L. (2013) 'Part III, politics', in: Rathje W.L, Shanks, M. and Witmore, C. (eds) *Archaeology in the Making: Conversations through a Discipline*. New York: Routledge.

Mitter, P. (1986) 'The Early British Port Cities of India: Their Planning and Architecture Circa 1640-1757', *Journal of the Society of Architectural Historians,* 45: 95-114.

Mol, H. (1979) 'Theory and data on the religious behaviour of migrants', *Social Compass* 26(1): 31-39.

Morgan, P.D. (1998) *Slave Counterpoint: Black Culture in the Eighteenth-Century Chesapeake and Lowcountry*. Williamsburg: Omohundro Institute of Early American History and Culture.

Nagapen, A. (1989) *Le catholicisme des esclaves à l'île Maurice*. Mauritius: Diocèse de Port-Louis.

Nelson, L.P. (2016) *Architecture and empire in Jamaica*. New Haven; London: Yale University Press.

Nemchand, A. (2014) 'The Trianon conservation project', *Souvenir magazine, 180th Anniversary of the arrival of Indentured Labourers in Mauritius.* Mauritius: Aapravasi Ghat Trust Fund.

Hume, I.N. (2001) *A Guide to the Artifacts of Colonial America*. Pennsylvania: University of Pennsylvania Press.

Peerthum, S. (2010) 'A History of the Old Labourers' Quarter of Trianon: A Rare National Point', *Aapravasi Ghat Trust Fund Newsletter,* 8, 10 and 12.

RCIM (1875) *Report of the Royal Commissioners Appointed to Enquire Into the Treatment of Immigrants in Mauritius: Presented to Both Houses of Parliament by Command of Her Majesty, 6th February.* London.

Porter, A.C. (2015) 'Identification and Analysis of Utilized Glass in Early Colonial Contexts: A Case Study from 17th-Century Rhode Island', *Technical briefs in Historical Archaeology* 9: 1-15.

Ramhota, P. (1998) 'Declining practice of worship at kalimai shrines in Mauritius', *The Eastern Anthropologist* 51(1): 41-51.

Rubertone, P.E. (2001). *Grave Undertakings: An Archaeology of Roger Williams and the Narragansett Indians*. Washington, D.C: Smithsonian Institution Press.

Seetah, K. (2015a) 'Objects past, objects present: Materials, resistance and memory from the Le Morne Old Cemetery, Mauritius', *Journal of Social Archaeology* 15(2): 233-253.

Seetah, K. (2015b) 'The Archaeology of Mauritius', *Antiquity* 89(346): 922-939.

Seetah, K. (2018) 'Climate and Disease in the Indian Ocean: An Interdisciplinary Study from Mauritius', in K. Seetah (ed) *Connecting Continents: Archaeology and History in the Indian Ocean World*. Ohio: Ohio University Press.

Seetah, K., Birch, T., Calaon, D., & Čaval, S. (2017) 'Colonial iron in context: The Trianon slave shackle from Mauritius', *Archaeological and Anthropological Sciences* 9(3): 419-430.

Selvam, S. (2012) 'Ramayana and Bhojpuri Hindus', in V. Teelock, A. Janoo, G. Summers, M. S. Rivière, & S. Nirsimloo-Gayan (eds) *Angajé: Explorations into the History, Society and Culture of Indentured Immigrants and Their Descendants in Mauritius*. Port Louis: Aapravasi Ghat Trust Fund.

Shanks, M. (2004) 'Three rooms: Archaeology and Performance', *Journal of Social Archaeology* 4(2): 147-180.

Singleton, T.A. (1985) *The Archaeology of slavery and plantation life*. Orlando: Orlando Academic Press.

Singleton, T.A. (ed) (2016) *The Archaeology of Slavery and Plantation Life*. London: Routledge.

Tamby, S. (2011) 'A scramble for souls: missionary activities in post-emancipation Mauritius (1840-1895) and its impact on contemporary society', in *Truth and Justice Commission Report 4: Part VIII – Economy and Society under Colonialism. Slavery and Indenture*. Port Louis: Truth and Justice Commission.

Teelock, V. (2001) *Mauritian history: From its beginnings to modern times*. Moka: Mahatma Gandhi Institute.

Trouillet, P.Y. (2012) 'Overseas temples and Tamil migratory space', *South Asia Multi-disciplinary Academic Journal* 6:1-24.

Vaughan, M. (2005) *Creating the Creole Island: slavery in eighteenth-century Mauritius*. Durham: Duke University Press.

Vlach, J. M (1992) *By the Work of Their Hands: Studies in Afro-American Folklife*. Charlottesville: University of Virginia Press.

Wilkie, L.A. (1996) 'Medicinal teas and patent medicines: African-American women's consumer choices and ethnomedical traditions at a Louisiana plantation', *Southeastern Archaeology* 15(2): 119-131.

Wilkie, L.A. (2000) 'Not merely child's play: creating a historical archaeology of children and childhood', in J.S. Derevenski (ed) *Children and Material Culture*. London: Routledge.

Younger, P. (2009) 'Mauritius: A Parallel Society', in P. Younger (ed) *New Homelands: Hindu Communities in Mauritius, Guyana, Trinidad, South Africa, Fiji, and East Africa*. Oxford: Oxford University Press.

Young People Living Multiculturalism in Contemporary Mauritius

CAROLINE NG TSEUNG-WONG

Introduction

Current world events are teaching us that an understanding of societies only in financial terms is incomplete and misleading without an understanding of social identities and the socio-political contexts that engender and challenge these identities. Globalisation has knit common markers across the globe (satisfying the human need for commonality) but at the same time has heightened (in)compatible differences across social identities which serve the human need for distinctiveness (Brewer, 1991). Everyday cultural diversity poses concrete social-conventional (e.g. should there be a consensual form of greeting others), moral (e.g. should female genital circumcision be accepted in the name of cultural beliefs) and personal (e.g. should I choose to befriend this individual) dilemmas to society and individuals. A pressing contemporary question is 'How best to manage cultural diversity'. Multiculturalism, a 'social-intellectual movement that promotes the values of diversity as a core principle and insists that all cultural groups be treated with respect and as equals' (Fowers & Richardson, 1996: 609), has been presented as the solution to manage cultural diversity by some (e.g. Parekh, 2000; Modood, 2007) and accused of exacerbating conflict by others (e.g. Barry, 2001). These opponents argue for a colour-blind approach instead, i.e. disregarding ethnic and religious categories and treating each person as a unique individual (Barry, 2001). However, the atrocities of genocides that permeate our common human history have taught us that it is neither easy nor acceptable to just ask people to make do of their social identities or choose one to the detriment of the others, especially when these social categories are important to who they are. Membership to various large-scale collective groups such as nations, ethnic and religious groups, means that at the level of the individual there is a fine, oftentimes compromising, balancing act to juggle in order to make sense (coherently) of one's multiple identities. How do young Mauritians articulate their social identities, mainly national and ethnic/religious, against a background of globalisation worldwide and mosaic multiculturalism (Eisenlohr, 2016; Ng Tseung-Wong, 2013; Ng Tseung-Wong & Verkuyten, 2015) locally?

Young Mauritians were born post-independence and therefore grew up only with markers of Mauritius as a nation-state such as the flag, national anthem, independence-day ceremony, currency, and national flower and bird, to name just a few. Because Mauritian history taught in the school curriculum does not describe, analyse and reflect on the period surrounding Independence, young people in general, can have a simple narrative of Independence in the form of 'Union Jack down, Mauritian flag up'. But the story of Independence is not that simple. People were divided on the question of Independence: on one side Indo-Mauritians (Hindus and Muslims) were pro-Independence and on the other side Creoles were afraid that Independence would equal to Hindu hegemony. The ethnic tensions culminated in the riots of 1967, and the emigration of many Creoles (mainly *gens de couleur*). In order to ensure a working government and appease ethnic tensions, the incoming government made sure that all components of Mauritian society were represented. And contemporary Mauritian mosaic multiculturalism was born.

Multiculturalism is a multi-level term that can be used at the descriptive level to denote the reality of cultural diversity of a particular setting; the individual level to reflect the membership of an individual to various cultural groups and how these are included in the self; and at the societal level to indicate the normative expectations for dealing with diversity and the political level of decision making (Wieviorka, 1998). While there are many strands of multiculturalism, the notion of multicultural recognition is a common underlying factor. As a cultural diversity ideology, multiculturalism denotes the recognition, respect and celebration of cultural groups and the participation of all components of society in an equitable manner (Berry, 1991). However, there is a retreat from multiculturalism in discourse in many western countries and Europe in particular (Goodhart, 2013; Vertovec & Wessendorf, 2010) to the point that the term can be considered 'toxically' charged, and 'interculturalism'[i] is now favoured by some, while others take a stronger position by rejecting any political concessions to religious, ethnic or cultural diversity. Yet, there are also countries (e.g. Canada, Mauritius) in which a form of multiculturalism has been fostered and institutionalised and where cultural diversity is part of the self-image. Multiculturalism is not seen as an accommodating gesture towards immigrants or minorities but as defining the society as a whole.

In the present chapter, I first briefly elaborate on the contribution of social psychology through mainly the social identity approach on our work on multiculturalism. Second, the chapter discusses on the multicultural norms and representations of the Mauritian nation held by young people. Third, I then examine empirical studies on the link between national and ethnic identities and consider the implications of dual identities.

Finally, I consider the importance of group representation in the Mauritian secular state and make final remarks on where Mauritius is fifty years post-independence.

Social Psychology Perspectives

The study of intergroup relations and identity is at the heart of social psychology (see Verkuyten, 2014). One major theoretical perspective that has informed research is the social identity approach derived from Social Identity Theory (SIT) (Tajfel & Turner, 1979). SIT posits that the social structure which is made up of social categories that stand in status and power relations relative to each other, precedes individual human beings. Individuals become psychologically connected to the social structure through their group memberships. The process of self-categorisation places the group in the person's head so that it becomes possible for an individual to think, feel and act in the name of the social group. SIT is insightful for (i) its insistence that an understanding of the social context with its collective ideological beliefs and theories about the social structure is primordial for an understanding of intergroup relations (Turner, 1999) and (ii) proposing that people are driven towards positive differentiation, i.e. maintenance of positive social identities formed through the processes of group categorisation and social comparison. Because individuals strive to maintain positive self-esteem, they prefer their in-group to be positively recognised, valued and respected. And this meaningful and positive social identity is protected and maintained by the individual group members. The implications of in-group identification have been extensively researched. For example, high in-group identifiers are more likely to show group-level responses compared to low-identifiers (see Ellemers, Spears & Doosje, 2002), in-group identification is an important condition for collective action (Reicher & Hopkins, 2001) and identification is linked to the endorsement of multiculturalism (see Verkuyten, 2006). However, identity threats can ensue when there is lack of identity distinctiveness or a devalued social identity which trigger identity-management strategies (see Tajfel & Turner, 1986). The social identity approach is therefore informative because 'multiculturalism is about group identities and status position, beliefs about the social system and requires an understanding of the nature of groups' (Verkuyten, 2006: 152).

'Diversity is who we are': Beliefs and attitudes about Mauritius

Multiculturalism in Mauritius emphasises mutual recognition and respect of differences. Group differences are maintained and group identity claims are regarded as mostly legitimate in public life. Although the Mauritian government does not have an official multicultural agenda, there are policies such as grants to cultural centres and language unions that point to a multiculturalism approach (Aumeerally, 2005). Diversity in Mauritius, to paraphrase Billig (1995), takes the form of 'banal multiculturalism' where symbols of difference self-evidently abound in the landscape and permeate everyday life. There are public holidays related to each ethno-religious group, religious places of worship anywhere, all cultures represented on Independence Day, different languages on radio and TV, and ethnically mixed neighbourhoods. These banal instances serve as reminders that 'diversity is who we are' and thereby normalize differences, 'they are so different to us' is viewed in terms of 'we are all different' (Ng Tseung Wong & Verkuyten, 2015).

Research from a large scale survey (N = 2327) found that adolescents of the three main ethnic groups (Hindu, Muslim and Creole) strongly and equally endorsed multiculturalism for Mauritius (e.g., 'In general, Mauritians should value the ethnic diversity in the country', 'In Mauritius, all the ethnic and religious groups should be recognized and respected' - Ng Tseung-Wong & Verkuyten, 2010; 2014). Furthermore, for the three ethnic groups the endorsement of multiculturalism was stronger for those who identified more with the Mauritian nation. Thus, those who have a relatively strong sense of national belonging were more in favour of the national ideal of 'fruit salad' multiculturalism. In an open-ended question to define what makes a person a Mauritian, the most common criteria given by the adolescents was 'respect and tolerance for other Mauritians' (van de Werf, Martinovic, Verkuyten & Ng Tseung-Wong, 2017). As social norms and beliefs regarding diversity are communicated and spread in a society, they become its 'cultural representations' (Guimond *et al.*, 2013; Moscovici, 1988) and convey the message 'this is who we are and this is what we do'. This idea of respect and tolerance for the other is illustrated in the following quote from one of the participants:

> *Mauritius is a country whose population consists of people from many different races, religion and cultures. A Mauritian would be one who's able to accept all the religion and cultures and respect them. A Mauritian is one who can adapt with any person irrespective of his age, gender, etc...a Mauritian should finally be devoted to the Mauritian culture.*

> (Female, 17, Hindu)

178

However, it is argued that people's preference for diversity ideologies is functional (Dovidio, Gaertner & Saguy, 2009): majority group members, and especially high identifiers, tend to endorse the ideology that supports the maintenance of their cultural identity and status and power position in society. Research in western countries has found that majority group members tend to prefer an assimilationist ideology and minorities prefer a multiculturalism ideology (see Verkuyten, 2014). In these countries, an ideology of colour blindness in which the emphasis is on individuals can be perceived by majority group members as rationalizing the disadvantage status of minority groups and justifying the majority's dominant position (Apfelbaum, Pauker, Sommers & Ambady, 2010; Neville, Awad, Brooks, Flores & Bluemel, 2013). In Mauritius, we found through both a survey (Study 1) and semi-experimental (Study 2) design that multiculturalism is non-threatening for the majority Hindu group (Ng Tseung-Wong & Verkuyten, 2016). Using survey data amongst 295 University of Mauritius students of which 140 self-categorized as Hindu (mean age = 20.72), the main hypothesis was that higher compared to lower Hindu identifiers would show more in-group bias (thermometer rating- in-group bias score computed by subtracting the in-group score from the average of the out-groups, i.e. Muslim and Creole scores) under colour blindness but not under multiculturalism. A two-step hierarchical regression analysis showed that endorsement of multiculturalism (e.g. of an item is 'It is possible for individuals to feel connected to both their cultural group and the national group') was associated with less in-group bias and ethnic identification was associated with more in-group bias. There was no association between endorsement of colour-blindness (e.g. of an item is 'At our core, all human beings are really all the same, so racial and ethnic categories do not matter') and in-group bias. As expected the interaction of ethnic identification with endorsement of multiculturalism was significant and results of simple slope analysis showed that for those who relatively strongly (+1 SD) endorsed multiculturalism, ethnic identification was not significantly associated with in-group bias whereas for the Hindu participants who had a lower endorsement of multiculturalism (-1 SD), the stronger their ethnic identification, the more the level of in-group bias reported. Therefore, Study 1 demonstrated that higher ethnic identification was not associated with more in-group bias for participants who strongly endorsed multiculturalism. This suggests that multiculturalism is non-threatening to Hindu participants but rather confirms and legitimise their dominant position in society.

To further test the argument that multiculturalism can have a reassuring and legitimizing effect for majority Hindu group members, in Study 2 we used a semi-experimental design to examine the causal impact of diversity ideologies and a control condition. Using the principle of lay theories activation (Levy, West & Ramirez, 2005),

179

participants randomly answered one of the four versions of the questionnaire in which they were encouraged to think in terms of multiculturalism, colour blindness, or polyculturalism (and a control condition in which no cultural diversity ideology was made salient). Our prediction was that activation of multiculturalism would make higher group identifiers not respond with stronger in-group bias whereas the activation of colour blindness and polyculturalism would trigger this response. After the experimental manipulation, the participants were presented with an in-group feeling bias measure (thermometer measure- similar to the one used in Study 1) and an in-group stereotype bias measure (rating on a five-point Likert scale of six different traits: honest, trustworthy, efficient, competent, friendly and likeable). The participants were 160 Hindus with a mean age of 21.24. The majority of participants reported living in rural areas (n =110). A between-subject analysis was conducted in which experimental condition was included as a factor and ethnic identification as a continuous centered variable. In line with our prediction, for both dependent variables, i.e. in-group feeling bias and in-group stereotype bias, there was a significant interaction effect between condition and ethnic identification. As expected and similar to Study 1, in the multiculturalism condition there was no significant association between ethnic identification and in-group bias but in all the other three conditions, the association was significant. Both studies therefore demonstrate that multiculturalism has a reassuring or buffering effect on the well-established link between ethnic identification and in-group bias. In the context of Mauritius, it is not possible for majority Hindus to claim 'we are all Mauritians, mainly like us' (See Devos & Banaji, 2005) because of their history as indentured labourers and the consensual social representation of Mauritius as a cultural diversity society (a 'fruit salad'). However, by claiming 'we are all different', they can actually ensure the state-promotion of Hindu-ness and maintain their political and public dominance which is related to their numerical size. While colourblindness in its French notion of *laïcité* might not necessarily jeopardise Hindus' access to resources and political power (i.e. colour blindness might not be a realistic threat), colourblindness does undermine the cultural group representation of the nation as a "fruit salad" or "mosaic" and thereby poses a symbolic threat to Hindus' distinctiveness and diasporic ancestral identity (Eisenlohr, 2006).

Compatible ethnic, religious and national identifications: Dual identities

According to SIT, social identities are social group memberships that are internalised as part of the self-concept and individuals can feel a sense of belonging and commitment to their group affiliations. Identification to social groups therefore has potent consequences at the individual and societal levels. Critics of multiculturalism have argued that diversity in cultural values, religion and cultural backgrounds make people less willing to sacrifice and share for the common good (Goodhart, 2013). For instance, European politicians often claim that minorities have divided loyalties and a lack of attachment to the host society- the Cricket test- and therefore are the 'weak links' in a cohesive society. But cultural diversity and multiculturalism are not antagonistic to a sense of unity that is shared through national identity- common belonging and commitment (Modood, 2007; Parekh, 2000). This emphasis on a shared sense of national identity is in line with the Common Ingroup Identity Model (CIIM) (Dovidio, Gaertner & Saguy, 2007) derived from the social identity approach. The CIIM proposes that an overarching shared sense of 'we' is positive for intergroup relations because previous out-groups ('them') become incorporated and become one of 'us'. Moreover, the CIIM also recognises that trying to replace ethnic or religious minority identities with only a sense of national belonging might not be feasible and desirable by minority group members who would then lose their sense of distinctiveness. This may heighten identity threats and intergroup tensions and conflicts (Dovidio *et al.*, 2007). Instead they propose that a dual identity is needed in which both ethnic and religious distinctiveness are present within a context of national connection and belongingness. Empirical research on the relationship between ethnic and national identities demonstrate that this relationship depends on the national context (see Deaux & Verkuyten, 2011).

Research amongst adolescents in Mauritius found that for all three groups (Hindus, Creoles, Muslims), participants reported high levels of ethnic group identification and even higher level of religious group identification (Ng Tseung-Wong & Verkuyten, 2010, 2013b). Importantly, these group identifications were not contradictory to a sense of national belonging. Across the three ethnic groups, the correlation between ethnic identification and national identification was significantly positive. Both majority Hindus and minority Creoles and Muslims preferred a dual identity whether measured as a self-identification choice (national-religious and national-ethnic) or as high national identification combined with high religious or ethnic identification (Ng Tseung-Wong & Verkuyten, 2010, 2013a). Furthermore, adolescents were more likely to report a dual identity (national-ethnic; 51.7%), than mainly national (32.4%) or mainly ethnic (15.5%). Additionally, when asked explicitly about how they saw themselves in terms of national and religious belonging, the majority indicated a dual identity: Hindu Mauritian (65.4%), Muslim Mauritian (50.7%), and Christian Mauritian (58.9%). When 'diversity is who we are', then it makes sense that most people view their national and ethnic/religious identities as compatible. In Mauritius, all ethno-religious groups are seen as making up the 'rainbow nation' to the point that being 'just Mauritian' can be problematic. Rather, being a good religious follower and practicing one's ethnic culture paves the road to being a good Mauritian (Eisenlohr, 2011).

Empirical survey data collected by Afrobarometer corroborates the adolescents' survey data[ii]. In the round 5 questionnaire collected in 2015(Q85B) and the round 6 questionnaire collected in 2014 (Q88B), the Moreno (1988) question was also used, i.e. participants (mean age = 43.66 and mean age = 40.64 respectively) were asked to indicate how they predominantly feel using five options ranging from 'I feel only Mauritian' (5), I feel more Mauritian than my ethnic group (4), I feel both Mauritian and my ethnic group (3), I feel more my ethnic group than Mauritian (2) and I feel only my ethnic group (1). In the round 5 questionnaire, taking data from only those who self-categorised as Hindus (n = 505), Creoles (n = 332) and Muslims (n = 244), the category most chosen by members of all the three ethnic groups was dual-identity- I feel both Mauritian and ethnic group (59.5% of the 1079 participants). Results for the round 6 questionnaire was similar: taking data from only those who self-categorised as Hindus (n = 536), Creoles (n = 296) and Muslims (n = 218) which represents 87.5 percent of the sample (N = 1200), the category most chosen by members of all the three ethnic groups was also dual-identity (56.9% of the 1050 participants). The correlation between a five-point measure and a combined three-point measure was high (r = .96 and r = .95). Therefore a scale with three discrete self-identifications – 'mainly nationals', 'dual identifiers' and 'mainly ethnics' is used for ease of interpretation.

Table 9: Percentage of participants in the three identity categories by ethnic group

	Adolescents data set (2007)			Afrobarometer Wave 5			Afrobarometer Wave 6		
	Hindu %	Creole %	Muslim %	Hindu %	Creole %	Muslim %	Hindu %	Creole %	Muslim %
Mainly Nationals	35	24	35	32.5	38.4	15.2	37.9	37.8	16.1
Dual Identifiers	54	58	47	64.1	50.2	62.7	57.8	49.7	64.2
Mainly Ethnics	11	18	18	3.4	11.5	22.1	4.3	12.5	19.7

As shown in Table 9, across the three datasets and the three ethnic groups, dual identity is the most chosen option by participants. It is noteworthy that in general the Hindus were least likely to consider themselves 'mainly as Hindus'. This is in line with research that found that majority group members are more inclined towards stronger national group identification (e.g. Staerklé *et al.*, 2010). Older Muslims compared to younger ones had lower percentages in the 'mainly national' category, indicating change towards a stronger sense of national identity amongst young Muslim Mauritians. Large survey data so far has shown that memberships to ethnic and national categories are not lived as an 'either or' option but rather are viewed as compatible identities. Feeling strongly for one's ethnic group and feeling strongly for the national group does not have to be contradictory, one is not 'disloyal' to either when the definition of the nation is in terms of cultural diversity.

Dual identities: Correlates and Implications

Dual identity is viewed as a positive concept with promising outcomes for (i) intergroup relations (Dovidio *et al.*, 2007), (ii) immigrants (and minorities) because by allowing them to 'feel both', dual identity is linked to better integration and less psychological distress in the immigration process (Nguyen & Benet-Martínez, 2013) and (iii) engagement in collective action to the benefit of their groups by minority group members (Simon & Ruhs, 2008). For instance, research in the Netherlands amongst minority groups showed that participants who reported a strict dual identity (both their ethnic group and Dutch) felt more at home in the Netherlands and scored higher on a measure of happiness than those who reported a singly identity only (Fleischmann & Verkuyten, 2016). In Mauritius, we found for all three ethnic groups that national identification was significantly and positively associated with both out-group evaluation and in-group evaluation. Moreover, national and dual identifiers rated the out-group more positively than ethnic identifiers (Ng Tseung-Wong & Verkuyten, 2010). Using cluster analysis to measure dual identity in terms of religious and national identifications, we specify a priory four clusters to match Berry's (2001) four identity positions. Our data did not map completely on the four theoretical identity positions. We did not obtain a 'national group identification' cluster (i.e. high on national identification and low on religious identification) but instead a 'neutral' position in which participants reported scale mid-point levels for religious and national identification. However, a dual identity cluster, a predominant religious cluster and an individual identifier cluster (low on both religious and national identifications) were obtained in line with the identity positions (Ng Tseung-Wong & Verkuyten, 2013a). The identity clusters were linked differently to global self-esteem. Dual identifiers reported higher self-esteem compared to the three other identity clusters. The religious identifiers and neutrals did not differ significantly.

Research so far points to the benefits of holding a dual identity: mainly for minorities and immigrants in western countries, but importantly for all ethnic groups in Mauritius. Dual identities satisfy the needs for both distinctiveness and commonality (Brewer, 1999) and allow individuals to maintain a sense of ethnic identification within a superordinate sense of national 'we'. In general, it has been found that the level of ethnic identification is higher than national identification (Phinney, Berry, Vedder & Liebkind, 2006) and Mauritius is no exception to this trend. But the findings on dual identity as the most preferred self-identification option and the most reported identity cluster derived from strength of identification to ethnic/religious and national categories, demonstrate that some level of national identification together with ethnic identification has positive intergroup and personal benefits. The implications are that it is not beneficial to Mauritian society to ask individuals to choose between their subgroup (i.e. ethnic) and superordinate (i.e. national) identities especially when the former is important to people self-definitions and the latter is an inclusive identity that incorporates diversity in its meaning. Brewer (1999: 442) pointed out that "In-group love is not a necessary precursor of out-group hate". When one reports feelings of pride, commitment and importance for his/her ethnic identity, one can also report positively on the same dimensions for the national category.

Group representations in a multicultural secular state: To be or not to be considered?

Societies are made up of social groups that stand in power and status differences relative to each other (Tajfel & Turner, 1979). Therefore, power involves decision making and raises issues of justice and fair procedures. These issues are more complex in multicultural societies because as Mansbridge (1999) asked 'Should Blacks represent Blacks, and Women represent women?' Is it democratic or fair that individual citizens only have a voice through their 'representative' cultural leaders rather than as individual citizens (Barry, 2001)? Using two contextual scenarios (school election of student council and national elections), we investigated adolescents' fairness judgments of three democratic procedures of decision making (representative democracy, equal group representation, proportional group representation), and one non-democratic form (cultural group oligarchy) in relation to ethnic identification, age and gender (Ng Tseung-Wong & Verkuyten, 2013b). Participants rated on a five point scale ranging from '1' very unfair to '5' very fair, four ways in which decisions can be made (i) in schools and (ii) in the country. For example, for the national context participants first read an introduction: 'Imagine that you could decide about the fairest way in which in Mauritius very important decisions are made. What is for you a fair and just way for making very important decisions? Please indicate the fairness of the following four ways': (i) 'The population elects 100 people and these 100 people make the important decisions' (representative democracy); (ii) 'All the different cultural or religious groups vote for their own representatives and these elected representatives make the important decisions' (equal group representation); (iii) 'All the different cultural or religious groups vote for their own representatives for making important decisions. But the larger the group is, the more representatives they can elect to make the important decisions' (proportional group representation); and (iv) 'Only the numerically largest cultural or religious group makes the important decisions' (cultural group oligarchy). Results showed that across ethnic and age groups, adolescents viewed representative democracy as fair and the non-democratic form (oligarchy) as unfair. This is in line with other research that has found that adolescents support democratic principles of majority rule and representative government (Ellenbroek *et al.*, 2012; Helwig *et al.*, 2003, 2007). Social cognitive domain theory indeed proposes that moral judgments based on rights principles hold true across cultural and national settings (Helwig, 2006; Turiel, 2002). However, there is an interplay between group membership and adolescents' beliefs about fairness and equality (Rutland, Killen & Abrams, 2010). In the national context, across ethnic groups, higher ethnic identification was associated to higher fairness rating of equal group representation. Of interest, are the findings that (i) Muslim adolescents rated equal group representation as fairer in the national context compared to Hindus and Creoles and (ii) Hindus did not judge proportional group representation as fairer compared to Muslims and Creoles. Actually in the national context, the correlation between proportional group representation and cultural group oligarchy was moderate (r = .52) and both forms were viewed as unfair. The ideological representation of Mauritius as a 'cultural mosaic' implies that all components can claim to be indispensable for the nation (Ng Tseung-Wong & Verkuyten, 2010) and unequal group-based decision-making procedure can be viewed as relatively unfair because all groups make up the national mosaic and should have an important say.

Results from the adolescent survey suggest that Muslims might be more open to the idea of group representation. This is corroborated by the wave 6 Afrobarometer data that showed ethnic group difference on support for electoral reform for the abolition of ethnic or religious representation in the national assembly (i.e. the Best Loser System). This item was measured on a scale of '1' strongly disagree to '5' strongly agree. There was a significant ethnic group effect, Welch $F(2, 496.73)$ = 22.53, $p<$ .0001. Post-hoc analysis using Games-Howell procedure showed that Muslims (M = 2.42, SD = 1.03) significantly differed from Hindus (M = 2.97, SD = 1.19) and the Creoles (M = 3.01, SD = 1.19). The latter two did not significantly differ from each other. In other words, Muslim participants showed less support for the abolition of ethnic/religious representation in parliament compared to Hindus and Creoles. However, in general it seems that participants from all three ethnic groups are not overwhelmingly in favour of the abolishment of ethnic/religious representation in the national assembly because for none of the ethnic groups is the mean score on the 'agree' end of the Likert-scale.

Minogue's (1987: 133) argument that 'Mauritian politics are above all, ethnic politics' resonates well with the above findings. On the one hand, this can be taken as a reflection of the pernicious place of ethnic representation in everyday living of Mauritians so that an electoral reform that would abolish ethnic/religious representation in politics is considered as an 'unknown' for all and bears the risk of unsettling the cultural diversity symbol that is very much ingrained in the collective consciousness and that has so far not done major 'harm', i.e. the sense of urgency for change is not high. On the other hand, this can also be interpreted as an illustration of the importance to ordinary people and especially Muslims, of knowing that the parliament has members who share the same ethnic/religious social identity as them because clearly these social identities are important to who they are. The real and symbolic notion of the government being composed of members that reflect the cultural diversity of the nation can be viewed as reassuring for individuals whose ethnic/religious identities are primary. People might not consider it legitimate and fair that members of parliament only represent the voice of, and work for their ethnic/cultural group but still consider it important that all cultural components of the society are seen in the national assembly. Ironically, this sense of representation and therefore sense of having a voice might be the deterrent to real societal change regarding discrimination based on minority group membership (see Saguy, Tausch, Dovidio & Pratto, 2009).

Are we there yet?

As children often ask when they are on their way to a much wanted destination: Are we there yet? Taking stock of social identities in contemporary Mauritius fifty years post-Independence, is a lukewarm exercise. Large scale survey data with representative samples of adolescents and adults suggest that in general Mauritians report high identification to their ethnic/religious category and this identification is not in opposition to their national identification. Moreover, most Mauritians report dual identities, feeling and being both their ethnic/religious and national categories. This means that the visibility of one's ethnic group in the national tapestry is not challenged across ethnic groups. Issues of integration, fitting in the dominant culture and feeling 'torn' between and being in a no-man's land which are often reported in portraits about immigrants or minorities in many settler countries do not find resonance in Mauritius. From this perspective, Mauritius has come a long way in 'getting along' and adolescents' compatible dual identities can be viewed as social cohesion strengths. It is no small feat that in general, young Mauritians negotiate their multiple cultural identities fluently and these cultural identities are not heightened and threatened in their daily lives. Because of the small geographical space, Mauritians are bound to be in contact with others from a different ethnic background and out of this intergroup contact, '*lakorité*' has emanated. *Lakorité* is a Kreol word with no roots in either English or French that denotes getting along with one's neighbours wherever one is, whoever the other is. However, because of this veneer of 'cultural diversity and tolerance', people rarely have the open and hard but necessary conversations surrounding ethnicity and unequal opportunities, prejudice and discrimination. These conversations are viewed as better avoided because they can disrupt the postcard image Mauritius and Mauritians have created for themselves. In so doing, Mauritian society misses the opportunity of healing past injustices, confronting the elephant in the room, and ultimately accepting equitable measures that might not necessarily be beneficial for some at the individual level but benefit society as a whole. The challenges for Mauritius are not necessarily in terms of the perceived right and recognition to culturally *be* or the 'clash of civilisations' (Huntington, 1993) as currently played out elsewhere but more in terms of economic disparity, inequitable distribution of resources and opportunities, political nepotism, violence, and illicit substance use, abuse and trade that cut across ethnic groups. There is as yet no special recipe to knock off these challenges but building trust, fairness, and integrity at micro- and macro-levels is a good starting point, especially if those in positions of power set the tone.

References

Afrobarometer. Retrieved from http://www.afrobarometer.org

Apfelbaum, E.P., Paulker, K., Sommers, S.R. & Ambady, N. (2010) 'In blind pursuit of racial equality', *Psychological Science* 21: 1587-1592.

Aumeerally, N. (2005) 'The ambivalence of postcolonial Mauritius: Policy versus practice in education: A reading of official and popular multiculturalism', *International Journal of Cultural Policy* 11: 307-323.

Barry, B. (2001) *Culture and equality: An egalitarian critique of multiculturalism.* Cambridge, UK: Polity Press.

Billig, M. (1995) *Banal Nationalism.* London: Sage.

Brewer, M. (1991). The social self: On being the same and different at the same time. *Personality and Social Psychology Bulletin, 17*, 475-482.

Deaux, K., & Verkuyten, M. (2014) 'The social psychology of multiculturalism: Identity and intergroup relations', in V. Benet-Martinez & Y.Y. Hong (eds), *The Oxford handbook of multicultural identity: Basic and applied psychological perspectives.* Oxford: Oxford University Press.

Devos, T., & Banaji, M. R. (2005) 'American = White?', *Journal of Personality and Social Psychology* 88: 447-466.

Dovidio, J.F., Gaertner, S.L., & Saguy, T. (2007) 'Another view of "we": Majority and minority group perspectives on a common in-group identity', *European Review of Social Psychology* 18: 296-330.

Dovidio, J.F., Gaertner, S.L., & Saguy, T. (2009) 'Commonality and the complexity of 'We': Social attitudes and social change', *Personality and Social Psychology Review* 13: 3-20.

Eisenlohr, P. (2006) *Little India: Diaspora, time and ethnolinguistic belonging in Hindu Mauritius.* London: University of California Press.

Eisenlohr, P. (2011) 'Religious media, devotional Islam, and the morality of ethnic pluralism in Mauritius', *World Development* 39: 261-269.

Eisenlohr, P. (2016) 'Religion and diaspora: Islam as ancestral heritage in Mauritius', *Journal of Muslims in Europe* 5: 87-105.

Ellenbroek, M., Verkuyten, M., Thijs, J., & Poppe, E. (2014) 'Adolescents' evaluation of the fairness of governmental decision-making procedures: A study in 18 European countries', *Journal of Community and Applied Social Psychology* 24(6): 503-517.

Ellemers, N., Spears, R., & Doosje, B. (2002) 'Self and social identity', *Annual Review of Psychology* 53: 161-186.

Fowers, B. J. & Richardson, F. C. (1996) 'Why is multiculturalism good?', *American Psychologist* 51: 609-621.

Goodhart, D. (2013) *The British dream: Successes and failure of post-war immigration.* London: Atlantic Books.

Guimond, S., Crips, R. J., De Oliveria, P., Kamiejski, R., Kteily, N., Kuepper, B., Lalonde, R. N., Levin, S., Pratto, F., Tougas, F., Sidanius, J., & Zick, A. (2013) 'Diversity policy, social dominance, and intergroup relations: Predicting prejudice in changing social and political contexts', *Journal of Personality and Social* Psychology 104: 941-958.

Helwig, C. (2006) 'Rights, civil liberties, and democracy across cultures', in M. Killen & J. Smetana (eds) *Handbook of moral development.* Mahwah, NJ: Erlbaum.

Helwig, C.C., Arnold, M.L., Tan, D., & Boyd, D. (2003) 'Chinese adolescents' reasoning about democratic and authority-based decision making in peer, family, and school contexts', *Child Development* 74: 783-800.

Helwig, C.C., Arnold, M.L., Tan, D., & Boyd, D. (2007) 'Mainland Chinese and Canadian adolescents' judgments and reasoning about the fairness of democratic and other forms of government', *Cognitive Development* 22: 96-109.

Huntington, S.P. (2006) 'The clash of civilizations?', *Foreign Affairs* 72: 29-49.

Levy, S.R., West, T.L., & Ramirez, L. (2005) 'Lay theories and intergroup relations: A social-developmental perspective', *European Review of Social Psychology* 16: 189-220.

Mahajan, G. (2005) 'Indian exceptionalism or Indian model: Negotiating cultural diversity and minority rights in a democratic nation-state', in W. Kymlicka & B. He (eds) *Multiculturalism in Asia.* Oxford: Oxford University Press.

Mansbridge, J. (1999) 'Should Blacks represent Blacks and women represent women? A contingent "yes"', *The Journal of Politics* 61: 628-657.

Minogue, M. (1987) 'Mauritius', in C. Clarke & T. Payne (eds) *Politics, Security and Development in Small States.* London: Allen and Unwin.

Modood, T. (2007) *Multiculturalism.* Cambridge: Polity Press.

Morrison, K.R., Plaut, V.C., & Ybarra, O. (2010) 'Predicting whether multiculturalism positively or negatively influences White American's intergroup attitudes: The role of ethnic identification', *Personality and Social Psychology Bulletin* 36: 1648-1661.

Moscovici, S. (1988) 'Notes towards a description of social representations', *European Journal of Social Psychology* 18: 211-250.

Neville, H.A., Awad, G.H., Brooks, J.E., Flores, M.P., & Bluemel, J. (2013) 'Color-blind racial ideology: Theory, training, and measurement implications in Psychology', *American Psychologist* 68: 455-466.

Nguyen, A.D., & Benet-Martínez, V. (2013) 'Biculturalism and adjustment: A meta-analysis', *Journal of Cross-Cultural Psychology* 44: 122-151.

Ng Tseung-Wong, C., & Verkuyten, M. (2010) 'Intergroup evaluations, group indispensability and prototypicality judgments: A study in Mauritius', *Group Processes and Intergroup Relations* 13: 621-638.

Ng Tseung-Wong, C., & Verkuyten, M. (2013a) 'Religious and national group identification in adolescence: A study among three religious groups in Mauritius', *International Journal of Psychology* 48(5): 846-857.

Ng Tseung-Wong, C., & Verkuyten, M. (2013b) 'Is cultural group representation a fair option? Adolescents' evaluations of forms of decision-making in multicultural Mauritius', *International Journal of Intercultural Relations* 37:727-738.

Ng Tseung-Wong, C. & Verkuyten, M. (2015) 'Multiculturalism, Mauritian Style: Cultural diversity, belonging and a secular state', *American Behavioral Scientist* 59: 679-701.

Parekh, B. (2000) *Rethinking Multiculturalism: Cultural diversity and political theory.* London: Macmillan.

Phinney, J., Berry, J. W., Vedder, P., & Liebkind, K. (2006) 'The acculturation experience: Attitudes, identities, and behavior of immigrant youth', in J.W. Berry, J. Phinney, D.L. Sam., & P. Vedder (eds) *Immigrant youth in transition: Acculturation, identity, and adaptation across national contexts.* Mahwah, NJ: Lawrence Erlbaum.

Reicher, S., & Hopkins, N. (2001) *Self and Nation.* London: Sage.

Rutland, A., Killen, M., & Abrams, D. (2010) 'A new social-cognitive developmental perspective on prejudice: The interplay between morality and group identity', *Perspectives of Psychology Science* 5: 279-291.

Staerklé, C., Sidanius, J., Green, E., & Molina, L. (2010) 'Ethnic minority-majority asymmetry in national attitudes across the world: A multi-level analysis', *Political Psychology* 31: 491-519.

Tajfel, H., & Turner, J. (1979) 'An integrative theory of intergroup conflict', in W.G. Austin & S. Worchel (eds) *The social psychology of intergroup relations.* Monterey, CA: Brooks/Cole.

Turner, J.C. (1999) 'Some current issues in research on social identity and self-categorization theories', in N. Ellemers, R. Spears, & B. Doosje (eds) *Social identity: context, commitment, content.* Oxford,UK: Blackwell Publishing Ltd.

van der Werf, F., Martinovic. B., Verkuyten, M., & Ng Tseung-Wong, C. (2017) '*What it means to be a national: A study among adolescents in multicultural Mauritius.*' (manuscript under review)

Verkuyten, M. (2006) 'Multicultural recognition and ethnic minority rights: A social identity perspective', *European Review of Social Psychology* 17: 148-184.

Verkuyten, M. (2014) *Identity and cultural diversity: What social psychology can teach us.* Oxon: Routledge.

Vertovec, S., & Wessendorf, S. (2010) *The multiculturalism backlash: European discourses, policies and practices.* Oxon: Routledge.

Wieviorka, M. (1998) 'Is multiculturalism the solution?', *Ethnic and Racial Studies,* 21: 881-910.

---

[i] Interculturalism has become the preferred term because it denotes an active exchange between cultures (see Barrett, 2016) but is viewed as more a change in rhetoric rather than actual policies (see Meer & Modood, 2012). These author argue that at concrete policy level, interculturalism and multiculturalism share much in common.

[ii] Afrobarometer website - www.afrobarometer.org

From Language to Religion in Mauritian Nation-Building

PATRICK EISENLOHR

Introduction

Linguistic diversity is closely connected to the building of modern forms of political belonging. However, there is no single, universal way of linking language-related differences to other differences of social and political character. Instead these links are historically contingent and take various forms. For example, difference in vernacular languages does not necessarily lead to the emergence of ethnic or national boundaries on their basis, and conversely, the sharing of the same or very similar vernacular languages does not preclude the emergence of such boundaries. As linguistic anthropologists and sociolinguists have for some time been pointing out, such boundaries based on perceptions of linguistic difference often come about as at least the partial result of language ideologies (Irvine and Gal, 2000). Such politically charged assumptions about language and language difference are historical, and therefore variable and embedded in particular socio-cultural contexts.

Mauritius is no exception to this. In its colonial and postcolonial history, different kinds of linking language-related difference to political forms of belonging have emerged and have become a key dimension of its nation building process. There is an enduring antagonism between two fundamentally different ways of imagining Mauritius through language difference that persists until today. These are, on one hand, a nation building paradigm that privileges a foregrounding of the different 'ancestral cultures' and 'ancestral languages' linked to particular different religious traditions among Mauritians, and on the other hand a more homogenizing vision of ethnolinguistic nationalism based on Mauritian Creole as the near-universally shared vernacular language of Mauritius. Ever since independence, the former has been the dominant of these two approaches to Mauritian nation building. As I will explain, the recent introduction of Mauritian Creole as an optional school subject in Mauritian schools ironically testifies to the final defeat of ethnolinguistic nationalism drawing on the notion of Creole as national language. Moreover, Mauritius can also tell us an interesting story with regard to the copying and 'pirating' of European and North American forms of political belonging and its language ideologies in the colonial and postcolonial world (cf. Anderson, 1991: 4, 87). This is because ethnolinguistic nationalism based on Mauritian Creole as a way of imagining a Mauritian nation through language difference is derivative of European models of ethnolinguistic nationalism, while the multiculturalist privileging of 'ancestral languages' with religious biases is a rather novel formation at odds with them.

As I will try to show, a discussion of these two modes of Mauritian nation building inevitably leads to the issue of religion, and its often veiled centrality in Mauritian nation building. This is because the dominant paradigm of postcolonial Mauritian nation building ultimately privileges a multicultural understanding of the Mauritian nation. As I will explain, in its highlighting of 'ancestral cultures' and associated 'ancestral languages', it establishes religion as the single most important element of communal differentiation among Mauritians. In fact, there is a strong connection between the now dominant multicultural mode of nation building and the strategy of gaining recognition through 'religionization' that Mauritians of Indian origin successfully pursued under colonial rule. This link has had great consequences for Mauritian nation building and has not yet gained the attention it deserves among scholars working on Mauritius. Even though this process of religionization that turned 'Indians' into Hindus and Muslims was closely linked to parallel developments in India, it was also a response to the situation Mauritians of Indian backgrounds were facing in colonial Mauritius. Religious differences are also related to the failure of the competing paradigm to break the dominance of a multicultural vision of the Mauritian nation. By this I mean the relative lack of success ethnolinguistic nationalism based on the almost universally shared vernacular language Mauritian Creole has had in Mauritius.

Linguistic diversity in Mauritius

Mauritius is widely known as a multilingual island nation. Mauritian multilingualism is complex and operates on multiple levels. To begin with, linguistic diversity in Mauritius is not, with some qualifications, a matter of distinct groups marked off from each other through different vernacular languages. Instead, there is one almost universally shared vernacular, Mauritian Creole, a language that is also usually considered the flagship of locally created cultural traditions in Mauritius. Other vernacular languages are in use as well, such as French, which is a home language for a small percentage of the population, as well as Bhojpuri, still used by less than a fifth of Mauritians, especially among people of north Indian descent in rural areas. There are still smaller numbers of Mauritians who use Hakka, Gujarati, and Kutchi as home languages. But all those using French, Bhojpuri, Hakka, Gujarati and Kutchi in everyday life also use Mauritian Creole, whose role as the predominant vernacular of Mauritius is uncontested. As in several other postcolonial states, notably in Africa, the language of the former colonizer, English, has been retained as official language in state administration and education. Mauritius experienced multiple layers of colonization, and French, the language of the colonizers from 1715-1810 continues to overshadow the significance of English in several respects, as it is the dominant language of media and the private sector economy. The importance of French is largely due to the dominant role Franco-Mauritian settlers and their descendants have always played in the island's economy, and their very important role in the politics of the colony even after the end of French rule until independence in 1968. A particularity of Mauritian linguistic diversity is the importance of so-called ancestral languages for local understandings of language and belonging. These languages, modern standard forms of Hindi, Urdu, Tamil, Telugu, Marathi, Arabic and Mandarin were rarely ever used or even known by any ancestors migrating from India or China to Mauritius, but emerged as important rallying points for emerging ethnic and ethno-religious identifications in Mauritius. They are officially recognized and supported by the state as school subjects, and the mostly religious organizations promoting these languages also receive state subsidies. Among Mauritians of Indian descent who comprise almost 70 per cent of the population and who claim these languages (with the exception of Mandarin) as their ancestral patrimony, these languages are closely tied to religious traditions and are predominantly used in religious contexts. They are hardly ever used in other areas of everyday life. Basic knowledge of Hindi and Urdu is relatively widespread among Mauritians of Indian origin, while knowledge of Tamil, Telugu, Marathi and Arabic tends to be minimal or absent even among those Mauritians claiming them as 'ancestral languages.' The main uses of these ancestral languages lie in ritual practice, and in the possibilities identification with these languages affords for the making of religious, and ethno-religious, and even sectarian boundaries. Despite their limited use and the often minimal knowledge Mauritians have of these languages, even if they are associated with them by virtue of their background, these languages are very significant because of their ties to religion. Their important role points to the prominent place of religion and religious diversity for Mauritian nation building. The latter has largely followed a markedly multiculturalist strategy in which the ongoing cultivation as well as official recognition of diasporic 'ancestral culture'" centered on major, standardized forms of religion play a supreme role.

Given Mauritian multilingualism, Mauritians often have large linguistic repertoires. They creatively draw on them in order to take stances, define situations, and to enact social, ethnic, and religious identifications in everyday life. To make matters more complex, this is not just a matter of code-switching from one defined language to another, but also involves considerable register variation within the vernacular languages Mauritian Creole, Mauritian Bhojpuri, and French. Perhaps most significantly, there is considerable sociolinguistic variation in the way Mauritians use Mauritian Creole. This often follows the dynamics of a 'creole continuum' (Rickford, 1987) that is also attested for many other settings where creole languages are used, in the Mauritian case ranging between 'basilectal' varieties of Mauritian Creole and its lexifier language French. The use of the creole continuum's intermediate varieties of "Frenchified Creole," corresponding to what creole linguists refer to as "mesolect," evokes middle class status and higher levels of education (Eisenlohr, 2006: 131-141, see also Chaudenson, 1993: 427 and de Robillard, 1989:153).

While the role of the former colonial languages - English and French - remains uncontested in the education system, the role of the main vernacular language Mauritian Creole in education as well as the teaching of the officially claimed ancestral languages has been surrounded by controversies. Despite its role as the dominant vernacular of almost the entire population, Mauritian Creole was denied official recognition in the past. In 2012, the language was finally introduced as a school subject on an optional basis. In contrast to Mauritian Creole's striking lack of recognition as compared to its dominant role in everyday life, ancestral languages claimed by Mauritians of Indian origin as well as Mandarin, claimed by Sino-Mauritians whose ancestors were Hakka and Cantonese speakers, have long enjoyed strong official support as subjects to be taught in the school system, a policy that was already in place in the final years of colonial rule.

Language and the nation

Certainly, giving greater recognition to Mauritian Creole has been tried before. In fact, on the 50th anniversary of Mauritian independence it is highly instructive to remember the abortive attempt to give Mauritian Creole official recognition during the festivities of the 15th anniversary of independence in 1983. Leaders of the government, at the time dominated by the Mouvement Militant Mauricien (MMM), had the national anthem sung in Mauritian Creole instead of English, an event that was also announced as 'the national anthem sung in the national language' in its broadcast by the state-controlled Mauritius Broadcasting Corporation (MBC). As Mauritians remember well, this caused a crisis, triggering a political upheaval along ethnic and religious lines. The vice-Prime Minister Harish Boodhoo dismissed the director of the MBC and the governing coalition fell apart soon after. In the following general elections the MMM, which had come to power in a landslide victory the previous year and whose leader Paul Bérenger was largely responsible for the controversial decision to performatively elevate Mauritian Creole as national language in the context of the Independence Day festivities, was defeated. The political resistance that doomed this 1983 attempt to give Mauritian Creole official recognition principally came from the Hindu state bourgeoisie

(Houbert, 1982-1983: 254-255; Eisenlohr, 2007). The latter do not monopolize, but clearly hold a dominant position in the Mauritian state apparatus. This raises the question of why representatives of this group were so opposed to giving official recognition to Mauritian Creole, the vernacular language of the overwhelming majority of Mauritians, including themselves. The question why the predominant vernacular language could not become the national language goes to the heart of the issue of language and religion in Mauritian nation building. Contrasting images of Mauritian Creole became linked to two opposed ways of imagining the nation through language differences.

For those promoting Mauritian Creole as national language, this move seemed a quintessential and overdue nation building strategy. Faced with a recently created postcolonial country that exhibited stark divisions along ethnic, racial, and religious lines as a result of its past as a plantation society, the leaders of the MMM at the time saw these 'communal' divisions as an obstacle to creating a 'real' nation, and therefore a deficit to be overcome under the slogan *enn sel lepep, enn sel nasyon* (one people, one nation).[i] For them, a nation that merited such a designation would have to adopt a strategy of internal homogenisation. Conversely, heterogeneity in terms of multiple ethnic, religious, and linguistic boundaries constituted a danger to this new nation. At the same time, standardizing a widely used vernacular language and turning it into an emblem of the nation had long been a strategy easily available for 'piracy,' in Benedict Anderson's terms (Anderson, 1991: 67). Ethnolinguistic nationalism would be the vehicle for creating a new and more homogenous nation and the solution for 'communalism' that pro-Mauritian Creole activists – for good reasons – attributed to colonial history and politics. At least since the early 19th century, European nationalists had promoted vernacular standardization, resulting in the growth of ethnolinguistic nationalism in often previously linguistically heterogeneous areas. According to this ideology, the possession of a shared and standardized vernacular turns people into a nation, entitled to self-determination. The standardized vernacular language is portrayed as the already existing 'natural' language of the people, not only downplaying linguistic innovation and erasure in the process of standardisation, but also typically sidelining substantial dialectal and sociolinguistic variation among those becoming a nation, let alone histories of long-established multilingualism. Attempts to standardize Mauritian Creole have for example all been based on 'basilectal' varieties of the language. In Mauritius, Mauritian Creole is not only shared by the vast majority of the population, but probably also the most significant locally created cultural element, thus an apparently ideal instrument for nation building when seen through the lens of European-style ethnolinguistic nationalism.

However, despite its wide distribution across ethnic and religious lines, Mauritian Creole has recognisable creators that are clearly identified with one of the ethno-religious groups of Mauritius. Born on the homesteads and plantations of 18th century Isle de France, academics and the wider Mauritian public agree that the creators of Mauritian Creole were slaves, predominantly from Africa but also Madagascar and India. Their descendants are nowadays squarely identified with the Creoles, a group of highly mixed but predominantly African and Malagasy origins and Christian by religion. This position was already voiced by Charles Baissac, the author of the first scholarly study on Mauritian Creole and one of the first systematic studies of Creole languages in general (Baissac, 1880: xii). It has largely remained uncontested until today. As a result, many Mauritians consider Mauritian Creole as more pertaining to the Creoles than any other group, despite its near-universal use (Rajah-Carrim, 2007; 2008).[ii] The post-independence attempts to standardize Mauritians Creole on the basis of its most basilectal varieties, maximally distant from French influences, have only contributed to this association, since for Mauritians these varieties indicate low socioeconomic standing. This in turn dovetails with common perceptions of Creoles as an underprivileged group in Mauritian society. That is, despite the fact of its use across nearly all communal boundaries in Mauritian society, most Mauritians accord Creoles greater 'ownership' over the language than to any other group. In addition, both the Creoles as an ethno-religious group and the language Mauritian Creole are locally referred to with the same term 'Creole' (*Kreol*). This perceived lack of ethno-religious 'neutrality,' predicated on a distinction between factual use and ideological ownership was one of the key reasons for the spectacular failure of the 1983 attempt to declare Mauritian Creole national language, and the political backlash against its perpetrators. In particular, the Hindu middle classes and the Hindu state bourgeoisie saw in the campaign for recognizing Mauritian Creole as national language a thinly disguised attempt at sidelining their centrality to the new postcolonial nation, placing Creoles, and thereby Christians in a privileged position in the national imaginary instead.

Hindu elites had at the time already successfully institutionalized a rather different regime of linking language and nationhood in Mauritius. Theirs is a vision of state-sponsored multiculturalism that highlights separate ancestral traditions brought from elsewhere over locally created cultural forms widely shared among Mauritians. According to them, Mauritius is already an established nation, albeit one that does not follow a model of nation building as homogenization. For them, the enduring deep communal divisions are not a deficit to be overcome on the road to a "real" nation. Instead, they view Mauritius as a mosaic of groups defined by their diasporic links to places of origin, especially India, as almost 70% of the population is of Indian background. Seen from this perspective, the public cultivation and celebration of such ancestral cultures is what makes people truly Mauritian in a country without an indigenous pre-colonial population. Accordingly, full cultural citizenship is achieved through the cultivation of such diasporic ancestral traditions pointing to origins elsewhere. For Mauritians of Indian background, the links of such officially recognized 'ancestral cultures' to the actual cultural and religious practices of ancestors who migrated from India to Mauritius is rather tenuous, as such 'ancestral cultures' emerged only after immigration from India had almost ended. They were the result of the profound impact modern Hindu and Islamic reformist movements have had among Mauritians of Indian origin since the 1910s and 1920s. In the final decades of colonial rule, such religious mobilizations that introduced modern, more standardized forms of Hinduism and Islam to Mauritius became rallying points for Indo-Mauritians' struggle for emancipation and enfranchisement in colonial Mauritius which at the time was dominated by a Christian elite that often looked down on people of Indian origin. Instead of mere cultural baggage brought from India, such 'ancestral cultures' were in fact new creations, a powerful response to the often difficult situation of most Indo-Mauritians under colonial rule. Like Creole culture, they should be understood as local creations. However, adherents of such ancestral traditions strongly highlight the Indian origins of the key elements out which they are composed.

The intertwining of language and religion in Mauritian nation building

An important official justification for the support of such 'ancestral cultures' is their supposedly stabilizing function for the 'social fabric' of Mauritius. According to official state discourse, these ancestral cultures with their religious foundations provide invaluable moral grounding in a society such as Mauritius that has undergone very rapid economic transformation and modernisation, helping to ensure the shaping of economically productive Mauritian citizens and their social cohesion. The fact that the strong promotion of such ancestral cultures also leads to the hardening of religious boundaries among Mauritians is usually sidelined by resorting to a Gandhian discourse that distinguishes between supposedly 'true' religion as the condition of possibility for a moral society, giving the impression that all religions are ultimately based on the same values, and religion's reprehensible political instrumentalisation that is known in Mauritius, as in India, as 'communalism.'[iii] This policy is inspired by the maxim 'unity in diversity' that characterised postcolonial nation building in India under Nehru (Peghini, 2016: 31-32), but takes a more optimistic Gandhian perspective on religion as the stabilising moral core of society and politics. Consider for example former Prime Minister Anerood Jugnauth's remarks at the opening of the Ramayana Centre in 2002: 'it [is] very important to perpetuate human values, particularly in the present context when crimes have increased, family breakups and divorces are frequent and moral commitment has lost its meaning.' Jugnauth went on to argue that only 'socio-cultural organisations,' which in Mauritian public discourse refer to politically well-connected religious organisations 'can in a real sense be the answer to today's social problems.' According to him, the Ramayana Centre 'would play a pivotal role for the moral and social uplift of the society at large.'[iv] Anerood Jugnauth also stated, in Hindi, that during his long term as Prime Minister of Mauritius, 'in politics and statecraft the Ramayana has been my greatest ideal (*rājnītī men rāmāyaṇ merā sabse baṛā ādarsh rahī hai*).'[v] The Ramayana Centre also is a good example of the important transnational dimensions of making Mauritian 'ancestral cultures,' as it was founded by an alliance of Mauritian and Indian Hindu and Hindu nationalist organizations. In June 2017 Indian Prime Minister Narendra Modi of the Hindu nationalist BJP and Indian Minister of External Affairs and BJP leader Sushma Swaraj sent congratulatory messages to the Centre on the occasion of the inauguration of its Ram temple (*Ram mandir*). The dense Hindu nationalist networks between Mauritius and India that have played a considerable role in shaping Hindu 'ancestral culture' go back to the 1970s and have from the beginning involved representatives of the Mauritian state apparatus, up the ministerial level (Eisenlohr, 2006: 36-44; 48-50).

Another implication of this regime of privileging ancestral cultures based on religious tradition is the marginalisation of those Mauritians who have no recognised claims on a diaspora-religion complex that would count as 'ancestral culture' in Mauritius. This of course primarily applies to Creoles. Official discourse on the virtues of ancestral cultures implicitly suggests that those, like the Creoles, who do not have recognised claims on an ancestral culture do not contribute to the stabilising of the 'social fabric' in the same way as other groups do. Seen from the vantage point of a discourse of 'ancestral culture,' they lack the moral resources to be socio-economically beneficial citizens. In addition, they also have no prestigious und useful connection to a major foreign power associated with a given 'ancestral culture,' such as the longstanding official connections between Mauritian Hindu organizations and India. This view of Creoles as both morally and economically lacking because of an absence of 'ancestral culture' is also rather widespread beyond official circles, at least among Hindus. During my field research among Hindu Mauritians in northern and northeast Mauritius, I often heard a fair number of my interlocutors compare themselves positively to Creoles. According to them, 'Hindu values', among which they considered to be family cohesion, thrift, and a willingness to sacrifice immediate pleasure for greater gains in the long run, had enabled them to experience considerable socio-economic mobility from very humble origins as indentured workers and small sugarcane planters. In contrast, they looked down on Creoles for 'having no culture,' which they also thought was responsible for lifestyles that led to Creole economic failure, unstable families, and shortsighted and imprudent spending patterns. In other words, in such popular renderings of the discourse of diasporic 'ancestral cultures' with religious biases, moral and economic superiority are talked about as closely intertwined.

The fact that 'ancestral cultures' claimed by Hindus of north Indian origin, Tamils, Telugus, Marathas, and Muslims very largely revolve around religious traditions and practices points to the often veiled centrality of religion for Mauritian nation-building and multiculturalism. In fact, the constitution divides Mauritians into four principal 'communities': Hindus (52%), Muslims (17%), Sino-Mauritians (2%) and the General Population (29%). The category General Population is composed of those who cannot be classified as Hindus, Muslims, or Mauritians of Chinese origin. These are largely Creoles and Franco-Mauritians, who are overwhelmingly Catholic. The small and multi-religious Sino-Mauritian community is the only one not clearly aligned with a major religious tradition (even though most Sino-Mauritians are also Catholics). Another ethnic category that transcends religious boundaries is Tamil. A considerable number of Mauritians of Tamil background are Catholics, there has been a lot of intermarriage between them and Creoles to the point that the boundaries between Christian Tamils and Creoles are often ambiguous. Nevertheless, in everyday and official discourse, the label Tamil is largely restricted to Hindu Tamils. Certainly, everyday discourse in Mauritius draws much more fine-grained ethnic distinctions. However, few of them cut across the boundaries of major religious traditions, with the exception of sub-distinctions among Sino-Mauritians.

The upshot of this is that religion is not the only, but clearly the most significant element in the boundaries between the 'communities' of Mauritius, whether seen through the lens of state discourse, or in the distinctions made among the larger public. The circumstance that Mauritians often use circumlocutions when referring to public and officially recognised religion is an indicator of the sensitivity of the issue, such as when talking about 'culture' when they mean religion, or mentioning 'socio-cultural organisations' when they mean religious organisations with considerable political influence and connections. Not only, but especially among Mauritian Hindus it is commonplace for politicians to publicly attend religious gatherings and events, usually with speeches that fuse religious themes with questions of state policy in a way serving the current interests of the politician in question, like Anerood Jugnauth did in the example above, especially at election time. The practice is as much criticised as it is impervious to any critique. The 'ancestral languages' Hindi, Tamil, Telugu, Marathi, Urdu and Arabic associated with the respective 'ancestral cultures' also primarily function as religious languages in Mauritius. When Mauritians switch to one of these languages, this can performatively mark the context of interaction in which this occurs as one of religious practice, or otherwise dedicated to the affirmation of religious belonging.

The slippage between Mauritian Creole and the Creoles as the largest non-Indian, and Christian ethnic group doomed the attempt to nationalise Mauritian Creole. Hindu elites responded to it by reinforcing longstanding trends towards ancestral and religious purity originally introduced to Mauritius by modern religious reform movements, such as the Sanatan Dharm and the Arya Samaj among Hindus of north Indian origin, and the Ahl-e Sunnat wa Jama'at (known in Mauritius as Sunnat Jamaat) and later the Deobandis among Muslims. At least among Hindus, this was also a driven by equally longstanding fears about 'creolisation.' This polysemic term merits closer attention. Hindu elites did not take this term to mean overall cultural changes in a plantation society, such as the adoption of cultural forms in for example food and language and new forms of social organisation that were locally created in a plantation setting by people with origins elsewhere. This understanding of creolisation is dominant among academics (Chaudenson, 2001; Trouillot, 1998; Vaughan, 2005; Eriksen, 2007: 156-157) and points to socio-cultural processes that virtually the entire Mauritian population has long been subject to. Instead, for many Hindu activists and also large numbers of Hindus without activist commitments, creolisation has meant 'becoming like Creoles.' For them, creolisation was a term evoking memories of oppression and disdain under colonialism when the Franco-Mauritian plantocracy often looked down on people of Indian origins and their religious traditions, and when there were also (largely unsuccessful) attempts to convert Hindus to Christianity (see Ramdoyal, 1977: 90). Creolisation in this view entails the loss of ancestral traditions, as usually happened as a consequence of slavery, with its brutal violence and disruption of family and socio-cultural ties. From such a perspective, the most significant of these disruptions is the loss of religion, and conversion to Christianity. In my research, Hindu activists often used the term 'deculturalization' to talk about these fears that the propagation of religiously based 'ancestral cultures' are supposed to counter (see Eisenlohr, 2006: 53-54).

In fact, in the literature on creolization there is much celebration of creolisation's openness and its embracing of diversity in the creation of new cultural forms, to the point that some have elevated creolization to the status of an inclusive ideal for the entire world (Bernabé, Chamoiseau and Confiant, 1993). However, creolisation, whether in practice or in academic theory, has difficulties in coming to terms with genuine religious diversity. In religious terms, Christianity appears to be its default position, despite some intermingling with other religious traditions. In the Creole cultural settings in the Caribbean and in the Indian Ocean, Christianity is the dominant tradition, while other traditions could in the past only survive through subordination and partial adaption to Christianity (e.g. Benoist, 1998). Cultural 'mixing' in the field of religion in these contexts of creolisation has historically meant the subordination and marginalisation of non-Christian religions, unless certain groups managed to break away from such dynamics of creolisation through often purist forms of religious mobilisation and revitalisation. This has been the case with Mauritians of Indian origin. In short, for the Mauritian context, this implied that creolisation could only be a phenomenon proper to a particular Christian ethnic group, but never be national. The discourses of religious mobilisation and the vindication of creolized cultural forms as emblem of the nation were opposed to each other. Given the demographic and political realities of Mauritius, the latter stood no chance. Instead of a characteristic of the entire nation, as in discourses about Mauritius as a 'Creole island' (Eisenlohr, 2009), creolisation is now widely seen as merely the defining property of a particular ethnic group in Mauritian society.

Despite the spectacular failure of the 1983 attempt to declare Mauritian Creole national language, there has been progress in the factual recognition of the language in a number of fields, such as education. An important milestone in the ongoing debates about standardisation and orthography of Mauritian Creole (Rajah-Carrim, 2008) was the 2004 issuing of *grafi-larmoni* (Hookoomsing, 2004), a new orthography designed under state sponsorship in order to create a consensual official version out of the different spelling systems already used. This was an important prerequisite for the 2012 introduction of Mauritian Creole as a school subject on an optional basis. The same period has also seen a growing vindication of Mauritian Creole as the ancestral language of the Creoles, conforming with the overall dominant multiculturalist setup of official Mauritian cultural politics. This trend, originating in the 1990s (Carpooran, 2003; 2005: 27-29) greatly accelerated after the riots of 1999, which were initially triggered by the death of Creole singer Kaya in police custody, first pitting Creole protesters against the Hindu-dominated police force and quickly leading to broader Creole-Hindu confrontations that in the end left four people dead and led to much destruction of property. Widely considered a manifestation of *le malaise Créole* (Boswell, 2006), the events led to calls and activism for greater political and economic inclusion of Creoles, but also to a stronger emphasis on Creole identity and its recognition, along the established lines of Mauritian multicultural nation-building (Harmon, 2014). Especially the introduction of Mauritian Creole as an optional school subject has followed this logic, as Creole is taught in the already existing time slots reserved for the teaching of the also optional 'ancestral languages.' As a consequence, the subject is mainly studied by students of Creole ethnic background, that is those students that would not normally be assigned to the study of either Hindi, Urdu, Tamil, Telugu, Marathi, Arabic or Mandarin (Auleear Owodally and Unjore, 2013: 215-216). Politically, the introduction is also linked to the protests of parents and organisations with Creole background against the fact that the results for the 'ancestral languages' of Mauritians of Indian and Chinese background in the Certificate of Primary Examination exams count for the final result, determining access to higher-quality secondary schools. The introduction of Creole, factually for students of Creole background, was widely understood as a compensatory move to address these grievances (Owodally, 2014: 324). And finally, the official ceremony for the introduction of the Creole language into the school curriculum in 2012 was held in the primary school of the village of Le Morne, a quintessential Creole locality in vicinity of Le Morne mountain, a UNESCO world heritage site commemorating the suffering of slaves and the resistance of maroons, and a focal site for identity of the descendants of slaves in Mauritius, the Creoles (Auleear Owodally and Unjore, 2013: 215). Thus a certain degree of official recognition of Mauritian Creole, a theme constantly argued about since independence, only came about once its proponents started framing the issue in terms of inter-ethnic justice and recognition, thereby overtly ethnicizing the Creole language. In contrast, earlier arguments about recognizing Mauritian Creole because it is already the informal national language, to use Thomas Eriksen's term (Eriksen, 1990), or the language of the working classes[vi] had hardly any effect. Mauritian Creole thus shifted from being a candidate for the role of national language, because of its near-universal use and its history of local creation, to being claimed as the ancestral patrimony of one ethnic group, in a bid to alleviate exclusion through recognition as a key part of the Mauritian multicultural mosaic. The way Mauritian Creole was officially introduced in Mauritian schools can therefore be understood as the ultimate victory of the dominant multicultural nation-building paradigm privileging 'ancestral cultures' over an ethnolinguistic nationalism centered on Mauritian Creole.

However, what distinguishes these more recent Creole activist bids for recognition and their claiming of Mauritian Creole as ancestral language is the lack of an appeal to religious alterity and difference. The latter is something that other groups that have been far more successful in gaining official recognition and valuation typically claim. These are above all the various ethno-religious groups of Indian origin who, taken together, constitute the great majority of the population. Despite the fact that Creoles are Christians and overwhelmingly Catholic, they do not claim recognition on a religious basis. This is because of enduring racial boundaries among Mauritian Christians that also powerfully contribute to Creole exclusion. In fact, Creoles are unable to replicate the very successful strategy of claiming ownership of a particular religious tradition, because the Catholic Church in Mauritius has from its very beginnings been under the control and domination of Franco-Mauritians. Also, many Sino-Mauritians are Catholics, as well as a number of Mauritians of Tamil background whose relationship with the Creoles is ambiguous. Claiming Mauritian Creole as ancestral heritage in a belated attempt to counter Creole exclusion under the current regime of Mauritian multiculturalism has therefore not had the same empowering results for Creoles compared to others claiming such languages. This is because the recognition and celebration of ancestral languages remains above all a recognition and celebration of religious traditions and religious difference. Under the dominant Mauritian regime of cultural policy, Mauritian Creole is thus doubly ineffective as ancestral language. As it is a locally created language native to nearly all Mauritians, it not only lacks fit with the long-established paradigm that ancestral languages are non-native, having origins elsewhere, and can be exclusively claimed by particular groups in Mauritian society. To make matters worse, despite the fact that Creoles are by definition Christians, the language many of them now claim as their ancestral heritage is also not clearly aligned with a particular religious tradition that Creoles could claim as their exclusive property.

Religionization as a strategy of recognition

The Mauritian nation-building policy of promoting religiously grounded 'ancestral cultures' has to be understood against the background of a long process of 'religionization' among Mauritians of Indian origin. This process is of key importance for a proper understanding of the role of language and religion in Mauritian nation building and the imbalances it has resulted in. Earlier, Indo-Mauritians were in their majority humble indentured workers and small planters widely looked down on among the white and coloured Christian elites of colonial Mauritius for being perceived as racially different and for their 'pagan' popular religious practices.[vii] In the course of rallying behind major, standardised religious traditions, Mauritians of Indian background managed to change their standing, gaining greater recognition by turning into respected representatives of the major 'world religions' (Masuzawa, 2005) Hinduism and Islam. As scholarship on South Asia has amply documented, present-day Hinduism and Islam in India do not stand in an unbroken continuity with a deep past, but are the product of powerful reformist movements in 19th century India. In many ways, the latter were a direct response to the colonial situation (van der Veer, 1994; 2001; Metcalf, 1982; Pandey, 2006; Viswanathan, 2003; Frykenberg, 1989). Especially the notion of Hinduism as a clearly identifiable, more or less bounded 'religion' is a product of this process that only began in the 19th century. Responding to Christian critiques of idol worship and practices deemed to be barbarian, an emerging Hindu middle class refashioned religious traditions along the lines of the Christian-influenced concept of religion. This entailed a greater focus on a limited number of sacred texts, a neo-Vedantist highlighting of philosophical foundations, and greater standardisation of religious doctrine and practice, often through Sanskritization. This newly standardised array of highly diverse traditions and practices then took the shape of an identifiable 'religion' also by making use of the emerging public sphere aided by modern transport and communications technology in colonial India. These dynamics of religious standardisation and reform through entering the modern public sphere were also particularly evident among Islamic reformers. For them, the turn to a newly emerging Indian Muslim public was particularly pressing because of the 'ulema's loss of patronage by Muslim dynastic states, especially after the failed anti-colonial rebellion of 1857. Both Hindu and Muslim reformers' stress on individual moral responsibility stemmed from this need to address a newly forming Indian public directly, bypassing state institutions, in an adjustment to the realities of colonial domination. This also resulted in greater intra-religious and sectarian competition. In short, colonial rule in 19th century India engendered a powerful response among Indian elites and middle classes that led to the highlighting of religious difference from the colonizer. This kind of self-assertion though religious mobilization also brought about a reconfigured religious landscape, resulting in standardized and competing 'religions' stressing the theme of personal moral reform. In relative terms, the dominance of modern Hindu and Islamic reformist movements in Mauritius became even more pronounced than in India. These modern religious movements were able to effect a far-ranging transformation of Indo-Mauritian society earlier than was the case in India. Among Mauritians of Indian origin, particularly Hindus of North Indian background and Muslims, it led to significant changes in religious practices and identifications so that the shared world of rural ritual practices that initially were more meaningful to indentured laborers and their descendants than the labels 'Hindu' and 'Muslim' gradually receded, turning 'Indians' into Hindus or Muslims of various sectarian affiliations.

Many Mauritian Hindus and Muslims have common origins in Northern India, the area that are now the states of Uttar Pradesh and Bihar. They shared the same harsh working and living conditions on the sugar plantations of colonial Mauritius and later lived side-by-side in the emerging Indian-dominated villages that dot the Mauritian countryside. Ritual kinship based on the memory of having traveled on the same boat (*jahaij bhai*) was common across religious lines and religious divides were much less significant than they are today. In the 19th century, religious and ritual practices of most Indo-Mauritians were often more influenced by a shared rural and regional background, albeit divided by reconfigured caste lines, than by awareness of belonging to two major separate religious traditions. The migration of indentured labourers from mostly rural districts was already in full swing when modern Indian religious reform movements were just emerging. As a consequence, these movements were initially not able to exert much influence among the migrants. This changed in the early 20th century, when Indian religious reform movements finally reached Mauritius, at a time when migration from India had mostly ended. In 1910 the Arya Samaj arrived in Mauritius, followed in the 1920s by the competing Sanatan Dharm movement, that was locally spearheaded by high castes (*Babujee-maraz*), and the Ahl-e Sunnat wa Jama'at (Sunnat Jama'at). The supremacy of the latter movement among Muslims, linked to the Kutchi Memon trader community began to be challenged with the entry of the Deoband-linked Tablighi Jama'at that were initially connected to the Sunni Surtees, another Muslim Gujarati trader community from the 1950s onwards. These movements spread very rapidly among Mauritians of Indian origin, reforming religious practice and above all raising awareness of belonging to Hinduism and Islam as major world religions. Among Muslims, this led to ongoing debates and concerns about ritual orthopraxy that resulted in the abandonment of a number of features of ritual life that were common well into the 20th century (Benedict, 1961: 142; Hollup, 1996; see also Bal and Sinha-Kerkhoff, 2007: 128; Jahangeer-Choojo, 1997). One consequence was that Mauritian Muslims coalesced into rival sectarian groups that mirror the broader landscape of Islam in South Asia. Even though these sectarian traditions have always opposed each other, it made their followers more aware of their membership in a global community of Muslims, following one of the world's major religious traditions. A rising concern with orthopraxy was also present among those Mauritians of north Indian background who started to think of themselves as Hindus, particularly among the followers of the Arya Samaj (Hollup, 1995), whose influence was soon challenged by the Sanatan Dharm movement. Having conducted fieldwork in 1955-1957, Burton Benedict described low-caste ceremonies in honour of Kali and minor guardian deities that involved animal sacrifice and possession (Benedict, 1961: 131-134). But he also wrote of an already strong trend towards Sanskritization replacing local, tribal, or caste tradition: 'The special practices of the low caste Chamars and Dusads are being abandoned for standardised Arya Samaji or Sanatani practices. Many distinctive ceremonies performed in former days have vanished within the last decade' (Benedict, 1961: 141). Nevertheless, the main emphasis of Hindu reformist movements was less on orthopraxy than on 'Hindu unity,' that is the spreading of the notion that there is a Hindu religion that unites many diverse ritual and sectarian traditions as well as religious practitioners of different castes and regions. The 'high' Sanskritic deities worshipped in temples that until 1986 were controlled by high castes (Eisenlohr, 2006: 222, 292-293) have become increasingly dominant. However, the tenacity of the popular cults at the multitude of smaller shrines known as *kalimai*, and the continued existence of low-caste rituals involving animal sacrifice such as *baharia puja* already described by Benedict are indicative of the limits of ritual standardization among Mauritian Hindus (Chazan-Gillig and Ramhota, 2009: 275-302). As happened among Muslims, religious reform and standardization also provoked the establishment of rival religious movements and associations among Mauritians of Indian background that had begun to identify as Hindus. These new divisions were less motivated by questions of ritual doctrine and practice, as was the case Muslims, but primarily emerged on regional (Eisenlohr, 2006: 234-238, Chazan-Gillig and Ramhota, 2009) and caste lines (Hollup, 1994: 302-303, 1995,; Eisenlohr, 2006: 98-99, 222, 278,; Chazan-Gillig and Ramhota, 2009), and nowadays are intimately connected to electoral politics (Chazan-Gillig and Ramhota, 2009). Nevertheless, and this is the crucial point, Hindu reformers were largely successful in grafting the label 'Hindu' on this diverse array of caste-based, regional and sectarian practices and affiliations.[viii] The stress on ideological unity, a common overall identity rather than unity of ritual doctrine and practice is also a hallmark of modern Hindu nationalist organizations, such as the Vishwa Hindu Parishad ('World Hindu Council') who since its foundation in 1964 has shown a particular interest in mobilising diasporic Hindus, including in Mauritius.

Among those beginning to identify as Hindus and Muslims, modern reformist movements also reinvigorated a connection with India, above all through regular visits of missionaries, the circulation of religious images and literature, and other links to the Indian public sphere. For Muslims, the presence of Gujarati trader communities who had settled in Mauritius as free immigrants with their own capital and who maintained dense business, kinship, and religious networks with India played a key role in facilitating the entry of the Ahl-e Sunnat wa Jama'at, and later the Tablighi Jama'at to Mauritius and the building of their institutions. Very importantly, all these Hindu and Islamic reformist movement enabled Mauritians of Indian origin to gain dignity as followers of a major world religion, with a global mission and presence (see Eisenlohr, 2012). These developments helped to spread more orthodox and purist ideas and practices about Hinduism and Islam in Mauritius and contributed to a shrinking of the old Indo-Mauritian worlds of shared sociability. The formally predominantly rural and regional ritual practices of Mauritians of Indian origin became more standardised while Indo-Mauritians began to align religious identities with the categories Hinduism and Islam.

In other words, since the first half of the 20th century Mauritians of Indian origins have successfully pursued a strategy of overcoming racial stigma as well as political and economic marginalisation through religionisation. It was this strategy that crucially informed the cultural policy of promoting ancestral cultures that was put in place in the final years of colonial rule. After independence, the newly dominant Hindu state bourgeoisie turned this into a model of nation-building casting Mauritius as a diasporic mosaic of 'communities,' with religion being by far the most important element of differentiation between such communities. One of the obvious imbalances built into this Mauritian regime of nation building is that the route to recognition through religionization has always been blocked for Creoles. As mentioned, Franco-Mauritian control of the Catholic Church made it impossible for Creoles to claim a religious tradition as their exclusive property in the same way as Mauritians of Indian origin were able to do with Hinduism and Islam. Also, despite its very important role in contemporary Africa, Christianity is not really considered 'African' in Mauritius, thus not suitable for the creation of 'ancestral' origins in the same manner as Hinduism and Islam are for Mauritians with Indian backgrounds. As a result, Creoles had no access to a comparable strategy of religionization in order to overcome racial stigma and socio-economic marginalisation. Not being able to claim property of a recognised 'ancestral culture' with a religious core put them in a marginal position in the dominant project of postcolonial Mauritian nation building.

Conclusion

In this chapter, I have discussed the main two modes of Mauritian nation building, focusing on their language ideologies and the role religion plays in them. The dominance of the multiculturalist model privileging 'ancestral cultures' and the apparent defeat of ethnolinguistic nationalism based on Mauritian Creole point to the centrality of religion in Mauritian nation building. I have tried to show how 'religionization' as a strategy of recognition has empowered Mauritians of Indian origin, who taken together constitute the great majority of the population. Even though a process originating in the first half of the 20th century, nowadays this strategy is also in line with an overall resurgence of public religion in many parts of the modern world, which some analysts have linked to the dynamics of globalisation (Csordas, 2009). In this sense, the centrality of religion to Mauritian nation building is also linked to the profoundly transnational quality of religious networks. Religious dynamics in other parts of the world, such as in South Asia, have had a deep impact on the Mauritian religious landscape and its social and political ramifications. The great imbalance in Mauritian multiculturalism as a nation-building strategy is that the Creoles do not have access to a comparable strategy of gaining recognition through foregrounding a link to a major religious tradition. The dominant imaginary of the nation as a diasporic mosaic mostly defined by religion sidelines them. The main tension in this Mauritian model of multicultural nation building is thus not only that it hardens religious boundaries among Mauritians, such as between Hindus and Muslims. Above all, it marginalises those who are not defined in terms of religious alterity and those who cannot claim exclusive 'ownership' of a religious tradition.

References

Anderson, Benedict. (1991) *Imagined communities: Reflections on the Origin and Spread of Nationalism.* London: Verso.

Auleear Owodally, Ambarin Mooznah. (2014) 'Language, education and identities in plural Mauritius: a study of the Kreol, Hindi and Urdu Standard 1 textbooks', *Language and Education* 28(4): 319-339.

Auleear Owodally, Ambarin Mooznah and Sanju Unjore. (2013) 'Kreol at school: a case study of Mauritian Muslims' language and literacy ideologies', *Journal of Multilingual and Multicultural Development* 34(3): 213-130.

Baissac, Charles. (1880) *Etude sur le patois créole mauricien.* Nancy: Berger-Levrault.

Bal, Ellen and Kathinka Sinha-Kerkhoff. (2007) 'Separated by the Partition? Muslims of British Descent in Mauritius and Suriname', in Gijsbert Oonk (ed) *Global Indian Diasporas: Exploring Trajectories of Migration and Theory.* Amsterdam: Amsterdam University Press.

Benedict, Burton. (1961) *Indians in a Plural Society. A Report on Mauritius.* London: Her Majesty's Stationary Office.

Benoist, Jean. (1998) *Hindouismes créoles. Mascareignes, Antilles.* Paris: Editions du C.T.H.S.

Bernabé, Jean, Patrick Chamoiseau and Raphaël Confiant. (1993) *Éloge de la Créolité.* (Edition bilingue). Paris: Gallimard.

Boswell, Rosabelle. (2006) *Le Malaise Créole: Ethnic Identity in Mauritius.* New York: Berghahn.

Carpooran, Arnaud. (2003) 'Reconnaissance et promotion du fait créole à Maurice: Bilan et perspectives', *Etudes Créoles* 26(2): 31-66.

Carpooran, Arnaud. (2005) 'Le créole à l'école à Maurice: Historique et évolution du débat', *Etudes Créoles* 28(2): 15-40.

Chaudenson, Robert. (1993) 'Français et créoles dans les aires créolophones', in Didier de Robillard and Michel Beniamino (eds) *Le français dans l'espace francophone. Tome I.* Paris: Editions Champion.

Chaudenson, Robert. (2001) *Creolization of Language and Culture.* London/New York: Routledge.

Chazan-Gillig, Suzanne and Pavitranand Ramhota. (2009) *L'hindouisme mauricien dans la mondialisation. Cultes populaires et religion savante.* Marseille: IRD/Paris: Karthala/ Moka: MGI.

Csordas, Thomas. (ed) (2009) *Transnational Transcendence: Essays on Religion and Globalization.* Berkeley: University of California Press.

de Robillard, Didier. (1989) 'Développement, langue, identité ethno-linguistique: Le cas de l'Île Maurice', in Francis Jouannet *et al.* (eds) *Langues, économie et développement (Tome 2).* Aix-en-Provence: Institut d'Études Créoles et Francophones/Didier Erudition.

Eisenlohr, Patrick. (2006) *Little India: Diaspora, Time and Ethnolinguistic Belonging in Hindu Mauritius.* Berkeley: University of California Press.

Eisenlohr, Patrick. (2007) 'Creole publics: Language, cultural citizenship, and the spread of the nation in Mauritius', *Comparative Studies in Society and History* 49(4): 968-996.

Eisenlohr, Patrick. (2009) 'An Indian Ocean Creole island? Language and the politics of hybridity in Mauritius', in Vinesh Y. Hookoomsing, Ralph Ludwig, Burkhard Schnepel (eds) *Multiple Identities in Action: Mauritius and Some Antillean Parallelisms*. Frankfurt: Peter Lang.

Eisenlohr, Patrick. (2012) 'Cosmopolitanism, globalization, and Islamic piety movements in Mauritius', *City and Society* 24(1): 7-28.

Eriksen, Thomas Hylland. (1990) 'Linguistic Diversity and the Quest for National Identity: The Case of Mauritius', *Ethnic and Racial Studies* 13(1): 1-24.

Eriksen, Thomas Hylland. (1994) 'Nationalism, Mauritian Style: Cultural Unity and Ethnic Diversity', *Comparative Studies in Society and History* 36(3): 549-574.

Eriksen, Thomas Hylland. (2007) 'Creolization in Anthropological Theory and in Mauritius', in Charles Stewart (ed) *Creolization: History, Ethnography, Theory*. Walnut Creek, CA: Left Coast Press.

Frykenberg, Robert E. (1989) 'The Emergence of Modern 'Hinduism' as a Concept and as an Institution: A Reappraisal with Special Reference to South India', in Gunther D. Sontheimer and Hermann Kulke (eds) *Hinduism Reconsidered*. Delhi: Manohar.

Harmon, Jimmy Desiré. (2014) *Heritage Language & Identity Construction: A Critical Ethnography of Kreol Morisien as an Optional Language in Primary Education within the Republic of Mauritius*. PhD thesis, University of the Western Cape.

Hookoomsing, Vinesh Y. (2004) *Grafi-larmoni. A Harmonized Writing System for the Mauritian Creole Language*. http://ministry education.govmu.org/English/Documents/Publications /arch%20Reports/hookoomsing.pdf, accessed 11 Sept 2017.

Hollup, Oddvar. (1994) 'The Disintegration of Caste and Changing Concepts of Indian Ethnic Identity in Mauritius', *Ethnology* 33(4): 297-316.

Hollup, Oddvar. (1995) 'Arya Samaj and the Shaping of "Egalitarian" Hindus in Mauritius', *Folk* 36: 27-39.

Hollup, Oddvar. (1996) 'Islamic Revivalism and Political Opposition among Minority Muslims in Mauritius', *Ethnology* 35(4): 285-300.

Houbert, Jean. (1982/1983) 'Mauritius: Politics and Pluralism at the Periphery', *Annuaire des Pays de l'Océan Indien* 9: 225–65.

Irvine, Judith and Susan Gal. (2000) 'Language Ideology and Linguistic Differentiation', in Paul V Kroskrity (ed) *Regimes of Language: Ideologies, Polities and Identities*. Santa Fe: School of American Research Press.

Jahangeer-Chojoo, Amenah. (1997) *La communauté musulmane de Port Louis. Une étude de géographie sociale*. Thèse de doctorat, Université Michel de Montaigne, Bordeaux III.

Masuzawa, Tomoko. (2005) *The invention of world religions, or how European universalism was preserved in the language of pluralism*. Chicago: University of Chicago Press.

Mérédac, Savinien. (1929) Petits entretiens sur notre patois', in *Centenaire de la Société Royale des Arts et des Sciences de l'Ile Maurice, 1829-1929*. Port Louis, Mauritius..

Metcalf, Barbara D. (1982) *Islamic Revival in British India: Deoband 1860–1900*. Princeton: Princeton University Press.

Pandey, Gyanendra. (2006) *The Construction of Communalism in Colonial North India*. 2nd edn. Delhi: Oxford University Press.

Parsuramen, Armoogum. (1988) *From Ancestral Cultures to National Culture: Mauritius*. Moka: Mahatma Gandhi Institute Press.

Parsuramen, Armoogum. (n.d) *Towards Green Horizons*. Beau Bassin: Mauritius Institute of Education/Curriculum Development Unit.

Peghini, Julie. (2016) *Île rêvée, île réelle. Le multiculturalisme à l'île Maurice*. Saint-Denis: Presses Universitaires de Vincennes.

Rajah-Carrim, Aaliya. (2007) 'Mauritian Creole and Language Attitudes in the Education System of Multiethnic and Multilingual Mauritius', *Journal of Multilingual and Multicultural Development* 28(1): 51-71.

Rajah-Carrim, Aaliya. (2008) 'Choosing a Spelling System for Mauritian Creole', *Journal of Pidgin and Creole Languages* 23(2): 193-226.

Ramdoyal, Ramesh Dutt. (1977) *The Development of Education in Mauritius 1710-1976*. Réduit: Mauritius Institute of Education.

Rickford John R. (1987) *Dimensions of a Creole Continuum: History, Texts and Linguistic Analysis of Guyanese Creole*. Stanford: Stanford University Press.

Teelock, Vijayalakshmi. (2017) 'The Legacy of Indentured Labour and the Mauritian Truth and Justice Commission: A Missed Opportunity?', in Maurits S Hassankhan, Lomarsh Roopnarine and Hans Ramsoedh (eds) *The Legacy of Indian Indenture: Historical and Contemporary Aspects of Migration and Diaspora*. London/New York: Routledge.

Trouillet, Pierre-Yves. (2014) 'Les lances de Muruga à Maurice: Trajectoires d'un hindouisme tamoul', in Catherine Servan-Schreiber (ed) *Indianité et créolité à l'île Maurice*. Paris: Éditions de L'École des hautes études en sciences sociales/Collection Purusartha.

Troulliot, Michel-Rolph. (1998) 'Culture on the Edges: Creolization in the Plantation Context', *Plantation Society in the Americas* 5: 8-28.

van der Veer, Peter. (1994) *Religious Nationalism: Hindus and Muslims in India*. Berkeley: University of California Press.

van der Veer, Peter. (2001) *Imperial Encounters: Religion and Modernity in India and Britain*. Princeton, N.J.: Princeton University Press.

Vaughan, Megan. (2005) *Creating the Creole Island: Slavery in Eighteenth-Century Mauritius*. Durham/London: Duke University Press.

Viswanathan, Gauri. (2003) 'Colonialism and the Construction of Hinduism', in Gavin Flood (ed) *The Blackwell Companion to Hinduism*. Malden, MA: Blackwell.

---

[i] In Mauritian Creole *nasyon* is a polysemic concept that covers other meanings besides 'nation.' In everyday life, Hindus more often use it to denote 'caste,' such as in *gran nasyon* (high caste) and *ti nasyon* (low caste). It can also be understood as a reference to 'African' or 'person of African phenotype,' or 'Creole,' depending on context. Eriksen (1994: 553-554) has pointed to the confusion this caused during political campaigns.

[ii] A widespread notion in colonial Mauritius was that Creoles speak the 'proper' Mauritian Creole while the Creole used by Mauritians of Indian background was deficient in comparison. For example, the Mauritian

writer Auguste Esnouf (1880-1939), writing under the pseudonym Savinien Mérédac distinguished 'the patois that the blacks speak among themselves' from 'different special *sous-patois* conditioned by the race of the interlocutor: Chinese, Indian, pseudo-Arab.' 'We are even forced to note that the Indian has introduced into the patois accented forms that really never existed before him [before the beginning of Indian immigration to Mauritius]. The Creole from our home [the Creole domestic servant] says: "Mo fine appèle li" (I have called him/her); the Indian "Mo fini appèlé pour li"' (Mérédac, 1929: 123). Esnouf used the common label for Mauritian Creole at the time, *patois*, denying it the status of a 'real' language, but nevertheless suggests that there are correct and ungrammatical ways of speaking it. Thus, at the time, the notion that Creoles speak the proper form of the language they invented was already established. Even though today hardly anybody in Mauritius would suggest that the Mauritian Creole spoken by Mauritians of Indian extraction is incorrect or deficient as Mérédac suggested almost 90 years ago, the stronger association of Mauritian Creole with the Creoles when compared to other ethno-religious groups in Mauritian society is still relevant today.

[iii] The policy documents of Armoogum Parsuramen, Minister of Arts and culture from 1984 to 1995 under Prime Minister Jugnauth are good illustrations of this official doctrine that identifies the promotion of 'ancestral' religious traditions with the strengthening of social and political cohesion. This is a key justification for Mauritian multiculturalist politics (Parsuramen, 1988, n.d.).

[iv] Ramayana Centre in Mauritius, Organiser (New Delhi), 8 September 2002.

[v] 'SAJ and values of Ramayana: from then to now and beyond', *Mauritius Times*, 23 August 2002.

[vi] Since the 1970s the Marxist groups LPT (*Ledikasyon pu travayer)* and *Lalit* have promoted Mauritian Creole as the language of the Mauritian working classes deliberately sidelining ethnic and religious identifications, publishing a considerable amount of literature and dictionaries in the language, in addition to devising an orthography for Mauritian Creole that is maximally distant from French.

[vii] Certainly, even among Hindus not all Mauritians of Indian background were of humble social standing, some succeeded in business and became owners of sugar estates. In the period up to the abolition of slavery, some even were slave owners (Teelock, 2017: 90-91)

[viii] A partial exception are Tamils, who reject the term 'Hindu' for themselves, which in everyday discourse is limited to Mauritian Hindus of north Indian origin only. From the perspective of the constitution, and for the purposes of the census they however count as Hindus. Many Mauritian Tamils also reject the term 'Hindu' for their religious rituals and festivals which they call 'Tamil' instead: 'The distancing of Tamils from a Hindu identity is particular to Mauritius. It does not exist elsewhere, neither in the Tamil diaspora, nor in Tamil Nadu, their land of origin, where 90% of the population is even officially of Hindu religion....' (Trouillet, 2014: 170).

Performative Historiography of the Mother Tongue
Reading 'Kreol' outside a Colonial and Nationalist Approach

GITANJALI PYNDIAH

Introduction

'Mezon kreol', 'kuizinn kreol', 'ti kreol', 'langaz Kreol' 'nou tou kreol' - colonial house, cuisine of blended influences, a Black person, the Creole language, we are all culturally mixed, are terms and expressions, written here within the standardised orthography, that are commonly articulated in contemporary Mauritius. The different semantic dimensions of the term Creole, to either denigrate or glorify reflect the colonial history of the term, which originally fed into a mechanism of establishing hierarchies within the plantation colony. In the context of Mauritius during the French and English colonial period (1710-1968)[i], 'Creole' was used to distinguish settlers born in the colony from the metropolitan French (Police, 2005). It later became a denigrating reference to categorise people of mixed races, or to denote people of African or Indian origins as a racialized marker of inferiority, justifying the economic exploitation of enslaved and indentured labour. The Mauritius islands[ii] have witnessed various countermovements of 'positivisation' (Police, 2005) such as the colonial appropriation of Creole (for literary purposes for example) as well as the post independence nationalist valorisation of the language (often intellectual) as acts of resistance to inherited colonial structures which still pervade postcolonial spaces.

This chapter aims at questioning what *being* or *becoming* creole entails through a decolonial approach. It first expands on the colonial present through the lens of decolonisation as a process of deconstructing inherited colonial aesthetics, epistemologies and historiographies. Focus is then made on the colonial denigration in parallel with appropriation of the Creole language, as well the nationalist activism of language valorisation. Thirdly, this chapter proposes a decolonial reading of Creole based on the oral, scribal, sonic, embodied and performative aspect of the language as mother tongue[iii], in contrast with literate culture and its appropriation within a colonial logic. In relation to thinking of the future of the Indian Ocean islands and considering that the colonial infrastructures of power inherited by the postcolonial state of Mauritius have contributed to the economic miracle enjoyed mainly by a comfortably rising conservative middle class, the reflection that this chapter raises is how to understand Creole cultures as potentialities of more decolonial humane societies, outside systems of exploitation, accumulation and consumption[iv]

Fifty years after Independence and during almost a century of political dismantling of colonial administration, contemporary Mauritius is still embedded in colonial structures, representations, geographies, historiographies and epistemologies (Boudet and Peghini, 2008; Collen, 2017; Edensor and Kothari, 2005; Eriksen, 1998; Forest, 2011; Hay and Salverda, 2013; Kothari and Wilkinson, 2010; Police, 2005; Selvon, 2001). While, in mainstream narratives of/on Mauritius, it is generally perceived that decolonisation was achieved after Independence, many scholars contest residual coloniality, without necessarily using the term 'decolonisation'[v]. The persistence of colonial epistemologies and historiographies in new nations is not unique to Mauritius and has been articulated and theorised by many writers and scholars, whose works fall in the postcolonial and decolonial cannon[vi], in reference to similar anti-colonial and supposedly 'post'-colonial situations. For example, the work of Sylvia Wynter, who comes from a Black radical anti-colonial tradition and who produces ontological work from the Caribbean (Jamaican) experience, remain fundamental to the decolonial critique. She refers to the symbolical date 1492 as representing the beginning of 'a founding politico-statal mercantilist economic system' based on racialised power structures of labour (McKittrick and Wynter, 2015: 46). Wynter informs us that by 1900, more than half of Asia, 98 per cent of Africa as well as most of the former slave plantation archipelago islands of the Caribbean (and the Indian Ocean islands) were under direct colonial rule. Understanding the epistemological shift of the 'post-1492 New World' is relevant to a reading of colonialism in the Indian Ocean region as the strategies of external, internal and settler colonialism were all deployed, since the seventeenth century, in the region to establish sovereignty over 'virgin' lands for capitalist exploitation. Within a decolonial historiography, the history of human contact on the islands was thus born at the inter-related junction of slavery-based merchant capitalism and external colonialism, which legitimated imperialist conquest as well as exploitative systems of labour. Within a few centuries of European colonialism, the islands were reduced to sugar plantation economies under Dutch exploitation colonisation (1638-1710), French settler colonialism (1710-1810) and English administration (1810-1968) dependent of enslaved labour from mainly East Africa (and India), then indentured and migrant labour from India and China after the abolition of slavery.

Critical literature on Mauritius reveals that 'official national symbolism in Mauritius is still closely linked to the colonial ideology and its symbols' (Eriksen, 1998: 11) and that the term postcolonial cannot be applied, in any definite way to the Mauritian context 'with the abiding [economic] presence of the French community following the country's Independence' (Mukherji, 2006: 4). The Franco-Mauritians are no longer the island's only elite, yet they remain the community with the highest socio-economic status, and the island's dominant business elite and as a small minority, they control about a third of the hundred top companies and five of the ten largest companies, and maintain control over large parts of the island's agricultural land (Salverda, 2015: 534). They also generate enclaves of exclusion and segregation reflecting 'the loss of their superior position, anxieties compounded by substantial demographic shifts and growing numbers of others entering their formerly exclusive enclaves' (Hay and Salverda, 2011: 237). Furthermore, based on research on representation, the 'mythical-history' of French settlers is given centre stage in national narratives of progress and simultaneously promotes the conception of a national history which proceeds from the group's history (Boudet and Peghini, 2008). For example, a specific private venture in Mauritius, the Blue Penny Museum funded by the Mauritius Commercial Bank, itself a financial institution founded on compensation received by ex-slave owners after the abolition of the European slave trade, portrays colonial history within a narrative of progress and consequently a 'myth of foundation' is perpetuated, which places colonisers as the founders of development and a civilising mission on the island. The same dialectical narrative is consistently repeated across colonial museums which have been nationalised after independence, namely the Natural History Museum in Port Louis and the National History Museum (colonial Naval Museum) in Mahebourg (Forest, 2011). The reports (specially the few papers addressing this issue) of the Mauritian Truth and Justice Commission (TJC), set up in 2009 to look into the consequences of slavery and indenture establish a historical link between colonial institutions (colonial epistemologies) and the memorial framework endorsed by the state[vii]. What is also problematic is the 'sweetening' of colonial history (Edensor and Kothari, 2005: 190) in the present within representations of colonisation, sanitised of its features of domination and oppression (Boudet and Peghini, 2008: 2), thus perpetuating colonial discourses which still intervene 'in the physical and social space of former colonies and ... continue to be mobilised in postcolonial contexts' (Kothari & Wilkinson, 2010). Edensor and Kothari analyse tourism as performance, from the specific study of a theme resort in Mauritius, the hotel *Sugar Beach* which itself evokes the banalisation of the system of economic exploitation that sugar plantocracies supported[viii]. They demonstrate the use of colonial forms of representation in capitalist ventures for the sake of tourism and illustrate how this setting is 'a strikingly dissonant image for those familiar with the inequities of Mauritian colonialism' (193). The history of the Creole language and the usage of the term Creole also reveals processes of colonial denigration and appropriation which still reverberate in contemporary Mauritius.

Colonising Creole

For more than a century during French colonisation (1710-1810), the different African languages in conjunction with French provided the initial cartography for the development of a Creole language on the islands. While most languages usually developed gradually, Creole languages exhibit an abrupt break in the course of their historical development from, what has been theorised as, the 'linguistic violence' (Arends *et al.*, 1994: 4) provoked by the institutionalised violence of slavery. A decolonial genealogy of the Creole language reveals that African tongues were figuratively 'cut out' (Anzaldúa, 1987: 34) under forms of epistemic colonialism, demonstrative of the linguistic violence or 'linguistic terrorism' on African languages under French cultural domination[ix]. In the process, an africanised language of communication emerged, which despite retaining close lexical links to the coloniser's tongue, subverted the dominant French dialects from Britanny (Chaudenson and Mufwene, 2001). For Jamaican theorist Carolyn Cooper, 'counter-colonising Creole tongues' involve seeing the reverse side of the coin that the Creole language 'africanise colonial languages [which] confirms the humanity of language creators as 'proactive bearers of culture, not mere zombies - passive receptacles of the will of the enslaving other' (1993: 174).

This phenomenon is visible in many postcolonial nations, where colonial languages have been adopted and valorised to the detriment of indigenous/native languages. The different aspects of language use, 'language of real life, language as communication in speech, and the written language' (Ngũgĩ, 1986: 13-15) is often inherent within the speaker's mothertongue which allows for a smooth transmission of the culture which the language carries.[x] This death of language, hence cultural traditions which languages carry, caused the deculturation (Ngũgĩ, 1986) of the African population, and in the process of a hundred years of bi-racial interaction (coercive or not), any attachment to a notion of 'Africanness' was severed[xi]. Discourses on indigenous languages have also long fuelled postcolonial and decolonial scholarship, especially in relation to a colonial system of knowledge which ascribed indigenous languages and cultural knowledge primitive status (Mignolo, 2009: 7). Scholarships in various fields, across continents demonstrate the violence of coloniality on indigenous languages which caused either their extinction, a reduction in their usage or neglect from nationalist policies (Mignolo, 2009; Ngũgĩ, 1986).

After the extinction of African languages in the Indian Ocean islands, a second erasure occurred, with the denigration of the Creole language by French settlers, as well as the later appropriation of the orality of the language and its conversion into a written form via a French poetic model when the islands passed to British hands. While the term 'creole' within plantation economies initially described French settlers born in the colony, it was later used by settlers as a racialized marker of inferiority denoting people of mixed races (mulattoes or 'gens de couleur') or of African or Indian origins. It was closely related to the Creole language which was consequently not considered as a full-fledged human language. In French Mauritius, when the ratio of French settlers to African slaves and biracial populations began to preoccupy officials, the term 'Creole' was defined in marriage legislations to represent an emerging mixed population (TJC, 2011: 107). Furthermore, within the plantation structure in the French colony of Mauritius in the eighteenth century, the varieties in the Creole language are situated within the structural segregation of the enslaved population on the plantation - plantation creole, fort creoles, maroon creoles - which further erased the geographical origins of their African ancestral culture, after enslavement and created divisions amongst the enslaved. Since the twentieth century, 'Creoles' and 'ti Créoles' (creoles of the rural working areas) in Mauritius have referred to people with African phenotype whose mother tongue is the Creole language (Boswell, 2006: 47), replicating colonial paradigms in the postcolony. Skin colour and language varietal differentiation, together with class differentiation also mark a conspicuous divide. In both French Caribbean and the Indian Ocean, the 'milat' population adopts the French colonial language as mother tongue, which in practical terms, represents 'the key that can open doors which were still barred to [them] fifty years ago' (Fanon, 2008: 25). French still remains the mother tongue of most of the Franco-Mauritians and the offspring of biracial relationships and later the rising urban bourgeoisie of Indo-Mauritians. The renunciation of Creole (or other respective ancestral languages) as mother-tongue and the relegation of its usage to a language of communication as well as the adoption of French as mother tongue are all 'hostages' of a Francophile culture, perpetuated later by the assimilation programme of the Francophonie. This reveals an 'inexhaustible solipsism' (Derrida, 1998: 1)[xii] which provokes the enunciator to defend the French language above his/her other linguistic and cultural (ancestral) traditions (Rambhujun, 1993). Adopting the language of the colonial culture **as mother tongue** also implies mimicking the culture of the coloniser (Ngũgĩ, 1986).

After the Napoleonic Wars, British sovereignty was established in the Indian Ocean, but under the negotiated 1815 Treaty of Paris, the French plantocracy, together with the Roman Catholic Church and other institutions, maintained the French Civil Code, language and culture. The colonial appropriation of the orality of the Creole language by francophiles under English administration in parallel with the denigration of Indian mother tongues is the third aspect of linguistic violence discussed here. Taking as example the first published poetry in Creole, written by French settlers between 1822 and 1831, a decade after the French were dispossessed of their political and statutory privileges, Police (2001: 9-10) observes that 'in their speeches, [there is] a certain attempt to legitimise symbolically - in language and music - their belonging to the administratively conquered territory'. In the literary field of the pre-Independence years, poetry in Creole was written by and for the petite bourgeoisie (Gauthier, 2017; Ramharai, 1993). In the first published colonial poetry in Creole, *Les Essais d'un bobre africain* (1822), the author François Chrestien describes the language as a 'naive patois of our favourable conditions'. The act of conflating naiveté to the Creole language, accentuated further by the 'favourable conditions' of the writer's position demonstrates a colonial gaze imbued in what has been articulated as 'imperialist nostalgia' (Rosaldo, 1889: 108-109) which describes 'idealised fantasies' designed to gloss over violence and brutality' of the civilising mission of colonisation and 'is a particular appropriate emotion to invoke in attempting to establish one's innocence and at the same time talk about what one has destroyed'. The spatiality of Creole knowledge is also invalidated by becoming an 'amusement for a francophone elite comfortably conscious of its own cultural and linguistic superiority' (Mooneeram, 2009: 51). The literature is, moreover, based on the burlesque as well as the textual structure of a French poetic model (use of conversation, rhymes and organised in couplets) in the format of song books (Police, 2001: 9). The history of Creole literature starting with colonial poetry, despite the process of positivisation which it represents (Police, 2005) inform the making of a colonial historiography.

The analysis of written Creole also reveals how colonial appropriation of the Creole language by francophiles under English administration ran in parallel with the strategic denigration of mother tongues brought by Indians during the system of Indenture on the island (Eisenlohr, 2006). Half a million Indians, impelled by indentured labour under British administration and French settlement (1810-1968), contributed to a shift in power dynamics and consequently changed the linguistic, social and cultural setup. Bhojpuri was widely spoken in the rural areas in the second half of the nineteenth century by the different linguistic communities that came from India as well as people of Chinese descent and the coloured population, especially on the plantations, while Creole became associated with the urban working class, lower Government offices and schooling, initially run by mostly missionaries (Eisenlohr, 2006: 208). As Civil posts required baptism and conversion to catholicism, most colonial schools used French or Creole as language of instruction, refusing to teach children of Indian origins, in their mother tongues. The expansion of Creole to the younger generation whose mother tongue was initially Bhojpuri and other Indian languages, spread through schooling, socialisation and the urban-rural mobility and brought an irreversibility to Creole as the main language of communication. In its orality and in its indigenous[xiii] incarnations, the Creole language initially spread in Mauritius, across class, ethnic, and religious backgrounds, and did not overpower Bhojpuri and other Indo-languages, as can be witnessed in the rural areas in the nineteenth century (Ramyead, 1985). At the time of independence, Mauritians spoke twenty-two ancestral/'indigenous' languages, with knowledge of a dozen more languages, identified as mother tongues of Indian ancestors of the population. These languages still play an important role in the cultural, religious and ritualistic set up of the different communities. Mauritian Creole (and its varieties) is the main language of communication across the Mauritius islands, but depending on the urban or rural nature of the setting, interaction on the streets (the physical spaces of the streets but also in the intimacy of the home) occurs in Mauritian Creole or in Bhojpuri (Asgarally, 2015)

Nationalist campaigns around language issues and movements of decolonisation promoted the Creole language as a tool for building national common denominators. A language consciousness was triggered after independence from the works of Dev Virahsawmy, a linguist of Indian origin, as well as language activists such as Ledikasyon Pu Travayer (an organisation actively involved in the standardisation of Mauritian Creole for literary and literacy purposes, and other language activists since the 1970s (Ah-Vee *et al.*, 2012). Five overlapping stages (Harmon, 2011) can be traced in the evolution of Mauritian Creole from around the time of independence until the language was eventually codified: (1) 1960s: nationalism around language as a marker of national unity; (2) 1970s: class struggle and trade unionism militating for the language to be employed for popular education and adult literacy; (3) late 1970s: golden era when cultural militants use Creole to revitalise music, theatre and the arts; (4) late 1990s: an AfroKreol movement, regrouping Creoles who appropriate the language as ancestral identity, which gains momentum after the death, in the hands of the police, of Kaya, a seggae artist; and (5) the codification of Mauritian Creole in 2004. A codified Mauritian Creole has, since then, been prescribed in certain schools, based on mothertongue literacy programs, which aim to facilitate the acquisition of literacy skills in the learner's mothertongue. The practicality of a Creole orthography that is close to French was argued to be better suited for educational purposes, to help Mauritians acquire literacy in their mothertongue (Hookoomsing, 2004). Nation building and decolonizing knowledge-making, through language, have been part of many postcolonial projects of decolonisation (Said, 1993: 97; Ngũgĩ, 1986), even if those solidarities are essentially grounded in an imagined basis (Anderson, 1983).

Nevertheless, despite a history of colonial positivisation of the language as well as the process of decolonisation which emanates from the nationalist valorisation of Creole, this chapter purports that decolonisation is not a historical rupture but a continuous process which started with forms of resistance to colonial culture since colonial times. In other words, to embrace being or becoming creole or to valorise the language as a post-independence movement entail understanding coloniality of power still in place in postcolonial Mauritius, undoing colonial structures which still marginalize certain communities with a plantation mentality and building life upon re-humanising the scarred colonial landscape. A decolonial reading is proposed here, from the perspective of building a performative historiography, based on the aspect of performance within the language and embodied knowledge/memory, rather than literate culture and appropriation by a colonial logic.

Performative historiography: The sonic landscape of the rootsical sega

The francophile appropriation of the Creole language, visible through the first texts written in the language and the nationalist valorisation of the language through codification imposed a new hierarchy which had not existed before: written literature over the orality, sonority, performance and musicality of the language. Creole languages have an oral tradition and continue to provide a relative autonomous repertoire of oral 'texts' existing independently of a tradition of writing as have been inventoried by Andon and Bastien (2014) - folk sayings, guessing games (riddles, enigmas), traditional narratives (folk tales, legends, myths), allegorical stories (parables), comical stories (known as grandmother's stories), songs (lullabies, children songs, the sega), verbal compositions (recitals, message songs) across the varieties of Creole within each specific island of Mauritius. Creative practices in the Creole mother tongue are read outside the paradigm of a colonial aesthetics and system of knowledge which defines and classifies the practice as 'folklore', 'past-time' or 'entertainment' (Police, 1998: 133). In this chapter, focus is put on the rootsical sega[xiv], a polymorphous performative art form consisting of dance, music, story-telling and song in the Creole language, rooted in practices indigenized or Africanized in the colony, which consist of a corpus of knowledge handed down through generations of practitioners.

The earliest archival reference to forms of 'festivities' among enslaved populations in French Mauritius is noted in the Code Noir (decree by the French Monarch which legitimates the chattel conditions of slavery) as early as 1723 (Police, 1998), within a decade into French settler colonialism on the island. It is speculated at this stage that these 'festivities', as well as spaces where escaped enslaved created livelihoods, could have entailed forms of community gatherings and rituals in which forms of sega practice was an integral part of. Written records of the sega appear as from the early nineteenth century where it was referred to as 'Chéga' or 'Tséga' (Assonne, 2014: 36; Police, 2001: 7) and was compared to the Brazilian Chica (Police, 2001) or a Mozambican dance with a similar name, meaning 'pull up or lift up one's clothes' in Swahili (Legros and Legros, 2015), and was rooted in the practices of enslaved African people during the eighteenth century (Andon and Bastien, 2014). Some ethnographic descriptions represented with the distant gaze of the European visitor (in 1801) in the colony reveal that sega practitioners among the enslaved were 'great compositors, able to improvise songs on the spot about anything that vividly strikes their imagination,' spending their Sundays dancing 'to forget the injustice which was their lot' (Selvon, 2005: 186). The practice was carried forward by the Creole population, referring to people of African or Malagasy origins, when they left the servitude of the plantation complex after the abolition of slavery.

The sega is furthermore a visceral experience of rhythm, beats, sounds, dance which produces decolonial archives of feelings and sensations, built on modes of expressions and aesthetics that subvert the objective historical archive and the colonial aesthetics in place. Remembering through performance encompasses the multiple historiographies which incorporate corporeality, affect and subjectivity, and their endurance, in the present, in forms of contemporary adaptation, imageries and memories (Fabião, 2012). A performative historiography is not a discussion on fictive vs. non-fictive aspects of historiography but rather, an experience of the perception of history and the phenomenology of narrative, which takes the body as paradigm (Fabião, 2012: 124).

The stark division between present and past is a 'narcotic' essentialism of western historiography (Fabião, 2012) as each past 'is contemporaneous with the present that it was, so that all of the past coexists with the new present in relation to which it is now past' (Bergson - cited in Fabião, 2012). The rootsical sega in Creole is thus read as an embodiment of a performative historiography where the re-arrangement of histories through creative practices enunciates haptic historiographies, which is the production of historical knowledge through visceral sensations. Brazilian performer and performance theorist, Eleonora Fabião (2012: 121) explains that performative historiography is a process or a series of processes, acts and corporeal engagement, as 'specific modes of acting historiography ... explor[ing] ways out of the well-known dichotomy between scientific history and literary history'. An event of the past is not a 'monolithic block' that has 'occurred' with no resonance in the present. It continues to exist in the present as consequences of that 'occurrence' in the past (Fabião, 2012: 124). Furthermore it is, according to Fabião

(2012: 121), about 'words' and about 'lingua' because in the Portuguese language, lingua means 'both language and tongue; its double meaning relates word and flesh, writing and muscle, speech and taste'. In the same way *lalang* in Creole means both tongue and speech (for example *lalang sal* - dirty tongue means 'dirty' language).

It is in that sense, that the performative approach to history is read in the melodious or the rhythmic sonic sega, as a tribute to remembering history and performing historical events, as forms of 'performatively oriented historiographies' (Fabião, 2012: 122). A genealogy of performatively oriented historiographies can be traced to historical forms of performances, such as the songs and dance of those enslaved in a period where oral and corporeal practices were forms of storytelling and history-transmitting in both agency and urgency. Singing and dancing in the Creole mother tongue is a re-enactment of the way that the rootsical sega was as an everyday practice of performing history. The sega creative practice - in its poetic forms, musical arrangement, instrumental range, the dance performance and the function of story-telling - continues to be performed today by a range of Mauritian artists. They rearrange the sega and mix different other musical traditions - jazz, blues, pop, Indian or Bhojpuri music for example - to fit its contemporary context. Depending on the range of rhythm in the various forms of sega, from trance-like slow music with focus on the vocalist to very rhythmic, it is accompanied by a specific sega dance movement, in which the upper body, specially the thighs, are stirred vigorously while the feet are grounded in slower motions, bringing both artists and audience into a participatory and visceral (sonic and visual) experience. The contemporary version of the sega dance, which tallies with eighteenth century descriptions of the practice, usually starts with the gentle swaying of the hips of the dancer to the slow and solemn tune which gradually rises to a tempo. The dancers then increase their movements, by bending the knees and lowering the body gently downwards while swaying the hips to the rhythm.

Julian Henriques (2001: xv), who theorizes sound (in particular the sonic culture of Jamaican sound systems) and the dancing body in relation to the reggae dancehall explains how sonic bodies, bodies which are fine-tuned with the sound, music and atmosphere, 'consist of a corpus of knowledge' handed down through generations of practitioners. In the sound system culture, 'sonic bodies are vocal, as well as musical' in a similar way that in the sega, the *chule*, the rhythmic cry of the singer (usually male) - who is also dancing - to increase the tempo of the dance, elicit the response of the other dancers to increase the rhythm of their movements (Henriques, 2001: xv). For Henriques (2001: xvi), sonic bodies are performative and highly skilled and are therefore 'knowing', knowledgeable and they 'make sense'. Unlike listening to the sega or observing the practice as a curious spectator which puts the body outside sound, sega dancers have their bodies 'placed inside sound' (Henriques, 2001: xvi).

Sonic bodies have to be heard, felt and given the attention of listening. It is of little use looking for them. Sonic bodies demand being approached in a certain way, one based on a relationship of mutual recognition and respect, as distinct from the positivist scientific paradigm of prediction and control. Sonic bodies produce, experience and make sense of sound. Sound, even as the playing of a recording is always 'live' at the point of hearing. Sounding has to be embodied as an event in a particular time and place, as distinct from being 'frozen' as a text or image whose embodiment is less immediate (Henriques, 2001: xvi-xvii).

The sonic body as a resistant container of what life throws at it, speaks of dance 'as a mode of theatrical self-disclosure in which the body speaks eloquently of its capacity to endure and transcend material deprivation' (Cooper, 2005: 1)[xv]. The female dancer in particular, whose body responds to the vibrating beat of the sega music and becomes one with the sound, resists conservative social norms and etiquette of the 'respectable' body as determined by colonial bourgeois norms. In other words the knowing body takes over. The sega dance is essentially a heterosexual space in which both men and women dance close together without necessarily touching each other. The licentiousness and pejorative qualifying terms such as erotic, noisy, vulgar, burlesque, carnivalesque and entertaining which often plague the sega dance and lyrics have been read within the lens of colonial (Christian/Indian) bourgeois aesthetics and epistemologies introduced in the colony and perpetuated in the postcolonial space with the aim at regulating taste and sensing. Instead the performative element of the sega is best understood as potentially a praxis of resistance to colonial servitude, correctness and 'purity' in the colony, as well as a participatory performance, which brings both dancer and audience in a poetic moment of intimacy and urgency. The sonic body of the enslaved, through the performative sega challenged, resisted and subverted colonial aesthetics, practices and epistemologies, hence became a carrier of decolonial knowledges.

Singing in the intonations of the Creole language and dancing to the tempo of a rootsical *sega* is also an experience which is situated in the historiographies of black cartographies of re-humanisation. Within a decolonial framework, performing the sega forms part of a process of self-creation rising from the lived experience of intimacy and humanhood of enslaved population who were, since colonial times, subjected to the controlled gaze of the coloniser. Auto-poiesis (self-creation) implies the praxis of creating possibilities of life and culture under regimes of oppression (Wynter, 2007), involving a logic outside of consumerism, spectatorship and voyeurism which the sega-vitrine (display sega, tourist/commercial sega) has so far portrayed as entertainment and burlesque. For Sylvia Wynter, the autopoetic field resonates in the sorrow songs, lumpen poetics of the blues or jazz of black people who indigenised and humanised the colonial American landscape with their music. While Mauritius had no indigenous populations, Africans auto-poetically instituted a Creole culture by indigenising and re-humanising the colonised landscape. Mauritian Creole and its varieties can be read as indigenous to the Mauritius islands, as they became the speakers' mother tongue and eventually were naturalised and became specific to its location for over three hundred years, originated from the new 'autopoetic languaging living system' (Wynter, 2007: 17) and modes of existence within a colonial structure. In that sense, it can be articulated that Africans and their descendants carried indigenous epistemologies within their Creole oral histories of resistance, resilience, survival and construction of a new re-humanisation process within the dehumanising system of colonisation. Cultural history is not found in 'writing' (referring to the culture of literature brought by colonization versus the generational knowledge ingrained in the orality of indigenous populations) but in people who humanised the landscape by peopling it with their imagination (Wynter, 1970). The notion of indigenisation refers to how African languages and practices in the language transformed into an auto-poetic languaging living system within the island colonies, under an oppressive regime.

Conclusion

The Creole languaging and knowledge system originates from a history which had resisted forms of capitalist exploitation of people of African origins and which was birthed in the process of building alternative livelihoods. While the nationalisation of the Creole language as language of communication potentially aspire to create markers of unity and reinforce a sense of citizenship, the language is still appropriated today by a comprador bourgeoisie (Amin, 2014) made of a privileged class of French, Afro-Euro, Indian and Chinese ancestry with common economic interest, to capitalise on selling a constructed idea of 'authentic' Mauritius for profit making. The Creole language is further utilised to strategically rebrand colonial products (for example vanilla tea, rum, biscuit manioc or the commodified dodo, the symbol par excellence of colonial exploitation and extermination in the Indian Ocean) as 'local products', with sellable attributes such as, 'Made in Mauritius' or 'Preserving Heritage'. This chapter proposes a decolonial reading of Creole based on a genealogy of rehumanisation which the language carries.

In this chapter, I elaborated on the residues of colonisation at the level of representation and the Creole language in Mauritius. The history of the language reveals the colonial denigration as well as colonial appropriation of Creole. Furthermore, this chapter proposed a reading from the perspective of a performative historiography as a decolonial praxis, by building a genealogy of the sonic and visceral creative practices carried by the Creole language as mother tongue which embodies decolonial aesthetics and knowledges. Focusing on the oral, scribal, sonic and performative aspects of the language, the rootsical sega in particular, in contrast with the sega-vitrine, it finally elaborates on the concept of being human, positioning the Creole nation as a potential space of ongoing decolonisation as well as reconstruction of more humane modes of living. In so doing, this chapter reveals how the language evolved from Creole geographies of struggle where decolonial spaces were produced through creative practices to regain the possibility of humanhood in a dehumanised environment. It proposes to position humanisation on the island at the centre of a historiography of the Creole languaging and knowledge system. This genealogy is also necessary as, I argue that, being creole or becoming creole cannot be incorporated in a postcolonial culture embedded in inherited colonial aesthetics and epistemologies, which continue to sustain narratives of progress based on a capitalist, patriarchal and racist system of knowledge.

References

Ah-Vee, A., Collen, L. and Kistnasamy, R. (2012) 'Victory Begins to be Won for the Kreol Language in Mauritius', *Le Mauricien*. [online] http://www.lalitmauritius.org/en/newsarticle/1335/victory-begins-to-be-won-for-the-kreol-language-in-mauritius/ (Accessed 10 May 2017).

Amin, S. (2014) *Samir Amin: Pioneer of the Rise of the South*. 1st edn. Cham: Springer International Publishing.

Anderson, B. (1983) *Imagined communities,* 1st edn. London: Verso.

Andon, V. and Bastien, D. (2014) *'Traditional Mauritian - Séga Tipik Morisien'*, First Inventory of Intangible Cultural Heritage for inclusion in the UNESCO Representative List of the Intangible Cultural Heritage. Port Louis, Mauritius: Prime Minister's Office. [online] www.unesco.org/ culture/ ich/doc/download.php?versionID=29662, Accessed 4 April 2016.

Anzaldúa, G. (1987) *Borderlands/la frontera*. SanFrancisco: Spinsters/Aunt Lute Book Company.

Arends, J., Muysken, P. and Smith, N. (eds) (1994) *Pidgins and Creoles: An Introduction*. Amsterdam: Benjamins (John) North America Inc.

Assonne, S. (2014) *Segatiers*. Mauritius: Editions de la tour.

Bogues, A. (2010) 'Introduction', in S. Wynter (ed) *The Hills of Hebron*. 2nd edn. Kingston: Ian Randle Publishers.

Boudet, C. and Peghini, J. (2008) 'Les enjeux politiques de la mémoire du passé colonial à l'île Maurice', *Transcontinentales* 6: 13-36.

Boswell, R. (2006) *Le Malaise Creole: Ethnic Identity in Mauritius*. New York: Berghahn Books.

Chaudenson, R. and Mufwene, S. (2001) *Creolization of Language and Culture*. 1st edn. London: Routledge.

Collen, L. (2017) '*Lindsey Collen at the University of Mauritius opens up the land question*'. Talk, University of Mauritius, [online] http://www.lalitmauritius.org/en/newsarticle/ 2005/lindsey-collen-at-the-university-of-mauritius-opens-up-the-land-question/ (Accessed 1 November 2017).

Cooper, C. (1993) *Noises in the Blood: Orality, gender, and the "vulgar" body of Jamaican popular culture*. Durham, NC: Duke University Press.

Cooper, C. (2005) *Sweet & Sour sauce: Sexual politics in Jamaican dancehall culture*, The sixth Jagan Lecture, Centre for Research on Latin America and the Caribbean, York University.

Derrida, J. (1998) *Monolingualism of the Other, or, The prosthesis of Origin*. United States: Stanford University Press.

Edensor, T. and Kothari, U. (2005) 'Sweetening Colonialism: A Mauritian Themed Resort', in M. Lasansky and B. McClaren (eds) *Arquitectura Y Turismo*. Barcelona: Editorial Gustavo Gili

Eisenlohr, P. (2006) *Little India: Diaspora, Time and Ethnolinguistic belonging in Hindu Mauritius*. Berkeley: University of California Press.

Eriksen, T.H. (1998) *Common Denominators: Ethnicity, Nation-building, and Compromise in Mauritius*. 1st edn. New York: Berg Publishers

Fabião, E. (2012) 'History and precariousness: In search of a performative historiography', in A. Jones and A. Heathfield (eds) *Perform, Repeat, Record: Live Art in History*. Chicago: Intellect.

Fanon, F. (2008) *Black Skin, White masks*. UK: Pluto Press.

Forest, C. (2011) 'Memory representations of slavery and indenture in Mauritius: towards the recognition of silent heritage', in *Truth and Justice Commission Report, vol. 4*. Port Louis, Mauritius: Government of Mauritius Printing.

Gauthier, E. (2017) 'La valorisation d'un héritage ancestral complexe: l'inscription du sega tipik mauricien sur la liste représentative du patrimoine', *Revue Internationale d'Ethnographie*, 6, [online] http://riethno.org/wp-content/uploads/2016/05/ART-6-Eglantine-GAUTHIER.pdf, Accessed 4 June 2017.

Harmon, J. (2011) 'AfroKreols' Quest for identity impacts on the future of Mauritian Creole', *Revue Haitiano-Antillaise* 7: 131–146.

Hay, I. and Salverda, T. (2013) 'Change, anxiety and exclusion in the post-colonial reconfiguration of Franco-Mauritian elite geographies', *The Geographical Journal* 180(3): 236–245.

Henriques, J. (2011) *Sonic bodies: Reggae sound systems, performance techniques, and ways of knowing*. New York: Bloomsbury USA Academic.

Hookoomsing, V. (2004) *Grafi-larmoni: A harmonized writing system for the Mauritian Creole Language*, Port-Louis: Ministry of Education. Available online at http://ministry-education.govmu.org/English/Documents/Publications/arch%20reports/hookoomsing.pdf (accessed 4 May 2017).

Kothari, U. and Wilkinson, R. (2010) 'Colonial Imaginaries and Postcolonial Transformations: exiles, bases, beaches', *Third World Quarterly* 31(8): 1395–1412.

Legros, V. and Legros, G. (2016) 'Séga... manchega: le serpent qui danse', *7LamLamèr* 14 January. Available online at http://7lameslamer.net/sega-manchega-le-serpent-qui-danse-1698.html#nb1 (accessed 4 July 2017).

McKittrick, K. and Wynter, S. (2015) *Sylvia Wynter: On being human as praxis*. 1st edn. Durham: Duke University Press.

Mignolo, W.D. (2009) 'Epistemic Disobedience, Independent Thought and Decolonial Freedom', *Theory, Culture & Society* 26(7-8):159–181.

Mooneeram, R. (2009) *From Creole to Standard. Shakespeare, Language, and Literature in a Postcolonial Context*. Amsterdam: Editions Rodopi

Mukherji, P. (2006) *Vertical Horizon: M. Nagalingum*. Mauritius: Mahatma Gandhi Institute.

Ngũgĩ, wa T. (1986) *Decolonising the mind: The politics of language in African literature*. Portsmouth, NH: Heinemann Educational.

Police, D. (1998) 'Séga et émancipation', in Cangy, J-C., Chan-Low, J, and M. Paroomal (eds) *L'esclavage et ses Séquelles: Mémoire et Vécu d'hier et aujourd'hui*. Port Louis: Ministère des Arts et de la Culture.

Police, D. (2001) 'Les pratiques musicales de la population servile puis affranchie de Maurice dans les écrits francophones des XVIIIè et XIXè siècles', in V. Teelock and E. Alpers (eds) *History, Memory and Identity*. Port Louis & Réduit: The Nelson Mandela Centre for African Culture and the University of Mauritius.

Police, D. (2005) 'L'évolution de l'identité créole en contexte mauricien', *Revi Kiltir Kreol* 5.

Quijano, A. (2008) 'Coloniality of power, Eurocentrism, and Latin America', in E. Dussel, M. Morana, I. and C. Jáuregui, (eds) *Coloniality at Large: Latin America and the Post-colonial Debate*. 1st edn. Durham & London: Duke University Press.

Rambhujun, H. (1993) 'La situation de l'écrivain mauricien', *Littérature Mauricienne*, 11, Paris: Ministère de la Coopération et du Ministère des Affaires Etrangères.

Ramharai, V. (1993) 'La littérature créole depuis l'indépendance', *Littérature Mauricienne*, 11, Paris: Ministère de la Coopération et du Ministère des Affaires Etrangères.

Ramyead, L.P. (1985) *The establishment and cultivation of modern standard Hindi in Mauritius*. Mauritius: Mahatma Gandhi Institute.

Rosaldo, R. (1989) 'Imperialist nostalgia', *Representations*, 26: 107–122.

Said, E. (1993) 'Resistance, opposition and representation', in B. Ashcroft, G. Griffiths and H. Tiffin (eds) *The Post-colonial Studies Reader*. New York: Routledge.

Salverda, T. (2015) '(Dis)unity in Diversity: How Common Beliefs about Ethnicity Benefit the White Mauritian Elite', *The Journal of Modern African Studies* 53(4): 533-555.

Selvon, S. (2001) *A Comprehensive History of Mauritius: From the beginning to 2001*. Port-Louis: M.D.S.

TJC (2011) *Truth and Justice Commission Report, Volume 1-4*. Port Louis, Mauritius: Government Printing.

Wynter, S. (1970) 'Jonkonnu in Jamaica: Towards the Interpretation of Folk Dance as a Cultural Process', *Jamaica Journal*, 2. Available online at http://www.dloc.com/ UF00090030/00010/36x?search=wynter (accessed 25 June. 2017).

Wynter, S. (2007) *'Human Being as Noun? Or Being Human as Praxis? Towards the Autopoetic Turn/Overturn: A Manifesto'*, Unpublished essay. Available online at https://www.scribd.com/document/ 329082323/Human-Being-as-Noun-Or-Being-Human-as-Praxis-Towards-the-Autopoetic-Turn- Overturn-A-Manifesto#from_embed (accessed 16 April 2017).

---

[i] Portuguese and Dutch colonial influences on the Indian Ocean islands (pre-1710) are irrelevant here due to the quasi-absence of cultural residues within contemporary Mauritius, in comparison to English and specially French epistemic colonisation.

[ii] Mauritius is mostly referred to and perceived as a singular island in the collective memory of mainland Mauritians. However, the postcolonial state of Mauritius consists of islands and archipelagos in the Indian Ocean, namely the main island of Mauritius, Rodrigues, Agaléga, Tromelin (co-administered by France and Mauritius), Cargados Carajos (commonly known as St Brandon islands) and the Chagos Archipelago including Diego Garcia which was illegally detached before Independence by the British Government and leased to the US for an army base.

[iii] This chapter does not minimise the importance of ancestral mother tongues of various sections of the population. It concentrates instead on Creole, as the only language which originates from the islands upon the colonial suppression of the undeniably many African languages carried by enslaved people from the continent.

[iv] See the reports in the four volumes published by the Truth and Justice Commission in 2011 which reveal the racism and economic inequality on the islands, especially around land ownership, ethnic and racial discrimination at work and social marginalisation. The work of Ramola Ramtohul and data collected by Genderlinks on the high rate of domestic violence in Mauritius reveal a hidden facet of gender based violence and exploitation. The Mauritius 2016 Human Rights Report gives the alert on police brutality and abuse of power, inhuman treatment perpetuated by the institution, societal abuse of women and discrimination against marginalised communities. The grassroots activism of Lalit Mauritius, http://www.lalitmauritius.org, provides ample information on the work done to tackle residues of colonialism on the Mauritius Islands. Lindsey Collen's talk as Guest Speaker for the Faculty of Social Sciences and Humanities at the University of Mauritius on 20 September 2017 reveals the structural colonial mentality still in place http://www.lalitmauritius.org/en/newsarticle/2005/lindsey-collen-at-the-university-of-mauritius-opens-up-the-land-question/.

[v] Decolonisation can be discussed in three overlapping phases. The first period is 'primary resistance' (Said 1993: 95) in which anti-colonial movements were legitimate tools to resist the violence of colonialism and to recover appropriated territory. Primary resistance also lied in the various individual movements of resistance against the colonial regime. The second period is 'ideological resistance', which according to Edward Said, author of the seminal text Orientalism (1993), represents a set of efforts towards the restoration of a sense of humanhood, dignity and freedom against oppression under the colonial enterprise and culminates in the implementation of the nation-state. However the lasting legacy of coloniality continues to impact the present, whether in bourgeois nationalism or neocolonial capitalism (Anderson, 1983; Mignolo, 2009; Ngũgĩ, 1986).

[vi] Postcolonial Studies emerged particularly from the works of Edward Said which brought light to South Asian scholarship in Anglo-American universities, and covered nineteenth and twentieth centuries European colonialism and their models of power. The decolonial critique looks at European colonial history since the symbolic date of 1492 and the coloniality of power still in place. A decolonial school emerged from the scholarship of South American scholars who cumulate the research of Caribbean scholars and indigenous studies from the Americas to New Zealand, articulate that the economic system of capitalism and post-independence coloniality of power (Quijano 2008), are residues of European colonisation of the 'global south' since the sixteenth century. Decolonisation is thus an ongoing process of

resistance against coloniality of power and encompasses a set of practices of de-construction, construction and re-construction at the level of epistemology, historiography and ideology, bringing class, caste, race, gender, ability & sexuality into dialogue.

[vii] In an extensive chapter, Corinne Forest, researcher at the TJC, explains the historical context of a 'colonial memorial framework' (2011: 803) in place in Mauritius, and establishes a link between memory from a colonial perspective and institutions which promoted scientific research in the colony such as the *Société d'Emulation* (1805), the *Société d'Histoire Naturelle* (1826), the Royal Society of Arts and Sciences (1846) and the Historical Records Committee, all created in the first half of the nineteenth century by the French and English elite and their network in the European metropolis.

[viii] Ethnographic descriptions of the resort, built in 'Mauritian colonial style, a distinct, Creole [meaning 'colonial' here] plantation - domain architectural form' and the staged shows designed to entertain mainly tourists coming from Europe, are revealing facets of the perpetuation of a colonial imaginary.

[ix] I use the metaphor of tongues being cut out to express the viscerality of the violence of being made ashamed to speak in one's mother tongue - 'Wild tongues can't be tamed, they can only be cut out'. Chicano writer Gloria Anzaldúa's writing on the epistemic colonisation of her 'wild' mother tongue - through shame, repeated attacks, discomfort, fear and guilt - is delineated as 'linguistic terrorism'.

[x] Similar to the experience of Creole languages in the Antilles and in Mauritius, Ngũgĩ recalls the 'humiliating experiences' of being caught speaking Gikuyu in Kenyan colonial schools, where English was rewarded and native languages demonised.

[xi] The homogenisation of what consists an Africanness is problematically maintained in this article, due to a lack of resources on the afro-genesis of the enslaved population whose linguistic origins remain unknown.

[xii] Franco-Maghrebian philosopher Jacques Derrida, in his seminal text *Monolingualism of the other, or, The prosthesis of origin*, reminds us that appropriation occurs 'historically, through the rape of a cultural usurpation, which means always essentially colonial, to appropriate it in order to impose it as 'his own'' (1998: 23).

[xiii] Sylvia Wynter develops the notion of indigenisation, by exploring the Jonkonnu folkdance, a creative practice brought by Africans to the Caribbean islands. She elaborates on the cultural process of 'indigenization' that the dance practice went through, by which dominated cultures resist, survive, and create new modes of existence (1970). In the context of Mauritius, the first Africans and Indians who were brought under Dutch slavery, are considered here as having indigenised the scarred colonial landscape (depleted of its indigenous forests and animals, such as the infamously extinct dodo bird). Within a decolonial historiography, the free Africans, after the departure of the Dutch, and the generations born on the island were thus the first people to indigenise the island before further colonial occupation. Wynter explains that 'while the 'creolization' process represents ... a more or less 'false assimilation' in which the dominated people adopt elements from the dominant ... in order to obtain prestige or status, the 'indigenization' process represents the more secretive process by which the dominated culture survives; and resists' (Wynter – cited in Bogues, 2010: xxiii).

[xiv] The rootsical sega of enslaved Africans (referring to the sega performed originally before its suppression and 'whitened' version through centuries of epistemic colonisation) is differentiated from the sega tipik (typical sega) which refers to a popularised form in the 40s-50s and inscribed on the representative list of intangible cultural heritage by the UNESCO. Carolyn Cooper (1993:5) uses the term 'rootsical' to determine creative practices which are rooted in black experiences of struggle. For example, Bob Marley sings 'in a language close to the English end of the linguistic continuum in Jamaica, but with clearly rootsical vibes'.

[xv] Carolyn Cooper theorizes from the angle of the sonic body in Jamaican dancehall.

Deconstructing Mauritian Literature

Julie Peghini

Introduction

In one of the masterpieces of Mauritian literature, *Polyte* (1926) by Savinien Mérédac, land is measured out in acres, cut up into fields, legacies, cemeteries. When land is made the measure of everything, everything becomes quantified and limited. The utopian state of happiness is here bound to the earth, to the act of constructing the authentic Self by uprooting the Other, by expelling the latter from his native soil, the Other being a stealer of land and a polluter of blood. The hatred felt by the Creole, Polyte, towards the Indian, Quincois, is paramount to this book, in a negative sense, as if Polyte's contempt and hatred for the Indian corresponded to self-contempt, self-hatred, an inability to ensure the continuity of his family line, his future and his rootedness. The idea of original purity is also bound up with this text, but in a sense similar to that of Pierre Renaud's concept of the *'même bâtardise'* (or same bastard status) and which is central to the work of one contemporary writer, Amal Sewtohul.

In a text posted with great humour on his blog, Amal Sewtohul attempted to re-establish what the two completely differentiated worlds of Indianness and Creoleness in Mauritius have in common. He provides a lucid analysis of a mutual confinement:

> *Am I the only one who sees similarities between Creole and Indian culture? Both seem marked by the fear of pollution (losing caste) [...] Yet, the naïve foreigner who ventures into these societies is in for a rude shock. Both Creoles and Indians, for a start, are obsessed with fair skins, and are cruelly racist societies.*

The literary approach to these questions is illuminating for the anthropologist interested in issues of national unity, both its construction and its future. To understand how far, fifty years after independence, the question of national identity has evolved in Mauritius, I will return to these two themes, of original purity and of the 'same bastard status', and how they have been tackled by writers. I will analyse literature as a place of symbolic expression of the most significant contradictions in Mauritian society: literary texts convey the perceptions of their authors regarding peaceful coexistence in

231

Mauritius. In this sense, such literary accounts can be considered as anthropological 'texts' from which can be extrapolated the thousand and one ways in which otherness can be produced in society, what Monder Kilani termed *'the invention of the other'* (2000). This is a process also discussed by Gérard Althabe, epistemologist of *'the otherness produced in exploratory situations'*, according to Ferdinando Fava (2014).

Michel Beniamino's distinctive approach to Mauritian 'ethnicity' is interesting in that he identifies three categories relating to key periods in the evolution of Mauritian literature. Although I prefer the term 'otherness' to 'ethnicity', I have applied a provisional classification to these three periods, a sort of typology of the situations described in the novels. These situations reveal the various ways of constructing potential otherness that engender a mechanism of negation of the Other, as a result of which socially affiliated communities can mutually establish themselves in relationship to each other. In the scenes depicted, there is frequently an inversion of identities and identity construction is then based primarily on negation.

All the novels presented thematically in this chapter describe complex situations in which relations lead to invariably irresolvable conflicts between protagonists involved. The nature of social ordering is revealed through three main themes: difference; the impossibility of breaking down established social boundaries; and, lastly, sites of liberation.

Negation of the Self, negation of the Other: *Polyte* by Savinien Mérédac

The contradictions and rivalries that arose at the time of abolition and the simultaneous arrival of Indian workers further aggravated the social anomie. Historians Toni Arno and Claude Orian have discussed this time of excessively rapid change and have highlighted the role played by external resolutions in the general and widespread solipsism of the various groups, who continued to adhere firmly to their pre-abolition social identities. Arno and Orian have argued that, without the arrival of the British and the development of the so-called 'coolie trade', the social system based on the taboo against sexual relations between groups of different origins would have changed in Mauritius, as it did in the West Indies:

> *...the social system of slavery functioned* [in the West Indies] *as a cover to hide the existence of transgressive tendencies.* [Whilst on the island of Mauritius, on the contrary] *the ethnic composition remained stable within the framework of a world which had closed in on itself.* (Arno & Orian, 1986: 66)

Polyte is an acute portrayal of the principle of withdrawal adopted by each group and the hardening of stereotypes that accompanied this process. The writer Savinien Mérédac (1880-1939), pseudonym of Auguste Esnouf, was born in Port-Louis in 1880. In parallel to his career as an engineer, he led an intense literary life. He founded a journal, as well as published essays, articles and interviews on the Creole language. In 1925, he wrote *Miette et Toto*, a book for children, followed by *Polyte* in 1926, a novel which is undoubtedly one of the great works of Mauritian literature. Polyte Lavictoire is a fisherman, a Black or 'Kaffir' from Grand-Gaube, sixty years old and a widower with no children, *'Thanks to this pitiful terrain Polyte feels rooted in his "Land of Mauritius"'.* (Mérédac, 1925: 12)

As far as Polyte is concerned, the Indian is the one who arrived from outside, as an invader. His use of the term '*Malabare*' signifies a rejection of any legitimate claim to the land. The '*Malabare*' is considered a '*stealer of land*' who supposedly bought '*land that was sold to him for a few dollars*'. Suspicion, born of a resentment against all Indians, eats away at Polyte whose greatest fear is that his land will be seized by a '*Malabare*' after his death. The negation of the Other can be seen as a double negation, both of the Other and of the Self, as expressed in the following metaphor:

> *Mal'bares! Feeble-hearted, rotten-hearted! Afraid of everything; for*
> *nothing, longouti dans pignons d'Inde!* (261)

In order to protect his land from any predation, Polyte decides to remarry Rébecca Sansdésir to have an heir.

Polyte's marriage remains barren during six years. Then one day, unable to go fishing because of a cyclone, he returns home to see the Indian, Quincois, leaving his house, when Rébecca was inside. The thought of adultery drives Polyte mad with rage. Some time later, he finds out that Rébecca is pregnant. Is the child his, or Quincois's? From the moment he is born, the child, Samuel, becomes the sole object of hate to the man who refuses to be his father. On the day of the child's fourteenth birthday, Polyte, along with Quincois, takes Samuel fishing during a storm, and Polyte drowns them both. This murder drives him into exile, and in the last chapter, it is Polyte himself who is forced to sell his land:

> *He turned his back without a word and set off towards the sea.* (315)

The plot of this novel is symptomatic of a particular fate in which everything that might have given Polyte an advantageous position – precedence on the island, his status as a native, his ownership of a plot of land – has had a negative effect, as if his contempt and hatred for the Indian had been compounded with self-contempt and self-hatred, an inability to ensure the continuity of the family line or his own future. Contempt for the Other and self-hatred, or it could be hatred of the Other and self-contempt. This is the irony expressed in the intransigent stereotypes of racial difference. Throughout the novel, Mérédac skilfully evokes the negation of the Other which takes place through a negation of the Self. The double process of identity negation is signified by the fact that nothing about this presumed adultery is ever made clear. Even at the end of the novel no more is said about the real or virtual nature of Polyte's imaginings; he is simply '*mad with jealousy*'. Nonetheless, we quickly understand that these two worlds, that in which Polyte has lived and that of the Indo-Mauritians, are incompatible. As far as Polyte is concerned, '*Indian blood, that's the stain that counts*' (17).

Was the child really born from adultery or is this only in Polyte's imagination? The doubt persists until the last page. The child had to die. But his death means exile. Polyte's death is a symbolic one. In this sense, the narrative is structured around a symmetrical and inverted account of the positions of the Black man and the Indian, both victims of the same impossibility: that of rising to the challenge posed by their condition of mutual rivalry. The hatred for the Other, which Polyte expresses towards the Indian, is extreme and candid; it is what prevents Polyte from considering Samuel as his son. Real or imagined, the paternal relationship could have provided a moment of recognition. For this recognition to take place, the primordial hate for the Indian would have to have been, if not challenged, then at least dulled in order to get past the taboo on sexual relations between the Creole and the Indian. The story plays out rather differently. The taboo on sexual relations between Polyte's Creole wife and the Indian, Quincois, is shown to be insurmountable. Everything takes place as if the identity of the Self could only be constructed through the elimination and the expulsion of the Other, a state of affairs which leads to the end of the family line in the narrative. Polyte's dramatic experience is emphasised by the fact that his symbolic death, as represented by his exile, evokes the absence of an original identity resulting from the enslavement of his ancestors, who came, as it were, from nowhere. Polyte goes into exile and thus meets the same fate as his ancestors.

The transgression of socially prescribed relationships

Le Sang de l'Anglais

Carl de Souza was born in Rose-Hill in Mauritius in 1949. Coming late to fiction writing, de Souza started writing novels in French in the 1980s. *La Comète de Halley* won the Pierre Renaud Prize in Mauritius in 1986. His first novel, *Le Sang de l'Anglais* (The Blood of the Englishman) was published in France in 1993 and won the ACCT prize (Agency of Cultural and Technical Cooperation). His second novel, *La Maison qui marchait vers le large*, published in 1996, recalled a landslide in Port-Louis and steered his writing towards tackling the topical issues of his country: *Les Jours Kaya* thus takes place during the 1999 riots and *Ceux qu'on jette à la mer* (2001), his fourth novel, recounts the journey of clandestine immigrants passing through Mauritius. His last novel, *En chute libre*, is a story inspired by badminton, a game brought over to Mauritius during the period of English colonisation.

The death of the father as a symbol for the moment of transition into a new social order brought by independence runs throughout Carl de Souza's first novel. *Le Sang de l'Anglais* takes place at the moment of independence, during the formative period when a new social order was established. De Souza tackles, metaphorically, the complementary and contradictory influences of the two colonial structures: French and English. The old social political order, introduced under English rule is summarised as follows (De Souza, 1993: 114):

> *To each his place, was that not what had maintained order up until*
> *now? Where would interracial mixing lead us then?*

Such is the explanation given by the narrator, Michel Saint Bart, who talks of the interior transformations and upheavals which he has had to face in telling his story, the story of a man who is living a second life, and who has now become '*open to everything happening around him*' (220). The tolerant man he has become allows himself to be touched by the Other. He notes that the social fault lines have changed, new values have emerged, leading to the birth of a new social order which goes beyond the old racist order. He is living a second youth.

The story is built on a duality, which bears witness simultaneously to the creation of a new political legitimacy through independence that establishes Hindu political power, and to the disintegration of the old social order. Because Michel Saint Bart does not immediately understand these social and political upheavals for what they are: the reconstruction of the social order. Initially, his story evokes the more or less radical resistance to the changes taking place, which becomes focused around the relationship he has forged with the 'Englishman', Hawkins, an outsider figure rejected by the White society to which he should belong. In fact, Hawkins confronts polite White society with the hated image of the English coloniser, playing a role that unsettles those who associate with him.

The issue of identity is seen to arise from the marriage of a British father with a Ladouce, an issue brought forward at the climax of the novel during the final confrontation between Hawkins, who has 'gone mad', and Michel Saint Bart, following which Hawkins commits suicide, having failed to kill his adversary.

Les Jours Kaya

The entire plot of De Souza's *Les Jours Kaya* [The Kaya Days], published in 2000 in the wake of the riots that occurred after the suspicious death in police custody of popular artist-musician, Kaya, stage name of Joseph Reginald Topize who was of mixed Creole and Hindu origins, also focuses on the possibilities of going beyond the rifts which divide Mauritian society. In the novel, the author evokes the real events by showing the conflict between the Creole population and the predominantly Hindu police force:

> *The girls from his neighbourhood (Creoles) had not been out for two days, their mothers kept them at home, they listened to Kaya's albums, the singer who had been mysteriously found dead in his cell, they tirelessly repeated these phrases calling for greater justice, for 'enlightened paths', whilst under cover of the fruit groves the lads threw rocks at the police stations and set fire to supermarkets.* (De Souza, 2000: 57)

The author describes the scenes of looting witnessed by Santee as she searches for her little brother Ramesh, evoking '*a village turned upside down*' (60), with fire blazing everywhere. The portrayal of anything relating to the process of violence, or to the consequences of the social tolerance of the groups of protesters calling for liberation, remains oblique. The protagonists pass through the burning towns of the Plaines Wilhems district led by a sole imperative: '*never turn back*' (114). This active temporality is punctuated by the author's own reflections on reality experienced as a suspension of time:

> *... it was a time which retained nothing, a time without memory.* [...]
> *These were new days when anything could happen.* (68-69)

A time without history. A time without ontological meaning. A time without ideological consequence.

The unity of time and place, the symbolic treatment of events, and the writing, like the choice of characters, are all elements that contribute to an almost structural representation of the way in which society functions. This is in contrast to the media reaction during the real events which constantly condemned both the ethnic and racial aspects of the conflict and placed pressure on all Mauritians, who were aware of the potential danger for social implosion. *Les Jours Kaya* has the metaphorical dimension of a dream in which can be imagined a reversal of the normally accepted relationships.

Valérie Magdelaine-Andrianjafitrimo has argued that the author's distinctive dreamlike depiction of real events in an imaginative context leads to a sense of 'social unmooring':

> *Based on real events, the novel is rooted in an all-consuming fiction that smooths over the contours of Mauritian society, which is diluted into an imaginary, surreal, even 'paranatural world'. The aberrations of a society in turmoil mean all reference points are lost along with the island's codes and stability.* (Magdelaine-Andrianjafitrimo, 2004: 154)

More than this social unmooring, what produces meaning, what affects identification at a fundamental level, with regard to the multicultural reality of society, is presented symbolically in the nature of the relationships between Indianness and Creoleness at the heart of the story. In order to do this, Carl de Souza has chosen a young Hindu woman as his main character, and it is she who mediates the meaning of these events. This choice was motivated initially by his own personal experience of the riots, in particular his response to the death of the Hindu caretaker at the school where he was the principal. De Souza wrote his novel all in one go in 2000, shortly after the events. By reversing the roles of the opposing protagonists, he found a way through his writing to process his feelings of that time as a school principal, his sense of responsibility for the safe return of all the young people under his responsibility to their homes, but also his feelings as a Mauritian who had lost one of his employees in the riots, another version of himself. During a candid interview, De Souza gave me an important key to understanding his work:

> *The little Hindu woman represents the rest of the country, all those who are not Creole, who watched the riots unfold in astonishment. I am close to the Hindu world, through my own history, through my father.*

Carl de Souza, close socially to the Hindu world, and haunted by the recent death of his Hindu caretaker, has conceived a form of 'liberation into the imaginary realm' by, in a sense, projecting the idea that historically erected social barriers were transgressed during this moment of 'suspended time'. De Souza has chosen to retrace the process whereby the conflict became generalised using a method of decentralisation, related in part to his family origins, and in part to his own personal experience. His position within his writing is portrayed through the eyes of the other, in this instance Santee, the young Hindu woman who leaves, at nightfall, in search of her little brother, Ramesh. The inversion of roles in the book and the transgressive situations described are imposed by a fluctuating reality, which goes beyond the limits of accepted relations, with the unexpected consequence, one actually experienced by the reader, of a blurring of established social categories. The main and secondary characters of the fictional plot are all in transgressive situations, caught in a reversal of roles in relation to those they are assigned in the everyday reality of society. The author presents us with a symbolic system of new relationships emerging from within this very society.

The main subject of the novel, represented by the transgression of society's primary sexual taboo in the union of a Hindu woman and a Creole man caught in the middle of the riots, is the author's transfiguration of the contradictory but not incompatible relationship between Indianness and Creoleness into the imaginary realm. But if de Souza found the words to write *Les Jours Kaya*, the taboo surrounding the events persists, once law and order is restored. The end of the novel is bleak: the mother, Ma, is dead; Santee and Ronaldo have most likely perished in the flames:

> ... they left him without returning to see him, without warning, so he doesn't know, but in his heart he knows, he knows very well, he'll admit it in the end, but will never be able to tell the police, who didn't come, or who came too late. (123)

Thus Ramesh ends up in prison, abandoned by his friends and family, although he is no more than a boy.

Beyond all barriers: *Histoire d'Ashok et d'autres personnages de moindre importance*

Amal Sewtohul was born in Quatre-Bornes, on the island of Mauritius, in 1971. After obtaining a degree in English and French literature from the University of Mauritius, he started out as a journalist for a Mauritian weekly newspaper, then became First Secretary at the Ministry for Foreign Affairs, and now serves as a diplomat in various countries. His first novel, *Histoire d'Ashok et d'autres personnages de moindre importance*, won the Jean Fanchette Prize in 1999. His second novel, published by Gallimard 'Continents Noirs' in 2009, was entitled *Les Voyages et aventures de Sanjay, explorateur mauricien des anciens mondes*. Amal Sewtohul revealed to me that Carl de Souza, a writer of the previous generation, had paid him the following compliment after reading his book: '*You are lucky, you know who you are*'.

An identity void

This is the story of a young Mauritian, born in 1975, who works for Virjanand doing cost analysis. He is a failure as an accountant, a failure all-round, in the highly competitive world of Mauritian society. The representation of the void, a concept central to the story, literally sucks Ashok into a metaphysical oblivion, expressed by the fact that he is teetering on the precipice of an identity void:

> *In fact, he aspired to escape from his identity, by becoming the opposite of what he was, a boy from a good family.* (Sewtohul, 2001: 72)

He is prey to an existential void, to the extent that, throughout the novel, he has great difficulty aligning himself with any one cultural movement. He doesn't know which side to choose, which cultural sphere to adopt, and this prevents him from finding himself. Work forces him to adapt to the business and financial culture which characterises Western societies. However, his interest in Priya, who is from a ritualised and highly codified culture, pulls him into a radically different world. Ashok would like to love like an Oriental and work like a Westerner. This contradiction manifests itself in his constant circling around an unanchored identity, which gives rise to repetitive and morbid behaviour. The failure of his relationship with Priya is the first consequence of his incapacity to choose a certain way of life rather than another.

Constantly ill at ease with others and constantly judged, Ashok is unable, in order to give any sense to his life, to satisfy his desire to be himself and even less to transgress the social barriers established by a segmented society. He considers two solutions to his existential problems: emigration and the accumulation of wealth. Emigration has once been a dream, even though the accumulation of wealth was supposed to resolve his existential problems. But even in his quest for wealth, Ashok seems doomed either to failure or to cynicism. He remains an artist despite himself. He has to find his path without the aid of material comfort. Presented in this way, the question of identity that Ashok fails to resolve highlights the central question to which the other characters gravitating around him in the book are also trying to respond.

Representing the Mauritian soul

Faisal is a Muslim, someone seemingly on the fringes of society, who Ashok meets during one of his long circular walks. He's a minor bourgeois artist (rather than a petty bourgeois artist), fighting against cultural disintegration. He thinks his efforts are necessary in order to unify the different cultures on the island, but Faisal's error seems to lie in the solitary nature of his action, he is working to unite the various cultures by distancing himself from other people:

> *I wanted to get out of Morcellement. I am looking for the soul of my country.* (201)

In his article, 'The Mirror Stage as Formative of the Function of the I', Lacan explains that the physical and psychological embodiment of 'I' is fragmented as long as it depends unconsciously on the mother's body. The mirror stage is what allows the child to consider himself as a whole. He moves from a fragmented to a unified image of himself, as perceived in the mirror placed before him. The work of the artist can be said to resemble the unifying principle of the reflection in the mirror: to look for the soul of a country is to want to understand the image it chooses to give of itself, a unified image, as if in a mirror. In the same way, to connect the fragmented elements of a divided country in a painting also means gathering each social entity within a frame, which then provides a unique image of the country.

Bearing this in mind, Faisal's fundamental problem is that he cannot remove himself from the portrait, nor can he put aside his own soul in order to understand the soul of the island. Thus the job of the artist is to eliminate their own portrait from the mirror, which otherwise attempts to make the artist themselves the reflection of a particular country or culture. Faisal can neither suspend his judgement nor provide an idealised and narcissistic image of the island.

Initially, Faisal works towards an intimate and sensual description of the reality he wants to portray. He has not yet grasped the political significance of things. His reflection leads him to feel a strange anxiety connected to the decay that he observes in his surroundings.

To try, as Faisal is doing, to clear your work of any false or idealised representation of the island of Mauritius is also to expose the indifference of the public. To present an image of the island that is too realistic, that is necessarily combined with symbolic evocations, and demonstrates the pervasive nature of corruption, is a major transgression. This is why stereotypical artistic creation plays such an important role even within cultural communities. Faisal is in rebellion against this type of artistic production and hopes to discover the soul of his country by forging something other than a conventional image generally accepted by the local 'establishment'. Such representations consider the artist as someone who might reveal the well-kept secret protected by a code of silence, someone who denies the people, considered as an ideal collective body, any narcissistic relief but who also works towards a representation that conforms to the island's constituted political order.

Thus the idealised image of Mauritian society is put to the test, tarnished by the reality of a young Hindu girl's experience of prostitution. Faisal takes the girl, who is exploited by her cousin, under his protection, thereby freeing her from the social domination of her family and relatives. In an act of revenge for liberating the girl from her alienation, the young prostitute's cousin sets Faisal's house on fire. Faisal expresses his feelings in relation to this act, and to his continual fight against the social evil of prostitution, through a painting which depicts the burning of his house:

> I, Faisal, I have finally found my painting: at the top there is a twisted moon, like the horse's head in Guernica, which turns towards an old colonial house ripped open by flames. The shingled roof rises towards the sky, suspended in the air like Goya's witches. In the middle of a strangely corrugated flame, the face of an old white woman, formed by a tongue of fire – and around the fire, upside down, like the jacks in a pack of cards, an Indian servant with a turban on his head, and a gardener dressed in tattered old clothes, carrying a bucket to extinguish the fire. Around them, the colour black: Port-Louis and its dull black, viscous, oily and rotten. Now, I think I can return to my house. (215-216)

The inhabitants of the island are liberated by the fire, as Faisal is liberated from his creative drought. The spectacular image he produces, that of a colonial house in Port-Louis enveloped by flames, belongs to a modernist urban aesthetic different from the usual clichés attached to the island and its blue waters; it is comparable to Picasso's *Guernica* or the paintings of Goya. The fulfilment of Faisal's quest through the image of fire affirms his role as a creator; he has become Mauritian, through art, by restoring the soul of his country. Symbolically, the fire represents this form of 'liberation into the imaginary realm'.

'The Maroon psyche'

Vassou is the last of the '*autres personnages de moindre importance*' (in reference to the novel's very appropriate title) to leave his mark on the reciprocal relativity of the identifications sought by the other characters in the novel, all of whom are positioned in relation to the main character, Ashok. Through Vassou the question of who can be identified with the self and who as the other is explored, a question imperative for every Mauritian, who in order to live well must accept the fundamentally multiracial nature of

241

the island, not in the limited sense of forming one or more alliances, but in terms of the locally-established political culture. For some people, like Vassou, the main point of reference is the spirit of the grandfather. Vassou is regularly visited by his deceased grandfather, Manikom's spirit, until Manikom succeeds in persuading Vassou to go and meet Léonard. Manikom is determined to help his grandson in his search for his lost identity:

Manikom accompanies Vassou to see his Creole Rodriguan friend, Léonard, who pronounces the following diagnosis:

> *He resembles you… But he does not know who he is… He's a Manaf.*
> *But he is too solitary. He must be brought to meet his brothers.*
> (155)

The term 'Manaf' used to describe the Hindu Vassou invokes more than a formal identity, that assigned to Creoles from the villages at the centre of Rodrigues, settled in the Roche-Bois suburb of Port-Louis on Mauritius or living in various villages around the coast of the island. It refers also to a process of 'social creolisation'. The quest for an identity goes beyond the question of geographical or so-called 'ethnic' origins, attempting to capture the true essence of the soul, the same essence for which Faisal is searching. Through his journey, which allows him to cross the many different worlds and regions of Mauritius, revealing the different forms of identities that have contributed to his own, Vassou discovers himself:

> *I can see that you are searching for your path. You are a Manaf. You*
> *are a Maroon. You must understand that it is not only the Creoles*
> *who became Maroons. There were also Indian maroons. White*
> *maroons, Chinese maroons, all sorts of maroons there are. All those*
> *searching for their freedom are Maroons. You will see for yourself.*
> (160)

Marronage then is by no means the sole preserve of former Black African or Madagascan slaves, but concerns all migrant populations affected by the expansion of empires, an expansion which led to the world being split between the great colonial powers. Marronage was thus the direct consequence of the trauma caused by encounters between peoples of different origins that were of unequal benefit to those involved, and ideally all examples of the phenomenon need be considered as a whole for any meaningful discussion to take place. 'The Maroon psyche II' (154-165), a very beautiful chapter of the novel, describes the trance experienced by Vassou, during which is expressed a form of 'social creolisation' expanded to include the whole of humanity.

Vassou's possession can be seen to encapsulate and bring together the ways in which the unique experiences of each culture, of each nation, might be unified in a shared representation of the same humanity. Vassou has a mystical experience as all the memories stifled by the violence of history re-emerge in him through the numerous metamorphoses to which he is subject. During his voyage of initiation, Vassou discovers all sorts of people who could be qualified as 'Maroons', each of their personal narratives contributing to the great historical narrative and to the history of immigration on the island of Mauritius. If marronage is a state of mind, then social creolisation is similarly cultural and political. The resurgence of all these memories allows the novel's central character, Vassou, to find the path into his future: liberation into the imaginary realm? Perhaps, but as well as this:

> *And thus Vassou drifted from one rebellious spirit to another, taking*
> *on a characteristic from each, a particular perspective. He became*
> *a Makondé hunting wild boar [...] then a Hungarian Jew [...] then a*
> *French revolutionary soldier [...] then a Gurkha fleeing India [...].*
> *Within each he felt a breath of life, a vital spirit, a dream* (164-169)

Thus is described a 'creolisation' which ushers in the dawn of a united world, where social, geographical and historical barriers might cease to have such importance.

Contemporary Mauritian literature is highly conducive to the construction of new non-essentialist representations of the Self and of the Other. This corresponds with the theories of the social theorist Jacques Rancière, which take into account the idea of the potentiality of art:

> *...the idea of the potentiality inherent in the innovative sensible*
> *modes of experience that anticipate a community to come.*
> (Rancière, 2000: 45)

The representations of otherness and the study of a certain symptomatology of the multiplicity of social relations that can be found in Mauritian literature are rich sources of inspiration. The final novel discussed here, *Histoire d'Ashok et d'autres personnages de moindre importance* goes still further in its analysis of the internal and external relations that take place during identity construction. It marks an epistemological rupture in the very conception of 'social creolisation' which may be seen as a privileged space for a new national imagination. Slavery is no longer viewed through the prism of the humiliations suffered by the victims of history, but is transfigured by it, to act as a reminder of those who resisted. From this perspective, the diverse encounters between different peoples, the building blocks of history in the making, which have structured our consciousness, in the end all share the 'same bastard status' that has structured Vassou's identity consciousness. The traumas of history should no longer be studied in relation to preconceived collective identities, but in relation to the nature of how identity is formed: the study of the obstacles or barriers to the emergence of social interaction should only be referred to in order to explore what in the present might constitute an 'us' in a broader sense, with the clear aim of unified action. Such research, sensitive to the importance of these new social bonds, could influence and demonstrate an expanded consciousness capable of exploring the limits of the contemporary world.

References

Arno, T. and Orian, C. (1986) *Île Maurice, une société multiraciale*. Paris: L'Harmattan.

Beniamino, M. (2005) 'Roman et ethnicité: voix et voies de l'identité à Maurice', *Francofonia. Studi e ricerche sulle letterature di lingua francese* 48: 61-72.

Chazan-Gillig, S. (2001) 'Les fondements du pluriculturalisme mauricien et l'émergence d'une nouvelle société', *Journal des anthropologues* 87: 139–168.

Geertz, C. (1973) *The Interpretation of Cultures*. New York: Basic Books.

Humbert, M. T. (1990) *A l'autre bout de moi*. Vacoas, Mauritius: Editions Le Printemps.

Kilani, M. (2000) *L'invention de l'autre. Essais sur le discours anthropologique*. Lausanne: Payot.

Lacan, J. (1966) *Le stade du miroir comme formateur de la fonction du Je*. Ecrits I, Points Essais, Paris: Seuil.

Madgelaine-Andrianjafitrimo, V. (2006) 'Histoire et mémoire: variations autour de l'ancestralité et de la filiation dans les romans francophones réunionnais et mauriciens', *Revue de littérature comparée* 2006/2, no. 318: 195-222.

Mérédac, S. (1926) *Polyte*. Port-Louis, Mauritius: The General Printing and Stationery Co. Ltd.

Ng Tat Chung, S. (2003) *Terre d'orages*. Port Louis, Mauritius: The Nelson Mandela Centre for African Culture.

Rancière, J. (2000) *Le Partage du sensible. Esthétique et politique*. Paris: La Fabrique.

Rancière, J. (2007) *Politique de la littérature*. Paris: Galilée.

Ramharai, V. (1990) *Les Interactions Sociales dans A l'autre bout de Moi de Marie-Thérèse Humbert*. Port-Louis: Best Graphics.

Sewtohul, A. (2001) *Histoire d'Ashok et d'autres personnages de moindre importance*. Continents noirs, Paris: Gallimard.

"For Mauritians, Joy; for Chagossians, Sadness"
Mauritian Independence, the Sacrifice of the Chagos Archipelago, and the Suffering of the Chagos Islanders

LAURA JEFFERY

Introduction: Excision, displacement and social suffering

Throughout the world, most of those forcibly displaced because of development, conservation, or military activities are already marginal people such as indigenous and tribal communities, the rural landless poor, and marginal urban residents (Cernea & McDowell, 2000). Even before undergoing displacement, such people may be already socially and economically marginal in multiple ways: they may belong to minority faiths or ethnic groups and speak minority languages; they may be geographically remote from the centre; they may be dependent on informal and often vulnerable livelihoods; and they may not be fully integrated into the formal economy (Cernea & McDowell, 2000). More often than not, this marginality is compounded rather than alleviated by displacement (Cernea & McDowell, 2000). In general, those who bear the highest costs of development, conservation, or military activities – those who are made to give up their land and other assets, to move their families, and to embark upon new lives and livelihoods elsewhere – tend to be among the least likely to benefit from subsequent infrastructural development (Cernea & McDowell, 2000; Chatty & Colchester, 2002; McDowell, 1996). This chapter looks ethnographically at such processes of marginalisation in the context of the Chagos islanders.

The Chagos Archipelago is a remote group of coral atolls in the middle of the Indian Ocean. The Chagos Islands were uninhabited prior to European colonial expansion in the Indian Ocean from the late 18th century onwards, whereupon the Chagos Archipelago was administered as a dependency of colonial Mauritius (Toussaint, 1974). French and later British colonists populated the islands with enslaved labourers and contract workers, mostly from East Africa and Madagascar via Mauritius. Throughout the settled history of the Chagos Islands, coconut plantations

245

were the economic base and main source of employment (Dussercle, 1934; Dussercle, 1935; Scott, 1961). Also known as the Oil Islands (Wenban-Smith & Carter, 2016), they relied almost entirely on the production of copra (dried coconut flesh) exported for the extraction of coconut oil that was refined for energy and used in the production of soap (among other products) in Mauritius and beyond. The population of Chagos rose steadily throughout the 19th century and hovered around one thousand people over the first half of the 20th century (Gifford & Dunne, 2014). By the 1960s, half of this population lived on the largest island of Diego Garcia, with the remainder divided between islands in the only other two inhabited atolls, Peros Banhos and Salomon (Gifford & Dunne, 2014: 38, 40).

In 1965, as part of negotiations leading to the independence of Mauritius in 1968, the UK Government excised the Chagos Archipelago from colonial Mauritius to form part of the new British Indian Ocean Territory (BIOT) (Boolell, 2006: 29-36; Chan Low, 2011; de l'Estrac, 1983, 2011). The excision contravened the 1960 United Nations Declaration on the Granting of Independence to Colonial Countries, which required the decolonising state to maintain the territorial integrity of the colony in question (see Robertson, nd).[i] A 1965 United Nations General Assembly Resolution on the Question of Mauritius specifically noted that the detachment of the Chagos Archipelago would constitute a violation of the Territory of Mauritius (Robertson, nd).[ii] In 1966 an Exchange of Notes between the UK and the US made the Chagos Archipelago available for defence purposes for fifty years in the first instance.[iii] Since 1971, the largest Chagos island of Diego Garcia has been the site of a major US overseas military base (Vine, 2009). The revised Mauritian Constitution has, since 1982, included the Chagos Archipelago as Mauritian territory, but the UK's response is that the Chagos Archipelago would be returned to Mauritian sovereignty only when it is no longer required for UK and US defence purposes (Allen, 2007; Robertson, nd). In 2016, the agreement between the UK and the US was automatically renewed for a further twenty years until 2036. Fifty years after independence, then, the decolonisation of the Republic of Mauritius remains incomplete.

Following the establishment of BIOT in 1965, and particularly from 1967 onwards, the UK government depopulated the Chagos Archipelago, first by preventing the return of islanders who had gone on trips to Mauritius and Seychelles, and later by restricting supplies, winding down work on the coconut plantations, and finally coercing the remaining islanders onto crowded ships. By 1973, between 1,328 and 1,522 Chagos Islanders had been relocated to Mauritius and 232 to Seychelles (Gifford & Dunne, 2014: 46). No support was offered to facilitate resettlement, and Chagos Islanders lacked contacts, education, training, and experience relevant to the job market in Mauritius. These challenges were compounded by the socio-economic marginalisation of Afro-Creoles in general (see Asgarally, 1997; Boswell, 2006; Eriksen, 1998; Miles, 1999) and Chagossians in particular (Botte, 1980; Dræbel, 1997; Jeffery & Vine, 2011: 94-97; Sylva, 1981; Walker, 1986: 21-22). In combination, these factors negatively impacted their ability to find adequate housing and jobs in Mauritius, and Chagossian families have consequently suffered disproportionately from the concomitants of unemployment and underemployment and of poor housing in disadvantaged neighbourhoods: low levels of educational achievement and high rates of poverty, physical and psychological ill-health, teenage and unplanned pregnancy, alcohol and drug addiction, prostitution, gambling, and crime (Prosser, 1976; Botte, 1980; Sylva, 1981; Madeley, 1985; Walker, 1986; Dræbel, 1997; Vine *et al.*, 2005; Jeffery, 2011). This resonates with the anthropological concept of social suffering: trauma, pain, and disorientation, generated by the abuse of political, economic, or institutional power, which are manifested in apparently individual and medicalised conditions that are at the same time profoundly interpersonal and social (Kleinman *et al.*, 1997: ix).

Struggles for compensation and the right of return

From the beginning, groups of Chagos Islanders have rejected both the fact and the terms of their removal from Chagos. In 1972, the UK government awarded the Mauritian government £650,000 with which to compensate the displaced Chagos Islanders, but this money was not distributed until 1978, following a Chagossian protest lasting several months (de l'Estrac, 1983: 37, 78). Each adult Chagos Islander was entitled to receive Rs.7,590, and Chagossian children under eighteen were entitled to between Rs.1,000 and Rs.1,500, depending on their age at the time (de l'Estrac, 1983: 77; Madeley, 1985: 7). Many Chagossian families (including all of those in Seychelles) received no money, and the sums proved to be 'hopelessly inadequate' (Madeley, 1985: 7). Chagos Islanders continued periodically to demonstrate in Port Louis to demand their right of return to Chagos, immediate compensation, decent housing, and jobs. In 1982, the UK government provided £4 million in compensation and the Mauritian government contributed land valued at £1 million. Each Chagos Islander received Rs.10,000 plus Rs.36,000 for adults or Rs.19,000 for children, much of which was used to pay off debts or pooled by families and put towards housing. Over one hundred Chagossian-headed households moved to purpose-built housing estates (*Cité Ilois*) or dedicated plots of land (*Morcellement Ilois*) in Baie du Tombeau and Pointe aux Sables, two neighbourhoods on the outskirts of Port Louis. The final instalments of Rs.8,000 were released in 1983, on condition that the recipients would

sign or thumbprint English-language 'full and final' renunciation forms to indemnify the UK government (Madeley, 1985: 10).

In 1997, a series of hitherto secret notes between UK officials were made available under the 30-year rule in the Public Records Act. These revealed that the UK government knew at the time of the displacement that the islanders were a settled population – rather than transient contract workers as they had then been portrayed – and that uprooting them was contrary to international law (Marimootoo, 1997). These revelations laid the foundations of a case against the UK government in the name of Olivier Bancoult, leader of the Chagos Refugees Group in Mauritius. In 2000, the High Court in London ruled against the UK government. In 2002, the British Overseas Territories Act awarded full UK citizenship to the Chagos Islanders and most of their second-generation descendants. Since then, several thousand members of the extended Chagossian community have migrated from Mauritius and Seychelles to the UK, mostly to Crawley (West Sussex), London, and Manchester. In 2004, however, a Chagossian compensation case was rejected, and the UK government bypassed parliament by using an Order in Council (a royal prerogative) to enact a new BIOT Immigration Order, which prohibited unauthorised people (including Chagossians) from entering any part of the Chagos Archipelago (Allen, 2009). In 2010, in response to a powerful campaign led by a coalition of conservation groups, the UK government established a no-fishing Marine Protected Area (MPA) around the Chagos Archipelago (see De Santo et al, 2011; Dunne et al, 2014; Harris, 2014; Jeffery, 2013; Sand, 2010). In 2015, the United Nations Permanent Court of Arbitration unanimously found that the declaration of the MPA was incompatible with the UK government's obligations under the United Nations Convention on the Law of the Sea (UNCLOS) with respect to Mauritian fishing rights, the eventual return of the territory to Mauritian sovereignty, and the rights of Mauritius to benefit from oil or mineral extraction activities in the region (Harris, 2015).

Meanwhile, in 2014, the UK government commissioned a resettlement feasibility study which concluded broadly that there were no insurmountable legal or environmental barriers to resettlement (KPMG, 2015; see Rotter & Jeffery, 2016). In June 2016, the Supreme Court in London ruled that the 2004 BIOT Immigration Order was lawful, but recommended that the UK government should review the right of abode in light of the resettlement feasibility study. In November 2016, however, the UK government announced that it had decided against resettlement on the grounds of 'feasibility, defence and security interests, and cost to the British taxpayer', and instead to fund a package of £40 million over ten years to improve 'access to health and social care and to improved education and employment opportunities'.[iv] Chagossian groups responded with dismay that the UK government was attempting to bribe them to give up their right of return, and pledged to reject the compensation package and continue to campaign. Demonstrations took place in December 2016 outside the British High Commission in Port Louis and outside the British Prime Minister's official residence at 10 Downing Street in London. In June 2017, the Mauritian government secured – by a massive majority of 94 for, alongside 15 against, 65 abstentions, and 19 who did not vote – a United Nations General Assembly resolution to seek an advisory opinion from the International Court of Justice (ICJ) on the sovereignty of the Chagos Archipelago. Also in June 2017, the Supreme Court in London heard the Chagos Refugees Group's appeal against the Marine Protected Area.

Having briefly outlined the relevant colonial and postcolonial political history, my purpose in the remainder of this chapter is to interrogate the implications of the excision of the Chagos Archipelago and the displacement of the Chagos Islanders for relations between the Mauritian state and the generationally extended and geographically dispersed Chagossian community. Firstly, I highlight Chagossian experiences of marginalisation and their consequent critiques of the Mauritian nation-building project. Secondly, I reveal similarities in their critiques of the different prospects for return and governance either as a controversial British Overseas Territory, or within the Republic of Mauritius, or via co-management. Thirdly, I conclude that the development of compelling objectives and strategies for the decolonisation the Chagos Archipelago will require outreach and consultation to incorporate diverse Chagossian perspectives.[v]

'Sacrificed for independence'[vi]

Seewoosagur Ramgoolam, the Mauritius Labour Party (MLP) politician and future prime minister at the centre of the independence negotiations in 1965, later reported that the UK government had coerced him into agreeing to the detachment of the Chagos Archipelago to ease and speed up the process of decolonisation (de l'Estrac, 1983: 9-11). He told the Mauritian Legislative Assembly's Select Committee on the Excision of the Chagos Archipelago:

> *A request was made to me. I had to see which was better – to cede out a portion of our territory of which few people knew, and independence. I thought that independence was much more primordial and more important than the excision of the island which is very far from here, and which we had never visited, which we could never visit ... if I had to choose between independence and the ceding of Diego Garcia, I would have done again the same thing.* (de l'Estrac, 1983: 22)

Mauritian politicians should never have been confronted with this ultimatum, and declassified documents reveal that the British would have excised the Chagos Archipelago with or without the agreement of Mauritian political leaders (Chan Low, 2011: 71-76), but the key point here is that Ramgoolam's account also reveals the extent to which the Chagos Archipelago and the Chagos Islanders were already marginal within colonial Mauritius. Most people in Mauritius knew little about the territory and its inhabitants, and the political elite 'considered that the excision of a distant archipelago, and the expulsion of some poor illiterate Creoles, was a small price to pay for state power, with British support, in decolonisation' (Houbert, 1992: 471). Ramgoolam is often affectionately referred to as 'father of the nation' (*père de la nation*) (Eriksen, 1998: 146; Teelock, 2001: 415), but in my experience, virtually every Chagossian would reject this accolade, retorting that Ramgoolam achieved independence only by allowing Mauritian territory and people to be violated through the excision of the Chagos Archipelago and the displacement of the Chagossians.

A conversation I had with a retired Chagossian woman and her elderly mother in Mauritius encapsulates some of the main issues. Ramgoolam, they told me, had 'sold the islands' in order 'to win independence'. Initially they asserted that independence was good for Mauritius because, as the mother put it, Mauritius 'became a grown-up'. Reflecting widespread concerns before independence that independent Mauritius would be dominated by Indo-Mauritians (see Boswell, 2006: 128; Eisenlohr, 2006: 197; Eriksen, 1998: 151; Salverda, 2015: 61-65), the daughter qualified that Indo-Mauritians supported independence because they wanted to get into positions of power. But, she said, Catholics were unhappy about independence, and that amongst Catholics, the Chagos islanders were the unhappiest because they lost their islands. Her mother concluded: 'for Mauritians, it's glorious, but for the islanders, it's sorrowful'.

Chagos Islanders argue that Mauritian independence was at their expense but not to their benefit since they were compelled to sacrifice their homeland, suffering displacement and ongoing marginalisation and impoverishment. It is therefore unsurprising that many Chagos Islanders are critical of the deal struck for Mauritian independence and of a nation-building project based on 'unity in diversity'. As expressed by Josephine,[vii] a Chagos Islander born in the 1940s:

> *Mauritian independence is something that has brought great sadness ... we have suffered too much. This whole community suffered, people died of sadness and poverty, all because of Mauritian independence. Mauritius got its freedom but we are still suffering, we have nothing, we're still slaving away... Mauritius got its independence and became a republic at our expense. The country was*

developed with a university and all that, all at our expense. [Look at] the courage of my elders, they suffered and died because of poverty and missing the islands. Look at our mizer nwar, our sacrifice for independence... Celebrate independence? Never! Can't do that.

This phenomenon is by no means restricted to Chagossians, which is perhaps unsurprising given that 44 per cent of the Mauritian electorate as a whole – and 95 per cent of the electorate in Rodrigues – voted for an anti-independence coalition in 1967 (Eisenlohr, 2006: 197; Eriksen, 1998: 10).[viii] Many marginalised people in the Republic of Mauritius – Chagossians and non-Chagossians alike – claim that they would have preferred to have remained under British colonial rule in order to access British citizenship, education, and welfare. One person praised Hong Kong for getting the UK to pay for 'development' before demanding 'independence' (that is, the return of Hong Kong to Chinese sovereignty in 1997).

It is also worth emphasising that many of the non-Chagossian but similarly marginalised people who I have encountered in Mauritius have reported that they too feel excluded from Mauritian nationhood because of historic ethnic discrimination and ongoing socio-economic marginalisation, as can be illustrated by a discussion during my conversational English class in Pointe aux Sables on the eve of the commemoration of 35 years of Mauritian independence in 2003. A teenager with two Chagossian grandparents told the class that he would be participating in the official flag-raising ceremony with his school. The teenager's father (both of whose parents were Chagos Islanders) said he does not celebrate Mauritian independence since 'Mauritius got independence because it sold my mother's land'.[ix] I asked the rest of the class to comment. One Mauritius-born young woman of Chagossian parentage said that she would be celebrating because, simply, 'I am Mauritian'. But another student – a young Mauritian man with no Chagossian ancestry – said that he does not celebrate independence because 'I am Mauritian, but I do not feel at home in my own country. There are a lot of social problems in Mauritius'. Many working-class Mauritian Creoles expressed a sense of exclusion from what they see as a dominant and discriminatory Indo-Mauritian nationhood. Experiences of exclusion contribute to a critique – widespread amongst Chagossians and other marginalised citizens alike – of a Mauritian nation-building project based on an unrealistic and idealised notion of 'unity in diversity'.

Prospects for governance and return

Fifty years after independence, the decolonisation of Mauritius remains incomplete. Amongst socio-political groups in Mauritius, the political party Lalit has been the most consistent in its commitment to unite campaigns for decolonisation through the restitution of the Chagos Archipelago to the Republic of Mauritius, demilitarisation through the closure of the US military base on Diego Garcia, and the right of return and freedom of movement for Chagossians and other Mauritian citizens (Lalit, 2002). Other critics take a pragmatic economic approach, querying the likelihood that the Mauritian government could sustain commitments to demilitarisation (given the opportunity to claim rent from the US) and to environmental conservation (given the prospects for commercial fisheries). Chagos Islanders and Chagossian groups have held a range of fluctuating perspectives concerning prospects for resettlement and governance of the Chagos Archipelago.

As detailed above, the Chagos Refugees Group (CRG) has launched a series of court cases in London over the past fifteen years to seek further compensation and the right of return from the UK government. At the time the smaller Chagossian Social Committee (CSC) and Mauritian critics – including politicians, journalists, and lawyers – accused the CRG of falling into a British trap, acting against Mauritian interests, and acquiescing to de facto UK sovereignty by campaigning for UK citizenship and taking cases to British courts (see e.g. Boolell, 2001; Lassemillante, 2001; Marimootoo, 2000; Minerve, 2000; Poché, 2000).[x] Following a succession of court cases against the UK that have not established the right of return, however, the CRG has recently increasingly aligned with the Mauritian government, which in turn declared its support for the right of return. Chagossians in Seychelles and in the UK, meanwhile, tend to favour the Chagos Archipelago remaining British territory. This section illustrates the similarities between their critiques of the different possibilities.

Two possible models within the Republic of Mauritius are the Outer Islands of Rodrigues and Agaléga.[xi] Chagossians favoured the much larger-scale model of the Rodrigues Regional Assembly, not least due to indications that life on the Agaléga Islands is being made increasingly difficult, as had been the case on the Chagos Archipelago prior to the final depopulation. Their critiques of autonomy within the Republic of Mauritius revolved around the fear that Chagos would become dominated by non-Chagossian interests. Josephine's principal concern was ethnic discrimination and the prioritisation of Indo-Mauritians:

> *The Mauritian government just looks after its own interests... With the British*
> *and the Americans, it's just seeking sovereignty... Then what will it do with the*

islands there? It could develop them. Who will it put there? It will put its Malbar [Hindus] there! Us? We'd stay here. We would. Sorry, but look here at Mauritius: they prioritise Malbar, nothing for Creoles.

Others were concerned by rumours about joint Mauritian and foreign tourist and fisheries business ventures and the possibility that the Mauritian government would allow foreigners to buy plots of land along with residence permits, thus extending the extant tradition of 'selling part of the patrimony in exchange for money'.[xii]

Chagossians who were relocated not to Mauritius but to Seychelles (and who may be Seychellois rather than Mauritian citizens), plus those Chagossians who have migrated to the UK since being awarded UK citizenship, are less likely to support autonomy within the Republic of Mauritius and more likely to support governance modelled on British Overseas Territories such as Falklands and Gibraltar (or, closer to Mauritius, the French overseas department of Réunion). For some, the rationale was that Chagos could benefit from British finance and infrastructure expertise. Others have been more critical of the governance of the British Overseas Territories: Fernand Mandarin, the late leader of the CSC, remarked to me that: 'the UK has abandoned them'. Crucially, Chagossian critiques of autonomy within the Republic of Mauritius mirror their critiques of British Overseas Territories: in both cases, Chagossians are concerned about being marginal to the economic preoccupations of a dominant power. A final suggestion is that Chagos could be co-managed, following the model of Tromelin, where marine resources and archaeological expeditions are co-managed by Mauritius and France 'without prejudice' to either country's sovereignty claim. But, again, co-management raises the prospect of joint Mauritian and British business ventures in which Chagossian interests would be marginalised. In any eventuality, Chagossians are understandably concerned that they would be confined to marginal roles such as manual labour of peeling coconuts (*plis koko*).

Fifty years since Mauritian independence, prospects for Chagos are in flux as a result of a multitude of factors including: the United Nations Permanent Court of Arbitration finding that the UK's declaration of a Marine Protected Area was unlawful; the United Nations General Assembly resolution to refer the Mauritian sovereignty case to the International Court of Justice (ICJ); ramifications of the UK's EU referendum in June 2016 (which could make British Overseas Territories ineligible for EU funding); the UK government's announcements in November 2016 that the US military base on Diego Garcia would remain until 2036 and that it had decided not to resettle the Chagos Archipelago; and the CRG's Supreme Court appeal against the Marine Protected Area. A potentially significant turning point came in September 2016, when the then

Mauritian Prime Minister Anerood Jugnauth invited the CRG leader Oliver Bancoult to accompany him to his first meeting with the UK Foreign Secretary Boris Johnson. And in 2017, CRG members were part of the Mauritian delegation to the United Nations General Assembly. In this context, it seems plausible that Chagossians in Mauritius may continue increasingly to support the Mauritian government as one of the few remaining avenues for the right of return. This is a pragmatic decision rather than an ideological realignment. As Chagossians insist, 'no government has helped us' and 'both states are guilty' of using the Chagossians as pawns in their tussle over sovereignty; for most Chagossians, however, sovereignty is less important than the associated right of return.

Inclusive decolonisation

I want to conclude by considering the diversity of opinion amongst some of my anti-imperialist research participants in Mauritius regarding the excision of the Chagos Archipelago and the status of the Chagos Archipelago as still disputed territory. One, who was critical of opposition to independence amongst the so-called 'general population', told me that Mauritians who are not interested in their own heritage and do not yet have their own identity or notion of 'the motherland' are weakened psychologically. Another determined that it was 'anti-national' for Chagossians to accept UK citizenship (even though Mauritius permits dual nationality; as Olivier Bancoult has asked rhetorically: 'if the British passport is such a threat to Mauritian sovereignty, why are there politicians with dual nationality?'). For some, reunification of the Republic of Mauritius is important both for Mauritians and for Chagossians as Mauritian citizens (although some Chagossians are, instead, Seychellois citizens). Other Mauritian perspectives chime more with Seewoosagur Ramgoolam's reflections on the relative insignificance of the Chagos Archipelago in comparison with Mauritian independence (de l'Estrac, 1983: 22). In the words of one Mauritian anti-imperialist intellectual, "my dear, nobody gives a damn about Diego Garcia". By contrast, a Mauritian academic opined that: 'Mauritians do not care about the Chagossians, and Mauritians have only been interested in the Chagos since the issue of Mauritian sovereignty was raised, so they care about the issue but not the people'. In my own experience, however, heartfelt sympathy amongst Mauritians for the plight of the Chagos Islanders is often tempered by a resignation that the Chagos Archipelago as a disputed territory is 'already lost'.

As a British anthropologist of postcolonial Mauritius, it is important for me to be 'on the right side of history' by condemning the excision of the Chagos Archipelago before independence and endorsing the reunification of the territory of the Republic of Mauritius as another step towards decolonisation. As the former UN appeals judge

Geoffrey Robertson QC has argued, 'the islands rightfully belong to Mauritius and should be returned to that nation' (nd). While strongly endorsing the principle of decolonisation, it is also important as scholars to remember that the nation is not a naturally occurring phenomenon but, rather, a historical and political phenomenon intimately connected in myriad complex ways to European colonialism (cf. Anderson, 1983; Chatterjee, 1993; Kedurie, 1960). The islands of Mauritius were populated via successive waves of European colonialism in the Indian Ocean (Teelock, 2001). Furthermore, a nation does not necessarily have naturally self-evident boundaries (Gupta & Ferguson, 1992: 11-12; Malkki, 1992: 26). Eriksen (1998: 143) noted that, 'being an island, Mauritius can easily be construed as a naturally bounded territory'. However, the Republic of Mauritius is not an island but a group of islands and archipelagos encompassing wildly divergent areas and population sizes of wildly unequal economic and political significance. The Republic of Mauritius is thus not a naturally occurring nation-state but rather an idea undergoing a process of constant negotiation and renegotiation.

That the Chagos Archipelago forms part of the Republic of Mauritius is of only secondary importance from the perspective of most native Chagos Islanders, who would identify primarily with the Chagos Archipelago in particular, rather than with the Republic of Mauritius in general. The Mauritius-born descendants of Chagos Islanders might identify principally as Mauritian rather than as Chagossian, although those Chagossians who were relocated to Seychelles do not tend to identify with Mauritius at all, and those who have migrated to the UK increasingly align with the UK. Furthermore, as we have seen above, many non-Chagossian Mauritians similarly dissociate from the Mauritian state and from Mauritian nation-building. This is a direct result of their experiences of historic ethnic discrimination and ongoing socio-economic marginalisation. Instead of dismissing this as an anti-national or colonised mentality that needs to be decolonised, I would be inclined to focus on their substantive pleas for the things that matter to indigenous and other marginalised peoples and their families: for some, the right to live on their ancestral homelands; for others, access to better welfare, healthcare, educational, employment, and other opportunities wherever they may (choose to) live.

Regardless of their differences of opinion regarding sovereignty, governance, and resettlement, most Chagossians agree that neither successive UK governments nor successive Mauritian governments have had the best interests of the Chagossian community at heart in the past, present, or anticipated future. The development of a close relationship between the MSM government and the CRG in 2016–17 may turn out to have been a significant turning point in mutually beneficial relations between the Mauritian government and the Chagossian community. But the onus remains on the Mauritian government to undertake outreach and demonstrate commitment not only to the sovereignty of the Chagos Archipelago but also to the welfare of the Chagossian community. The development of compelling objectives and strategies for the decolonisation of the Chagos Archipelago will require consultation to incorporate diverse Chagossian perspectives on key issues such as governance, immigration, resettlement, environmental conservation, and the US military base on Diego Garcia.

Acknowledgements

The research on which this chapter is based was funded by the UK Economic and Social Research Council (award numbers R42200134267 and RES-063-27-0214) and the Leverhulme Trust (ECF/2006/0122). I am grateful to the many Chagossians and Mauritians who have so generously shared their time and their opinions with me, and to Sean Carey, Thomas Hylland Eriksen, Vinesh Hookoomsing and Ramola Ramtohul for their insights.

References

Allen, S. (2007) 'Looking beyond the Bancoult cases: international law and the prospect of resettling the Chagos Islands', *Human Rights Law Review* 7(3): 441–482.

Allen, S. (2009) 'Reviewing the Prerogative of Colonial Governance', *Judicial Review* 14(2): 119–128.

Anderson, B. (1983) *Imagined Communities: Reflections on the Origins and Spread of Nationalism*. London: Verso.

Asgarally, I. (ed) (1997) *Étude pluridisciplinaire sur l'exclusion à Maurice*. Réduit, Mauritius: Présidence de la République.

Axel, B. K. (2001) *The Nation's Tortured Body: Violence, Representation, and the Formation of a Sikh "Diaspora"*. Durham: Duke University Press.

Boolell, S. (2001) 'The fall out of the Bancoult case', in *Le Mauricien* (27 February). Port Louis.

Boolell, S. (1996) *Untold Stories (a collection of Socio-Political Essays) 1950–1995*. Stanley, Rose-Hill: Éditions de L'Océan Indien.

Boswell, R. (2006) *Le Malaise Créole: Ethnic Identity in Mauritius*. Oxford: Berghahn.

Botte, F. (1980) *The 'Ilois' Community and the 'Ilois' Women*. Unpublished report.

Cernea, M.M. & C. McDowell (eds) (2000) *Risks and Reconstruction: Experiences of Resettlers and Refugees*. Washington DC: World Bank.

Chan Low, J. (2011) 'The making of the Chagos affair: myths and reality', in S.J.T.M. Evers and M. Kooy (eds) *Eviction from the Chagos Islands: Displacement and Struggle for Identity*. Leiden: Brill.

Chatterjee, P. (1993) *The Nation and Its Fragments: Colonial and Postcolonial Histories*. Princeton: Princeton University Press.

Chatty, D. & Colchester, M. (eds) (2002) *Conservation and Mobile Indigenous Peoples: Displacement, Forced Settlement, and Sustainable Development*. Oxford: Berghahn.

de l'Estrac, J.C. (1983) *Report of the Select Committee on the Excision of the Chagos Archipelago (No. 2 of 1983)*. Port Louis: Mauritius Legislative Assembly.

de l'Estrac, J.C. (2011) *L'an prochain à Diego Garcia...* Stanley, Rose-Hill: Éditions de L'Océan Indien.

De Santo, E.M., Jones, P.J.S. & Miller, A.M.M. (2011) 'Fortress conservation at sea: A commentary on the Chagos marine protected area', *Marine Policy* 35: 258–260.

Dræbel, T. (1997) *Evaluation des besoins sociaux de la communauté déplacée de l'Archipel de Chagos, volet un: santé et education*. Unpublished report.

Dunne, R.P., Polunin, N.V.C., Sand, P.H. and Johnson, M.L. (2014) 'The Creation of the Chagos Marine Protected Area: A Fisheries Perspective', *Advances in Marine Biology* 69: 79–127.

Dussercle, R. (1934) *Archipel de Chagos: En Mission, 10 Novembre 1953–11 Janvier 1934*. Port Louis: General Printing & Stationery Co Ltd.

Dussercle, R. (1935) *Archipel de Chagos: En Mission, Diégo–Six Iles–Péros, Septembre–Novembre 1934*. Port Louis: General Printing & Stationery Co Ltd.

Eisenlohr, P. (2006) *Little India: Diaspora, Time, and Ethnolinguistic Belonging in Hindu Mauritius*. Berkeley: University of Chicago Press.

Eriksen, T.H. (1998) *Common Denominators: Ethnicity, Nation-Building and Compromise in Mauritius*. Oxford: Berg.

Gifford, R.D. & Dunne, R.P. (2014) 'A Dispossessed people: The Depopulation of the Chagos Archipelago 1965-1973', *Population, Space and Place* 20: 37–49.

Gupta, A. & Ferguson, J. (1992) 'Beyond "culture": Space, Identity, and the Politics of Difference', *Cultural Anthropology* 7(1): 6–23.

Harris, P. (2014) 'Fortress, Safe Haven or Home? The Chagos MPA in Political Context', *Marine Policy* 46: 19–21.

Harris, P. (2015) 'Britannia rules the waves? The law of the sea, the British Indian Ocean Territory, and the Chagos Islanders' right to return', *Anthropology Today* 31(3): 18–19.

Houbert, J. (1992) The Indian Ocean Creole islands: Geo-politics and decolonisation. *The Journal of Modern African Studies* 30(3): 465–484.

Jeffery, L. (2011) *Chagos islanders in Mauritius and the UK: Forced Displacement and Onward Migration*. Manchester: Manchester University Press.

Jeffery, L. (2013) '"We are the true guardians of the environment": Human-environment relations and debates about the future of the Chagos Archipelago', *Journal of the Royal Anthropological Institute* 19: 300–318.

Jeffery, L. & Vine, D. (2011) 'Sorrow, sadness, and impoverishment: The lives of Chagossians in Mauritius', in S.J.T.M. Evers & M. Kooy (eds) *Eviction from the Chagos Islands: Displacement and Struggle for Identity*. Leiden: Brill.

Kedourie, E. (1960) *Nationalism*. New York: Praeger.

Kleinman, A., Das, V. & Lock, M.M. (1997) 'Introduction', in A. Kleinman, V. Das and M.M. Lock (eds) *Social Suffering*. California: University of California Press.

KPMG. (2015) *Feasibility study for the resettlement of the British Indian Ocean Territory Volume 1*, London: KPMG LLP.

Lalit. (2002) *Diego Garcia in Times of Globalization*. Port Louis: Ledikasyon Pu Travayer.

Lassemillante, H. (2001) 'Chagos: les intérêts mauriciens sont menacés', in *Le Mauricien* (1 March): p.7. Port Louis.

Madeley, J. (1985) *Diego Garcia: a contrast to the Falklands, London, Minority Rights Group report no.54*. London: Minority Rights Group.

Malkki, L. (1992) 'National Geographic: The Rooting of Peoples and the Territorialization of National Identity', *Cultural Anthropology* 7(1): 24–44.

Marimootoo, H. (1997) 'Diego files', in *Week-end* (weekly, 25 May 1997–10 August 1997). Port Louis.

Marimootoo, H. (2000) 'M. Olivier Bancoult lance, à nouveau, un appel à l'unité les Chagossiens', in *Week-end* (22 December): p.69. Port Louis.

McDowell, C. (ed) (1996) *Understanding Impoverishment: The Consequences of Development-Induced Displacement*. Oxford: Berghahn.

Miles, W. F. S. (1999) 'The Creole Malaise in Mauritius', *African Affairs* 98(391): 211-228.

Minerve, J. (2000) 'L'archipel des Chagos: affirmons concrètement notre souveraineté!', in *Le Mauricien* (15 November): p.7. Port Louis.

Poché, J.M. (2000) 'Maurice réclame l'ouverture immédiate des négociations sur sa souveraineté', in *Le Mauricien* (7 November): p.4. Port Louis.

Prosser, A.R.G. (1976) *Visit to Mauritius from 24 January to 2 February: Mauritius – Resettlement of Persons Transferred from Chagos Archipelago*. Port Louis: Government of Mauritius.

Robertson, G. (n.d) *Who owns Diego Garcia? Decolonisation and indigenous rights in the Indian Ocean*. Unpublished manuscript at
  http://www.austlii.edu.au/au/journals/UWALawRw/2012/1.pdf

Rotter, R. & L. Jeffery (2016) '"We no longer have faith and trust in anyone": Misadventures in community consultation on the future of the Chagos Archipelago', *International Development Planning Review* 38(4): 383–403.

Salverda, T. (2015) *The Franco-Mauritian Elite: Power and Anxiety in the Face of Change*. Oxford: Berghahn.

Sand, P.H. (2010) 'The Chagos Archipelago: Footprint of Empire, or World Heritage?', *Environmental Policy and Law* 40: 232-242.

Scott, R. (1961) *Limuria: The Lesser Dependencies of Mauritius*. London: Oxford University Press.

Sylva. H. (1981) *Report on the Survey on the Conditions of Living of the Ilois Community Displaced from the Chagos Archipelago*. Port Louis, Mauritius: Government of Mauritius.

Tatla, D. S. (1999) *The Sikh Diaspora: The Search for Statehood*. London: UCL Press.

Teelock, V. (2001) *Mauritian History: From its Beginnings to Modern Times*. Moka: Mahatma Gandhi Institute.

Torabully, K. (1995) *Kot sa parol là? Rôde parole*. Vacoas, Mauritius: Editions Le Printemps.

Toussaint, A. (1974) *L'océan Indien au XVIIIe siècle*. Paris: Flammarion.

Vine, D., Sokolowski, S.W. & Harvey, P. (2005) '*Dérasiné: The expulsion and impoverishment of the Chagossian people*'. Unpublished report.

Vine, D. (2009) *Island of Shame: The Secret History of the US Military Base on Diego Garcia.* Princeton: Princeton University Press.

Walker, I. (1986) *Zaffer pe sanze: Ethnic Identity and Social Change among the Ilois in Mauritius.* Report produced for Mauritius Indian Ocean Committee.

Wenban-Smith, N. & Carter, M. (2016) *Chagos: A History. Exploration, Exploitation, Expulsion.* London: Chagos Conservation Trust.

---

[i] http://www.un.org/en/decolonization/declaration.shtml

[ii] https://documents-dds-ny.un.org/doc/RESOLUTION/GEN/NR0/218/29/IMG/NR021829.pdf?OpenElement

[iii] http://treaties.fco.gov.uk/docs/fullnames/pdf/1967/TS0015%20(1967)%20CMND-3231%201966%2030%20DEC,%20LONDON%3B%20NOTES%20BETWEEN%20GOV%20OF%20UK%20&%20NI%20&%20GOV%20OF%20USA%20CONCERNING%20AVAILABILITY%20FOR%20DEFENCE%20PURPOSES%20OF%20BRITISH%20INDIAN%20OCEAN%20TERRITORY.pdf

[iv] http://www.parliament.uk/business/publications/written-questions-answers-statements/written-statement/Lords/2016-11-16/HLWS257/

[v] This chapter is based on sustained ethnographic engagement with the extended Chagossian community since 2002, on topics ranging from the politics of victimhood (e.g. Jeffery, 2011) to debates about environmental knowledge and sustainable resettlement (e.g. Jeffery, 2013).

[vi] 'Chagos, les sacrifiés de l'Indépendance?', *L'Express* 19.03.07. Available online at https://www.lexpress.mu/article/chagos-les-sacrifi%C3%A9s-de-lind%C3%A9pendance

[vii] The name Josephine is a pseudonym. In this paper, only the Chagossian leaders Olivier Bancoult and the late Fernand Mandarin are identified by their full real names.

[viii] Rodrigues is the second largest island in the Republic of Mauritius. Over 90% of the population of Rodrigues are Roman Catholics of African descent (Boswell, 2006: 48). Since the 1970s, an independence movement has campaigned against internal colonialism within the Republic of Mauritius (Eriksen, 1998: 166).

[ix] Resistance to the commemoration of independence is widespread amongst minorities such as separatist groups: for instance, diasporic Sikh nationalist movements, among others, have marked Indian Independence Day with protest (Axel, 2001: 197; Tatla, 1999: 128).

[x] This chapter focuses on the Mauritian side of the story, but here I would articulate a parallel critique of how successive UK governments have deployed the Chagossian community as mere pawns in their varied attempts to safeguard the US military base on Diego Garcia.

[xi] The Agaléga archipelago comprises two Outer islands in the Republic of Mauritius dominated by the coconut industry (like colonial Chagos) and inhabited by a predominantly Roman Catholic population of African descent (like colonial Chagos and present-day Rodrigues).

[xii] The Mauritian poet Khal Torabully complained: 'Mem si nou ti kapav vane bane vagues/nou pa ti pou hésité./Sa mem la mer fine casse gomon'/'Si nous pouvions vendre les vagues,/Nous n'aurions pas hésité./Voilà pourquoi la mer s'est sauvée.' (Torabully, 1996) [If we could sell the waves,/We would not have hesitated./This is why the sea escaped. (My translation)]

nursery assistant living in Watford, Hertfordshire, who positively embraces a Mauritian identity in large part because of its well-deserved reputation as a 'paradise' holiday destination. 'Oh, I'm always ready to tell people I meet that I'm Mauritian,' she says. 'I'm quite dark skinned so people know I'm not "English" and want to know something about my background. Nowadays everyone's heard of Mauritius.'

What are we to make of two UK-born young women who exhibit two very different attitudes to being classified as 'Mauritian' but do not self-identify as 'English' because of their skin colour? Accounting for these differences can be partly based on factors that go into the calculation of ethnic self-identity – Aasmah's chartered accountant father is (Gujarati) Muslim and her mother, a housewife, is (Bihari) Hindu, while both Shakti's parents are (Bihari) Hindus who have now retired after working as nurses in the NHS – but also because of their relative socio-economic status, leisure interests and perceptions of the future. With Aasmah, apart from times when she feels boxed in by a classification system in which she feels obliged to reduce herself to a specific 'nationality', she objects to self-identifying as 'Mauritian' for at least two reasons. Firstly, it tacitly acknowledges that there are different types (or categories) of UK citizens, and secondly, because being 'Mauritian' acts as a sort of conceptual drag on a future defined not, she hopes, by tags such as gender, nationality, 'race' (or ethnicity) but through her educational success (including fluency in French) leading to a career in London's financial sector. By contrast, Shakti, who has already mapped out for herself a career path in pre-school education, uses her Mauritian identity as a useful bit of currency to engage with other young people in her busy (largely secular) social life in 'safe', ethnically-mixed spaces such as bars, clubs and house parties in and around her hometown.

Aasmah's and Shakti's narratives about self-identity lead to a further point about the construction of so-called hyphenated social identities – for example, British-Asian, British-Sikh, British-Muslim or British-Pakistani-Muslim – which, because of the UK's multiculturalist policies (initiated in the mid-1960s), throws up dual or multiple identities as different groups of ethnic minority people take into account official concepts of 'self' based around single or dual nationalities, as they move over time from outsiders to insiders, from migrants to citizens. This often leads to the creation of novel, hybrid socio-cultural identities (Eade, 2016). It is revealing, though, that in everyday conversation I have never heard anyone of first or second-generation Indo-Mauritian heritage, who lives in the UK and travels on a UK passport, self-identify as 'British-Mauritian' – or for that matter 'British-Muslim', 'Mauritian-Muslim' or 'British-Mauritian-Muslim'.

Because discussions about self-identity rarely, if ever, take place between different generations of Indo-Mauritians, first-generation, self-identifying 'Mauritians' tend to assume that their UK-born children automatically self-identify as 'British'. The reality can be more complex and self-identity reflects a number of factors, including country of birth, generational status, peer and age group. For instance, I have interviewed some older second-generation Indo-Mauritians, who, like Shelina Permalloo, feel that as they move into middle age they are on a journey towards defining themselves as less 'Mauritian' and more 'British'. However, the most common pattern for older second-generation people involves switching between 'British' and 'Mauritian' identities, according to the social situation or context. For example, UK-born Sunil, 45, a solicitor, the son of retired NHS nurses, finds that identity switching happens not only on his frequent business trips to Mauritius but crucially also whenever he feels disempowered by being classified as racially 'other' in the UK. 'Sometimes I feel Mauritian and sometimes I feel British,' he explains. 'When I'm in Mauritius I feel British and when I'm in England I feel Mauritian. But at the end of the day in this country [UK] you'll always be judged on your skin colour. There's no getting away from that. I've been called "Paki" so many times – in fact, it happened the other week while I was sitting in my car in a traffic jam near where I work in London. I said to the [white] guy: "Thanks mate for trying to tell me who I am but actually I'm Mauritian".'

However, teenage and young adult second-generation and all third-generation young people interviewed tend to self-identify as 'British'. The exceptions are young people who were either born in Mauritius and then came to the UK before the age of 15 (1.5 generation), or those who were born in the UK but then lived for several years in Mauritius before returning to the UK as young teenagers. Another group of self-identifying Mauritians (including profiles on Facebook or other social media) consists of those under 25 who live in areas of relatively dense Mauritian settlement in London or elsewhere, and feel part of a distinctive, spatialized Mauritian 'community' (Vaughan & Arbaci, 2011), maintain at least some degree of religious observance, eat Mauritian-style food several times a week, and are fluent Kreol speakers. This pattern of self-identifying as 'Mauritian' is strongly reinforced amongst those who make regular holiday trips to Mauritius and stay with maternal or paternal kin.

Apart from Shelina Permalloo, Indo-Mauritians have a low profile in the UK. The relatively small population size, the absence of parliamentary representatives, pop stars or sporting heroes known to be of Mauritian heritage, as well as the fact that people of Indo-Mauritian origin often physically resemble those from other south Asian groups means that Indo-Mauritians have never been classified or identified by national or local institutions in the reified way that Sikhs, Hindus or Muslims have often been (Baumann, 1996). Frequently mistaken for other south Asians from the subcontinent Mauritians have no specific place in the galaxy of identities in the UK. Indeed, the absence of a socially, culturally or politically powerful category of 'Mauritians', defined as such and then courted by mainstream organisations in the UK, goes a long way in explaining why the vast majority of Indo- and other Mauritians in the UK do not feel an obligation or consider there is an advantage in constructing a 'public' hyphenated identity.

The practice of classifying oneself as 'Mauritian' is of relatively recent origin and the use of the term for self-identity purposes has for many years been much stronger in those who left than in those who live in Mauritius. Certainly, before people started going abroad in large numbers for study or work from the mid-1960s onwards, self-identity was largely based on belonging to a particular, largely endogamous group – Franco-Mauritian, Sino-Mauritian (Hakka or Cantonese), Creole (including gens de couleur) or Indian (the last segmented by religious affiliation; ancestral regional origins such as Bihar, Gujarat or Tamil Nadu; class and caste; and sometimes political loyalties). But the new form of self-identity as 'Mauritian' for those in the diaspora was significantly amplified by everyday interactions with people with other ethnic self-identities, as well as the introduction in 1969 of a significant new piece of material culture, the navy blue Mauritian passport.

Mauritians in the UK

Today the vast majority of older, first-generation Indo-Mauritian professionals – dentists, doctors, lawyers or chartered accountants – residing in metropolitan areas, including Bradford, Manchester and Newcastle upon Tyne, occupy large houses in affluent, suburban areas relatively near their places of work. A similar residential pattern can be found among those who make a living running large nursing or residential care homes outside London. Those who work in London's financial or legal sector mostly live near rail or underground stations in the capital's more affluent outer suburban areas, such as Finchley, Sidcup or Southgate, and commute. By contrast, most Indo-Mauritians in London running small businesses, such as insurance brokers, travel agents, cafes or small residential care homes, as well as those working as nurses, and their families, tend to live near their places of work in what were once the capital's more affordable inner or outer suburban areas, such as Leyton, Tooting or Wood Green. Significantly, these clusters of Indo-Mauritians are close to one or more large NHS hospitals.

There are also smaller populations of Indo-Mauritians to be found just outside London in places where NHS psychiatric institutions, often the successor institutions of Victorian asylums, or other specialist hospitals, such as 'mental deficiency colonies', were once located. For example, the Hertfordshire city of St Albans, the nearby village of London Colney and the North Watford-Leavesden area, where there are several large NHS general hospitals, smaller privately-run hospitals, and a number of NHS psychiatric and learning difficulties facilities, are home to a population of several thousand Indo-Mauritians. A similar pattern of clustering of Indo-Mauritians is found around NHS hospitals in the Epsom and Redhill areas of Surrey.

Because of the dynamics of chain migration, religious affiliation has played a significant part in the clustering of transnational Mauritians employed in nursing. While Hindus are the numerically dominant group residing in east, north and south London, the majority of Muslims are to be found in specific parts of north London and surrounding areas, such as St Albans, London Colney and Watford-Leavesden. Although no temples or churches have been established by Hindu or Christian Indo-Mauritians, Mauritian Muslims have been instrumental in setting up mosques in three locations, namely Edmonton, Leyton and London Colney. Yet whatever their religion or wherever they live, Indo-Mauritians, like most other transnational south Asian groups, are (or strongly aspire to be) owner-occupiers rather than social housing or private sector tenants (Peach, 1998).

First wave

Indo-Mauritian immigration to the UK started in a significant way in the late 1950s, especially after the introduction of Commonwealth scholarships for high-academic achievers. Because of the colonial connection, however, a small number of Mauritians had come to the UK before this period. Indeed, the pursuit of upward social and economic mobility, even if latent, has long been a core value for almost all Indo-Mauritian groups. This can be traced back not only to their ancestors' journey from the subcontinent to work as indentured labourers (beginning just before the abolition of slavery in 1835), but more specifically to the 1860s when a few Muslim, and a much larger number of Hindu men, obtained the status of sirdar (foreman or overseer) and purchased small parcels of land from cash-hungry Franco-Mauritian landowners, anxious to maintain their living standards when global sugar prices collapsed (Bates and Carter, 2017).

Unsurprisingly, those having the financial wherewithal to aim for educational success and status have opted to study in countries with a globally-prestigious university system. Some Indo-Mauritian students as well as those from other ethnic groups, especially those studying French, went to France, the old colonial power, but most journeyed to the UK, the colonial power until Mauritius's independence in 1968. In turn, these pioneers helped establish a bridgehead for a second wave of sojourning students, mainly male but some female, coming to UK universities, some of who on their return to Mauritius went on to launch political careers, work in educational fields or otherwise contribute to civil society.

Second wave

Medical professionals

Yet there were a small number of Indo-Mauritians, mainly men, aiming to become high-earning professionals in that second migration wave, who settled in the UK – though that was almost certainly not their intention. In many cases, funding their studies at UK colleges and universities involved selling some or all of their ancestral land to male siblings or other members of the extended family. While this strategy should not be seen as a case of 'burning their bridges' in terms of returning to their homeland, it was certainly transformative in terms of both their social status and sources of income. By moving abroad, these young men were no longer socially or economically active members of small, close-knit, relatively affluent family planter groups. In fact, because of their successful passage through the UK education system they became members of individualistic, well-remunerated high-status 'Western' professions.

A second factor in Indo-Mauritian dentists and doctors committing to live in the UK was the length of study and the requirement to complete one or more years work experience after qualification. This meant that at least some of these young men, free (to some degree) from the classification system and social controls imposed by their family and ethnic group in Mauritius, established 'serious' relationships with British women, especially when compared to other Mauritian students, who also had romantic liaisons but had come for shorter periods of study, which meant that they were more likely to return their homeland. Furthermore, the income levels that these newly qualified medical professionals earned at that time were much higher than those available in the colony of Mauritius.

The success of these medical professionals, and the expectation that their children would have enhanced life chances by growing up in UK, tended to offset to a large extent the loss of socio-cultural identity or membership of the extended family group, and, importantly, the comfortable lifestyle had they returned to Mauritius. Furthermore, the entry of Indo-Mauritians into socially and economically powerful professions in the UK conferred other stable forms of identity based not on ties of kinship but instead on friendship with work colleagues or others of similar socioeconomic status. For instance, despite the prevalence of middle-class racism, Indo-Mauritian medical professionals were often invited to become members of the local Rotary Club or golf club. Membership of such voluntary organisations counterbalanced or even trumped those available (or from which they were excluded by Franco-Mauritians) in their homeland.

Typically, the British women (of lower socioeconomic status) whom these Mauritian medical professionals married, gave up their jobs and became full-time homemakers. This meant that the internal design of the household as well as all-important ongoing order-creating household rituals were controlled in large part by middle- or working-class British-born women (Martin, 1984; McIntosh and Zey, 2004). The result was that children were effectively socialised into the local version of 'respectable' British society. It is also noteworthy that while the surnames or 'family' names of such children remained Indo-Mauritian, those selected as first forenames were typically 'English' or 'British', though the less visible second or third names were often chosen to mark Indo-Mauritian heritage. In addition, English, rather than Kreol, was the day-to-day language in these mixed-race households.

Significantly, self-identifying as 'Mauritian' became in many social contexts a background rather than a foreground feature of these male medical professional lives. Indo-Mauritian doctors and dentists were often very popular with their patients. This had little to do with 'personality' and much with their socio-cultural upbringing. 'Here in Mauritius, you must realise that we walk on eggs continuously,' noted one Maltese expatriate married to a Mauritian after a decade of residency on the island some years ago. This observation accurately reflected (and continues to reflect) the complexities of negotiating everyday ethnic diversity on the island (Eriksen, 1992: 121). However, the flip-side of being obliged to continuously walk on ethnically diverse eggs is that generations of people raised in Mauritius from almost all ethnic groups acquire a skill-set, that was (and continues to be) immensely useful in dealing with people from different socio-economic or ethnic groups. Indeed, most Mauritian doctors and dentists are seen as 'sympathetic' and 'welcoming' by their patients. Put another way, Mauritian medical professionals have always tended to possess a good bed- or drill-side manner.

Although the offspring of these pioneering, ethnically mixed relationships visited Mauritius for family holidays one or more times as children, none I have encountered self-identify as 'Mauritian'. Today, as adults with their own households, the relationship of the second-generation to their fathers' homeland, particularly in the

270

absence of ownership of land or other significant economic assets, has almost disappeared. As with many Britons, ongoing identity is driven more by experiences in other life worlds, especially those associated with work, family and leisure. As Alan, a 60-year-old dentist, who works at a prestigious address in London's Marylebone, and who made a single trip to Mauritius in 1972 with his parents and two siblings, tells me: 'My [Hindu] dad was from Quatre Bornes and came to study dentistry in the UK. He then met and married my [British] mum so I was born and have spent all my life in the UK. I don't have any contact with any remaining family in Mauritius. Really, I don't regard myself as "Mauritian" in any sense. I regard myself as "British".' He pauses, smiles and adds: 'Whatever that means.'

Nurses

The NHS has long depended on the recruitment of English-speaking workers from abroad to sustain its health services. In 1949, a year after its foundation, the Attlee Labour government launched a formal recruitment drive targeting specific Commonwealth countries, such as Jamaica, Malaysia and Mauritius, to supplement the long-standing recruitment of nurses from the Irish Republic who, by this time, were unable to fill all NHS vacancies.

As already noted, there is no official data available from UK healthcare organisations concerning the number of Mauritian-born men and women who have worked or are currently working in the NHS or the private sector. However, the 2000 Mauritian census estimated that 4531 nurses, making up 63 per cent of the nursing profession, were working abroad, and of that number, 4042 were employed in the UK (Sward, 2015: 344). Although the situation of nurses working in healthcare systems overseas has sometimes worked to Mauritius's advantage if those returning had learnt innovative skills (Klopper and Uys, 2012), it has been estimated that some 700 highly qualified nurses, around 20 per cent of the workforce, left Mauritius for the UK between 2000 and 2005. Few have returned (Sward, 2015: 344). Not surprisingly, the Mauritian authorities protested strongly to the UK about the hugely detrimental effect on the country's healthcare system by the brazen 'stealing' of its qualified staff. This episode explains in large part why the NHS no longer 'officially' targets nurses from Mauritius (or other 'developing' countries, such as Bangladesh, the Seychelles or Sri Lanka). Nevertheless around 6000 qualified nurses are currently recruited annually on work permits by the NHS, which can be converted into 'indefinite leave to remain' and then UK citizenship. This continues to make a nursing qualification an attractive proposition for Mauritians aiming to migrate to the UK. However, the evidence from my fieldwork suggests that in the last few years most Indo-Mauritian nurses who have settled in the UK have done so for reasons of family reunification.

Unlike many countries where nursing is a female-dominated profession, in Mauritius nursing has long been perceived as 'a highly attractive employment opportunity' by young, well-educated men and women (Hollup, 2014: 12). This explains why there are roughly equal numbers of male and female nurses currently employed on the island. However, the first Mauritians, often Creole or Sino-Mauritians, who migrated to the UK in the 1950s and early 60s to train as nurses were almost exclusively male. Some returned to Mauritius to work in senior positions in nursing or other parts of the public health sector (Hollup, 2012: 13). These pioneers were soon followed by mixed gender and mixed ethnic groups, with Indo-Mauritians rapidly becoming the majority. Few in these later cohorts returned to their homeland. Unlike Indo-Mauritians from more affluent backgrounds studying dentistry or medicine, these young men and women, equipped with a good secondary school education, did not require much in the way of finance to fund their studies because at that time, the shortage of nurses was so acute that students received a salary while training.

Respondents who started work as nurses in the NHS in the late 1960s and 70s stated that the single most important factor in their decision to emigrate was the lack of suitable work for people with their level of education. 'There were no jobs for us in Mauritius at that time,' says Sita, 69, a retired psychiatric nurse living in Epsom, Surrey. 'Women like me had very few options at that time so we decided to try our luck over here.' This 'push' factor was compounded by social and economic uncertainties concerning what would take place after Mauritius' independence in 1968, including among well-educated Hindu Mauritians, members of the majority community, who it was widely believed at the time would likely benefit in terms of jobs at the expense of minority ethnic groups. In fact, Hindu respondents told me that they were keen to migrate to the UK before or shortly after independence because they thought that they would never again get the opportunity.

Like their pioneer dental and medical compatriots, many early Indo- and other Mauritians coming to work as nurses in the NHS had no grand plan regarding where they would settle. This explains why small numbers of Mauritians can be found near NHS hospitals throughout the UK, though the demand for labour and the pattern of chain migration meant that most early and even later recruits settled in or just outside London (Lingayah, 1991: 8; Mannick, 1987: 8). Undoubtedly, most early migrants saw themselves as 'sojourners' rather than 'settlers', though interviews also revealed that there were others who simply wanted to see what opportunities arose over time. It is evident, too, that were significant status gains for the individual and their family by working in the UK. 'If you went back to Mauritius for a holiday,' says Deepak, 72, a retired psychiatric nurse living in Tooting, 'people would say, "He's from London!" And they would lower their voices [in deference]. Also, if you were a parent and you said, "My son is in London", it was one up on the neighbours.'

Coming to live and work in the UK was undeniably transformative in terms of social and ethnic identity. Respondents stressed that while in Mauritius they could not be anything but aware of their and others' ethnic identity, in the UK their ethnicity became significantly less important, especially in the workplace. Furthermore, the vast majority of respondents reported that because they were often asked about their origins or heritage by British or other foreign healthcare workers and patients, it meant that for the first time many began to strongly self-identify as 'Mauritian'. For some Indo- Mauritians this was a liberating experience. 'When you lived there [Mauritius] you were whatever you were – Hindu, Muslim, Creole or Chinese,' explains Deepak. 'But when you're here [UK] you are 'Mauritian'. People ask, 'Where do you come from?' and you say, "I come from Mauritius, I'm Mauritian". In fact, people in my group didn't talk about their [ethnic] group any more. Most of us weren't into politics or anything like that so we mix, we go to parties, we have a drink. And some people intermarried. In my group, a Hindu married a Muslim.' For others, though, a specific ethnic (and caste) identity, though under-communicated to their compatriots or others with who they interacted, continued to be a relevant factor in the way they conducted their lives – not so much in terms of the romantic liaisons in the nurses' home but certainly in their choice of marriage partners, the food they routinely ate (including the observation of food taboos regarding the avoidance of beef or pork) or the consumption of alcohol.

In terms of social bonding early migrants to the UK interviewed revealed that cooking and sharing Mauritian-style food was not at that time a particularly significant factor in maintaining a sense of in-group, primarily because they lived as single people on hospital premises, often ate in the hospital canteen and did not routinely have access to the type of kitchen or dining facilities that could cope with a large number of people dining together. Instead, for Deepak and others, it was music and dance that was crucial in social bonding for Mauritians and, indeed, with other health workers of similar status at staff dances in the hospital social club (see McCrae & Nolan, 2016: 207-226). 'We all liked music and some of us played instruments so we formed a band,' recalls Deepak. 'Of course, we played séga but we also played the stuff we were hearing on TV and the radio as well.'

Depending on geographical location some Hindu or Muslim nurses married local men or women, often fellow nurses, but the dominant pattern for the first-generation of Indo-Mauritians, was to have an arranged or semi-arranged marriage with a suitable partner with the wedding carried out with both extended families in

273

attendance in Mauritius before the couple returned to work in the UK. The households these Indo-Mauritians established were quite different from those involved in 'mixed race' marriages in higher socio-economic groups (or in cases where Indian, Creole or Sino-Mauritians nurses married partners who were British or other nationalities). While male surnames were preserved after marriage, forenames were more or less the same as if they had continued to reside in Mauritius. The exception was among Indo-Mauritians who belonged to Christian denominations, such as Anglican or Presbyterian, or sects, like the Seventh-Day Adventist Church. In such cases, UK-based parents selected 'Christian' or 'British'-sounding names that reflected the customary usage in their respective socio-religious groups in Mauritius.

Indo-Mauritians who came to the UK to work as nurses from the 1980s onwards did so not so much to escape the prospect of long-term unemployment as with the previous generation but rather to find better or different work opportunities commensurate with their educational qualifications than those available in their homeland as the process of industrialisation gathered pace. Interviews revealed that what was particularly important for those migrating in the mid-1980s onwards was not solely about improving living standards but crucially also the life chances of their (born or unborn) children 'This country has made me who I am today,' says Iqbal, 55, who lives in Leyton. 'I qualified in two areas of nursing, psychiatric and learning difficulties, and then got a degree in autism studies. It's given my wife and my children a lot, too. My wife has a good job [as a psychiatric nurse in a secure unit]; my oldest daughter has just qualified as a doctor; and my youngest daughter is about to go to university to study pharmacy. And, as my daughters remind me, had they lived in Mauritius they wouldn't have got where they are today without private tuition.'

Iqbal also tells me that although he and his wife hold British passports, they continue to self-identify as 'Mauritian' because 'we were born and grew up in Mauritius'. However, he claims that his two UK-born daughters self-identify as 'British'. One important reason for this, he thinks, is that he and his wife communicated with their children in English. 'We didn't want to confuse them,' he explains. 'If either of us [inadvertently] spoke Kreol we would tell each other off!' Nevertheless, like other Indo-Mauritians in his social group, food cooked in the household has always been thoroughly Mauritian in style and thus an important marker of 'Mauritian' identity.

Unlike other retired nurses who have inherited land in Mauritius and subsequently built properties, Iqbal has no plans to do so or return permanently or for part of the year to the place of his birth. 'I've lived here for more years than I have in Mauritius,' he says. 'If I spend four weeks there it's very nice but living there for six months would be very different. I know people who've gone back to Mauritius full of

274

hope and then they just can't settle – they end up coming back to England. Mauritius is a tiny country and in many ways, it's still a developing country.' In addition, Iqbal points out that consultations with doctors working in private practice in Mauritius, which is customary behaviour amongst all middle-class groups, have to be paid for, and an important financial consideration for returnees (like himself) with one or more chronic medical conditions, such as type II diabetes, cardiovascular disease or musculoskeletal problems. Although Iqbal thinks Mauritius has much to teach the UK and other countries about the positive aspects of ethnic diversity, he is nevertheless critical of Mauritius's Hindu-dominated political system and the negative impact on the life chances of those from minority groups, including his own group of Sunni Muslims of north Indian heritage (Calcuttiyas). 'Multiculturalism is good in Mauritius,' he says. 'But what I don't like is that the prime minister always has to be a Hindu. It shouldn't be like that – being prime minister shouldn't be based on race or colour. The job should go to the best person. Corruption is big in Mauritius, too. If you are a Hindu and unemployed you can go to a minister and you will get a job.'

Iqbal's reluctance to return to Mauritius also reflects the fact that many UK Indo-Mauritian households have moved on from what social anthropologist Thomas Hylland Eriksen usefully terms a 'traditional, sociocentric concept of personhood', common among first generation migrants, to a more 'reflexive, individualist one', much in evidence among members of 1.5, second and third generations, because of their greater exposure to mainstream institutions and the popular culture of the (European) society in which they have grown-up (Eriksen, 2015). This shift towards greater individualism is often most clearly expressed in young ethnic minority people's awareness of and relaxed attitude towards cultural diversity and hybridity. In turn, this reflexive, individualist process, amplified by upward social mobility and affluence, invariably changes the family dynamic and perceptions of what younger and older members consider is involved in the 'good life'. 'My daughters have visited Mauritius three times now,' says Iqbal. 'To be honest they find it a bit boring. You know what it's like – everything shuts at five o'clock. They prefer to go on holiday to Disneyland in Florida, or Canada or Dubai. Really, my daughters are the reason I have decided not to make [property] investments in Mauritius. It might be different if my parents were still alive but they passed away some years ago. Definitely my home – my family's home – is here in the UK.'

Like the children of other first-generation ethnic groups in the UK, who have rejected employment in specific occupational niches favoured by their parents, it is very clear that 1.5, second or third generation Indo-Mauritians no longer view nursing as a good career choice. Put simply, nursing is perceived as 'mum's and dad's work' and children strongly aspire to semantic-type occupational opportunities in high-status professions (Gellner, 1998: 28). Nevertheless, because of the strength of family bonds many 1.5 and second-generation Indo-Mauritians resident in London or the Southeast, whose parents are or were nurses, prefer whenever possible to live in the same area. (In a small number of cases this has resulted in multiple-family households.) However, this pattern is changing for many in the third generation, partly due to the fact that young people pursuing careers in the digital economy take for granted that they need to be geographically mobile, and partly because the significant recent rise in property prices in London and the South-east means that many are obliged to look further afield in their quest to find affordable housing.

Recent migrants

Until visa restrictions were imposed in 2008, a significant number of Indo-Mauritians came to the UK to work in adult care homes in the previous decade or so. This migration wave typically involved nuclear family units where one parent, usually female, had found work in a residential adult care home and became the 'breadwinner'. Because of the layered dynamics of chain migration, these self-identifying 'Mauritian' migrants gravitated towards the ethnically diverse, 'safe' neighbourhoods of London where previous generations of Indo-Mauritian migrants had settled. The male and female children of these new migrants, often without much in the way of formal academic credentials, have (like Mauritian-Chagossians in Crawley) found a variety of jobs, including working as cashiers, shelf stackers or cleaners at major supermarket groups, located in or nearby their area of residence in the capital's outer suburban retail parks. Others, usually female, are employed as cleaners in local hospitals or, following the example set by their mothers, also often work as carers in residential care homes.

Self-employment in retail, hospitality or other sectors has traditionally been high among lower socio-economic migrant groups compared with their white British counterparts (Hall *et al.*, 2017: 9). Many previous and more recent Indo-Mauritian migrants, especially males, exemplify this pattern of employment. In particular, small businesses have been established in the last decade or so which have exploited the significant increase in the population size of Indo-Mauritians in specific areas of London, and the growth of an 'internal economy'. For example, some men work in small teams to renovate properties, or install windows or burglar alarms in the capital. Work is typically found initially within and then outside the ethnic boundary by word-of-mouth recommendations – relatively easy to come by for reliable tradespeople in densely populated suburban areas. Other Indo-Mauritians have taken advantage of the recent increase in the size of the Indo-Mauritian population by exploiting the demand for Mauritian branded foods, spices and drink, which often play a crucial role in reminding many first-generation migrants of 'home'. This has led to a significant proliferation of Mauritian-themed cafes, food stalls, bars and retail outlets in south, east and especially north London.

Not all recent Indo-Mauritian migrants have remained in the UK. After a few years some, especially the unskilled from older age groups, have returned to Mauritius because they miss their family or find the weather too depressing or, crucially, find that property prices are out of reach. Sometimes returnees will leave behind other family members – typically teenage or young adult sons or daughters who either want to make a go of it in the UK or simply want to extend their stay in order to work and save before returning to Mauritius in a few years' time. Even in the absence of regular holiday visits, family ties are often well maintained by the exchange of gifts transported by relatives or friends travelling between Mauritius and the UK, and utilising one or more elements of the e-diaspora – texting, email, Facebook, Instagram, or Skyping (Low, 2015:13-15).

Conclusion: A chance to dance

New forms of expressing Mauritian identity are increasingly available to Indo-Mauritians, especially for those in lower socio-economic groups (as well as middle-class university students), who live in or near areas of Mauritian settlement in the capital. Many families, for example, attend religious events celebrating Diwali, Holi or Eid, or attend the (secular) annual Mauritius Open Air Festival (billed as 'The Biggest Mauritius Festival in Europe'). Successor to earlier events that began in the 1980s, the festival has been held in Down Lane Park, and more latterly in Gunnersbury Park, on the third Sunday in August most years since 2010. Fieldwork reveals that the vast majority of festivalgoers are of Indo-Mauritian heritage and that, like similar small-scale UK festivals catering for specific transnational groups, there is a high level of 'integrative' or 'celebrative sociality' (Rusu & Kantola, 2016). At the festival, for example, those born and raised in Mauritius will meet old friends or acquaintances with who they will be delighted to converse in Kreol, and purchase gâteaux piment, samosas, and chicken or other curries, as well as Mauritian flags, for their children or grandchildren. In addition, those attending can dance, sway or clap along to leading Mauritius-based Creole DJs and séga musicians, such as Mr Love, Alain Ramanisum or Linzy Bacbotte. In sum, the festival experience acts a powerful reminder to those who self-identify as 'Mauritian', whether they live in Leyton, Tooting or Wood Green, that they are indeed Mauritian and can be proud of being so, while also communicating to their younger, mainly self-identifying 'British' kin that, however fleetingly, part of a park in north London has been ritually – almost magically – transformed into little 'Mauritius'.

Acknowledgements

I am grateful to John Eade, Dalton Exley, Jonathan Freeman, Laura Jeffery, Linda Jowsey and Christopher Knowles for feedback and comments on earlier drafts of this chapter. I would also like to thank the many Mauritians in the UK, Mauritius and elsewhere who took the time to share their views and opinions with me. In this regard, I would particularly like to express my gratitude to Jacques K. Lee.

Notes

The names and some biographical details of some respondents have been changed to protect their identities.

References

Bates, C. & Carter, M. (2017) 'Sirdars as intermediaries in nineteenth century Indian Ocean indentured labour migration', *Modern Asian* Studies 51(2): 462-484.

Baumann, G. (1996) *Contesting Culture: Discourses of Identity in Multi-Ethnic London*. Cambridge: Cambridge University Press.

Eade, J. (2016) 'Economic Migrant or Hyphenated British? Writing about difference in London's East End', in S. Gupta and T. Ominiyi (eds) *The Cultures of Economic Migration: International Perspectives*. London: Routledge.

Eriksen, T.H. (1992) 'Containing conflict and transcending ethnicity in Mauritius', in K. Rupesinghe (ed) *Internal Conflict and Governance*. London: Palgrave Macmillan.

Eriksen, T.H. (2015) 'Person, time and conduct in Alna', *Nordic Journal of Migration Research* 5(1): 11-18

Gellner, E. (1998) *Nationalism*. London: Phoenix.

Goodchild, S. (2013) 'Being Mauritian: A sociolinguistic case study on the transmission and use of Mauritian Creole in the UK', *Newcastle Working Papers in Linguistics*.

Hall, S., King, J. and Finlay, R. (2017) 'Migrant infrastructure: Transaction economies in Birmingham and Leicester, UK', *Urban Studies* 54(6): 1311-1327.

Hein, P. (2004) *Options for migration policies in the long term development of Mauritius*. Geneva: International Labour Organization.

Hollup, O. (2012) 'Nurses in Mauritius motivated by extrinsic rewards: a qualitative study of factors determining recruitment and career choices', *International Journal of Nursing Studies* 49(10): 1291-1298

Jeffery, L. (2011) *Chagos islanders in Mauritius and the UK: Forced displacement and onward migration*. Manchester: Manchester University Press.

Klopper, H. & Uys, L.R. (2012) *The state of nursing and nursing education in Africa: A country-by-country review*. Indianapolis: Sigma Theta Tau International.

Lingayah, S. (1991) *A comparative study of Mauritian immigrants in two European cities: London and Paris.* London: Mauritians' Welfare Association.

Low, K.E. (2016) 'Migrant warriors and transnational lives: Constructing a Gurkha diaspora', *Ethnic and Racial Studies* 39(5): 840-857.

Mannick, A.R. (1987) *Mauritians in London.* Mayfield: Dodo Books.

Martin, B. (1984) '"Mother wouldn't like it!": Housework as magic', *Theory, Culture & Society* 2(2): 19-36.

McCrae, N. & Nolan, P. (2016) *The Story of Nursing in British Mental Hospitals: Echoes from the Corridors.* London: Routledge.

McIntosh, A. & Zey, M. (1989) 'Women as gatekeepers of food consumption: a sociological critique', *Food and Foodways* 3(4): 317-332.

Nayeck, J. (2009) *Circular migration – The case of Mauritius.* International Conference on Diaspora for Development. Washington DC: World Bank.

Peach, C. (1998) 'South Asian and Caribbean ethnic minority housing choice in Britain', *Urban Studies* 35(10): 1657-1680

Rotter, R. & Jeffery, L. (2016) '"We no longer have faith and trust in anyone": misadventures in community consultation on the future of the Chagos Archipelago', *International Development Planning Review* 38(4): 383-403.

Rusu, M.S. & Kantola, I. (2016) 'A time of meta-celebration: Celebrating the sociology of celebration', *Journal of Comparative Research in Anthropology and Sociology* 7(1): 1-22

Sward, J. (2015) 'International Recruitment: Current Trends and Their Implications for Small States', in W.H. Khonje (ed) *Migration and Development: Perspectives from Small States.* London: Commonwealth Secretariat.

Vaughan, L. & Arbaci, S. (2011) 'The challenges of understanding urban segregation', *Built Environment* 37(2): 128-138.